DEAR MR. SMALLWOOD

DEAR MR. SMALLWOOD

Confederation in the words of those who lived it

Edited by Sonja Boon and Vicki S. Hallett

MEMORIAL UNIVERSITY PRESS

Library and Archives Canada Cataloguing in Publication

Title: Dear Mr. Smallwood : confederation in the words of those who lived it / edited by Sonja Boon and Vicki S. Hallett.
Names: Boon, Sonja, editor | Hallett, Vicki Sara, 1974- editor
Description: Includes bibliographical references and index.
Identifiers: Canadiana (print) 20250296705 | Canadiana (ebook) 20250296721 | ISBN 9781990445248 (softcover) | ISBN 9781990445255 (EPUB) | ISBN 9781990445262 (PDF)
Subjects: LCSH: Smallwood, Joseph R., 1900-1991—Correspondence. | LCSH: Newfoundland and Labrador—History. | CSH: Newfoundland and Labrador—History—1949- | CSH: Newfoundlanders—Correspondence. | LCGFT: Personal correspondence.
Classification: LCC FC2175 .D43 2025 | DDC 971.8/04—dc23

Cover design by Randy Drover
Copy editing by Iona Bulgin
Page design and typesetting by Alison Carr

Published by Memorial University Press
Memorial University of Newfoundland and Labrador
P.O. Box 4200
St. John's, NL A1C 5S7
www.memorialuniversitypress.ca

Printed in Canada

31 30 29 28 27 26 25 1 2 3 4 5 6 7 8

Table of Contents

INTRODUCTION

Sonja Boon and Vicki S. Hallett

Ordinary People in Extraordinary Times

DEAR MR. SMALLWOOD is a book about the lives and stories of everyday Newfoundlanders and Labradorians as they navigated what was arguably the biggest political transition of their lifetimes: the entry of the former nation of Newfoundland into Confederation with Canada. In short, this is a book about ordinary people living in extraordinary times.

A collaborative project that brings together archival materials, personal reflections, poetic and visual responses, and scholarly essays, *Dear Mr. Smallwood* moves discussions beyond the polarizing figure of J.R. Smallwood and recentres the conversations about Confederation to consider how Newfoundlanders and Labradorians understood themselves and their world at the time of Confederation. To do this, we draw on one of the province's richest archival treasures, the letters written to J.R. Smallwood during his time as premier, and more specifically, those letters written between 1948 and 1952, all of which are housed in the Archives and Special Collections Division of the Queen Elizabeth II Library, Memorial University.[1] In the course of that four-year period alone, thousands of letters, from every electoral district in Newfoundland and Labrador, made their way to Smallwood, both as he championed union with Canada prior to Confederation, and later, after the cause was won.

Sidonie Smith and Julia Watson have observed that "[i]n the details and immediacy of lived lives of such autobiographical narrators, the political and

1 The letters to Smallwood, organized by electoral district and by year, can be found in the District Files, J.R. Smallwood Collection, COLL-075, 1.1.01–1.1.50, Archives and Special Collections (ASC), Queen Elizabeth II Library, Memorial University.

cultural context of the historical past become vivid and memorable."[2] Indeed, the letters to Smallwood, as unique expressions of people's hopes, dreams, discontents, and desires, open a window onto Newfoundlanders and Labradorians as political agents, citizens who looked to Smallwood to make good on his many and varied promises. In their letters, these correspondents both articulated their current living situations and imagined their futures, looking for ways to improve not only their own lives but also those of their communities. We're excited to share about 250 of them with you.

Numerous books have been written about Newfoundland and Labrador's entry into Confederation. Some have focused on the politicking that led up to the 1948 referenda.[3] Others, meanwhile, have considered the figure of Joey Smallwood.[4] Others, still, situate Confederation within the broader history of Newfoundland and Labrador.[5] Confederation also "haunts" the literature of Newfoundland and Labrador, as numerous writers consider "[t]he lost possibility of a politically autonomous Newfoundland nation that Confederation signalled."[6] Certainly, Wayne Johnston's critically acclaimed *The Colony of Unrequited Dreams* (1999) offers one example of this. But none of this work considers the vast trove of letters written to Smallwood. Indeed, the letters to Smallwood remain a "virtually untapped"[7] source of insight into Newfoundland and Labrador political identity.

---

2 Sidonie Smith and Julia Watson, *Reading Autobiography: A Guide for Interpreting Life Narratives*, 2nd ed. (Minneapolis: University of Minnesota Press, 2010), 14.

3 See, for example, Raymond Benjamin Blake, *Canadians at Last: The Integration of Newfoundland as Province* (Toronto: University of Toronto Press, 1994); Raymond Blake and Melvin Baker, *Where Once They Stood: Newfoundland's Rocky Road towards Confederation* (Regina: University of Regina Press, 2019); David MacKenzie, *Inside the Atlantic Triangle: Canada and the Entrance of Newfoundland into Confederation 1939–1949* (Toronto: University of Toronto Press, 1986), https://doi.org/10.3138/9781487576493; Greg Malone, *Don't Tell the Newfoundlanders: The True Story of Newfoundland's Confederation with Canada* (Toronto: Alfred A. Knopf, 2012).

4 See, for example, Ray Argyle, *Joey Smallwood: Schemer and Dreamer* (Toronto: Dundurn, 2012); Richard J. Gwyn, *Smallwood: The Unlikely Revolutionary* (Toronto: McClelland & Stewart, 1999).

5 For example, Sean Cadigan, *Newfoundland and Labrador: A History* (Toronto: University of Toronto Press, 2009).

6 Ian Moffatt, "Confederate Hauntings: The Spectral Legacy of Nationhood in Contemporary Newfoundland Fiction" (master's thesis, Memorial University, 2015), 2.

7 Sonja Boon, "'I Am Very Badly in Need of Help': Promises and Promissory Notes in Women's Letters to J.R. Smallwood," in *Creating This Place: Women, Family, and Class in*

In *Dear Mr. Smallwood*, our interest lies not in Confederation as an historical event. Nor does it lie in Confederation as a fictional trope. Rather, we are interested in the relationship between Confederation and life narrative. Drawing on the thousands of letters written to Smallwood, we consider how Newfoundlanders and Labradorians represented themselves and made meaning of their lives, that is, we focus on the stories they told about themselves and this rapidly changing place they called home. Taken together, these letters are a vital source toward imagining a collective autobiography of Newfoundland and Labrador.

People wrote to Smallwood from all over: from places with names imposed by settler colonization and from places with names that would, in the context of resettlement, disappear from maps in the not-too-distant future. Some lived in communities whose original names were never formally recognized. Further, while Newfoundland became a province in 1949, Labrador would not formally be added to the name of the province until 2001. As a result, the names Ktaqamkuk, Nitassinan, and Nunatsiavut appear nowhere in these letters to Smallwood, even as those names were always there, spoken in communities, lived in tradition, waiting to come back to wider consciousness. Such absences are stark in the settler-colonial archive and are a reality that shape our (mis)understandings of the past. They speak volumes about who and what we remember and who and what we (sometimes deliberately) forget. Contributors Shruti Raheja, Vicki S. Hallett, and Patricia Way all speak to these absences, listening for the silences that ring in those not-so-empty spaces.

The stories shared in the letters to Smallwood are the stories of this place we now call Newfoundland and Labrador. They are about desires and hopes and dreams. They are about grief and loss. They are about seemingly insurmountable challenges. More than this, they are about a commitment to this place and its possible futures.

"not enough for sweetening for their tea": Notes on the Perils and Promises of Early Twentieth-Century Newfoundland and Labrador

By the mid-1940s, after ten years of Commission of Government, having endured the tragic losses of World War II, and facing the economic downturn of

---

St. John's, 1900–1950, ed. Linda Cullum and Marilyn Porter (Montreal and Kingston: McGill-Queen's University Press, 2014), 223.

the fishery and forestry sectors, the Dominion of Newfoundland was at a crossroads. New technologies were shifting how people lived their lives: the way they did their jobs, the way they communicated, the way they travelled, and also, the way they saw themselves in relation to the wider world. The arrival of Canadian and American soldiers, meanwhile, along with the construction of military, naval, and air bases during World War II, shifted the economic expectations of entire communities and the cultural grounds beneath people's feet.[8]

The country had been under Commission of Government since 1934, its concerns directed by a group of seven unelected commissioners appointed by the British government. In the 1930s as the Depression took hold, and the Commission's policies for economic and social reform failed, poverty deepened, and labour activism increased. In the words of Sean Cadigan, "[t]hroughout Newfoundland, the working poor, especially loggers, continued to voice their discontent, and crowds continued to gather in protest against poverty and inadequate relief through the late 1930s."[9] The war brought significant economic uplift as prices for fish, lumber, and minerals shot up, and jobs associated with the building and maintenance of American and Canadian military, air force, and naval bases across the island and in Labrador paid good wages, though not as good as they might have been without the interference of the Commission of Government.[10]

With the influx of Canadian and American soldiers and money came an influx of new culture, as well. As people mingled in the social life created at and around military installations, new relationships, both personal and political, were formed and would more closely bind Newfoundland to North America as never before.[11] The cost of living would increase for everyone, while the standard of living would increase for many.[12] Access to health care improved as new hospitals

8 For those interested in delving further into some of the issues we introduce in this section, the Heritage Newfoundland & Labrador online public history project (https://www.heritage.nf.ca/) provides excellent short essays, as well as videos and images, that provide further context.

9 Cadigan, *Newfoundland and Labrador*, 214.

10 Cadigan, *Newfoundland and Labrador*, 228. For more on life in St. John's during World War II, see Steven High, ed., *Occupied St. John's: A Social History of a City at War, 1939–1945* (Montreal and Kingston: McGill-Queen's University Press, 2016).

11 Letters from war brides and widows form an intriguing subset of letters to Smallwood, as their concerns generally transcended the policies put in place by the newly elected provincial government. For more on this, see Boon, "Badly in Need," 228–30.

12 Jenny Higgins, "Economic Impacts of WW II," Heritage Newfoundland & Labrador, 2007, https://www.heritage.nf.ca/articles/politics/economic-impacts-wwii.php.

were built, but overland transportation links would be slower in coming, meaning continued struggles for those farthest from infrastructure and fiscal resources.[13]

Despite the Dominion's positive postwar balance sheet, the economic and social outlook of Newfoundland was uncertain. The boom years of the war were over, and the associated demand for many of Newfoundland and Labrador's resources plummeted. Prices for salt fish crashed and work in the lumber woods was irregular, back-breaking, and poorly paid.[14] Returning veterans, loggers, and merchant mariners could also not be assured of financial solvency. Nor, indeed, could widows. As "A worker & Widow" wrote in 1949, the widow's pension in pre-Confederation Newfoundland was paltry: "the sum they were receiving by The Commission of Government was not enough for sweetening for their tea."[15] The return of pre-war economic woes was unpalatable for many, as was the continued suspension of democracy.

Deepening the uncertainty was the reality that the British Empire was crumbling, and its oldest colony could no longer be financially supported. Faced with increasing crises, a National Convention was established in 1946 (forty-five elected representatives would serve: forty-four from the island, one from Labrador). In addition to reporting on the economy, the National Convention was tasked with considering possible "future forms of government," which would be presented to the electorate in the form of a referendum.[16] "Active debate defined the political culture of these transitional years," writes Sonja Boon. "In newspapers, on the radio, and from the pulpit, politicians, community leaders, and average Newfoundlanders promoted their perspectives."[17] The stakes were high, as was the rhetorical register. For some, and particularly the merchant class in St. John's, responsible government was the only viable option; they did not want to be dependent on Canada and its social programs. Anti-confederate and St. John's West representative Major Peter Cashin claimed at one point in the debates that a conspiracy existed "to sell this country to the Dominion of

---

13 For example, see the letter from "A disopinted Confedrate" in Carbonear-Bay de Verde district (p. 106, this volume) as well as essays by J.T.H. Connor and Heidi Coombs, later in this volume.

14 See Terry Bishop Stirling's essay, later in this volume.

15 Letter from "A worker & Widow" to Joseph R. Smallwood, May 22, 1949, St. John's West district (p. 349, this volume).

16 MacKenzie, *Inside the Atlantic Triangle*, 168.

17 Boon, "Badly in Need," 225.

Canada."[18] But for Joseph R. Smallwood, the representative for Bonavista Centre, "Canada was the promised land."[19]

This was not the first time that a union with Canada had been proposed. As J.K. Hiller writes, "[w]hether Newfoundland and Labrador should remain as an independent political entity, or join the federation of the other British North American colonies, was an issue from 1864 to 1949."[20] But never before had it been championed by such an impassioned advocate, a man with great political savvy and a well-known radio program to boot. As host and writer of *The Barrelman* from 1937 to 1943, Joseph Roberts Smallwood became a household name across the Dominion. It was through this platform that Smallwood built his reputation as an "expert" in Newfoundland culture, styled himself as the voice of the people, and laid the groundwork for his political career.[21] Smallwood was already a "gifted writer, speaker, and organizer; ... well read, well travelled, well rooted in the political culture of Newfoundland, and had boundless energy and self-confidence"[22] by the time he took up the mantle of the Barrelman. He would go on to put his talents, energy, and canny use of radio broadcasting to use in the two referenda to decide Newfoundland and Labrador's political future.[23] In his own words,

18 J.K. Hiller, "The Newfoundland National Convention, 1946–1948," Heritage Newfoundland & Labrador, 1997, https://www.heritage.nf.ca/articles/politics/newfoundland-national-convention.php.

19 Blake and Baker, *Where Once They Stood*, 258.

20 J.K. Hiller, "Newfoundland and Canada: 1864–1949," Heritage Newfoundland & Labrador, 1997, https://www.heritage.nf.ca/articles/politics/confederation-1864-1949.php.

21 Philip D. Hiscock, "*The Barrelman* Radio Program, 1937–1943: The Mediation and Use of Folklore in Newfoundland" (PhD diss., Memorial University, 1994).

22 Melvin Baker and Peter Neary, "Joseph Roberts Smallwood: A Biographical Sketch, 1900–1934," *Newfoundland and Labrador Studies* 33, no. 2 (2018): 401.

23 The radio was the centre of family life in mid-twentieth-century Newfoundland and Labrador—in the words of Jeff A. Webb, "a sort of aural hearth" (*The Voice of Newfoundland: A Social History of the Broadcasting Corporation of Newfoundland, 1939–1949* [Toronto: University of Toronto Press, 2008], 3), and many correspondents would have listened to Confederation debates. Many correspondents mention radios in their letters, among them a twelve-year-old girl from Fortune Bay & Hermitage district, who observed of her own community, "The people of this little settlement Listens in to your addresses over the Radio" (p. 148, this volume). Reflections by Vicki S. Hallett and Patricia Way, and Gemma Hickey, later in this volume, reference the influence and importance of *The Barrelman*.

> I had spent many years broadcasting and I knew the magic of it. The sheer, sheer magic, especially in a place like Newfoundland with so many isolated people. Radio, I've always contended, was invented by God especially for Newfoundland ... It was meant for a remote and isolated people who never met. Who never saw each other. Radio was the great unifying thing.[24]

Smallwood's fiery speeches, delivered over the radio, at the National Convention, and in person during his tireless touring of the island, were no small part of his success. In a January 23, 1948, speech to the National Convention, for example, Smallwood offered an impassioned defence of Confederation, positioning the battle as one between a small, wealthy, privileged elite that had too long held the reins of power and "the people," an oppressed majority eager and ready to see substantive change. As he stated,

> mark this well, this is not 1869.[25] This time the people are going to know the truth. They are not going to be smothered with the lies and propaganda of 1869 ... this time the anticonfederates are not going to get away with it, not even if every millionaire, half-millionaire and quarter-millionaire in the country rallies to the side of the anticonfederates. The day is gone when their money-bags will tell our people how to vote. That day is gone, and we live in a different age. Our people are no longer in the mood to bow down and almost worship a man just because he has managed somehow or other to make a great fortune for himself. They no longer measure a man's patriotism or his loyal heart by the money he has in the bank. When we say we have a stake in the country we no longer mean how much money a man has, but how many children he has, what is the size of his family, what is his love for the country. When we talk of "men of substance" today, we include something more than money. Our people are on the march in their tens of thousands. They have formed great trade unions and co-operative societies, and cannot

24 Qtd. in Webb, *The Voice*, 142.

25 In the 1869 general election, "the central issue was whether or not Newfoundland should join the Dominion of Canada." J.K. Hiller, "The Confederation Election of 1869," Heritage Newfoundland & Labrador, 1997, https://www.heritage.nf.ca/articles/politics/election-confederation-1869.php.

> so easily be bluffed any more. They have learned a lot the past few years, and they ask questions, questions that they never dared to ask in the bad old days ... They are not so easy to bluff as our fore-fathers were in 1869, and our anticonfederates are going to find that out in 1948 when the referendum takes place.[26]

"Joey" personalized politics in a way few others before him in this place had, and people connected with him, negatively or positively, in turn. His promises and grandiose vision of a modernized future played upon social schisms, ancient grievances, hopes and fears, both real and imagined. Knowing the difficult realities of seasonal work and the allure of both social security and cold hard cash, Smallwood built the myth of "'have not' will be no more" long before Brian Peckford,[27] with orations like these:

> I don't know how many children of under 16 there are in Victoria today, but in 1945, when the Census was taken, there were exactly five hundred.[28] Five hundred children under the age of 16, and I suppose today there are more. Every one of those children will get the Family Allowance—$5, $6, $7 or $8 to every child every month of the year, according to their ages. Taking it at an average of $6 a month for all the children, that would put $3000 a month into Victoria every month of the year—three thousand dollars to the children of that inland town in Conception Bay—Rain or shine,

26 "Newfoundland National Convention, 23 January 1948, Debates on Confederation with Canada," 1865–1949 Confederation Debates, 2023, https://hcmc.uvic.ca/confederation/en/lgNFNC_1948-01-23.html. The famous "Anti-Confederation Song" was written during the debates over the 1869 referendum and framed it as a choice between independence or succumbing to the "Canadian Wolf." See Edith Fowke, "The Anti-Confederation Song," *The Canadian Encyclopedia*, August 11, 2014, https://www.thecanadianencyclopedia.ca/en/article/quotthe-anti-confederation-songquot-emc and Vicki S. Hallett's reflection on letters from the Placentia-St. Mary's district, later in this volume. For more on the 1869 debates, see James K. Hiller, "The Debate: Confederation Rejected, 1864–1869," Heritage Newfoundland & Labrador, 1997, https://www.heritage.nf.ca/articles/politics/confederation-rejected-1864-1869.php.

27 For details of Premier Brian Peckford's provincial government, see Jenny Higgins, "The Peckford Government: 1979–1989," Heritage Newfoundland & Labrador, 2011, https://www.heritage.nf.ca/articles/politics/peckford-government.php.

28 Victoria is a small community near Carbonear, in Conception Bay.

> good times or bad, winter, spring, summer and fall, all the year round, month in and month out, three thousand dollars of cash would go into Victoria to the children. That is what Confederation will do for Victoria.[29]

As Karen Stanbridge has observed, through repeated concrete references to social programs such as the Family Allowance, Smallwood linked not only children's health, happiness, and well-being—and thus the future promise of Newfoundland and Labrador—but also parental responsibility directly with Confederation.[30]

After two years of boisterous public debate, the first referendum, on June 3, 1948, offered the electorate three options: a return to responsible government, a continuation of Commission of Government, or union with Canada. With a slight plurality of votes for responsible government but no clear majority for any of the three options, a second referendum was held just over a month later, on July 22, 1948. This time, there were only two options: responsible government or Confederation. Confederation came out on top, with a small majority of 52 per cent, a result carried by communities beyond the Avalon Peninsula. On March 31, 1949, the Dominion of Newfoundland became the tenth province of Canada, and two months later, on May 27, 1949, the first provincial elections were held.

The Terms of Union negotiated between Canada and its newest province would significantly impact all aspects of life in Newfoundland and Labrador, and its reverberations continue to be felt today. Specificities of taxation, control over natural resources, health care, and social programs were all hammered out between the two entities. The influence of religious institutions guaranteed the retention of Newfoundland's denominational education system, while control over fisheries management became a federal matter.[31] Formerly British subjects became citizens of Canada, and that included all Indigenous peoples.[32] Significantly in this regard, without consultation of Inuit,

---

29 Joseph R. Smallwood, undated speech, COLL-075, File 4.01.007, ASC.

30 Karen Stanbridge, "Framing Children in the Newfoundland Confederation Debate, 1948," *Canadian Journal of Sociology* 32, no. 2 (2007): 185.

31 Melvin Baker and Peter Neary, "Negotiating Final Terms of Union with Canada: The Memorandum Submitted by the Newfoundland Delegation, Ottawa, 13 October 1948," *Newfoundland and Labrador Studies* 33, no. 2 (2018): 459–506.

32 For more on how this erasure impacted and continues to impact Indigenous peoples in the province, see the essays by Dave Lough and Andrea Procter and the excerpt from Joe, O'Neill, Bound, and Thorpe's "Newfoundland Mi'kmaw Resistance

Innu, or Mi'kmaw groups about their future as enfranchised Canadians, the Terms of Union made no reference to "aboriginal people or Indian affairs" and the Indian Act was not adopted in the province.[33]

The turbulence of this period, the political intrigue, and the considerable stakes involved factored directly into the referendum results. The citizens of Newfoundland were receiving messages from politicians, clergy members, their neighbours, and the media, and these messages also—and unsurprisingly—found their way into the letters and telegrams sent to Joseph R. Smallwood.[34] Newfoundlanders and Labradorians cast their ballots and wrote their own letters based on a myriad of factors, but their opinions about Joey played no small part. Indeed, numerous correspondents echo not only Smallwood's politics but also directly reference his phrasing, positioning themselves among the "toiling masses" he spoke about in his speeches.[35] Histories of financial hardship or security impacted their imaginings of the future, and their allegiances to local religious and cultural traditions coloured their views of Smallwood, Confederation, and Canada writ large. Those views were rarely ambiguous, as evidenced by the reams of missives gathered in the archives. Reading them opens a unique window on the ways that Newfoundlanders and Labradorians were responding to the promises and perils of their times.

Lives, Letters, and Life Writing

As scholars who work in the field of autobiography studies, we are interested in the ways that individuals and communities represent themselves and their lives, and how they understand and make meaning of those selves and lives in relation

---

and Vibrancy in a History of Erasure," all later in this volume.

33 David MacKenzie, "The Indian Act and the Aboriginal Peoples of Newfoundland at the Time of Confederation," *Newfoundland and Labrador Studies* 25, no. 2 (2010): 176. The issue of the Indian Act was also raised by a correspondent whose telegram is short and to the point: "DO ANY OF OUR NFLD CITIZENS COME UNDER THE INDIAN ACT WOULD APPRECIATE HAVE ACT PUBLISHED REPLY" (p. 223, this volume).

34 See, for example, an impassioned letter from a man from Green Bay district (p. 170, this volume) who was concerned about the possible role of religion in shaping the outcome of the first referendum. For more on the kinds of messages directed toward the electorate, see Stanbridge, "Framing Children."

35 See, for example, selected letters from St. Barbe and Trinity South.

to the world in which they live. In this book, we use the term *life writing* to capture the myriad forms of autobiography that emerge in the letters to Smallwood, from letters and telegrams to poems and prayers, petitions, receipts, birth certificates, and more, all of which can be seen as forms of what Sidonie Smith and Julia Watson term "everyday" autobiography.[36]

But we also understand our contributors' personal and individual responses to the letters—whether in essay, poetic, or visual form—as instances of life writing. These responses, which are designed to be personal rather than scholarly interventions, write back to the original letters and offer insightful, intimate, and sometimes vulnerable reflections not just on this place but on their changed understandings of themselves and their relationship to this place as a result of reading the letters.

Letters are a unique form of life writing. In contrast to diaries, for example, which focus intimately on the self, letters are relational documents: correspondence requires both a sender and a recipient. Letters are about social relationships, that is, about how individuals imagine their identities in, through, and with others. Letters are about individuals, yes, but they are also about communities: about social, cultural, political, and geographical relationships.

Until recently, when alternative forms of relationship building such as email, texting, and social media became dominant, letters were ubiquitous to social relations. From intimate personal messages shared between lovers, newsy briefs shared among family members, and eager children's letters to Santa, to business letters, letters to the editor, published letters shared between famous authors and even epistolary novels, letters have been central to how we have imagined our relationships with others and also to how we have sustained those relationships.

As this broad range and variety suggest, letters are an intriguing genre because they blur the distinction between public and private lives. We might want to think of letters as intimate documents. And yet, as Margaretta Jolly argues, letters exist in an in-between space: they are a "tantalizing form of writing's engagement with life, where public and private, professional and personal are … happily confused."[37] This is evident in the letters to Smallwood—where

36 Sidonie Smith and Julia Watson, eds., *Getting a Life: Everyday Uses of Autobiography* (Minneapolis: University of Minnesota Press, 1996).

37 Margaretta Jolly and Liz Stanley, "Letters as / not a Genre," *Life Writing* 2, no. 2 (2005): 91.

Newfoundlanders and Labradorians leveraged sometimes deeply intimate and personal life stories in a bid to improve their life situations.[38]

The letters to Smallwood are not epistles shared between literary greats, or even intimate letters shared between partners. Rather, these letters are largely practical and pragmatic: most were written with the purpose of resolving material concerns and problems. But they are also aspirational: their presence reveals the commitment Newfoundlanders and Labradorians had to this place and to its possible futures, and to working toward improving the conditions in which they and others lived.

The letters to Smallwood are of interest for a number of reasons. First and foremost, they give insight into a tumultuous period in Newfoundland and Labrador history—not from the perspective of political leaders, but rather, from the perspectives of the everyday folks who were living through it. In this way, they are important testimonies that say "We matter," not just as individuals, family members, or community members but also as political agents. Indeed, numerous correspondents reference their voting intentions in relation to the issues they raise in their letters. At the same time, there is an inherent vulnerability in these exchanges, as correspondents shared sometimes very personal and intimate aspects of their daily lives with the premier.

The letters give slices of insight into the regional peculiarities of this place: what was important to folks in Grand Falls, in the forested interior of the island of Newfoundland,[39] was different from what was important to folks in St. Barbe or White Bay districts, who lived along the remote northern coast of the province, and thus very far from necessary infrastructure.[40] What mattered in St. John's East and West, the only urban districts in the new province,[41] meanwhile, was not necessarily relevant to those living in rural, outport communities in Burin or Burgeo-La Poile.

---

38 See, for example, Heidi Coombs's reflection on a letter from the White Bay district, later in this volume.

39 For more on the issues facing forestry workers in central Newfoundland, see Terry Bishop Stirling's essay, later in this volume.

40 See, for example, a fraught series of telegrams between a resident in White Bay district, and Smallwood requesting an emergency boat or plane to transport his wife to hospital. For more on the specific medical concerns along the Northern Peninsula, see Heidi Coombs's essay, later in this volume.

41 For example, young women in St. John's East and St. John's West wrote Smallwood seeking clerical work, which would not have been available in smaller, rural communities.

The letters also offer insight into questions of gender, class, and employment. While men were more likely to write in search of work so that they could support their families,[42] many women wrote as mothers or widows, with some requesting financial support for clothing that would allow their children to go to school.[43] Middle-class correspondents in urban St. John's wrote about different kinds of employment than their rural counterparts.

Disability is a factor as well. Newfoundlanders and Labradorians had fought in two world wars,[44] and even at home many men worked in physically demanding and often dangerous industries such as fishing, sealing, forestry, and factory work, all of which took a toll. One man recounted his own experiences in the fishery in a 1949 letter to Smallwood:

> I was washed overboard, and was rescued by some of the crowd, but got badly frozen when left in the snowdrifts until my shipmates travelled several miles to get assistance. I was so badly frozen that I spent several months in the hospital at St. Pierre & St. John's I lost some of my fingers, and what are left are knarled and out of shape also my feet are in much the same condition.[45]

Poverty, meanwhile, contributed to malnutrition, while geographic isolation and economic precarity resulted in limited access to health care. As a result,

42 In a 1949 letter, a man in Grand Falls district details his work history, including both the periods when he has been working and his subsequent fruitless search for work, and "trust[s] that [Smallwood] will do something" (p. 165, this volume) for him.

43 A widow from Burin district wrote Smallwood to ask him to send clothing and footwear for her family, and even included a list of items and sizes. For more on the intersections of gender and class in Confederation-era Newfoundland and Labrador, see Linda Cullum's essay, later in this volume. See also Linda Cullum, "Below Stairs: Domestic Service in Twentieth-Century St. John's," in Cullum and Porter, *Creating This Place*, 89–113, and "'It's Up to the Women': Gender, Class, and Nation Building in Newfoundland, 1935–1945," in Cullum and Porter, *Creating This Place*, 179–201.

44 One man from Placentia-St. Mary's district (p. 253, this volume) wrote Smallwood in April 1949, indicating that he was a veteran of World War I and "physically unfit for work."

45 See also a letter from a man from Burin district who shared details about his "physical inability" (p. 86, this volume) that was the result of a shipwreck, and a woman from Harbour Grace district who wrote to request financial support to open a "Candy Shop" (p. 195, this volume), as her husband had been suffering from work-related silicosis and was unable to provide.

tuberculosis rates were high—much higher than in Canada, the UK, and the USA[46]—and many died, or experienced lifelong aftereffects.

In addition to this, local cultures and religious belief were very important. The pulpit was a site of political rhetoric. Roman Catholic archbishop Edward Patrick Roche, for example, came out forcefully on the anti-confederate side.[47] The Provincial Grand Lodge of the Loyal Orange Association, in response, encouraged Protestants to resist this influence.[48] Some districts, such as Placentia-St. Mary's and Ferryland, were overwhelmingly Catholic; others, such as Twillingate and Burgeo-La Poile, were almost wholly Protestant.[49] While eventual referendum results have conventionally been linked to religious affiliation, and while the anti-confederate cause was bolstered in sermons from Roman Catholic pulpits, that equation is not necessarily as neat and tidy as it might at first look, and as Vicki S. Hallett examines in her reflection on the letters from Placentia-St. Mary's, individual letters suggest a much more complex matrix was at play.

Finally, the letters offer written records of local dialects and in this way exist as vital testaments to local ways of living, thinking, and being. Many of the correspondents had limited access to formal education and this is reflected in spelling, capitalization, and punctuation. And yet these seemingly "inconsistently written" documents can give incredible insight into how people spoke: they are material markers of dialects that are slowly disappearing. They attest to the

---

46 According to a 1947 publication, in 1945, "the number of cases of active pulmonary tuberculosis was estimated as being between 3 and 4 percent of the population, which is three or four times the incidence in England" (H.N., "Review of Tuberculosis in Newfoundland [1945] by T.O. Garland and P. D'Arcy Hart," *The British Journal of Tuberculosis* 41, no. 1 [1947]: 30). For more on the history of tuberculosis in Newfoundland and Labrador, see Keith Collier, "Fighting Tuberculosis in Newfoundland and Labrador," Heritage Newfoundland & Labrador, 2011, https://www.heritage.nf.ca/articles/society/fighting-tuberculosis.php. For more on health care in Confederation-era Newfoundland and Labrador, see the essays by J.T.H. Connor and Heidi Coombs, later in this volume.

47 For more on Archbishop E.P. Roche, see Hans Rollmann, "Edward Patrick Roche," Heritage Newfoundland & Labrador, 1999, https://www.heritage.nf.ca/articles/politics/biography-edward-roche.php.

48 J.K. Hiller, "The 1948 Referendums," Heritage Newfoundland & Labrador, 1997, https://www.heritage.nf.ca/articles/politics/referendums-1948.php.

49 For more detail on religious affiliation at the time of Confederation, see "Referendum Voting Trends by District," Heritage Newfoundland & Labrador, https://www.heritage.nf.ca/articles/politics/denominational-percentages-statistics.php.

specificity of each writer and each region in this province. We encourage you to read the letters out loud to recover some of the embodied experience of dialect.

What can we learn from reading letters? As Kylie Cardell and Jane Haggis observe, letters can "[give] insight into the private lives of famous or notable people."[50] Our interest, however, is in the social role of letters, that is, in the relationships imagined and articulated through letters. The letters to Smallwood document relationships that individuals built with Smallwood—as premier, as radio host, as hero or villain of this place. Premier or radio host, hero or villain, the Smallwood to whom the people of Newfoundland and Labrador directed their letters was a mythical, larger-than-life being. But he was also, for better or for worse, the person best placed to respond to their material concerns.[51] Smallwood capitalized on this. Building his populist political brand as defender of the "toiling masses," he invited constituents across Newfoundland and Labrador to share their concerns directly with him, and it's clear that correspondents took up this invitation. In the words of a man writing from Burgeo-La Poile district in August 1949, "I was at the meeting here when you came and you told us if we wanted to write to you just to call you Joey, so I am taking the chance to write you hoping you will be able to do something for me."[52] Another correspondent from Bonavista North district, writing in October of the same year, echoed this sentiment: "you told us in your speech here ... anything we want to know about just write and ask you."[53]

And yet, we can't read letters as wholly transparent documents; just as we need to consider the truth claims in social media posts, for example, so, too, do we need to consider the stories we read in letters. Letters are exchanges, but they are also performances that depend on audience reception. In other words, letters—unlike other forms of intimate life writing such as diaries or autobiographies—are about reciprocity. Because of this, it's important to consider the possible motivations of letter writers and also their awareness and understanding of their audience.

---

50 Kylie Cardell and Jane Haggis, "Contemporary Perspectives on Epistolarity," *Life Writing* 8, no. 2 (2011): 129.

51 Smallwood responded to many—but certainly not all!—of the letters sent to him. In some instances, we have included his responses so readers can get a sense of the nature of the politician-constituent relationship. But as Jennifer Morgan's exploration of a series of letters written by a widow in St. John's suggests, many correspondents were frustrated by the inadequacy or complete lack of replies.

52 See p. 67, this volume.

53 See p. 34, this volume.

Does this mean that correspondents are lying? Absolutely not. But letter writers are storytellers and storytellers shape and frame their stories for their audience, highlighting some aspects of their stories, while downplaying or even ignoring others. Although we are not focused on Smallwood, he is nevertheless an invisible presence in each and every letter. In his radio broadcasts and on the hustings, Smallwood actively invited constituents to share their concerns with him,[54] and those who chose to write knew they had to convince the new premier of the relevance, importance, and seriousness of the issues they were bringing forward. Some correspondents were particularly tenacious. Contributor Jennifer Morgan, for example, introduces us to a widow who wrote not just a single letter to Smallwood in the first two years following Confederation, but at least eight! Many correspondents used flattery. Some correspondents, as Angela Antle discovered, offered quantifiable and verifiable details as well as supporting documents (including bills, petitions, and more). Others used deception.[55] And some couldn't contain their venom.[56]

The sheer volume of letters included in the Smallwood collection gives an illusion of completeness, that is, readers might assume that every single letter that Newfoundlanders and Labradorians ever sent to the premier was kept and filed away. However, this is not the case. In some instances, letters were forwarded to other departments or offices and only Smallwood's reply remains. It is also likely that some letters were misplaced, destroyed, lost, or otherwise waylaid, either in the premier's or other Cabinet offices, or even before they arrived at their destination.

There are other issues to consider as well. Those who wrote to Smallwood ranged from children to the elderly. They lived in St. John's and they lived in the tiniest, most remote outport communities. Some had extensive formal education; others had none. Some were Protestant. Others Catholic. Still others likely tangled with faith. Some were Indigenous. Some were new immigrants. Some were not. Some were poor—very poor—while others were solidly middle class. This breadth is refreshing. But it's also deceptive in that it can obscure the absences. Largely absent from the correspondence, for example, are the individual

---

54 Thousands took up Smallwood's invitation; however, some were insistent on their rights to privacy. In the words of "A Confederate," "I would prefer not to have this broadcast" (p. 382, this volume).

55 See, for example, Boon, "Badly in Need," 241, n. 74.

56 See, for example, a letter from St. John's East dated April 1, 1949, in which the author compares Smallwood to Judas Iscariot (p. 325, this volume).

voices of the most privileged. Thus, while some merchants wrote in in their formal capacities as business owners, very few wrote personal letters. This suggests that they likely had other avenues through which to approach the premier with issues of personal or private concern. The voices of those who could not write are also absent. Those who were illiterate, ill, hospitalized, and/or otherwise institutionalized usually appear only in letters written by others on their behalf (although we include a few notable exceptions in this book).[57] Others, meanwhile, may have chosen to fly under the radar rather than to advertise their social precarity. Finally, we must also consider that not all Newfoundlanders and Labradorians communicated in English (let alone in its written form). Among this group, we might include some Indigenous and newer immigrant communities.[58] Contributors Miriam Wright and Robert Hong observe that some 400 Chinese men immigrated to Newfoundland in the decades preceding Confederation. Of them, forty sought Canadian citizenship in 1949. And yet, we have been unable to find any letters to Smallwood from Chinese Newfoundlanders in the districts of St. John's East and West or Harbour Main-Bell Island between 1948 and 1951.[59] Thus, while we can—and should!—celebrate the incredible diversity and richness of this collection of letters and the stories they reveal, we should also be mindful of the stories that remain unwritten and unspoken, and therefore, unheard.

A Collaborative Quilt

Much like the process of collaborative quilting, the construction of *Dear Mr. Smallwood* has been a group effort. We invited more than thirty contributors to participate in this project. Some contributed scholarly essays; others, meanwhile, wrote personal reflection pieces. Each of our contributors brings a unique history and relationship to this place, and thus to the letters and the broader historical period

57 See, for example, a letter sent by a longtime patient in the Waterford Hospital, then known as the Hospital for Mental and Nervous Diseases (p. 352–53, this volume).

58 Very few letters directly reference Indigenous concerns. Among the letters gathered here, one woman identifies herself in the letter as "Eskimo" and wants to know what Smallwood is going to do for the people of Labrador (p. 243, this volume). Another correspondent from Humber district asked about the Indian Act (p. 223, this volume).

59 It is, however, possible that some of these men may have sought in person meetings with the premier.

in which they were written. They are students, researchers, artists, business owners, poets, teachers, activists, craftspeople. They are young. They are old. They can trace their family history in Newfoundland back ten generations or more. They arrived in this place within the last twenty years. Some live here. Others yearn for it. They are Indigenous, settlers, immigrants.

What our contributors have in common is a deep and abiding love and passion for Newfoundland and Labrador, its histories, and its peoples. And that love and passion shines through in the letters they chose, in the reflections and writings and visual art they share, and in the scholarly essays they have written. In their journeys with the letters, all of them learned new things about this place. "I'll never forget my experience reading them," noted one contributor, "and I will be going back again to do it again sometime for my own pleasure." As another observed, "This project changed me."[60]

Together, the letters, reflections, and essays that comprise this book can be seen as a layered patchwork quilt. The letters to Smallwood—a small sampling of 250 chosen by contributors from an archival collection of thousands—are the colourful swatches that reveal not just the individual voices of Newfoundlanders and Labradorians of all ages at mid-century but also the beating life narrative—the collective autobiography—of this place itself.

We asked reflection contributors to read letters from a single district, pick out those that impacted them most, and then to write about what inspired them. For some, the task was intensely personal. They have or had family connections to the area about which they were reading, and familiar family names appeared like magic as they read. For others, the task was one of novel engagement and of learning about Newfoundland and Labrador in a unique way. Their letter choices are individual, but taken together, they create a vibrant and colourful whole. Alongside the letters, our contributors stitched personal reflections, sharing intimate, poetic, and visual responses not only to the letters but also, in some cases, to their own family histories. In form and approach, the diversity of our contributor reflections—which include poetry, visual art, autobiographical pieces, and essays—mirrors the diversity of the original letters, which included poetry, song, birth certificates, receipts, petitions, and more. The original letters and contemporary

---

60 Jasmine Paul, "I'll never forget my experience reading them and I will be going back again to do it again sometime for my own pleasure," Twitter (now X), 5:13 p.m., January 13, 2023, https://twitter.com/jnp709/status/1614012753684975627, and Andreae Callanan, "This project changed me. Thank you for welcoming me into it! I can't wait to see everyone's work," Twitter (now X), 8:14 p.m., January 13, 2023.

reflections, personal rather than scholarly in nature, are the heart of this project, and function almost as kitchen-table conversations, bringing the concerns and passions of past and present together. Taken together, these letters and reflections are a complex quilt top, rich with patterns and memories.

While the letters and reflections form the core of this book, we also include short, more scholarly essays that provide further information and historical context. An editorial introduction, plus an orientation to the Smallwood collection, "A Contextual Note from the Archivist," written by Archives and Special Collections archivist and division head Colleen Quigley, begins this final section. This is followed by a series of essays written by scholars and activists that provide a set of signposts about some of the more specific social, cultural, and economic conditions that pervaded in the lead up to the Confederation debates and referenda. Writers take up health care (Connor; Coombs), work and work conditions (Bishop Stirling), and community (Cullum). In some instances (Procter; Wright and Hong), these essays point to forms of political identity and political agency that are not visible in the letters to Smallwood. To follow our quilt metaphor, these essays are the batting upon which the multifarious swatches of letter and reflections were sewn.

But as vibrant as this quilt is, it's also a very specific and particular quilt stitched by the specific and particular contributors who came together for this project. Different editors and different contributors would have made different choices, and those choices would have resulted in a very different—though equally rich and colourful—quilt.

Our collaborative quilt offers a reframing of the story of Confederation. Unlike any book that precedes this one, *Dear Mr. Smallwood* invites readers to reflect on the stories they might think they know about this time, about these events, and about the peoples of this place, and to consider them anew. It asks that we consider the lived experiences of voters, some of whom would be exercising the franchise for the first time in the referenda of 1948, and many others of whom had not voted since 1933, and what a potential union with Canada might have meant to them and their communities. While those meanings were varied, they were united around one central reality: change. Significant changes were occurring, and there were more in store, of that all correspondents were certain.

Whatever your background or attachment to this place, we invite you to visit the Smallwood collection, to read these letters, and to build relationships with those who shared their hopes, dreams, passions, and disappointments with Smallwood. Perhaps you will find old family connections, perhaps you will experience new familial feelings. We think you will feel part of this place as never before.

A note on transcription. We asked contributors to transcribe letters exactly as they found them, that is, to maintain original spelling, capitalization, and punctuation. We also asked them to mark unclear words or phrases with empty square brackets. After receipt, we and a research assistant checked transcriptions against the originals and made any necessary changes. In some instances, we turned to social media to crowdsource suggestions for unclear or illegible words and phrases that left us all stumped. Where things remained illegible after this point, we have marked them in this book as "[illegible]."

We present the transcribed letters in three different fonts from the Nexus typeface family. Handwritten letters (the vast majority) appear in sans serif italic (*Nexus Sans Italic*). Telegraphs are presented in a stylized sans serif (NEXUS TYPEWRITER PRO) in capital letters, as they originally appeared. Typewritten letters, as well as responses from Smallwood, meanwhile, appear in a font that mimics the look of typewriter lettering (Nexus Mix Pro Regular). The introductions, reflections, and essays appear in a standard serif (Nexus Serif Pro).

In a few instances, following a practice outlined by Karina Vernon in *The Black Prairie Archives: An Anthology*, we have chosen to maintain the lineation of the original letter, which results in a long, narrow strip of transcribed text, rather than in transcribed text that flows across the page. As Vernon asserts, such a process "amplifies the possibilities for reading the texts in other ways—for instance, as found poems."[61]

A comment about ethics and privacy. While those who wrote to Smallwood likely understood that their letters would be handled by different government secretaries and officials, and while some indicated that they didn't want their letters read on the radio, many likely could not have imagined that their letters would end up in a publicly accessible archival collection at Memorial University. Some correspondents—such as "a drunkards wife," "The girl

61 Karina Vernon, *The Black Prairie Archives: An Anthology* (Waterloo: Wilfrid Laurier University Press, 2020), 49. See, for example, three letters written by [name redacted] from Fox Cove, in the district of Placentia West (p. 267–68, 272, 273–74, this volume), and a letter from [name redacted] in St. John's East (p. 328–29, this volume).

given a raw deal," and a "Worried Widow"—actively chose anonymity even as they brought their concerns forward. Other letters, meanwhile, included details of possible criminal or potentially libellous nature. These, we have left in the archives. Finally, we note that in some instances correspondents use terms that are considered derogatory today, although they were common at the time they were written. We have chosen to maintain the terms as they appear in the original letters.

Except in instances where we were able to reach out to descendants of correspondents, we have redacted all correspondent and community names. In most cases, we have chosen to cut the names entirely; however, where there was more than one signatory to a letter, we have noted this with square brackets.[62] When correspondents were writing in their official capacities as teachers, members of the clergy, doctors, nurses, or union leaders, we indicated their roles, but not their names, in their signatures. Where correspondents identified specific communities within the body of their letters, we redacted these using phrasings such as "[my community]" or "[neighbouring community]," or we used an ellipsis ("..."); we made our decisions based on what we felt would make the letter flow most smoothly for readers. Regardless of redactions, all letters remain within the larger district from which they were sent.

Where correspondents included names of family members, doctors, nurses, and so forth *within* their letters, we redacted them, using either square brackets or an ellipsis depending on readability. The only exception to this is when correspondents identified politicians, as these men were public figures whose words and actions are often integral to understanding the meaning and context of the letters. Where politicians' names appear in letters, we also include a footnote to identify their political party and district.

Where correspondents included multiple names in their letters, such that writing "[name redacted]" would have resulted in confusion for readers, we used pseudonyms. We have included footnotes whenever pseudonyms are used. Some correspondents, for example, "Widows of the West End," chose their own pseudonyms. In these letters, we have honoured their pseudonyms but redacted the name of their community.

We have included several examples of Smallwood's responses to the letters he received, because these letters and telegrams give a sense of the nature and

62 See, for example, a letter from Labrador district dated April 5, 1949 (p. 238, this volume).

timeliness of his responses. In these instances, we have followed the same principles we previously outlined: we redacted correspondent and community names, but maintained Smallwood's name.

We transcribed all letters as faithfully as we could. Where we felt that additional context was necessary to understand the letter, we included that information in footnotes.

We engaged in extensive outreach—via public events, a website, radio broadcasts, and social media—to identify possible descendants of correspondents. Ultimately, we were able to reach out to only three families—represented in two letters. We are grateful to these families for granting us permission to include their parents' full letters in this collection, and we acknowledge this permission in footnotes.

We began this project in 2019, before Snowmageddon and before the global pandemic. As a result, our individual and collective research and writing journeys have been tumultuous, challenging, overwhelming, and sometimes completely upside down. Our thanks to all our contributors for their commitment, curiosity, and energy. It's been a delight to work with you all and to read and learn through your eyes. Our deepest thanks to the descendants of O. Parsons, O.E. Taylor, and Ethel Dempsey, who granted us permission to include their names and full letters in this book.

Our thanks, too, to Colleen Quigley, Linda White, Paulette Noseworthy, and the rest of the staff at Archives and Special Collections, who went above and beyond to support this project, even offering special hours to make access possible in pandemic times; Elizabeth Dane and Tóbin Boon-Petersen for proofreading work in the early and late stages of this project respectively; Andrea Procter for scanning all the letters from Labrador to make them more easily available for transcription; Linda Cullum for information about the Fishermen's and Workmen's Protective Union in Burin; and to those participants who transcribed letters from more than one district. Thanks, too, to those in the social media world who offered a range of possible interpretations for particularly challenging transcriptions. We also want to thank those who were interested in being part of this project but who had to withdraw for a variety of reasons over the course of more than three long pandemic years.

Our thanks to the anonymous reviewers who offered helpful commentary that strengthened this work and to the tireless staff at Memorial University Press—Fiona Polack, Sharon Roseman, Alison Carr, Randy Drover, Heather Patey, and copyeditor Iona Bulgin—who answered endless questions, put out fires (sometimes big ones!), designed the perfect cover, typeset this book, and took care of the tiniest of details. Thank you to the *Canadian Historical Review* for granting us permission to reproduce an excerpt from Mi'sel Joe, Sheila O'Neill, Jessica Bound, and Jocelyn Thorpe's "Newfoundland Mi'kmaw Resistance and Vibrancy in a History of Erasure," which appears in *Canadian Historical Review* 104, no. 3 (2023): 315–42, and to the J.R. Smallwood Foundation and the Federation for the Humanities and Social Sciences for the publication subvention grants that make the publication of this book possible.

Even more than this, our deepest thanks go to the Newfoundlanders and Labradorians who chose to put pen to paper to write to the premier between 1948 and 1951. Thank you for giving us a window into your lives. Thank you for sharing your concerns, hopes, and fears and for pushing for a brighter future for yourselves and those who would come after you, and in this way, for making Newfoundland and Labrador the place it is today.

BONAVISTA NORTH

"I know you will do your best for me."

Vicki S. Hallett

"I KNOW YOU WILL DO YOUR BEST FOR ME." This phrase was common to the point of ubiquity in the collection of letters sent from the district of Bonavista North to Joseph R. Smallwood in the years 1948–50. Scrawled on tiny scraps of paper or typed on company stationery, the phrase at once evokes the writers' confidence in the letters' recipient, offering subtle praise for their faithfulness, while simultaneously pleading for that faith to be rewarded.

First as Confederation's greatest advocate, and later as Newfoundland's first provincial premier, Smallwood inspired the people of this district to write copious letters and voluminous petitions for local improvements they hoped to make. The sprawling district held J.R. Smallwood's hometown of Gambo, the place where his grandfather David Smallwood had set up the island's first steam-powered lumber mill in 1863.[1] It was the district in which he had cut his political teeth and would be elected as its first Member of the House of Assembly. It was a district defined by the two key extractive industries of fishing and logging, industries which had provided livelihoods for generations of Newfoundlanders, but were floundering at mid-century.

The Labrador floater fishery, stalwart supplier of salt cod for over two centuries, had all but disappeared, and by 1954, the last of the schooners, my

1 Ursula A. Kelly and Meghan C. Forsyth, *The Music of Our Burnished Axes: Songs and Stories of the Woods Workers of Newfoundland and Labrador* (St. John's: ISER Books, 2018), 5.

grandfather's among them, would be out of the water forever.[2] The lumber woods were also no longer the assured source of income they had once been for families in Bonavista North. All lumber mills, including the giant Anglo-Newfoundland Development Company, had seen business decrease from their height at the end of the nineteenth century.[3] Men were finding less and less work in the lumber woods, both those employed year-round and those fishermen who relied on it to supplement their income in the fall and winter.[4]

"I know you will do your best for me." People wrote the phrase at the end of their letters, a way of signing off that held Mr. Smallwood to account for the story they had imparted. Sometimes the story was brief, a few lines to convey the writer's dismay at the rising cost of groceries. One man inquired about the "right selling price" of a tin of milk, as he thought nineteen cents far too dear. Could Mr. Smallwood double-check this, while not making his name "known to the trading co."?

Others were hoping that their disabled child who was approaching adulthood might qualify for some kind of benefit, as the aging parents were finding it too difficult to keep body and soul together. Widows wrote of their struggle to feed themselves and their children on pennies a day. A widow with six children wrote to Smallwood on February 27, 1949, that she was "starving" and "always a cheque back" in her debt to the merchant.

Entrepreneurs, new and seasoned alike, wrote narratives detailing their business ventures and their relative success or failure. Could Mr. Smallwood do something to get the government involved to help local sawmills process more lumber in the area? Was there any help available for an enterprising fellow looking to open a new store? Might there be work building the new road or at the airport in Gander? Perhaps he could find a buyer for the twenty-five sticks that were cut and dried out back? One man tried to inveigle Smallwood into helping

---

2 W.A. Black, "The Labrador Floater Codfishery," *Annals of the Association of American Geographers* 50, no. 3 (1960): 267–95.

3 "The heyday of the lumber mill era on the island was the last decade of the nineteenth century and coincident with the completion of the Reid Newfoundland Railway." Kelly and Forsyth, *The Music*, 4.

4 We use the terms "fisherman" and "fishermen" throughout this book to denote people involved in the fishing industry. We recognize that the gender specificity of these terms does not reflect the current realities in the fishing industry; however, we use them because they were the most common terms in mid-century Newfoundland and Labrador.

with his new venture and used his existing company letterhead to lend gravitas. His entreaty included the slightly more sophisticated, "I am confident that you will do your utmost for me in this matter."

A skipper wondered whether there would be any compensation for gear destroyed in a monstrous gale on the Labrador the previous summer. What about those Unemployment Insurance benefits? Surely those would be extended to the fishermen, for how could they continue "to take such a gamble" without access to the same benefits as other workers?

Still others were making intrepid waves in new directions. One woman was convinced that a telephone would help her and others in the community more effectively market their vegetables. Another involved Smallwood in her fight to get financial support from her husband, who was seeking a divorce. This mother of three went so far as to send Smallwood copies of his lawyer's correspondence and ended her letter with the familiar phrase, "I trust that you will do your best for me."

The phrase signalled Newfoundlanders' brand of politics. Personal and deeply felt, it opens up a relationship bounded by trust. It is both naive and calculating in its simplicity. It asks a good turn, but not before offering a compliment. It imbues Mr. Smallwood with those qualities he claimed to have: trustworthiness, sway with the bigwigs, and a determination to fight for the people. The people believed it, as far as it went. They had done their best for him, supported Confederation, the Liberal Party, and most of all Smallwood himself. Now, they were placing their faith in him, that he would do his best for them.

Aprial the 1
1948

Mr. Smallwood

Thanks very much for your kind litter it was very nice of you to right me will this as been a very exsighting day here and I am very proud of you going through so much trouble and work to get newfoundland into confederation to do good for the poor piple witch has suffer so much I often praied that god would give you strength and bring you through and I am glad he heard my prayer and I hope newfoundland will live bitter no more dole I have seen dark days on the dole with my children around me I often cried down tears and I have work hard trying to bring up 12 children but I lost some I have done all kinds of work now I am not able to do any work but I am trusting in god that he will help me through alowing you will do your best for every poor widow[5] *who cant work please exsuise my righting I haven't much learning*

Sincely Yours

5 For more on supports available to widows, see Gina Snooks's reflection, later in this volume.

Feb 27 – 1949

Dear Mr. Smallwood:

I am a widow residiend of [my community] with six children ranging from two yrs to fifteen yrs.

My only support is from the D.P.H.'s Welfare a cheque of $35.00 monthly.[6]

This small amount is not enough for me to live on. And as the present time, I am starving.

I am always a cheque back. I mean by this that when I get my cheque it is owed to the merchant that supplies me.

I am asking you now sir could you obtain some help for me please – could you make my case known to some of your friends and get a few cash donations and send me.

This would help me and very much.

Should you be able to do anything for me in this respect I would be deeply grateful.

I remain,
Yours Sincerely

6 Department of Public Health.

May 7/49

Dear Mr. Smallwood

I am sending you a bill of a tin of Suncrest milk which I received. As far as I know the right selling price is 15¢.

If there is anything done about this price I would like for my name not to be known to the trading co. Yours truly

Come as quickly as possible
Big reception for you

[Attached to this letter is a receipt from the Fishermen's Union Trading Co. Ltd. for "1 tin milk 19¢"]

May 26/49

Joseph R Smallwood
St. Johns

Dear Sir: -

I am a farmers wife and we are living in a settlement with only one phone which is not in working order all the time and we are sometimes cut off from all connection thus causing a very great inconvience especially in the fall when we and also all the farmers are trying to make shipment for their vegetables.

I made application for a telephone nearly two years ago and have not received one yet[7] *Could it be possible for you to see to this and see that my application be granted thus enabling us to get connection all the time through one phone or the other. And this would be a great convience for us farmers and also all our buyers as we could get communication with all parts of Nfld.*

Please will you try to do your very best for us and see that my application be granted thanking you very much as wishing you every success in the future

Yours truly

7 For more on the history of telephone communications, see Jenny Higgins and Luke Callanan, "Post-1949 Communications and Transportation," Heritage Newfoundland & Labrador, 2008/2019, https://www.heritage.nf.ca/articles/society/post-1949-communication.php; Newfoundland Telephone Company, Ltd., *Along These Lines: A History of Newfoundland Telephone* (St. John's. Newfoundland Telephone Co., 1979).

July 8th, 1949.

Hon. J. R. Smallwood,
Premier,
ST. John's

Dear Mr. Smallwood:-

I know that you are a very busy man and will be busy for the next four years, but I feel that as the time is passing, I am anxious to know if I am going to get that permission to start a store at Gander, which I have pestered you so much about. I am confident that you will do your utmost for me in this matter.

I would also like to mention here, that daily the old people of this place are making enquiries as to when they are giong to receive their old age pensions, as the invistigators are very slow in getting around, to make matters worse, those who are against us are trying to convince those old people that its all of a bluff. To speed matters up would it not be a good suggestion to have some reliable man in the place have the applications filled and sent the department concerned.

Yours very Sincerily,

July 13/49

Dear Sir,

I am writing you concerning my crippled son he haven't got any pension yet I have had is papers sent in since the first part of June. [Name redacted] told me he would see about it but I never heard from him his father was killed in this war and I get a pension if youd ask [him] you would get Particulars from him I lived at [community] but now I am removed to [another community] would you be able to get this money for him as the poor boy needs it badly as he is a cripple & there is times when he needs something to eat more than I can get for him. I didn't know who else to write to & I know you will try & do your best for me as you do for everybody else.

Hon. JR Smallwood
St. Johns *August 8 1949*

Dear Sir,

As you have been our friend for the past two or three years and it as present our Primeminister I think it my pleasure in writing you to get your opinion on some way to get a engine for us as you told us in your speech here at [my community] anything we want to know about just write and ask you and as I would like to know what our new goverment could do in that way to help out the fishermen I taught I would write and ask you our old engine we have been running for years is just about worn out or anyway she is not fit to be trusted and in order to carry on the the fishery we have got to get a new engine we want a eight HP Atlantic to suit our boat and they are at a pretty high price for a fisherman to buy we have been fishing all of our life or at least 15 years and cannot raise the money to buy a new 8 HP Atlantic engine as you know a fisherman with any gear is always a big expence year before last we build a new motor boat cost us over one hundred dollars so I think when a man got to slave at the fishery all the summer and when it is over in the fall got to look for a job for the winter to get money for to buy a engine for to go fishing they next summer it is time to forget it the only thing is into it when a man is fitted out for fishing he is never stuck weather he makes any money of not he got a chance it have been a very poor fishery here this summer the catches ar low you will have to excuse me for writing you but I don't think it is mutch harm we have got a new goverment and not all of we people know what it can do so will you please write me at your earliest convenience and let me know what you can say about it so I think I have said all for this time

Yours Sincerely

Oct. 14th, 1949.

Hon. J.R. Smallwood,
Premier,
St. John's.

Dear Sir,

Since my visit to St. John's, I am daily confronted with a question which is causing some trouble. I am fully aware that the question arising is not one that I should be looking to you for a definite ruling on; but so many have been looking for the correct procedure that I ask you if you will set me right, so that I then advise the parties concerned correctly.

Here is the obstacle some people here that were employed with the A.N.D. Co.,[8] have been discharged from work due to the Company slowing down, they have applied for Unemployment Insurance and have received their first cheque, and the A.N.D. Co., office here have definitely refused to sign their application form; although they were their last employer; It leaves those men in a box; I have also been given to understand that they will not place stamps in the employee's books; What can such people do? I take it that the Company is not registering their employees. What I would like to ascertain is what must such men do? If their employer will not sign they will loose their unemployment insurance. With such a slowing down in both the Company's Operators due to the sterling exchange. It is too bad to see those men cut being off from Unemployment Insurance because of the attitude of their Employer.

I am at present looking around for something myself; I was thinking you might have something to offer; If you have I would gladly accept.

I felt like writing Hon. W.J. Keough on his action over the rabbits, which is definitely a step in the right direction, a mistake of past governments but I am happy that he has made the right move: Further to this I would like to see his Department take necessary steps to save the rabbit and partridge by offering a bounty on crows, foxes and weasels which are over running those areas; and no young life can exist.

Trusting you are keeping fit,

Yours truly,
(Sgd).

8 The Anglo-Newfoundland Development Company, established by English newspaper-publishing brothers Alfred and Harold Harmsworth, concerned about the availability of printing paper in Europe, was incorporated in St. John's in 1905. It opened its first pulp and paper mill in Grand Falls in 1909.

23/11th/49

Honourable Prime Minister Nfld
J.R. Smallwood
St. John's

Dear Sir:-

A few days ago, while at St. John's I thought to get an interview with you for a few moments, but failed, as you happened to be to a meeting at that time as I was informed by the finance minister on. Mr. Quinton.[9]

What I want to know is this, have you any hope for Labrador fishery? You may say that's a silly question to ask, to my point of view, it is a serious one. My point is this, The fisherman and the farmer are all in the one boat, they receive no unemployment insurance, neither do they come under the assistance act. Do you really think that fisherman is going fishing & take such a gamble, as you know fishing is always a gamble, when if they get work for thirty days they come under the assistance act and if they work for six mths they come under the unemployment insurance act.

"Hon Sir" I can tell you, ninety percent of the fisherman that Ive been in contact with, that is the chief topic and as we got a lot of unemployment in our country today, I, greatly afraid we will have a larger number in the spring unless someone works fast.

Here is another thing I wish to draw your attention too, which is making the matter worse, two thirds of the floaters[10] *on the northern Labrador lost from one to three cod traps in the storm of Aug. 9th/49, & one third of these men cannot place their gear without help as the cost of twine , rope, leads is high & those who can purchase gear is failing to do so under present conditions, as they don't know if they will get men enough to operate or not.*

9 A veteran of World War I and later manager of Fishermen's Protective Union Trading Company branches, Herman William Quinton was first elected to the House of Assembly in 1928, representing Bonavista. He later served in the Commission of Government (1947–49). In 1949, he was elected as Member of the House of Assembly for Burgeo-La Poile and served as finance minister. In 1951, he was appointed a federal senator.

10 For more on the floater fishery, see Jeff Butt, "Labrador Fishery," Heritage Newfoundland & Labrador, 1998, https://www.heritage.nf.ca/articles/exploration/labrador-fishery.php.

What about the "workmens compensation act" is that still going to remain in force, for the owner of the vessel to pay all premiumns? If so, you can rest assured that a very small portion of vessels will operate next year.

I have been master for twenty one years, and it looks very much like I am to the end of my rope, as I was one of the unfortunates, who lost my cod-traps & two other vessels of this place shared the same fate.

"Honourable Sir" I know you are a very busy man, & I consider you are up against a hard year, for your first year in office but if the mean time, please give this a little consideration, and reply at your earliest convenience in the light as you see the Labrador fishing industry

I Remain

Yours Truly

BONAVISTA SOUTH

Confederation Promises, Confederation Prayers

Julia Laite

I REMEMBER MY GRANDPARENTS' supper table, on Sundays after they'd moved to Holyrood in the early 1990s. I can close my eyes and smell it: roast chicken, boiled turnip, apple dumplings, and the woodstove down in the belly of their bungalow. This table was the place where I cut my political teeth, where I learned to think and debate, where I first got my hunger to know, understand, and become a historian. The topics at hand were on many families' lips in those days, and they mostly swirled around Newfoundland and Labrador's place in Canada. The cod moratorium and Crosbie and the way Newfoundlanders were being depicted in the national press. The coastal boats and rural depopulation and resettlement.

> (Tell me about floating the house, I'd ask for the hundredth time, and then I'd listen as though to a litany: the spruce rollers, the oil drums, the put-puts, and the sheer wonder of the collaborative work and collective madness of moving a couple hundred people—houses and all—from Silver Fox Island to the mainland towns of Northwest Bonavista Bay).

And, of course, we spoke about Joey Smallwood and Confederation.

Back then, I was pasting "Newfoundland Republican Army" stickers to my guitar case and toying with being a separatist. I had been firmly warned by my mother: don't say anything against Joey or you'll break your grandfather's heart. My grandfather voted for Confederation and told me in no uncertain terms he'd vote the same way a thousand times. My grandparents loved their tiny island, but Canada promised social mobility for their children. On March 31, 1949, they must have celebrated. My grandfather, a gifted writer himself who counted Smallwood among his heroes, may have penned a few passages of his own.

The letters to Smallwood from the Bonavista Bay area reveal ordinary folks of modest means like my grandparents bearing witness to immense change, from Plate Cove to Princeton, Summerville to Greenspond, Lethbridge to Bonavista.[1] I'm struck by how seriously these writers took their democracy: asking clear questions about social and economic policies, demanding a hearing for their concerns. Some of us today could learn a thing or two.

These concerns included isolation and poverty. One man from a small outport community asked for an apartment in Gander. "There's not much company for us out here now," he wrote, mourning the urban migration of the young folks who were emotional, social, and economic lifelines. Another begged for a school—or at least a bit of shelter for the kids marching two miles to the current one in poor weather. Others noted the disappointments, the forgotten constituencies, and the broken promises. A man requested relief money from the sealers' fund, while the memory of witnessing eighty men dying in front of him on the ice still played out in his mind.[2] "We voted for confederation and we cannot get a job of work hear," wrote another man. A sixteen-year-old boy, having just lost his father after an unsuccessful operation, was told by the local relieving officer he now had to go out to work. "If only I could get some help whereby I would be able to get to school this winter," he wrote, "nobody knows what a blessing that would be to me." A sixteen-year-old girl with an ailing father and brother begged for help so that she too could keep going to school.[3]

---

1 For more historical context about the Bonavista peninsula, see, for example, Clayton D. Cook, *The Bonavista Peninsula of Days Gone By* (St. John's: Jeff Blackwood & Associates, 1999).

2 The sealing disaster of 1914 has been examined in numerous forms, from novels and films to scholarly work. Among this work is Cassie Brown's classic *Death on the Ice: The Great Newfoundland Sealing Disaster of 1914* (Toronto: Doubleday, 1988). See also the National Film Board's *"I Just Didn't Want to Die": The 1914 Newfoundland Sealing Disaster*, directed by Joe MacDonald (2018), and Jenny Higgins, *Perished: The 1914 Newfoundland Sealing Disaster* (Portugal Cove-St. Philip's, NL: Boulder Publications, 2013).

3 For more on the history of health care in Newfoundland and Labrador, see the

A farmer wondered, what thought has been given to the farmers of Newfoundland? What are the new regulations and policies? "I won't vote for Canada onless I get that clear," he stated. A shopkeeper (like my grandfather was for a time) who knew that "a better way of living cannot come to us all at once" noted that the price of food had not—as promised—fallen. Cheese, for instance, was still sixty cents a pound.

> (My grandmother would often recall how her mother returned to Silver Fox Island from domestic service at a merchant mansion in St. John's with a taste for Stilton. She'd wrap up the ordinary cheddar from the store in cloth and set it on a shelf to let it grow fustier and would eat it with great satisfaction.)

The letters also shine with a hope I'm sure my grandparents would recognize. Hopes of new schools, new places to live, engines for fishing boats, and a baby born on Confederation Day. One man from the district wished for better protection for the forests and wildlife: "Every pond in this locality carry a good supply of trout, and if looked after would multiply rapidly, as well as Otters, and beavers ...," he wrote. Another man dreamed of getting a wool carding and spinning machine and launching a local sheep-farming industry in Eastport.

Most striking perhaps is the anonymous "Confederation Prayer" for the new Canadians, in which god and country and Joey Smallwood appeared entangled in an entreaty for unity, a common cause, and a better life. "The toil and labour of this my dear land has left its mark that will be carried to the grave, but the love shall never die," went the prayer. "Thou who doeth all things well, has united this land of ours with a greater land to make a greater people."

My grandparents' children around that Sunday supper table were testament to their dreams of social mobility come true. Out of at least a half-dozen generations of Newfoundland fisherfolk, and before that dozens more generations of landless labourers in England's West Country, their own five children emerged as professionals. They went on to become a teacher, a social worker, a naval architect, a computer programmer, and a government worker. Their grandchildren, meanwhile, collected even higher degrees. But out of all of them,

essays by J.T.H. Connor and Heidi Coombs, later in this volume, as well as J.T.H. Connor, Jennifer J. Connor, Monica G. Kidd, and Maria Mathews, "Conceptualizing Health Care in Rural and Remote Pre-Confederation Newfoundland as Ecosystem," *Newfoundland and Labrador Studies* 30, no. 1 (2015): 115–40.

only my mother and one of my cousins still live full-time in Newfoundland and Labrador.

Many promises went unfulfilled. There is no deeper a reminder of this than the loss of my grandparents' sixth child in the late 1960s, my mother's youngest brother. Andy died a likely preventable death, miles from proper health care. After that, the lines of worry never really left my grandparents' faces, and I feel this intergenerational loss each time I hold my own feverish sons. The better way of living couldn't, of course, come all at once. But for some it didn't come at all.

> ("Every time I speak to my sisters," my grandmother told me a few months before her death, "we go back together to Silver Island." She could remember it just as if it were yesterday. All the stories, all the people. She would never change her mind about having left, she tells me. She knows it was the right choice. But still, more and more these days, she finds herself returning to the island. To that past world that—for better, surely?—was so decidedly undone.)

For Jacob Harrison Button (1929–2016) and
Olive Meta Feltham Button (1932–2021)

N.F.L.D
Confed.
Association
158 Water Street

June 14 – 48

Dear Sir:-
I Have lisened to & read the terms of union with canada. with great intrest but I never yet read or Heared any thing concerning the farmer of this country as I am a farmer Started to poineer farm in 1938 & up to this date under the good manigement of commison coverment. & interest in the farmer I Have made a success of it. up to this date I got in ruff pasture & cultivet ruffly 20 acres & under our present goverment I can make a go of it. now I would like to get some infermation on farming under confederation law. I no nothing about canada. But I read the family Eearl quit a lot & I figer by letters that I Have read. that under confed I woul Have to close the gate & go elswear seeking a job. on June 3rd. I voted for commision. now I no about responsible gov in the pass but I wont vote for canada onless I can get it clear. How I will be taxed under canada law. I can only do it now & I work in the lumbering wood winter time & my wife do the chores during that time. I will be looking forward to getting information on the above quiston I have asked. & thanking you

Signed

Dec 30th/48

Mr. J. R. Smallwood.

Dear Sir

First of all I must congratulate you for the wonderful job which you have done for the entry of Nfld into Confederation. It was no easy task for you I know. Well Mr. Smallwood what I am writing you about is concerning an apartment at Gander. If I could get one there I would move in some time this Spring. So I thought I would write you as I know you will intercede for me. I would not want a very large one because there is only the two of us. [Name redacted] my nephew is working at Gander and has his family there so I would like to go in there to live. There is not much company out here for us now. Trusting I will hear from you in the very near future and that you will do your best for me. Here's wishing you all the Best for 1949.

Sincerely yours

April. 9/49

Dear Mr. Smallwood

I am writing you today because the news that is rumoured about Bonavista. Any baby born on Confederation Day means something. My baby boy was born on April 1st at noon. Is this Confederation Day. The 1st of April or March 31st? I just wrote you to see if it means anything. Reply when you receives this note (please.)

I am glad to know that you are Premier of Newfoundland.

Congratulations

Signed

April 22nd/49

Mr. J. R. Smallwood
St. John's.

Dear Mr. Smallwood,

I'am writing you concerning the game in this district, and to know if you would be interested in appointing someone in its interest. The Country around here is very thickly forested, and ponds are very plentyful, and it carries a great varaity of game, but sorry to say an awful lot of it bes destroyed in ways it should not, and if someone was appointed to look after it, it would mean an find thing, for the tourest industry of this country.

Every pond in this locality carry a good supply of trout, and if looked after would multiply rapidly, as well as Otters, and beavers, and in some cases these poor animals have it very uncomfortable during the Summer, as people with boats in the ponds trouting, and cutting wood disturb them a lot, and this certainly should be checked. There are als a good supply of birds in these ponds, and these should be looked after to see that their nests are not destroyed and the young birds when they first go to the water.

The forest carries a good supply of rabbitts, partridge, and moose, and which a lot is destroyed during the Summer period when they should be guarded and left to multiply, and as you already know that tourist means a great deal to this country. I think it only right to have these things guarded for their interest.

However Mr. Smallwood I hope you don't look this matter over, and if you should appoint someone for the wellfare of all the above mentioned. I would be very thankful to accept the opportunity.

Thanking you. I'am,
Yours Very Truly

best of luck with your Campaign

April 25 / 49

Hon J R Smallwood

Dear sir
you will see that I am not highly educated and I find it hard to explain my troubles But excuse my mistakes now sir I voted for confederation and a Better way of living But I know it cannot come to us all at once
now sir I understand there is a drop in Prices. well sir I have some Proof here that this dosnt aply to [my community] and I think sir that this thing should Be considered you see I am a very anxious confederate
now sir you can see for yourself when you look at those copies note the difference in our Prices from one date to the other confederation havent taken any efect
no sir I am sure you wont agree with those Prices these articles I mention is what ive Bought from this this store on the two Pictular dates

yours very truely

anxious confederate

FU TRADING CO LTD[4]
[community name] April 22 /49

solo 5 lb Butter 35 CTS
1 Plug Beaver 29
1 Big Ben 27
10 lb sugar 13
oats 30 cts Per gal
tea Red Rose 12
Cheese Per lb 60
Fat B Pork 35[5]
Milk Per tin 18 sun crest

---

4 The Fishermen's Union Trading Company was a commercial enterprise established by the Fishermen's Protective Union. Founded in 1911, it enabled fishermen to work co-operatively to buy supplies and sell their catch.

5 Fatback pork.

wire nails 20
dried apricots 39

FU TRADING Co LTD
[community name] April 7 /49

Flour Per 8 75
Solo Butter Per lb 35
Red Rose tea 120
Sugar Per lb 14
light Beaver tob 29
wire nails 22
am Bay milk 18 ½
cheese 60 cts

May 1st

1949

To Hon JR Smallwood

Prime Minister of the Province NFLD

Dear Sir

I wish to bring to your atention our sitution in regards of school here in long beach we have seven children of school age and the school at [community] is two miles away and its too far for children to attend school as ther is no livures along the way and in bad weather there is no place to take shelter and we cant any family Allowance for our children unless they attend school and we here in [our community] earn our liveing Indepent of any Government assistents and we havnt a phone or Post office or any government service what ever and to be fair sir I think we are Entitle to have a school here in [our community] and I thrust that when you and your Government is Elected that you will do your best to see that we get a school here....

and I Congralate you on the success you have made

I remain

Yours Truly

May 23rd
1949

Dear Sir

I am writing to see if you could do something for me I am 16 years old and I am going to school and I have no way getting any thing my father is not able to work he only gets a order from the R. O. a month we have a wonderful job to get anything from the R. O.[6] *he wont give only just when he like. I have one Brother and he dont be well so he is not able to feed the family and I like to hold on going to school but if I dont get some thing I will have to give up school my father is getting old and he have been turn down by the Doctor not able to work so I would be very thankful if you would do something for me.*[7]

Yours Truly

6 Relieving officers managed government relief programs in local communities. As part of their role, they policed the activities of dole applicants and recipients. As numerous letters show, relieving officers held considerable power in communities.

7 As Jenny Higgins observes, the educational system was poor and illiteracy rates were high at Confederation. Many schools lacked running water and electricity, many teachers were untrained, and poverty meant that many students were malnourished and/or kept home by parents (Jenny Higgins, "Education 1949–1968," Heritage Newfoundland & Labrador, 2011, https://www.heritage.nf.ca/articles/society/education-1949-1968.php).

TO:

HON J R SMALLWOOD

ST JOHNS

KEEP GOING [COMMUNITY] RIGHT TO YOUR BACK KEEP CASHIN HIGGINS AND BROWN AT ARMS LENGTH.

[FOUR NAMES REDACTED].

JUL 2 1949[8]

8 Many correspondents chose to send telegrams to Smallwood. These particular correspondents reference Peter Cashin, John G. Higgins, and William J. Browne, all of whom were prominent anti-confederate voices, with Higgins apparently "[hanging] black crepe, a symbol of mourning, over the door of his house" on the day Newfoundland and Labrador entered Confederation (Bert Riggs, "Jack Higgins: Newfoundlander Through and Through," Heritage Newfoundland & Labrador, 2000, https://www.heritage.nf.ca/articles/politics/jack-higgins.php). Both Cashin and Higgins were elected to the House of Assembly in 1949, Cashin as an Independent (Ferryland) and Higgins as a Progressive Conservative (St. John's East). That same year, Browne was elected as a federal MP for the Progressive Conservative Party (St. John's West). For more on the anti-confederate movement, see Peter Cashin, *My Fight for Newfoundland: A Memoir*, ed. Edward Roberts (Paradise, NL: Flanker Press, 2011), and Jeff A. Webb, "The Responsible Government League and the Confederation Campaigns of 1948," *Newfoundland Studies* 5, no. 2 (1989): 203–20.

Aug 5th 1949

Dear Sir

I am writing to you to see would you get me a Engine for my little schoner she is a eleven tons it will have me to get more fish and I would be fishing longer in the fall and go about where the fish is plentyful I have a codtrap and moter Boat for fishing all I need is a Engine about twenty horse power • 20 • h • p If I dont pay for the engine in two years you can take it and sell it

Hoping to here from you soon

I remain yours

Aug 24/1949

Hon J.R. Smallwood

Dear Sir
I am Interested in Purchasing a wool carding & spinning machine. Which I believe would be a profitable undertaking with a fair chance at expanding. Seeing this is a farming area it would encourage the raising of more sheep and thousands of woolen garments & socks could be made localy which have to be purchased elsewhere & so for as I know there is neither one on the east coast for here they have to send it on the west coast it would cost approximatie eight thousand dollars $8000.00. So I would be please to know if the Dept of Development of Industries would consider giving me a loan for to purchase the above mentioned machine.
yours truly

Sept 7th / 49

Mr Smallwood

Dear Sir

I don't suppose you expects to get a letter from me. but I daresay that you remembers me as you know that I was a good friend to you while you was here at [my community], I am so glad to know that you are standing in the place where you are. The reason I am writing to you, I want to know would you oblidged me by interceding to see if you could get a bit of distaster money that I suffered for 36 years ago. on the ice, 80 men passed away before my eyes, I didn't receive enything from the fund sinse that time.[9] *I know if there's enyway to get it you will kindly do so I know there were lots of men that did receive the money, but I didnot have enyone to see into it for me. I suppose you will find out the amont of money that's given. a quarter, I will apperacate it it very much*

Please reply

Yours Sinserely

9 This correspondent is likely referencing the sealing disaster of the SS *Newfoundland*, in which 132 sailors were stranded on the ice in blizzard conditions for two days. Seventy-nine of those men died. For more, see Jenny Higgins, "The 1914 Sealing Disaster," Heritage Newfoundland & Labrador, 2007, https://www.heritage.nf.ca/articles/politics/sealing-disaster-1914.php, and *Perished.*

Oct 28th, 49

Hon J. R. Smallwood
Premier of Nfld
St. John's
Dear Sir,
Sometime ago you received a letter from [my community] concerning my father, ... who at that time was seeking admittance to the General hospital for an operation. Since then he has been operated on but his operation was'nt a success and he passed away on Wednesday, last. Beside my mother he has left a family of five of which the youngest is two years and I, the oldest, am sixteen. Last year I completed successfully Grade X at school and had every hope of finishing Grade XI this year; but according to the relieving officer at [community] I will have to get out now and work. If only I could get some help whereby I would be able to get to school this winter, nobody knows what a blessing that would be to me. My other brothers will receive their family allowances and my mother, I suppose will receive her widow's allowance; but that will not be enough to help me out. Up until now I was receiving five dollars a month in my father's monthly govt. cheque. If only I could get that much now I would be able to go to school. Anyway, I can't see how I could go away and leave her this winter, with a family of small children to look after. I would no ask for any help, Mr. Smallwood if I did'nt have one more year to go to school. I would be more than glad to go out an earn my own. Please, Mr. Smallwood, try to help me and I will always be grateful to you. Hoping to hear from you soon.
Yours sincerely,

Honourable J.R. Smallwood[10]
St. John's

Dear Sir: -

I am enclosing, that which I have written myself. You may please read it and if you think it unworthy you can destroy it. I wrote it for past time and I thought I would send it along to you.

Sincerely Yours

Confederation Prayer

Thou has slept my child and peace did attend thee, but now the night is o'er, a new day is dawned, and as your eyelids doth uncover your dreaming eyes thou wilt enter into a new era. Thou art not a new born son, but that little yesterday has passed away, the great April day is come when you are a Canadian too my son. Wake up! and behold your mother, standing on the threshold of Heaven with a gentle smile to receive her Angel. You are alone with your mother and our God, So give your mother a kiss and your God a prayer my Son!

The great God who art ever near can see me now. Kneeling by her side gazing into her face, and when I see the silvery hair hanging over that wrinkled brow how easy it is for me to recall the past of my native land. The toil and labour of this my dear land has left its mark that will be carried to the grave, but the love shall never die. The seed has been scattered in many parts that the roots which has taken such a strong-hold on mankind will carry on down through the Ages. They have hungered, they have thirst, but mother nature provided for them, and at times they have survived by the breath of air and the ray of sunlight. But the good God who have given us the example to carry on, let us accept it then take our lead without knowing the burden of it. The God of our forefathers is our God too, then if we lack courage we lack confidence in Him, for they that loveth not knoweth not God, for God is love. Father after father have trodden in the footsteps of their native land, and grant O Lord that as the footsteps of one generation after another has led to a better forsight, that ours may be made brighter by the change

10 This letter is both undated and unsigned. Where letters are undated, we have placed them chronologically at the end of each district's letters, unless the letter's contents make it possible to approximate the date.

that has been wrought upon our land. Thou who doeth all things well, has united this land of ours with a greater land to make a greater people, for we are one great flock of our Father's land and He is the great shepherd of the fold. So O Lord teach me to say, "Take hold of my hand thou fellow Canadian, let us be united to fight side by side for one common cause and one common good of our people." Help us to love each other as we ought to, to love our great land the flag that fly o'er it, the empire we are part of, the king and all the rulers of our land, hit above all to love Thee. The great common love have always combined the old Canada with the new, even in our world destruction where they fought side by side for on common cause. Grant O Lord that with such a great union our love may be made more thorough than ever before, that all loving Thee may take up our cross daily and follow after Thee. Then when our path on earth is trodden, our task is o'er, we after serving Thee as we ought may come to that great life eternal, that Thou has promised unto all those that are worthy of it, and Thou wilt say unto me and to others, "Well done thou good and faithful servant." Accept this we beseech O Lord our humble prayer in our own simple words in honour of this my dear land, Newfoundland.

BURGEO-LA POILE

If Only I Could Casually Brain Dump on Joey Smallwood via Messenger at 2 a.m.

Joanne Harris

JOEY. Damn dude, I read letters to you from two different districts—Burgeo-La Poile and Bonavista South. It is wild what was different and what was the same across regions, as well as what is relevant today, now, ACROSS TIME.

Seriously, the then and now issues list, without analyzing too deeply:

communication infrastructure
health care services
economic security
access to education
affordable groceries
properly paved roads

That's it, some pretty essential stuff (which is also kinda global scale issues, but we'll stick to NL today).[1] The only things missing that would make this a

1 For more on the history of economic insecurity in Newfoundland and Labrador, see, for example, Seantel Anaïs, "(Mal)Nutrition, and the 'Informal Economy' Bootstrap: The Politics of Poverty, Food Relief, and Self Help," *Newfoundland and Labrador Studies* 24, no. 2 (2009): 239–60; Jenny Higgins, "Great Depression—Impacts on the Working Class," Heritage Newfoundland & Labrador, 2007, https://www.heritage.nf.ca/articles/

wholly modern list is the fishery, crime/drugs, more emphasis on housing, and climate change.

Seriously though, I really didn't expect the letters to feel so eerily relevant. Some of them were utterly heartbreaking, knowing they wouldn't get the urgent help they wrote to you, begging for. But even that felt familiar—recently there was a story in the news of a young woman who, desperately needing better mental health care services, died because she couldn't make it to the hospital in time. The ambulance had to travel hours down a highway without cell service, and because of this lack of service the family couldn't drive to meet the ambulance without risking missing it. That story gutted me, same way the letters begging for a doctor to be sent, for space in the "mental hospital" or "sanatorium" did.[2] People now are desperate for a doctor, for a space in mental health and addiction programs. The hospitals are at capacity; there aren't enough doctors or nurses. Same problems, different century, eh?

But I have to say, as much as some of it was very grim, the hope was uplifting, inspiring. Absolutely amazing how keen people were for their bright new future under Confederation. I really hope they saw things change for the better in their lifetime, that their hope wasn't wasted. Because damn, what a beautiful thing, to have such hope and optimism. I have no such hope for my future in this province. I really question myself some days for continuing to live here and tough out the uncertainty. Living here is getting difficult: it feels like all systems are in disrepair and won't be getting better under the continuing succession of questionable leadership. And we still haven't felt the full impact of Muskrat Falls yet (ahhhh!). I think I am just hedging my bets that this is a safe(r) place to face whatever climate change will bring in my lifetime.

I do think the letters cast some perspective on all the grimness. There may be something to learn from the sense of community that was present. As often

---

politics/depression-impacts.php. For more on the history of education in Newfoundland and Labrador, see, for example, Frederick William Rowe, *The History of Education in Newfoundland* (Toronto: Ryerson Press, 1952); Katherine McManus, "Before the 'Fogo Project' There Was Florence O'Neill: A Glimpse of Early Adult Education and a Dedicated Advocate," in *Weather's Edge: Women in Newfoundland and Labrador*, ed. Linda Cullum, Carmelita McGrath, and Marilyn Porter (St. John's: Killick Press, 2006), 36–47; Marilyn Porter, "'She Knows Who She Is': Education Girls to Their Place in Society," in Cullum and Porter, *Creating This Place*, 146–78; and Andrea Procter, *A Long Journey: Residential Schools in Labrador and Newfoundland* (St. John's: ISER Books, 2020).

2 For more on health care in Confederation-era Newfoundland and Labrador, see the essays by J.T.H. Connor and Heidi Coombs, later in this volume.

as people may have asked for something personally benefiting them, they very often alluded to others experiencing a similar plight and the need for something to be done. And then there are all those letters asking for something for the community—safer roads to schools, a phone, a post office.[3] Knowing that people voluntarily kept postal services operating without compensation, that they wanted a phone in their community so fishermen stranded in bad weather could call to let their families know they were safe, that made me think. Yeah, we need government services to keep going, but we really do need each other, our communities, to advocate for what we need, keep each other going. Things look grim, but we'll probably get by, together, by strengthening community bonds.

This feels like a bit of a tangent, Joey, but before I leave you alone I want you to know I had hoped to do a bit of extra research for this, but that grand ambition went sideways when the whole pandemic thing happened. Essentially, I wanted to look at Indigenous presence (or lack thereof) in the letters because Joey, SIR, decisions you made with the Terms of Union SUCKED.[4] Really made things for the Indigenous peoples in what is the province of Newfoundland and Labrador. So. Much. Fun. Seriously, there should be a course taught at Memorial about it, but there isn't because that's just how much work there is to do working through and unravelling the entire big messy socio-political Indigenous-Settler narrative of the province.[5]

---

3 For more on telecommunications and postal history in Newfoundland and Labrador, see Robert Cuff, "Telegraphy," Heritage Newfoundland & Labrador, 2001, https://www.heritage.nf.ca/articles/economy/railway-telegraph.php, and K.W. Hoffmann, *History of Telecommunications in Newfoundland* (St. John's: Newfoundland Historical Society), 1978.

4 The Terms of Union make no mention of Indigenous peoples, a situation which has had long lingering aftereffects, from questions around the provision of health care to, more recently, taking responsibility for the effects of residential schools. This absence has also made it challenging to settle land claims and work toward self-government. For more on this, see, for example, Sébastien Grammond, "Equally Recognized? The Indigenous Peoples of Newfoundland and Labrador," *Osgoode Hall Law Journal* 51, no. 2 (1960): 469–99; Maura Hanrahan, "The Lasting Breach: The Omission of Aboriginal People from the Terms of Union between Newfoundland and Canada and Its Ongoing Impacts," *Royal Commission on Renewing and Strengthening Our Place in Canada* (St. John's: The Royal Commission, 2003), 207–78; MacKenzie, "The Indian Act."

5 For more on colonialism, Newfoundland settler identity, and self-indigenization, see Susan M. Manning, "Contrasting Colonisations: (Re)Storying Newfoundland/Ktaqmkuk as Place," *Settler Colonial Studies* 8, no. 3 (2018): 314–31.

Anyway, sorry to dump all this on you, but I had some thoughts. Do with them as you please. Thanks!

Oh also, you are some lucky Twitter and Facebook weren't a thing when you were campaigning or in office. If the anonymous and sass-filled letters are any indication, you would have been DRAGGED on the reg, and it would have been hilarious. Gotta appreciate a fine tradition for sauce. Ok, promise I am done now. Bye.

June 9 = 1948

Dear sir
I am a criple man and by your papers you send out around or going to Help out criples and i want to know if that is so. i am one that like to get some Help. i been cripled every sence i was a baby. throu sickness i was 10 years old when i give up the crutch. i am 51 years old now i have 4 children at home. i am a fisherman. goes in an open boat all winter and i got my foot chilled and now i cant stand the cold they wont give me a job on the fish plant so i cant mak a living for my family. i am asking for Help pleas from [name redacted] to Mr. Smallwood.

JANY 12TH, 1949.

J. R. SMALLWOOD ESQ.,
ST. JOHN'S
DEAR SIR;

I WONDER WOULD YOU HAVE THE TIME TO ENLIGHTEN ME ON THE FOLLOWING.

I AM A TELEGRAPHER AND POSTMASTER HERE, MY DAUGHTER IS ASST P.M.. WHEN UNION TAKES PLACE I UNDERSTAND POST OFFICE WILL BE SEPERATED FROM TELEGRAPHS, THE LATT2R COMING UNDER CAN. NATIONAL RAILWAY AND THE FORMER UNDER THE FEDERAL GOVT.

I INDERSTAND ALSO THAT IN SETTLEMENTS SUCH AS THIS (WE SERVE APPROX 1800 PEOPLE FROM [COMMUNITY] TO [COMMUNITY]) POST OFFICES GO OUT ON TENDER, THE QUESTION IS COULD I TENDER ALTHOUGH I WOULD BE A TELEGRAPH OPERATOR OR COULD MY DAUGHTER AGED 16 TENDER. IT COULD BE MORE ECONOMICALLY RUN THAT WAY

WOULD APPRECIATE A REPLY, WITH VERY BEST WISHES FOR 1949.

YOURS RESPECTFULLY,

Jan 22/48[6]
Mr J Smallwood
St Johns,
Dear Mr Smallwood:

I wrote Secretary Dept Posts & Telegraphs sometime ago Asking for telephone to be connected with [a community]. The road leading to that place is difficult to travel in the winter especially when the fishing boats have to harbour there in case of bad nights, and their families do not know if they are still out or not. [This community] is the port they sell their fish. I was told you would be the right man to write to. Please do your utmost and see that we get a telephone
connected, it does not take a fortune to put some here, only a few poles, wire and the telephone. I may say I worked with the Anglo telegraphs for ten years, and would have the telephone put in my house and would handle all messages. This little Settlement voted solid for You so I think you should do your best & try & get us a telephone
Hoping to hear from you soon
Thanking you.
Yours Truly

6 Given the other letters that this woman wrote Smallwood, the date should probably read 1949; it is possible, however, that because it was January, she—like many of us!—miswrote the year.

April 12th, 1949

To Mr J. R. Smallwood

St. John's.

Dear Sir,

Glad to know we can now safely say we are Canadians.

We are now looking forward for a better future, in hopes we will have it better than ever we have experienced it before.

We, the people of [our community] know little about good times. The population of our town is 123 people. My husband is a fisherman, and we are very sorry that you could not visit these small settlements.

There is no post-office in this settlement, but mail has been taken in a dwelling house. When these people left [our community] and went to another town, we decided that we would take the mail. But, we were told that there was no payment for handling the mail.

I have been handling the mail for 17 months, and hasn't been paid a cent. Now due to our big change, and better outlooks I should think that I should be paid for doing this work. I collect in money for all C.O.D[7] parcels and duty parcels, registered letters, and the usual mail. This is a lot of work, and I really think it is worth something.

I am satisfied to do my best, and I think it is only right to get a little payment for this job.

I am sure you will do your best for me, as well as the rest of the people.

We have our mail brought to us in a small boat. We are unable to go onboard to get our mail, so it must be brought to my house and under my responsibility. I am satisfied to do as I am doing, but I would like to receive a payment for the work.

Yours truthfully,

7 Cash on delivery.

19th, May, 1949

Dear Joey,

I am writing you a few lines to inquire if there is any chance of a job for me on Railway Wharf here I have 6 youngsters and have done nothing for about six or seven months. There is two and three out of some familys working up there so I think it is pretty bad when there is plenty married men walking around doing nothing and two and three checks coming into one household. Joe I am willing to take anything they give me to do but it is no use for me to go up there as I have tried and tried. They took on a few lately but it was mostly all young fellows some of them their father's working up there already. I don't grudge any young man their job as every one as to live but when there is two and three sons working and all these checks coming in one house when I and many more like me can't make one check. My two sons they had to go to Halifax to work 4 years ago so why can't there be something done on the wharf here to make it fair for everyone. Joe I hope you don't mind me writing you but I was at the meeting here when you came and you told us if we wanted to write to you just to call you Joey, so I am taking the chance to write you hoping you will be able to do something for me Wishing you the best off luck when Election comes of hope you get in as you deserve

Hope to hear from you in answer to this letter
And oblige
Yours Faithfully

May 24/49

Mr J. R Smallwood
St Johns
Dear sir

I wrote you sometime ago re telephone for [our community] and explained everything in regards to the use of the fisherman. Mr Quinton visited this place couple weeks ago & will tell you he was welcomed very much. I also told him about the phone & he promised it would be looked after if the Liberal Govt got in which I hope it will.

I dont say there will be much money coming in from the phone as its mostly for the fishermens use in case of stormy weather. I could handle all telegrams etc as I was formerly a telegraph operator with the Anglo company for ten years & if a p. office should be considered I could have all at my home. Would I be allowed something for looking after this as I would be cleaning all the time with people back & forth? It will only be a few days before we all know whats what. Am anxious for this to go into effect immediately. Pls write me at your earliest. Yours very truly

A series of telegrams between a woman and J.R. Smallwood, concerning her husband's health.

HON J R SMALLWOOD
ST JOHNS
HUSBAND SERIOUSLY ILL SINCE FRIDAY SEVERE PAINS IN HEAD AND EARS RUNNING TEMPERATURE WOULD LIKE YOU SEND DOCTOR IMMEDIATELY REPLY

MAY 25 1949

MAY 25, 1949

BRING YOUR HUSBAND [TO COMMUNITY] HOSPITAL IMMEDIATELY

J.R. SMALLWOOD

MAY 25, 1949.

SENDING PLANE TO BRING HUSBAND TO HOSPITAL SOON AS WEATHER CONDITIONS PERMIT.

J.R. SMALLWOOD

HON J R SMALLWOOD
ST JOHNS
NO BOAT HERE TAKE HUSBAND HOSPITAL WANT DOCTOR COME IMMEDIATELY HIS CASE VERY SERIOUS

MAY 26 1949

HON J R SMALLWOOD
ST JOHNS
HUSBANDS CONDITION MUCH WORSE PLEASE RUSH PLANE WEATHER HERE GOOD

MAY 27 1949

MAY 27 1949.
WEATHER FOGGY HERE PLANE LEAVING AS SOON AS WEATHER CLEARS BRING YOUR HUSBAND EITHER TO GANDER HOSPITAL OR HERE WHEREVER HE CAN LAND. DOING ALL POSSIBLE HELP YOU.
J.R. SMALLWOOD

HON J R SMALLWOOD
ST JOHNS
IF PLANE UNABLE COME URGENT YOU ARRANGE BOAT BRING DOCTOR FROM [COMMUNITY] HUSBANDS CONDITION VERY GRAVE BEEN DELIRIOUS TWO DAYS BLEEDING FROM NOSE AND MOUTH

MAY 28 1949

MAY 28, 1949.
TRYING TO ARRANGE [DOCTOR] COME TO YOUR HUSBAND FROM [COMMUNITY].

J.R. SMALLWOOD

June 3/49
Premier Smallwood
St. John's
Dear Sir:

Some years ago I was cast away while fishing on the Rose Blanche Banks. It happened in the month of February. And I, with other members of the crew were driven ashore on the plates of St. Pierre.

I was washed overboard, and was rescued by some of the crowd, but got badly frozen when left in the snowdrifts until my shipmates travelled several miles to get assistance. I was so badly frozen that I spent several months in the hospital at St. Pierre & St. John's I lost some of my fingers, and what are left are knarled and out of shape also my feet are in much the same condition.

I have fished in this condition now for many years, but this year my hands practically gave out and the doctor advised me to do no more fishing. I have a large family & get the dole. I cant manage to live on this small amount.

I understand that there is a pension allowed cripples now that we are under Confederation. The Ranger here can voucher for my condition. Please advise me if there are any help for me.

Yours Sincerely

June 5th /49

Dear Mr. Smallwood.

I though I would write and ask you a few questing which I would like to fine out. there may not be any thing you can do for me, about what I am going to asked you. I would like to know if Newfoundland have got Canada prizes. which I know she have in some places. So I though I would make it my biseness to send you a few of my bills. as I am only a fishmen as you know the most of we men is on the south west coast. as we got a hard job to make a liveing, that the prize every thing is here to day. So just figer out these few bills, I am sending. please tell me where I am going to fit in to when I got to pay taxes as same as they do in Canada. and lots other men like me. as I do realy think that those goods are to hige. so that is the only way to fine out. so I think that is all for this time so please answer me.

Yours truly

June 21

1949

Joseph Smallwood

Dear Sir all wee poor Widows thought wee would get our pensions before the children got there allowance has wee where more in need than the children at this present time some off the big girls or working on the plant earning money and get their allowance too I ham a crippel 6 years ago I have a lame harm ever sence I had 3 opperation in Grand Bank hospital with the cancer I had my left breast cut of if you thinks I ham telling you false please write to [the doctor] at Grand Bank and he will tell you all about it that my home [community] and I goes around to work But I cant do much all my families or all for themselves all grown up an gone there his a poor cripple woman close bye me and no help and only got 10$ a quarter till this New year the give her 15$ she been a cripple ever since 1930 her name his [redacted] I hope you will do better than this for us all I vote for you hope I could do more

please answer

HON H W QUINTON
ST JOHNS NF
YOU PROMISED US PHONE MEN READY START OPERATIONS RUSH REPLY[8]

NOV 15 A.M.

8 In addition to this letter, which is addressed not to Smallwood but to H.W. Quinton, the MHA for Burgeo, this correspondent wrote a number of letters to Smallwood, including the first letter we've included from this district, and the telegram that immediately follows this one.

HON J R SMALLWOOD
ST JOHNS NF
PLEASE DO UTMOST RE TELEPHONE FOR [OUR COMMUNITY] AND ADVISE

NOV 26 1949

Dear Sir: -

Please let me give you a word picture on a very small margin of the present conditions in [our community].

First I would like to speak of the respected age, who have received such a bitter disappointment with regards to the old age pension.
They say, "what we can't understand is why did the kids get their allowances so quickly and we have to wait so long?"

Another fact has been noticed. The road repairment now proceeding takes on men for two weeks only.
Then they must give it up to give the other guy a chance. This may seem and may be selfish, but why should a family man have to come off the road work, to let a single young fellow get his two weeks work.

I'll admit the young fellow may need a dollar as well as the married man. With that I guess you will agree, but since you do not who's who the young fellow may have a father plus a brother or two working with the Railway.

Speaking of the Railway there are men, stevedores, who work their job as a convenience. Work four or five days and then take a day or two off. At least that's what some of their fellow workers say. While one man has to make his weeks pay do him a period of five or seven, another man takes in sometimes $400., as a total for him and his son.

Since we are at the Railway Centre, lets look in on the Railway boats. The S.S. Cabot Strait and the S.S. Burgeo. It is rumored that four brothers are on one of these boats and one receiving his monthly baby bonus plus his monthly pay (understood relieving).

Now while the prompt receival of the baby bonus has amazed the old people, this is what I question, Is it fair for the old, to tell the truth about their age to gain support, and not – to date, and for another or possibly others to gain their baby bonus support and to put on their age with the result gain a monthly pay.

These are the present problems in [our community] which most people believe could be solved.

It is also my belief that such matters could be solved if the right authorities inquired

Thank you,

An Observer

BURIN

Nothing, Everything

Kate Lahey

AS I MAKE MY WAY ACROSS campus on a duckish St. John's day, I find myself hoping to find my Nan in the archives. Throughout my life, whenever I was away from her, we always wrote letters to one another. She kept every letter that I wrote to her and I kept every letter that she wrote to me. My Nan passed away in the summer of 2020, but about a year earlier (or previously?), another family member threw away all of my letters to her. Because my family is burdened with intergenerational trauma, mental health issues, addictions, and alcoholism, I was unsurprised and yet also heartbroken at the loss of the letters. I hold on to the ones that I received from her as an unreciprocated archive, half of which is now gone forever. The echoes of the lost half can be implied in the unanswered questions, small references, and the back and forth of conversation that rest among the half I do have. I have been learning to listen to the inferences of silence.

Sitting in the comforting quiet of the archive, I make my way through the boxes of letters placed on my research desk. I can't help but hope to hear her voice among the many lines that speak of familiar places, in familiar penmanship, in familiar dialect. But I know that I won't. Born in 1932, my Nan was too young to be writing to Joey Smallwood from her homestead in Taylor's Bay. And yet, I flip through letters with hopeful anticipation, searching for family names like Hillier, Haskell, Bonnell, or family communities like Taylor's Bay, Point au Gaul, Lamaline. Carrying the family secrets that I do, I am scared of what I might find, or what I won't find, reflected back to me in these letters.

Struggling to survive among addictions, poverty, illness, death, domestic violence, and sexual abuse while subsistence-living on the lands and waters, my Nan's family did not have the time, faith, resources, or ability to write to Smallwood. Still I search for whispers of her life, a beautiful spectacular life, among these relics. Holding her endless stories close to my heart, I read these letters through the lens of the difficult knowledge passed down to me in oral story, culture, family dynamics, and relationships.

My Nan always said, "we had nothing and we had everything." Making my way through these letters, the nothingness is everywhere. Letters from abandoned widows, starving mothers, maimed fishermen, and disabled young women seeking education reflect the dire socio-economic circumstances of many in Newfoundland, while their pleas for help are littered with hopefulness and the humanity of their personal narratives. It is easy to see the destitution, poverty, trauma, and suffering in this collection of letters, as it has always been looking at my family, past and present.

By contrast, I struggle to feel the everything, but bring my Nan's lessons of compassion and grace to my reading practice. Amid these letters I am also able to see love, laughter, faith, joy, hope, dreams, protection, and wisdom. Many letters speak about the promise of social assistance, better roads, and public services. A single mother living in poverty writes a list of clothing she dreams of providing her children. A young woman with a disability writes about her dream of pursuing higher education and independence from her parents. As an autistic person, I sometimes see things in black and white, struggling to make sense of the messy, in-between, colourful spaces that echo around us, between us and within us. It is my Nan, and the historic, cultural, and familial dynamics that informed her knowledge, that have helped me sense the queer, contradictory ephemera of family trauma and memory, to see the everything in the nothingness. Indeed, resilience and hope are structures that we inherit.

In a powerful letter written anonymously by "a drunkards wife" (April 29, 1949), I hear the familiar and ongoing suffering of alcoholism, domestic violence, poverty, hunger, childhood sexual abuse, illness, and death that punctuate my family's past and present. The author writes, "my home is a hell to me through the cause of liquor." I hear the nothingness. But I also hear the everything. In writing on behalf of the women and children in her community, I hear the drunkard's wife's act of collective care, a breaking of silence, an act of revolt, a dream for a different future, and ultimately hope. In another letter, written on behalf of an orphaned, disabled sixteen-year-old, I see that teenager's big dream of attending school. Yet another letter reveals the story of a father maimed while fishing, who has "been fighting against impossible odds and [has] now come to the point where [he] find[s] it impossible to carry on," even as he works a farm and writes in hope of financial support. Mothers ask for underwear. Widows ask for food. Writers of all kinds hope for social and economic change. Finding the everything in the nothing is, my Nan reminds me, an activation of resilience. Seeking to find moments of abundance and love within trauma and suffering helps us to survive. Ultimately, these letters ask me to read them with the care, empathy, and radical hope that account for the paradoxes and possibilities that have defined, and continue to define, life in Newfoundland and Labrador.

March 4 / 49

Dear Sir

I am taking the pleasure to write you a few lines

Well Mr Smallwood my husband was a Veteran of World I King & Country and I am not recognized as a war veteran widow at all or my dear little orphan children[1] *I have one boy 12 yrs one boy 10 one little girl 7 yrs she was 3 months old when her daddy was killed in the mine here I find it hard now as my compensation is all out now and my boy [redacted] age 18 havent earned a cent since the first week in Dec when the job he was at closed down.*

I was wondering if you could send me some clothes for the children & [illegible]. breeches & pants & 2 suits of and Fortman underwear each & my little girl age 7

A coat to fit a child age 7 & a bit of stuff for dress & underwear or flannette.

breeches & underwears age 12 yrs

size 36 breeches I hardly know what size windbreaker

Age 10 32 breeches & a windbreaker to fit this age

boys age 12 rubber boots or lace up boots size 6

age 10 rubber boots or lace up boots size 4 ½ or 5

Girl age 7 shoes & garters size 10 ½ or 11

I like to get a pair of shoes for myself size 8 & garters 8 & a few yds of flannette for myself to make shirts for boys. I would like to get also a couple suits of underwear for myself pants size 52 or 54 & singlets large.

Hoping you will do something in this aspect for me

Yours

---

1 As outlined in the Introduction, children figured strongly in Smallwood's campaign speeches, and the Family Allowance—or baby bonus as it was colloquially known—was very welcome in Newfoundland and Labrador homes. For more on the Family Allowance, see Edward Roberts, "How the Baby Bonus Came to Newfoundland," *SaltWire*, September 29, 2017, https://www.saltwire.com/atlantic-canada/federal-election/how-the-baby-bonus-came-to-newfoundland-28364/. See also Mathieu Mondou, "Social Assistance in Newfoundland and Labrador," in *Welfare Reform in Canada: Provincial Social Assistance in Comparative Perspective*, ed. Daniel Béland and Pierre-Marc Daigneault (Toronto: University of Toronto Press, 2015), 239–54.

April 24th 1949

Dear Mr Smallwood:

(Premier)

I am very glad indeed to have Confederation restored upon us what the majority of us have worked for especially yourself which the people of [our community] are very proud of.

Well Sir I am a crippled man myself. I am 40 years of age married with 3 children.

I was born a cripple both hands and feet.

My family get dole, not myself. I receive a pension at $10.00 per quarter so you can see I am having a hard time. So I was wondering how much Better Confederation will make it for me. I have heard about family allowances and old age pensions over the air but not anything about the cripples. When you was at [our community] last Spring (1948) I met you if you can Remember I asked you what could be done for cripples under Confederation, you told me there was a grant for them so I still beleive that is correct. I know every thing can't be done in a month or two, but I know we people wont be for-gotten. Also will the Dole system be any better than at present. So God knows we suffered enough with it.

I never want to have to go through it again. So I'll bring this letter to a close

Wishing you every success

I would like for you to answer and tell me, what it will be.

Yours truly

April 27th 1949

Hon Sir J R Smallwood

Dear Sir

we the fishermen and labourers of this Town regret that when you was hear at [our community] we could not get the chance to give you a hand shake and congraulate you on your big fight you have put up and have won it may God bless you and all of us and make our country and town and viligaes a better place for us to live in but I must say sir we poor people as a whole would like for you to put some one hear to look after the price of everything we think they are black marketing and over charging as they have been doing in days gone bye and we would like to have a good magistrate hear so as we could get right and justice on both sides there are lots I could tell you sir if I could get a chance to talk to you I am 64 years old and go fishing with one legg now we are under Confederation will I get any thing for been diabled or will I not if you had time I would like you to let me know some time I know you are a busy man now at this time so I will be dropping you a few lines once in a while.

yours sincerly

April 29 1949

To Mr J. Smallwood
St. Johns
Dear Sir

I make my first appeal to you & trust it will be a success as it concerns me very much & I also hope it will meet your approval

What I wish to speak on is very near to my heart it concerns the Bootleggers of [my community] I must tell you its a real hot bed for them & have been for the past years as you say there will be a great many change in many things & Im asking you to change the smuggeling & put down the Bootleggers in [district] ... especially my home is a hell to me through the cause of Liquor if it was not brought from St Peire my husband could not by it he cannot go to St Peire to get he can by it every day near his home the cullers do be sent out to keep this thing down but it makes no difference to the small boats such as dorys & so the captains of these little boats take clearances they go without them & many times when its to rough for the cullers to stay out in the Bay coming on night they go in to Grand Bank or Lamaline for a harbour during the night thats just the time for Mr Bootlegger to make their dash for home I trust these big Canadian Cullers will stay in the St Piere waters or out in the Bay to prevent & keep Liquor from being brought to our homes breaking the hearts of mothers & wives & causeings so much unhappiness & want in many homes where unity & comfort could reign you can send this letter to any of your paper to be published as I dont care I hope you will get busy right away to make a bright spotlight in many of our homes I can tell you much more its up to you to find out in your self dear sir I sign my self

A drunkards wife

Ps this letter is sent from [district]
... & its a true Statement please work on it right away[2]

2 For more on the history of alcohol and bootlegging in Newfoundland and Labrador, see, for example, J.P. Andrieux, *Rumrunners: The Smugglers from St. Pierre and Miquelon and the Burin Peninsula from Prohibition to Present Day* (Paradise, NL: Flanker Press, 2009), and Sheilah Roberts Lukins, *Bottoms Up: A History of Alcohol in Newfoundland and Labrador* (St. John's: Breakwater Books, 2020).

April 30th / 49

To

Premier J R

Smallwood

Dear Sir

I am writing to you to see if you could Possibley do anything for me regarding my order I have been on Permant relief for three years I had an operation and since then cannot do any work I get $40 a month for eight of us so you can imagine what I can buy from this. I never got a garment of clothing I was to the Ranger several times but still received nothing nor I never got a nob of coal from relief so all I have to depend on for everything is this mere $40. So I would be very grateful to you if you would try and get a raise for me or see that I would get help with clothing or fuel. Hoping to hear from you in the near future regarding this & wishing you every success in the future

Thanking you

I remain

May 3rd 1949

Dear Sir

just a word with regards to my husband & baby, I got a baby 1 year and a half old i don't get any relief for him, what is the reason of that, he eats the same kind of food the other children eats still he don't get any relief, i want to know if you can put him on his father check we get 15.00 for five of us and we are nearly starved to death, my baby is getting thin and pale looking he is hungry he only get bread and tea three times a day, and that is no good to a baby, and i dont get any relief my self i got to go on beach and have a sick man home to nurse a baby and another small child beside, if i could get a bit of relief for my self and baby i would stay home and give my sick husband a chance to go out around and get the fresh air,

Hon. J.R. Smallwood,
St. John's. *June 7, 1949.*

Dear Sir:

If you will excuse the intrusion on your time I should like to inform you regarding my situation. I am in my forties and owing to my physical condition I am unable to do any amount of work. As a matter of fact I have been depending on the government for assistance for a long time and with a large family I have been finding it difficult to exist. However, your hard work in bringing in family allowances has meant a great lot to me.

Some years ago I was shipwrecked on the Canadian Coast and I went in peril of my life to save the schooners crew which I did and as a result I have spent a long time in hospital and have been incapaciated ever since. I shall inclose a write up regarding the shipwreck then I am sure you will understand what accounts for my physical inability. If you need certification of the above you may write to Mr. [name redacted] or the Salvation Army Officer here at [my community] and I am sure they will furnish the necessary information.

I would appreciate it if you would let me know at your earliest convenience whether there is any legislation that will give me assistance in this time of need.

Sincerely yours,

June 9 1949

Dear Mr Smallwood

I am writing this little note to you to let you know that I am a cripple so that if there be anything give to the cripple I like to get something as I have no father to look out to me and I cant very well work I lost my leg when I was only 13 years old and I never got a thing from the government and I am twenty eight and still single I have a old wooden leg and that not very light to tro around so I cant very well earn my own so if the cripple pension be give out I would like to get one.

Hope to received answer soon I remain your truly

July 16th / 49

M. J R Smallwood
St. John's

Dear Sir

As you seem to be the poor man's friend, I am writing you to see if you can do anything for me Three years ago I had the misfortune to lose my right arm, and since then have been trying to make a living for myself & family on a small farm. As you can readily see it is impossible for me with one arm to plant and raise enough to support my family which consists of myself, wife and three children.

I can manage to do something but not enough and I am writing you to see if you could arrange that I be granted a monthly pension sufficient to enable me and my family to exist and enjoy some small comfort in this life.

I have been fighting against impossible odds and have now come to the point where I find it impossible to carry on.

Kindly use your influence on my behalf.

Yours truly

P.S. I would refer you to the Ranger[3] *or [name redacted] should you need to enquire into the merit of my case.*

3 The Newfoundland Ranger Force provided government services, including policing, in remote and northern parts of Newfoundland and Labrador from 1935 to 1950. See Jenny Higgins, "Newfoundland Ranger Force," Heritage Newfoundland & Labrador, 2007/2015, https://www.heritage.nf.ca/articles/politics/newfoundland-rangers.php.

July 21st 1949

Premier Smallwood
Liberal Headquarters
St. John's.

Dear Sir:

It is with much hope that I take the time to write you. All during the time before polling day I have heard of all the things the Liberal party would do for the people, yet not one mention was made of helping the Deaf people. And the Deaf no matter if they are over sixteen years old they need and should have an allowance. Because of their handicap, deaf people depend on their parents several years longer than the normal child because they are slow to learn. Moreover they are not too eager to take jobs with other hearing people because they do not understand them well enough.

I myself am deaf-mute. I was taken ill with menegitis at the age of 8 years and the result was being left stone deaf. But I managed to overcome by handicap to a certain point. I went to school here at home and passed grade nine. My last two years have been at the deaf school at Halifax. In June of this year I received my second diploma. Somehow, I don't care to return there to school. This is no doubt due to my remaining at home in my earlier childhood. I was 14 when I went away to school.

Although I'm totally deaf I have a good voice and can talk very well. But I cannot lipread. For two years Ive tried to lip read well but with no success. My parents are [names redacted] of [my community].

Don't you think a thought should be given to us deaf-mutes. I'm sure our fathers and mothers would be glad of an allowance for us.

Hope my time is not wasted
I am yours to oblige

April 25/50

Dear Sir -

There is a matter I would like very much to bring to your attention if you would not think it to much trouble to listen to me. As you know ever since world war II a merchant navy man are not classed as a war veteran and like myself there are hundreds to day left a cripple and receiving no help from any source while the army navy and air force are receiving benefits from several sources as man to man Sir do you think this is fair. I have been unable to do very little work for two years now and I am receiving no help whatsoever. I think the merchant navy played a big part as well as the other forces and I don't see why we are not entitled to benefits as well as others as the Premier I would appreciate it very much Sir if you would try and see if you could be of some assistance to me in this respect and oblige.

Yours Very Truly

CARBONEAR-BAY DE VERDE

On Archives as Time Travel: How Letters to Smallwood Transported Me Back in Time

Jasmine Paul

MY ADVENTURE BACK IN TIME through the Smallwood letters began with a trip to the city. I booked three days at the archives, where I spent my time reading through four folders of letters and telegrams sent to Smallwood and the form letters his office sent in reply.

Reading the letters was emotional work and I had to take breaks to reflect. On the third day, my sister came to read the remaining letters with me, and we took photos of sixty-three letters which we then uploaded to my computer. From those, I selected twelve to transcribe. But the letters were only the beginning of my journey back to the early days of Confederation. For context, I researched the timeline of Confederation, read newspapers published at the time, and used 1945 census data to check the name spellings and to estimate ages of the letter writers. The census was particularly useful in identifying the first names of the women, most of whom signed using their husbands' names.

The content of the letters varied, but there were recurring topics: questions about new social programs; inquiries about work, the fishery, agriculture, and the election; and requests for housing, money (either given or as a loan), as well as for objects like bicycles. There were also letters addressing concerns and complaints. The paper on which the letters were written was lined or unlined, or taken from stapled notebooks. They were written in cursive in ink. Very few were typewritten. The idiosyncratic approach to capitalization stood out to me, as it wasn't confined to standard English orthography, but the quality of penmanship and spelling in general suggests that this was intentional, and not at all because of poor understanding. Vernacular speech also comes through in some letters.

Both men and women wrote to Smallwood, with many women signing with their husbands' name. Ages of the writers varied from sixteen to over seventy, but the average was about fifty. In some cases, it is possible that people relied on others to transcribe their words for them, and in these cases, the person who signed the letter was not the person who wrote it.

While each of the files held a large volume of letters, it is unlikely that everyone in the district was represented in them. At the time, writing letters was the most affordable way for most people to communicate. People with capital and connections had other ways to reach the premier; for example, they had the option of travelling to meet with Smallwood in St. John's or of communicating with him by telephone. Interestingly, some of the writers expressed their wishes not to have their letters printed or read over the radio, a nod, perhaps, toward Smallwood's own popularity as a radio host of *The Barrelman* for seven years. While I chose not to transcribe any of those letters, I wonder how those correspondents would feel about my reading their letters, all these years later. Would they have sent the letters had they known they would be retained and later donated to the archives as part of the Smallwood collection? Would they have changed how or what they wrote about?

Of the recurring topics, there were some specific requests or inquiries. Some people asked for infrastructure and gear to help them in the fishery, such as slipways, chains, and lines and inquired if support would be extended to fishermen in the event of a poor season. Farming was also a popular topic, with people asking for help with getting land, fencing, and seed. One man wrote to Smallwood in October 1949, wanting to know why he was unable to ship a barrel of potatoes to Toronto. Others asked for things many of us would take for granted today: a bike, a radio, or even electric lights.

Beyond practical letters about infrastructure, work, and supplies, there were some more unusual letters. One correspondent, "A Strong Confederate," sent a letter and two poems on April 24, 1949. He requested typewritten copies and feedback or money if the poems were good. There was no reply, so I can't be sure that he ever got the typewritten copies he requested. Another correspondent, who wanted to know where he could get the best stock of pigs, received a robust reply from Smallwood, who wrote that he himself had also previously imported "many thousands of young pigs from Prince Edward Island" and proceeded to offer advice on how to ensure the best quality of pig.

Other queries were more personal. One woman asked for help finding the birthdate of her boarder, so that she could help the woman apply for Old Age Pension. A correspondent who signed as "disopinted Confedrate" wrote in detail about the increase in the price of apples, observing that prices hadn't gone down since Confederation. Another man, meanwhile, asked if he could take a stick that had been left by marine works to use aboard his boat as a mast. Of all the letters, the most distressing was from a woman who reported that when she went to the relieving officer for help with her grandson, an illegitimate child, she was told to drown him in the brook! This letter stuck with me and created a lot of questions about relieving officers.

Using an archive is like time travel. Reading letters written by people who detailed their specific hardships put me in touch with the past in a way that is very different from reading books or documents that generalize about the past. Newspapers, books, and government documents outline the policies in place surrounding Confederation, but the letters in the Smallwood collection tell the story of how the policies really worked for people and what their experiences really were in trying to use them.

Smallwood promised hope and help, and these letters of request show that while people believed him, they were also willing to hold him accountable by reminding him of their vote. Sharing personal and private details of their lives was intended to communicate to Smallwood how desperately he and his help were needed. For the readers of today, the letters offer an intimate look into the past that can deepen our understanding of how much those promises meant and how much people believed or wanted to believe that this one man could make all the difference.

Mar 4th/49

Mr J R Smallwood

St. Johns

Dear Mr Smallwood:-

Re your letter some time ago. + it was very grateful of you to ask me to keep in touch with you from time to time. Well Mr Smallwood I am asking you for some information concerning buying young bigs this spring.

I want to Import Eighty or a Hundred young bigs this spring, + I want a good stock at the lowest price I can get, so if you could direct me to any one particular, please advise me, + I would be very much obliged.

Thanking you, hoping to drop in to see you sometime next month

Yours truly

Apr. 24, 1949.

Hon. J.R. Smallwood,
Premier of Nfld,
St. Johns.

Dear Sir,

I hope Mr. Smallwood that you will find time to read these two little poems. They were composed locally. Please if you have time send a reply to this letter saying how you liked it. I would like for you to send me a copy back (typewritten). I hope that you will soon pay a visit to Victoria. I will assure of a good reception when you come. Hoping to see you in the very near future.

Yours Truly
A Strong Confederate

P.S. If this is worth anything to you Please send to me what It is worth. Remember their is an another election coming and my vote is yours. [Our community] is 98.9% for the Liberal Party.

Welcome to our Island
It was on the 31st of March,
as we clearly understand,
That Canada so kindly accepted Nfld.
I hope dear friends, it will be
best for all who are concerned
For our dear old colony's
Freedom, for which our
Hearts have yearned.

———

The critics are downhearted
because they've lost the spoil
Their outlook seems to beaten
We'll never see them smile
But let them smile or let
them gruff, it will never do
no good.

for we are all Canadians
now, Thanks to Joe Smallwood

So let us join together now,
and lend a helping hand.
As friend to friend with Canada
who have joined with Nfld.
To help us in our struggles
And make our lives anew.
Something the graballs of the
Past never tried to do.

Now three cheers for dear old
Canada, who have set our island
free. From Grudge + Greed + plunder
and gave us victory.
I know It will be well for us,
when we boldly take our stand
side by side with Canada
Ride her in Nfld.

Now give a cheer to those who
helped to make our lives anew
That spend much in planning the
best thing for to do. To help
the poor + needy, orphans and
widows too.

Now here's a hand
for our trusty friend
The one that we all know
who did his best to beat
the Rest.
His Name is Uncle Joe

A FUNERAL

MY FRIENDS SO DEAR AND DID YOU HEAR,
THE LATEST GOING ROUND,
OF A FUNERAL THAT IS TAKING PLACE,
OVER IN ST. JOHNS TOWN.

DON JAMIESON[1] IS THE LEADER OF THIS VERY SPITEFUL GANG
HE SAYS WE'LL MAKE A CASKET, AND TRIM IT UP SO GRAND
TO SHOW TO ALL THE PEOPLE THE DEATH OF NFLD.

THEY SAY HOW WE WILL GET ALREADY, AND DO NOT BE TOO SHY.
TO SHOW OUR DEEPEST SYMPATHY YOU MUST WEAR A BLACK TIE,
SO ON THE 31ST OF MARCH WHEN EVERYTHING IS STILL,
WE WILL TAKE OUR FLOWERED CASKET, UPON SIGNAL HILL.

BUT WHEN THEY WERE GOING DOWN THE STREET,
ALL DRESSED IN FUNERAL FASHION, THE COVER FROM THE CASKET
POPPED, AND OUT HOPPED PETER CASHIN.

OUR FRIENDS HE SAID IT IS NOW THAT NFLD HAS DIED,
IT WAS WHEN I MADE MY PLUNDER AND THE HUNGRY CHILDREN CRIED,
SO ITS JUST AS WELL FOR US TO GIVE UP AND HAVE NO MORE TO SAY,
FOR VENGEANCE IS MINE THE GOOD LORD SAID AND I SURELY WILL REPAY.
BUT WE DON'T CARE NOW WHAT THEY SAY, OR WHO THEY TRY TO KILL,
THEY CAN TAKE THEIR CASKET DOWN TO HAIDES AND NOT TO SIGNAL HILL.

FOR WE ARE ALL CANADIANS NOW, WE WILL HAVE A BETTER CHANCE,
TO GET A BITE WITHOUT BEING ATE OR CROAKED AT LIKE A FROG.
SO HERE'S GOOD LUCK TO NFLD OUR ISLAND HOME SO DEAR,
SO COME ALONG CANADIANS, YOUR WELCOME OVER HERE.

---

1 Don Jamieson, a well-known radio personality, was a strong anti-confederate who campaigned in favour of economic union with the United States.

April 27/49

To

The Hon. J. R. Smallwood

St John's

Dear Sir,

I havin't a Radio + can afford to get one. I am wondering if you could arrange to get + send me a small battery Radio. I would appreciate it very much. I have four votes which will be cast in your favor when that time comes.

Thanking in [illegible]

Yours very truly

May 17th, 1949.

Dear Mr. [name redacted],

I beg to acknowledge receipt of your letter and to inform you that the Premier is at present out of town, but upon his arrival back your letter will be placed before him for his attention.

Sincerely yours,[2]

2 This response was likely from Muriel Templeman, J.R. Smallwood's longtime personal secretary. For more on Muriel Templeman, see Colleen Quigley's essay, later in this volume.

May 1st/49

Hon J.R. Smallwood

Dear Sir,

I have living with me an old lady who was taken from the Poor house about fourteen or fifteen years ago, She is cripple, deaf, and has poor eyesight, has no understanding in fact She is in bed at the present time I have her on board and lodgings from the Government.

She told me that she belonged to [a community] in Bonavista Bay. She doesn't know her age or when her Birthday is.

Now that we have Confederation (Thanks to you) and old age pension has come up I want to try and get her age to know if she is entitled to a pension. You know how to go about it better then I do. So will you please try and get her age for me so that she may get her old age pension.[3]

I am a poor woman, my husband hasn't (evne) earned a cent since last Summer, we are not on relief have only one to get family allowance for, my husband has gone to Canada to seek employment. we are for the Liberal Party and if I am spared we'll vote for Dr. Pottle on May 27.

I guess I am a namesake of his.

hoping Mr Smallwood that you will succeed and wishing you a great success. I remain

yours Sincerely

P.S. I am sorry I did not give you the old ladies name. Its [redacted].

3 For more on Old Age Pensions in Newfoundland prior to Confederation, see James G. Snell, "The Newfoundland Old Age Pension Programme, 1911–1949," *Acadiensis* 23, no. 1 (1993): 86–109, and Mondou, "Social Assistance."

May 5, 1949.

Hon. J.R. Smallwood,
Premier of Nfld,
St. John's.

Dear Sir,

We have in our house four (4) votes. Those were given for Confederation, and will now be given for the Liberal Party, but I think that with all the money that is being given away, I should be able to get about twenty dollars ($20.00) in order to get the electric lights in my home.[4]

I am a poor man, and can't afford to get the Electric Lights. Why should I not get twenty dollars, when others are getting thousands?

Yours respectfully,

4 Among the many benefits that Smallwood promised Confederation would bring was electricity to the rural areas of the province. For more on this, see Michelle McBride, "Electrifying the Island," Heritage Newfoundland & Labrador, 2001, https://www.heritage.nf.ca/articles/economy/electrifying-island.php.

June 6th 1949

Premier J.R. Smallwood
St John's

Dear Sir,

First of all I want to congratulate you for pulling the big majority of voters on polling day.

I wonder if you would be able to help me out in getting a 3.H.P. Acadia Engine for to go fishing the year. I know for one practically new for one hundred dollars. I can't afford to get this Engine myself so if I don't get some help I will have to stay ashore this summer. Will you please let me know if you can give me any help as soon as possible.

Wishing you good success in the coming Elections,

Yours truly

June 21/ 49

Hon Jr Smallwood
Prime minister .

Dear sir;
theare is some sticks Hare that is not in use, they are only spoling; I mean getting Rotten. they Belong to the merene Works; I use a Boom and mast to Land my fish; + my mast is Brok. can you tell me to get one of those sticks or point me to the Right Auttority; I am grately in need of one

You will oblige me By so Doing. yours turly

Aug 28 1949

Dear Sir,

I am a poor boy and my father was sick. 26 year and was not out of [our community] I have a sister and she is sick with the azma. We cannot only get enough to eat. I was getting the baby bonus for a few months and then when it was Stop with the money I had to get a suit of clothes because my father could not earned any money for me to get one.

Last year I had a bicycle and earned enough of money to pay my fees and buy book for another Grade. I am in Grade 9.

Well on Summer Vacation I had misfortune with my bike and it was broken I could not get it fixed because it was broken too much too fix. My father said would you kindly See could you get a bike for me.

In the election time my father and mother voted for your Canidate because we said that you could help us in distressed. My Father and Mother would appreciated it very much. If you cannot get me a bicycle I will have to stay home from school. I thought I would get my Grade 11. If I had the bike I would earned plenty of money carrieing mail and going long distance quickly for ~~me and a~~ people who want to do things Quickly

Mr Smallwood see what you can do one all the family will be glad but if you cannot help me we will be sorrow. I hope you will see and do what you can for us

Yours Sincerely

[name redacted] .. Father and Mother

Oct 2/49

Premier Joseps
Smallwood

Dear sir just a short while ago i had a letter from my son in toronto asking me to send him up a barrol of patotoes and vegetables for the winter so i went to the station master in carbonear to find out what i could do and he told me that i could not send it out of the country i taught it funney as we ar all called canada now and i would like to know why we are bared from sending patotoes there for a food as well as have them come in please let me know by return mail as i would like to get them off before the frost takes then

[illegible] oblige yours
truely

date 1161949[5]

Hon J R Smallwood

Prime Minister

Gentlemen could you or would you tell me if the Goverment is doing anything in the way of Goverment supply for the fishery.

I have a Cod trap and in order to go too the fishery I want 150 lbs of line to put in it I am not in a position to buy this but if there is aney goverment gaurentee I would like to get it for the past few years I have bee ingaged at other imployment but as work is scarce I would do the next best thing go fishing, I was over at your liberal Convention as a delegate and I congatulate you on the great Liberal

Victory

I remain

yours truely,

5 In some instances, it is unclear whether correspondents are writing dates in month/day/year format or in day/month/year, and the letter contents do not offer any further insight. In these instances, we have chosen to organize them chronologically as month/day/year.

Premier J R Smallwood

Dear Sir,

I am writing to know when we are going to get the cheap living we were Promised before Confederation

Now Mr. Smallwood I want to talk about apples for instances why have we got to Pay So much for apples when they are so Plenty and cheep in Canada. When I was a Boy all I would want was one cent to get a apple a day and two cents would get a real large one you know that as well as I do and when my Boys and girls was growing up that was around 25 or 30 year ago they could get the same and oranges also only 25 & 30 cents per dozzen I could give my children say 5 children 2 cents each that would be only ten cents and they would have a nice lunch a real large apple every day that was when we hade Bad Responsible goverment then we hade Comission Goverment and a child had to Pay 6 and 7 cents for one apple if they wanted one and what Poor family could give Six or Seven children 6 & 7 cents a day a great many of them had to do without ~~them~~ apples O yes the rich children could get all right

Now we are the 10 Province of Canada and we Still have to Pay 30 to 40 cents per dozzen for not very large apples every child Still has to have 4 or 5 or 6 or 7 cents to get an apple for lunch. and all other fruit a lot of it coming from Canada it makes me Sick to hear all the Preaching about TB give the poor children the chance to buy cheep apples & oranges and other fruit. they are getting the Baby Bonus with one hand and the Merchants and grocers taking it with the other its the merchants and Shop Keepers that is getting the Benfit of Confredration they don't Pay any duty and asking just as much as they always did I heard of one Shop Keeper saying if he hade to Pay hevey taxes he was getting it of SomeBody So I guess the Poor will always be Poor. and as for work the toiling masses didint vote for Work they only wanted Baby Bonus & old age Pensions. The only employment I can hear of is Beer taverns getting Set up in every Place that will mean more Poor homes and hungry Children after all I guess Peter Cashin was the only man that did tell the truth. [two words illegible]
A disopinted Confedrate. [community name]

FERRYLAND

Hiking the Campaign Trail

Elizabeth Dane

BEGINNING JUST OUTSIDE the capital city of St. John's and ending just after Trepassey, the Southern Shore runs along the easternmost edge of the Avalon Peninsula on the island of Ktaqmkuk, colonially known as Newfoundland. Boasting a myriad of colourful rural communities, high populations of seabirds (including the beloved puffin), and annual visitations from a plethora of whales and icebergs, the Southern Shore is considered an integral part of the Newfoundland tourist experience. It is also home to the East Coast Trail, which spans 336 kilometres from Topsail to Cappahayden. The Trail consists of a series of twenty-five paths, all of which are connected by what the East Coast Trail Association calls "community walks." In these walks, hikers trek anywhere from fifty metres to eight kilometres through towns such as Cape Broyle, Bauline, Tors Cove, and Renews to get to the next trailhead. Since its inception in 1994, the East Coast Trail has become an increasingly popular destination for locals and tourists alike. For many, the attraction rests not only in the awe-inspiring views found along the coast but also in the communities themselves. Many leave the experience with the quintessential impression of Newfoundlanders: an extremely friendly, generous, and quaint people. Indeed, residents of the Southern Shore have been known to offer rides, water, food, and encouragement to hikers as they traverse through their backyards.

After moving to the island in 2014, I was introduced to the Trail in the spring of 2017. Like others, I was taken by its undeniably unique geography, history, and culture. In the summer of 2022, I decided to embark on a solo thru-hike of the Trail in pursuit of a communion of sorts between me, nature, and these communities, which are far more nuanced than their stereotypical representations suggest.

I too was offered (and accepted) many offerings from residents of the Southern Shore during my thru-hike. Indeed, having moved to the island at seventeen, a come from away with no familial ties to the island, I have been extremely privileged to find myself surrounded by welcoming and generous people, many who, over the years, have become family. It's true that Newfoundlanders often are very friendly and generous people, and, for many Newfoundlanders, it is also true that their way of life remains similar to so-called simpler times of days gone by. But Newfoundland identity transcends far beyond the realm of simplicity. Rather, it exists somewhere within complex and painful histories of colonialism in tandem with the myriad traumas inherent to living on an isolated island surrounded by the cruel mistress Atlantic. Life on this island is characterized by hardship, both pre- and post-Confederation, evident in the letters that Newfoundlanders wrote to Joey Smallwood.

During my thru-hike, I found myself thinking about the letters from the Ferryland district and about what it might have meant to be a Newfoundlander living on the Southern Shore during the early years of Confederation. The Ferryland district was predominantly Catholic, ergo, Joey Smallwood and his Liberal Party struggled (and failed) to get their votes, both provincially and federally.[1] Smallwood infamously threatened the voters of the new Canadian federal riding of St. John's West (of which Ferryland was a part), saying:

> I don't need you. I've been elected. But you need me. I'm sitting on top of the public chest, and not one red cent will come out of it for Ferryland unless Greg Power is elected [to Ottawa]. Unless you vote for my man, you'll be out in the cold for the next five years ... Those

1 In the 1949 provincial election, the Ferryland district elected Peter Cashin. Cashin, a staunch anti-confederate who ran as an independent before joining the Progressive Conservative Party in 1951, took over 2,500 of the approximately 3,300 votes cast. Cashin was not new to politics: he was first elected in 1923 as a Liberal-Labour Progressive, and then moved to the Liberal Party, where he served as minister of finance from 1928 to 1932. For more on the Liberal campaign in Ferryland, see a petition from several Liberal voters expressing their concern about party support for their candidate, Augustus Greene, later in this section.

> settlements which vote against Greg Power will get nothing—absolutely nothing.[2]

Certainly, the power of guilt was nothing new for the Catholic population of the Ferryland district. However, when presented with the option, guilt with the promise of eternal paradise would presumably take precedence over guilt with the promise of Canada.[3] As such, Greg Power was not elected.

From the letters, it appears that the residents of the Ferryland district were well aware of the animosity their government felt toward their region. One man writes, "we want to live as well as anyone else," while another acknowledges that "it seems no one bothers About how we get by." Those who found themselves in need of governmental services were thus forced to plead and bargain for their basic needs: schooling, health care, welfare, employment, road repair, etc.

Perhaps in an attempt to make their causes more worthy of or sympathetic to Smallwood's attention, many began or ended their letters with statements of support and best wishes for the premier. In one community, the promise of votes appeared to function as a form of currency that might pay for the settlement's electricity: if Joey could fix up the road, then one correspondent said he would guarantee the successful election of the next Liberal candidate in the Ferryland district. In this district, a relationship with Joey was necessarily transactional, as forsaking the church had to yield some kind of worldly benefit. Eventually, it did: these days, as part of the larger Irish Loop Drive, the Southern Shore Highway has become a tourist destination in its own right. Similarly, the community walks of the East Coast Trail are easily reached and completed, posing little to no threat to hikers.

For some contemporary hikers, the community walks along the East Coast Trail are a charming way to immerse themselves in rural Newfoundland, whereas some view them as a necessary yet irksome traipse, useful insofar as they allow them to get back on the real trail. For others, the walks offer an intriguing glimpse into Newfoundland history and culture. Monuments along these walks commemorate tragedies such as Beaumont Hamel, the massacre of nearly all the soldiers in World War I's Newfoundland Regiment; the SS *Florizel*, a 1918 shipwreck that killed ninety-four people, including a three-year-old girl; as well

---

2 Qtd. in Gwyn, *Smallwood*, 15.

3 Religious affiliation was an important aspect of voter identity; however, it was not the only one. For more on this, see Vicki S. Hallett's reflection, later in this volume.

as the newly erected tribute to the equally beloved and troubled son of Newfoundland, Ron Hynes, a prolific Ferryland-born singer-songwriter who struggled with severe drug and alcohol addiction until the end of his life. The absence of monuments related to Confederation or to Smallwood might offer insight into the tensions that exist between that which is shown and that which is known. Indeed, that these roads which once posed a genuine threat to the livelihoods and safety of locals are now part of a tourist experience might be a more authentic glimpse into this disparity between what we believe to be and what is actually quintessentially "Newfoundland." Not merely an idyllic place with quaint people, nor simply a pleasant spot for a drive or a hike, it is a place where residents are forced to negotiate with their government for their safety and basic needs. In peeking behind the curtain of Newfoundlandia, we are compelled to move beyond the kitschy jellybean-row souvenirs, the knitted socks, the screech and the screech-ins. In doing so, we reveal histories characterized by economic, cultural, and personal hardships, largely informed by historically incompetent leadership. Together, these have created what is arguably the most authentic Newfoundland tradition: a fraught relationship to authorities who prioritize curating tourist experiences over the health and well-being of their constituents.

June 16/48

Hello Joey

How are You not in Jail yet Ha Ha Too Smart for that. i Was Sorry that i Was Sorry that i Was not at home. When you Were. But i am sure that my good Wife gave you a nice lunch, she always takes it up for Joey. You Will i am sure Be sorry to Know i am not Well. i have a strained heart, angina Pectorious is sat in. i am not allowed to Perform any manuel labour from now on and after the summer is over i Will not do any supplying for the fishery. i give the fishermen everything the Want. and i am going the same. But i Wish that i did not do it this Year if i had no credit out i could take a complete rest. come up to see us some Sunday evening or Holiday after noon. You would meet the West Coast Captains and there men. They will Be taking ice Salt & general Supplies here. Bring Mrs with you come anytime you … my Doctor he tells me not to work. let me Know if you get this get your son to drop a line for You hoping to see you sometime soon

With all Best Wishes

From Your Sincere Friend

April 20th 1949

Dear Mr. Smallwood,

Last week I called at your office twice but I did not get to see you. My business was concerning the [school] at [my community name]. I am teaching at [this community] sixteen years owing to the small number in attendance the school was closed Feb. 25th until Sept. The school was opened here for five months. I am unemployed since Feb 25th. There was always a school kept at [my community] no matter how small the number as the nearest school is seven miles from here Mr. Smallwood I know you will agree that those children are entitled to education. Could you do anything in the matter to have the school re-opened for the next two months?

Before closing I wish to congratulate you and I wish you continued success.

Kindest regards,

Thanking you in reply.

I remain

Yours sincerely

[Teacher]

April 24th 49

To Hon J. R. Smallwood
Prime Ministers Office
St Johns

Honorable & Dear Sir,

To begin, I congratulate you on your recent appointment to Premiership of Nfld now Canadas Tenth Province, through your untiring and indefatigable wrestle for the betterment of us Nfldrs as a people. I beg now to put my problem before you. I have in my care a grandchild, the illegitimate child of my daughter [Josephine];[4] (The Father [Walter], made his get a way under the pretense of going to America to make the nescessary arrangements for their marriage) he did not return, My daughter the childs mother is at present [on the mainland] she went there in Nov , [...] she has been three times in hospital twice with a Nervous break down and on the other occasion for the Removal of a Tumor, I have never received one cent from the Dept of Child Welfare towards the up-keep of this child, My (second) husband is only a stranger to both the Mother & child, While we do all we can for the child, we cannot give her the nesessary additional requirements I went personally to [Mr. Arnold]'s office & couldn't see him for a day or so & of course couldn't wait over, then I wrote him & was informed that there was nothing coming to me (at least from their direction). Then I interviewed Mr. [O.P. Morgan] R.O.[5] at [community] (where I was then residing, & he told me that No 1 there was a Monetary stipend granted for caring for such children, No 2 there was an allowance for Milk Supply, Clothing & Cod Liver Oil, None of these have I recieved & I've knit articles & hooked rugs & made sale of them in order to buy milk & shoes for the child, I also wrote the Commissioner of P. H & W[6] of that time & my letter was ignored anyway I recieved no answer or got no results. and as far as I can find out, It was the R. O here in [my community] who was the cause of this little delicate bit of humanity being deprived of the priveledges that others in the same category enjoyed. Just on account of an old family grudge an innocent, harmless little mite is made to suffer, So far I have not recieved the Baby Bonus, but I know thats coming, as I only moved to [my community]

4 Because the correspondent names four different people, we have chosen to use pseudonyms for ease of reading.

5 Relieving Officer.

6 Public Health and Welfare.

from [another community] last week & I asked the P. M[7] there to see that any mail for me would be forwarded to [my community] & as soon as I get the B Bonus[8] I will write that Dept & notify them of my change of Address.

This grand child of mine is both undersize & underweight & I would very much like to get a Pass for free transportation to the Child Welfare Clinic to have her examined by a Doctor. Trusting that you will see to it, that the proper person will take the proper steps in this matter referred to above, and although [my community] is part of the Southern Shore, I can assure you, that you and your Party have many supporters here, including myself.

Thanking you in anticipation

I Remain

Yours Very Sincerely

7 Postmaster.

8 Officially known as Family Allowance, the baby bonus was one of a series of benefits to which Newfoundlanders and Labradorians were entitled upon Newfoundland and Labrador's entry into Confederation. The first cheques were sent out within a few weeks of Confederation in 1949. For more on this, see Roberts, "How the Baby Bonus Came to Newfoundland."

APRIL 25, 1949

HON. J. R. SMALLWOOD,
PREMIER OF NEWFOUNDLAND,
ST. JOHN'S.

DEAR SIR:

THE SOUTHERN SHORE ROAD IS IN A DESPERATE STATE OF DISPAIR, NO CONSTRUCTION WORK HAVING BEEN DONE FOR OVER FIFTEEN YEARS FROM THE GOULDS TO TREPASSEY, EXCEPT ORDINARY MAINTENANCE BY PATROL MEN AND NOW AND THEN A FEW MEN AND A TRUCK, MORE PARTICULARLY DO I MENTION THE ROAD FROMTHE JUNCTION OF CAPE BROYLE ROAD WHICH LEADS TO TOR'S COVE AND BAULINE SETTLEMENTS. KNOWING YOUR ABILITY AND ENERGY TO GET THINGS DONE, I HAVE EVERY CONFIDENCE THAT IF YOU ONLY PASS THE WORD TO THE RIGHT DEPARTMENT, SOMETHING SUBSTANCIAL IN THE WAY OF ROAD IMPROVEMENT WOULD BE ACCOMPLISHED IN A SHORT TIME.

I OPERATE A TAXI SERVICE FROM [COMMUNITY] TO [COMMUNITY] DAILY AND I ASSURE YOU THAT ANYONE DRIVING OVER THIS ROAD IN ITS PRESENT CONDITION IS RISKING SERIOUS DAMAGE TO HIS CAR. IF YOU SAW THIS ROAD YOURSELF I AM SURE THAT THERE WOULD BE NO NEED FOR ME TO WRITE YOU ABOUT IT.

PUT A GOOD MAN ON YOUR TICKET IN THIS DISTRICT AND WE WILL RETURN HIM AT THE HEAD OF THE POLLS.

ANY FAVOR YOU CAN DO FOR US ON THIS MATTER WILL BE GREATLY APPRECIATED AND WILL DO MUCH TO FURTHER THE CAUSE OF THE LIBERAL IN "FERRYLAND DISTRICT"

I REMAIN, SIR,
YOURS TRULY,

April 29/49.

To

Premier J. R. Smallwood,

Colonial Building,

St. John's

Dear Sir,

There have been several letters written in from here concerning the Breakwater here at [my community]. But so far there has been nothing done about it.

With the condition it is in now it is impossible for us to get over to our fishing premises. This cliff is about two hundred feet high & the people got to get over it all hours of the day & night. And its too late to have it repaired when there is someone killed, & its really impossible for people to get over it safely.

So I trust you will take this matter in hands & have the work completed in the very near future.before the men goes fishing.

I remain

Yours Truly

Apr. 30th/49

Mr. J. R. Smallwood.
Premier of Nfld.

Dear Mr. Smallwood,

The people of this settlement wish to draw your attention to the fact that they are without electric light in this settlement which is only one mile from the settlement of [...] which has electric light. We feel sure you can do something to help us in this matter and when your party is represented here during the coming elections you can be assured of our votes.

There are twelve families in this settlement who are desirous of having their houses and fishing premises lighted and it would be such an asset to the people who sometimes have to work all night in the stages at fish during the summer. Our fishing premises which are quite near the houses could be easily lighted.

This is the sole request of the people of this settlement who would wish to shun the burden of buying batteries for radios if they could have electric ones which would cost less and we would also be able to partake of the modern electric conveniences of every day life.

We are all aware that most of your Promises during the Convention have materialized and we feel sure you will give our cause your immediate attention

Signed on behalf of the people of this settlement by

May 7th. 1949.

HON. MR. J. R. SMALLWOOD,
ST. JOHN'S.

Dear Sir,

We, the undersigned voters of [our community] are disappointed at the apparent lack of support which is being given to our Liberal Candidate, Mr. AUGUSTUS GREENE.[9] Is this due to the fact that Confederation received such a small number of votes in the past Referendum? If so, then we would to point out that many of these votes were cast solely for Responsible Government with a view to attaining Economic Union with the U.S.A., whilst many other voters were influenced by sources better known to yourself; but we emphatically state that the majority were not cast for Mr. Peter J. Cashin. And now that all this is water under the bridge, we strongly urge, Sir, that we definitely believe that there is a strong possibility of Mr. Greene being elected for the Liberal Party provided he is given the necessary support that he is in need of, and that the same support given other Districts should apply to the Southern Shore.

We also believe that our best chance of getting our full share of the benefits received under the new set-up is by breaking the Cashin stranglehold on this District and electing a Liberal member.

SIGNED.
[fifty-five names redacted]

Dear Sir:

These are some of the representative citizens of [our community] but by no means all that are at present behind Mr. Greene, but as my time was very limited I could not manage to see the many others who would have been to glad to affix their names to this petition.

Sincerely Yours

9 In the 1949 provincial election, Augustus Greene received 456 votes. In second place, he was nonetheless far behind Peter Cashin, who won the district with 2,506 votes.

June 11th 49

To

Hon J. Smallwood

Dear Sir

I want to know if there are anything can be done with the bridge here in this small settlement which separates us from all comunication with the rest of the Island. We have a mile this side of [our community] which was the main road going to [another community] Years ago & was always kept up by the high road, with one months work every spring as a secondary road now this Year, theres nothing seems to be done [name redacted] was here in April & told me he would put the other section men to work he would Come here & put me to work also & altho I wired the dept since I never got a reply from them or [name redacted]

Each fall my orders are take away the cribbing so as the ice have a chance to force its way through when the river rafters, so its away yet & theres no truck can take a load across in safety. Fishing time is here now & I cant work on road before Sept, but I could fix up the bridge so as we can truck our fish over it during Summer, I do hope you will use your influence & see the matter is fixed up. We are off the main road & nobody seems to know much about us.

Trusting you will do your best as its important we want to live as well as anyone else

You will oblige

Yours very truly

July 10th
1949

To Hon. J. R. Smallwood
The Premier
St Johns

Dear Sir,

I am appealing to your sense of honour & Justice, I want you to kindly take into consideration my case of unfortunate circumstances which I will state here for your consideration, well to begin with I am completely crippled and handicapped in every way due to a T. B. hip condition which I developed when quite a kid, now to add to this my right leg seems to be giving out and I am forced to exist on five dollars per Month which isn't enough to feed a cat, can you credit that Mr Smallwood, now I have a delicate daughter who is working in a store for small money and she can barely scrape by on what she gets, as she always got to be taking tonics etc to keep her on her legs at all as she so delicate, I am living home here with my Mother and my little girl, now in all sincerity Mr Smallwood do you consider five dollars per Month enough for any human being to exist on, to say nothing of nourishment for me in my state of health, what I want you to do for me is, will you try & increase what I am getting say about $15 or $17 per month, I would get by on that much alright and I am not telling any lies when I say that I am urgently in need of assistence, will you get an increase in that 5$ for me a cripples pension will be O.k. I think they should get a chance as well as their more fortunate friends if I could get fiftheen or seventeen dollars $15 or 17 dollars would be fine for me, you understand as well as I do that there never was any one in the Govnt for me or any one like me to apply to for assistence before now we never had a right Governemnt before thats why cases such as mine were unheeded, I am expecting to get a run out to the City soon & I hope to have the pleasure of seeing ~~to~~ you and too congratulate you on your great success in the past election

Thanking you in Anticipation

I am dear Sir

very Gratefully & Respectfully.

Aug. 3. 1949

Hon. J. R. Smallwood
Premier of Nfld
St. John's

Hon. Sir

Regarding the announcement of the refund of money to persons who paid for Streptomycin treatment at the Sanatorium, I wish apply for refund of some.[10]

My daughter ... was administered this treatment to the value of six hundred and seventeen dollars ($617.00) the receipts of which I have on hand and shall furnish them when necessary. At present I am in need of this money as the fishery is bad and I have a heavy hospital bill to pay.

Your consideration of the matter of Streptomycin is indeed worthy of the highest commendation and shows your ardent desire to serve the people.

Trusting a reply at your earliest convenience

I remain,
Respectfully yours,

10 Streptomycin was an experimental drug that became the standard treatment for tuberculosis. Families had to pay for this at first. See J.G. Kidney and E. MacLaughlin, "Streptomycin in the Treatment of Pulmonary Tuberculosis: A Presentation of 11 Cases Treated with Streptomycin at the Newfoundland Government Sanatorium," *Journal of the Medical Association of Eire* 22, no. 127 (1948): 3–8. For more on the history of tuberculosis in Newfoundland, see Keith Collier, "History of Tuberculosis and Its Presence in Newfoundland," Heritage Newfoundland & Labrador, 2011, https://www.heritage.nf.ca/articles/society/tuberculosis-newfoundland.php and "Fighting Tuberculosis in Newfoundland and Labrador."

Aug 24/49

Premier Joseph
R. Smallwood

Dear Sir.

At this time, I would like to make it known to you About the Conditions of our roads here to our homes on the south side of [our community]. Its hard for one to explain just how awful these roads are and it seems no one bothers about how we get by, However my brothers and likewise myself are fishermen and we work very hard and Im sure we turn in more to the Government then lots of others I know who are getting there local roads done not only to there home but to there gardens ect - It wouldent cost so very much to put a road along there about - Seven or eight hundred dollars would take care of it. just widing & graveling that all we bought a truck couple months ago and we got to leave it a mile from our homes
We can just manage to walk on that terrible road we are endangered especially at winter time if at any time you may be here … would you kindly take time to look it over and I'm sure you will say, its the worst you ever seen on the whole Southern shore.
Dont think i dident vote for you i certainly did and glad I did
So please write and let me know what you can do for me

I remain
Sincerly

April 30th 1950

Your Honour,

This letter is a personal one, Concerning my situation in life, What I have done, and what I am trying to do, And I trust that you will read it and do your best to help me solve my problems.

I am a young Veteran age twenty four. I served in the Cdn. Army for three years I was wounded in Italy in Sept. 1944, after my Discharge I returned to N.F.L.D. because I loved my Island home, I had to take up fishing because I couldn't get anything else to do.

What I am after now is the contract of the mail from [a community] to [my community]. Which I understand will be out on tender in July, My Dad is the telegraph operator here in [my community] getting a salary some where in the vicinity of one Hundred Dollors, and with six of us to feed almost all year round is very small I am getting after the mail because I think Im intitled to it, I used the tool's of war to defend our country. then why shouldn't I be given the rest of the tool's of peace to make a decent living, I am well aware that this problem faces many Newfoundland Veterans. But I think something should be done to help us. And who should be better to ask for help than the Premier of the Country.

I know and am well aware that the odds are against me. Because I know there's men after it who has lots of money and who supported you in your fight for Confederation. But I wish to be straight forward even if it cost me this contract which I'm after. So I might as well tell you I didn't support Confederation, or I am not a Liberal supporter, But still I give credit where its due, I know you don't mind me telling you these things. If you do, well Ive just got to take it the hard way as I have always done.

I am simply asking for a fair brake. I fought for and lost most of my blood fighting for Freedom. And I ask for a chance to live. is this to much to ask for? Or is one friends with the money in the front line with jobs to choose from. We had Brains enough to win the war then haven't we the Brains to run these simple jobs.

Your Honour I trust you'll help me all you can, And hope at least that you will answer this letter.

In closing I wish you the Very Best of luck in your work as Premier of this Province.

I remain
Your Obedient Servant,

FOGO

The Barrelman

Gemma Hickey

ON TOP OF AN ANTIQUE WOODEN TABLE in the house where my father was raised, two books lay side by side: *I Chose Canada* by Joseph R. Smallwood and the Bible. Given how Smallwood was viewed in my grandparents' household, he may as well have authored both. On more than one occasion, I remember my grandmother referring to Smallwood as "the saviour of our province," so it was only fitting that the 3D image of him, distributed in the early 1970s, be hung next to Jesus on the wall in the hallway. My grandfather talked about Smallwood as if he knew him personally and, like many, affectionately referred to the province's first premier as "Joey."

It's no wonder many people from my grandparent's generation felt such a kinship to him. Before becoming a politician, Smallwood hosted his own radio show called *The Barrelman*. The name originated from the byline in his publication and was a play on the position of lookout historically located at the top of a ship and resembling a barrel or bucket. On naval vessels, protective platforms were eventually constructed to replace these earlier designs. Smallwood figuratively positioned himself as this province's lookout man. The show aired over the course of seven consecutive years with the intent of "making Newfoundland better known to Newfoundlanders." For six nights a week, people gathered around their radios as Smallwood's voice blared like a beacon across a sea of electromagnetic waves.

I rode the trains from time to time with my grandfather, a railwayman, in my youth. During those rides, he spoke about Smallwood as if he were a superhero. Before "Canada joined Joey," as my grandfather put it, the railway was publicly owned and as a result many workers fell on hard times. When he told me that Smallwood took up their cause and walked across Newfoundland on the railbed, the look of pride on his face imprinted itself on me. I adored my grandfather, so I told him that when I grew up, I was going to walk across Newfoundland to help people, too. Cancer took my grandfather in 1989 (long before I learned that Smallwood had used a trolley for part of his walk), but on July 2, 2015, I kept my promise to him. I began my cross-island walk in Port aux Basques and set out on the Trans-Canada Highway, the paved highway that replaced the railway. One month later, I ended my walk at the Mount Cashel Memorial in St. John's. I thought about my grandparents during my walk, especially as I passed the town of Gambo and took a short rest in the parking lot dubbed "Joey's Lookout," where a large black and white wooden cut-out of the Barrelman himself keeps watch over his hometown.

Reading the letters of people who lived in the Fogo Island district was like peeping through the front window of their homes. I felt like I was trespassing at first, but as I read on, a feeling of familiarity ensued. The nostalgia was real. Struggle is universal. I imagined my grandmother as a little girl in her small rural town living with her six siblings and parents in a two-room shack that had no electricity or running water. My grandmother rarely talked about her upbringing, but when she did, she referenced Smallwood's radio show. Perhaps the fifteen minutes of airtime provided the family with some form of escape.

The letters to Smallwood revealed incredible hardship and mainly focused on bread-and-butter issues such as jobs, disabilities, pensions, wages, equipment, transportation, and so on. At first glance, the letters appear worshipful, but there is an undertone of agency in exchange for votes. Some letters contained more than one signature. For example, in an April 1949 appeal to Smallwood, three men explained that they each had large families and, over the winter months, all were bordering on starvation because their "orders" were discontinued. Their situation was not unique. Many in the district were destitute and couldn't afford to feed or clothe their families. They had no access to a local hospital, and schools weren't centrally located. Many children had to walk miles each day to attend class and were consequently forced to stay home when the trek became too dangerous during certain times of the year.

Smallwood replied to most of the letters he received, but outside of expressing empathy, there wasn't much he could do. In the year prior to Confederation, he encouraged people to write when his government was officially elected because he'd be in a better position to help them at that point. After Confederation, he referred people to their district member, Gordon Janes, or to the representatives of national companies such as the Canadian National Railway or the Labrador Mining & Exploration Co. Ltd.

I grew up hearing so many colourful stories about Smallwood that when he died in 1991, I remember experiencing a deep sense of loss. Thinking about Smallwood today, I believe he had a vision for this place, but I also believe that this vision became clouded when the pedestal of his own creation prevented him from seeing past himself. The Barrelman wasn't a saviour or a superhero. He was a mere mortal like the rest of us. Looking back, I see now that I mourned the myth not the man. His ship had sailed.

Dec 31st. 1948

Mr. J.R. Smallwood
St. John's

Dear Sir

I have living with me my wife's Sister who is both deaf and dumb … and who at present receives the sum of $10.00 per quarter from the government which totals $40.00 per year. Under Confederation what will she receive? I have never seen any provision made in any of the terms regarding a person of that kind. I suppose there must be some allotment for such persons and if there is a form to be filled in I would be very pleased to receive one.

You know that $10.00 per quarter is not sufficient to clothe and feed someone.

Please give this your carefullest consideration. Trusting to hear from you as soon as possible. Congratulating you on the victory you have won.

Yours in the fight for freedom

January 15, 1949.

Dear Mr. [name redacted]:

I have considered your letter carefully, and I must agree that the amount of $10.00 per quarter paid to your wife's sister is a scandalously small amount. She comes in a class of where there are many hundreds in our country. Practically nothing is being done for them now, but I am looking forward eagerly to the day, not many months from now, when I can do something for them. I would be glad if you would write me on this matter sometime after March 31.

Sincerely yours,
J.R. SMALLWOOD.

April 16/49

Hon. J.R. Smallwood .P.M.
St. John's

Dear Sir
Whe the undersine apeal to you on Behalf our families During the Winter months I was geting $40.00 per month for 8 in family & [James Wimslett][1] $35.00 for 7 in family in March we recived the above amount for April The R.O. [Edward Brinley] cut our orders from the above amount to $20.00 twenty Dollars per family to the amount of $2.50 Per head for 8 in family Per month & Little over $2.50 for 7 in family for [James Wimslett] Per month whe dont understand why our orders was cut in half & others git a full order for the same month [James Wimslett] got sick wife with a nursing baby [Arthur Pile] with Sick Wife & nursing Baby With our orders reduced Part of our families must starve whe got children going to school so whe canot see any thing to do but Keep them home as we are not going to send them to school hungry thear is no Employment to be had & thear will not be any until late in May so if we cannot git any more Relief our Families must certainly starve is this the Dept orders or is [Edward Brinley] R.O. doing it on is one authority Will you Please interceed for us as our families is in a semmy starvation condition & canot live a month on $2.50 Per head Please Reply

I Remain yours Truly

1 Because there are four separate names in this letter, and because it was signed by three individuals, we have chosen to use pseudonyms for ease of reading.

Hon. J.R. Smallwood,
Premier Newfoundland, *April 21st/1949*

Sir,

Referring to a cottage Hospital on Fogo Island.[2]

We the People of [our community] after Navigation closes are completely cut of from all Hospitals until the reopening of Spring. Therefore we the Drs Committee of [our community] urgently request to you for to interest the right authority to help and errect a cottage Hospital on Fogo Island.

Yours Sincerly,

Secty Drs Committee

2 The cottage hospitals were a series of small hospitals spread across Newfoundland (not Labrador or the Northern Peninsula, which were served by the Grenfell Association) that opened between 1936 and 1954. These hospitals had between twelve and forty beds and were staffed by a doctor and a team of nurses. While more serious cases were still sent on to St. John's, the cottage hospitals could take care of many common complaints, including minor surgeries. For more on the cottage hospital system, see J.T.H. Connor's essay, later in this volume, as well as Keith Collier, "Cottage Hospitals and Health Care in Newfoundland," Heritage Newfoundland & Labrador, 2011, https://www.heritage.nf.ca/articles/society/cottage-hospitals.php; Connor, Connor, Kidd, and Mathews, "Healthcare as Ecoystem"; Gordon S. Lawson and Andrew F. Noseworthy, "Newfoundland's Cottage Hospital System: 1920–1970," *Canadian Bulletin of Medical History* 26, no. 2 (2009): 477–98; and Edward F.J. Lake, *Capturing an Era: History of the Newfoundland Cottage Hospital System* (St. John's: Argentia Pilgrim, 2010).

Apr. 23rd

19/49

Mr J R Smallwood

St. John's

Dear Sir:-

It gives me great pleasure to write you this letter although I haven't much education and am not able to put it together very good, but I will try and do my very best to explain to you that I am living in [a community] on the South Side on the South east end of [a harbour]. its called where there is no road and never has been one. And there has not been much hopes of getting a road, It's A terrible bad place I have reared A family of six children from the age of 19 years down to the age 3 years. All but one of these the youngest have went to school. Most of there time half way to their kneese in mud. And water all along by [name redacted] fence certain times when the water is low they beats around a Ban of rocks which is enough to kill any child I have. Three children attending school now, most of the time they have to walk through mud and water and climb fences. And do it all: Now sir dont you think with me that this is very unfair but I am not the only one who has this to do lots of other children has the same to do to connect with the road that leads to the school, my three children has lost several days of school since Spring came owing to the conditions of this walking through mud and water where there is about 4 or 5 hundred feet of road wanted 3 hundred feet mud and water the remainder of it sticks and stumps and rocks. I have been living here for fourteen years now and have had it very difficult to get my Boys and girls to school and I have them that is very interested in going to shool. And I am interested in putting them to school, but its very discouraging Sir, during the School period the children have the three Winter months they can walk on ice and as soon as the ice is gone they have to take to rocks and mud and water untill school closes in June month. Then in the fall when school opens again they have Sept oct nov Dec doing the same thing again and the children get beat out and loose lots of days from school. I taught it would be wise to write you concerning the matter we are living in hopes that we are going to be treated better now than ever we have been before, When you gives my letter consideration would you write me concerning this affair this road will not interfere with any persons primises its outside of all fences to come as far as my frontage

Thrusting your reply in the near future and

Thanking you.

I remains sincerely

April 29 1949

Mr
J.R. Smallwood
Premore

Dear Sir
As I am a criple I am writing you to know what you can do to help me, I will explain to you my condition, two years ago I broke the spine of my back and had to take an upration on the same I had two feet of a cut, in my back and lege, I had a bone taken out of my lege and put in my back and sewed in with silver wire, I was in hospitable for eight months on my back in the grace hospitable in St Johns and now I am home a criple, I want to know what you can do for me as I am a married man.

Dear Mr. [name redacted]:

Thank you very much for your letter. Unfortunately at the present time there is really no actual position for cripples who cannot work for themselves, and just now my Government has no power to do anything in this matter as it is not an elected Government, but after we are an elected Government, which will be after May 27th, it is my intention to see that something is done for such cases.

With very best wishes.

Sincerely yours,

J.R. SMALLWOOD
PREMIER

April 30th/49

Hon. J. R. Smallwood
St. John's.

Dear Sir:

I wish to express my sincere thanks for the invetation to attend the liberal convention, but sorry I could not attend because of a severe cold, also sorry we have no delegate there, because the man that is gone, stood on the wrong side last year, he talked against Confederation, so he is in the wrong place.

Now sir the people around here on the Straight shore, want something they have been trying to get for the past twenty years, and that is a connection with the Railway, so as we can travel. Steamers or passenger boats are not much good to us, because the harbour is too rough to land in stormy weather, so we want a road or railway, which I would suggest should connect with the railway at Gander airport, which is only forty miles away. Now sir if you want your election to be a success in these parts, give us the road, and further sir, I hope the people who fought for Confederation, will be recognised before those who tried to down it, we have some of them here, I have fought with all my powers to put down responsible government, and Sir there is a position here I would like to fill, and that is the office of releiving officer, the man who fills it now fought tooth and nail against Confederation, and I think sir it's time to change it, it's no use fighting for a thing, if you don't gain anything by it. I am proud to be one of the crowd who fought for confederation with you, and won the victory over the crowd who tried to keep us down as we have been for the past eighty years, Sir here we havent advanced in our roads system from what we had in our grandfathers time, and sir I think it's time we had something done, now take away our steamers, and give us a road, I would like to be able to talk these matters over with you in person.

You are getting great praise for what you have done sinse you have been in office, we are proud to know you are controlling prices, and its time, that means votes, and more votes, give us the road and you get the majority here. Sir I am with you now for the Liberal party.

Wishing you success in the future as in the past. Now sir I hope the confederates dont be forgot, there are some of us here that carry a big influence.

Wishing you every success
Yours very truly,

Mar 12 19/50

To Premier JR Smallwood

Dear Sir

I am writing you conserning unemployment as I am a labourer and am out of work I am drawing unemployment assistance and that will soon be out it is rumoured around hear that there will be lots of work down on the labradour this Summer if that is So I would like to get a job down there can you tell me where to apply to get a job I would be much oblidge if you can expecting to hear from you soon

---

March 23rd, 1950.

Dear Mr. [name redacted]:

Thank you very much for you letter. If you write the Labrador Mining & Development Co., Ltd. Montreal in connection with work on the Labrador they will give you any information you require.

Sincerely yours,

J.R. SMALLWOOD
PREMIER

4-2-50

To

Premier Smallwood

St John's

Dear Sir:-

Am a fisherman and am looking forward to the coming season when I shall be able to resume my work again.

I am a cripple now for 6 yrs and fishing is the only thing that I can do to earn a livihood for my family.

I am suffering from a varicose ulcer leg. I have a certificate from a doctor which states I am unable to work.

Of course I am working on relief work.

Now my problem that I am writing about is that I havent an engeine for next summer if I am spared to want one. The one I used last year is given out so I was wondering if you can in some way help me to secure an engiene for the coming year.

The size of engiene is 6 ½ HP Acadia.

Am looking forward of hearing from you soon.

I am yours

Faithfully

May 10 19-50

Mr. J.R. Smallwood
Premair

Dear Sir I am writing you on behalf of my unemployment assistance for the pass Winter I was imployed with the A.N.D Co, I spent 77 Day at work was layed off when the wood was finished and on arriving home I applied for my assistance for which I thought I was entitled after paying the fee asked, But I receaved a letter & this week telling me I didn't work enough now who can I work when I was layed off now Mr Smallwood I am in need of this money I don't expect the six months fee But I do want what I have payed for and worked for it is not my fault I dident work the 295 day I couldint get the work to and I understand men who have done less work than have already got their assistane so hoping to get some money soon

I remain sincearly

May 22nd, 1950.

Dear Mr. [name redacted],

Thank you for your letter. The Unemployment Insurance Department have certain rules and regulations to follow and which they cannot change for anybody. A person must work a certain number of days before he can qualify for Unemployment Insurance or assistance. Apparently you did not work long enough and under those circumstances I am afraid you are not eligible for it.

Yours sincerely,

J.R. SMALLWOOD
PREMIER

June 4 1950

Dear Sir

My object in writing you is to find out in what attitude the government is taking in making Loans to fishermen to help them. I am interested to know if they would be Loaning money to men for boat and Engines as I am very anxious to get a boat and Engine for the fishry I would have been fishing this Summer on my own if I could have got Some finianicil assistance to get a boat and Engine. There are two brothers of us both experince in the fishing industry for the Summer we have decided to fish with Some one else But if we could get a boat and Engine by fall I guess we would start on our own another reason for having Some would be that I have boys that in a few years may be some help to me trusting you will give a consideration and reply in the near future I am farternally yours

---

June 13th, 1950

Dear Mr. [name redacted]:-

Thank you for your letter and I note all you say. At the present time there is no fund in the Government from which amounts can be paid for the purpose you ask for. We have passed an Act in the House called the Fisherman's Assistance Loan Act, but the Board has not yet set up, and will not be for a while yet. Just as soon as it is you will hear all about it.

With kind regards,
Sincerely yours,

J.R. SMALLWOOD

FORTUNE BAY & HERMITAGE

Yours truly, yours very truly

Andreae Callanan

SO, WHEN I TELL HER *I don't know what this place will*
look like in the end, what I mean is *you*
and I and everything could vanish in an instant. Please
don't misunderstand: I don't wish to give
the impression that I'm always this
catastrophic of mind. It's just that it's happened before. *Your*
great-grandmother was born in a tsunami, I tell her, careful
in my recollection of details. For your consideration:
my daughter and I walk under blue and
cloudless skies along an overpass. Let
the record show: she obliges me
by listening. Or: she appears to listen. *You know—*
no, wait, hang on—I can't remember if
I already told you this part. The wedding band I
wear is a hundred and fifty years old. I am
not sure my grandmother was justified
in handing off something so precious, in
handing to me our family's history, in making
me the clumsy keeper of this
keepsake from a home long washed away. I request

a recount. I am not cut out for this. When I try
to see myself in this story, my focus scatters. For
once in my life, can I just pay attention? God
is in the detail. God is the detail. For argument's sake,
let's say there's this wedding band, which was given to
me. It's all that survived, more or less. I send
my aunt photos of the ring when she asks me
to. She wants to save the family's history to hand along.
I am embarrassed by my fat fingers and my
deep-etched palms. My grandmother dodged widow-
hood by divorcing twice. Check
mate. I had wanted my daughter to know her as
well as I had. I got distracted. The details are gods. I
am embarrassed by the inelegance of my hand. I need
to remind myself that my hand writes me into the story, that it
too is my family's history, for what it's worth. So
when I tell my daughter *this place is bad*
but it could always be worse, what I
mean is *none of us knows what another is thinking.* Am
I cut out for this? If a gold ring had once been yours,
would you want the likes of me to have it? Truly?

My daughter listens—appears to listen—as I
try to make her see herself in this story. She ought to know
where we've come from. I ought to know. *You*
and I ... well ... that which we are, we are.
That's Tennyson. Closer to home? *I am the*
king of my own little island. What man
wouldn't lust for the power to
make such a claim? I write
a book of poems and dedicate it to
my grandmother. I write about
my place in our story, and about the things
that have distracted me from all I'd meant to do.
So, when I tell my daughter *you are your*

mother's daughter, what I mean is *you are the best*
thing that could have happened to me. I mean to
say *you are the reason I came back here.* I mean, *oblige*
me while I tell you one more story. Oblige me.

Notes on "Yours truly, yours very truly"

My early attempts to "write back" to these letters, and even to "write about" them, fell flat. What could I possibly say that the letter writers hadn't already expressed perfectly? So, I decided to take a new approach: I would write *into* them. I was inspired by a poetic form called the "golden shovel," which was developed by the American poet Terrance Hayes to honour the late Gwendolyn Brooks. A golden shovel poem borrows a line or lines from a source text and arranges the words from those lines, in order, as end-words for a new poem. The lines of the new poem merge with the source text along the poem's jagged right margin (the part of the poem I always refer to as the "coastline"). Given the subject matter, the form seemed exceptionally fitting.

Rather than use an existing poem as my source text, I chose lines from three letters written by women to J.R. Smallwood. I have taken liberties with the punctuation, but the words are exactly as they appear in the letters.

The line "that which we are, we are" comes from the poem "Ulysses," by Alfred, Lord Tennyson; "I am the king of my own little island," from Smallwood.[1]

1 Qtd. in Gwyn, *Smallwood*, 238.

June 22/th/1948

Dear Mr Smallwood.

hear a note say I am for Confederation I am vote for it once and I am marking my X for it again you See. letter forward to you By My Husband where he was here for 2 days leave From Canada asking you about voteing he will Be on Grand Banks high Seas then so he Send on to you pass his hand writing over for Canada Do your Best we had go [community] for polling Day we were made fun of they called us Confederation woman told us mark our X for respontable government one women Said God Dame the respontable government and peter Cashin too The Said [our community] people voteing for family allowance. But I said look here. I has no children I am not voteing for family allowance. And I said can you sware who we are voting for. I was mad my blood and all others like wise Please put this in your paper. They had at [that community] Mr Grosbie[2] *up their windows But at [our community] polling days flags were flying for Mr. Smallwood People here not voteing anymore unless the can get it here this only Small place all men was able work is at Canada. the onely men leave here what is to young to work or to old and every one at Canada. I am calling St. John's Summer. if I knew your address I called see your family. I hope we get Confederation with Big Victory I read your papers every mail I get them*

Your truly

if you printed for us about what happen at [that community] Don't Sign our name

2 Likely Chesley Arthur Crosbie (Ches), a prominent anti-confederate.

Jan 2nd 19/49

Mr. J. R Smallwood

Dear Sir;

I am a widow with five children and I haven't any support except twenty dollars I get from the government and this small amount is not sufficient to support a large family I have a very poor home and have no means to keep it up. as I am a member of confederation I thought I should write you. I would like to get your advise to know if there is any widows allotment. I feel sure mr Smallwood you will give me a satisfactory answer. My husband was lost on the S. S. Caribou 19.42 almost 7 years ago[3] *and I have had to work hard to try and Raise my Family with the few dollars I get from the Govt. you know mr Smallwood what our old Responsible Govt is like and what it has done for the people of this country. will you be kind enough to let me know if the widows are entitled to any more under confederation.*

I am yours very
Truly

3 The passenger ferry SS *Caribou* ran between Port aux Basques, Newfoundland, and Sydney, Nova Scotia. In October 1942, after leaving Sydney, it was torpedoed by a German U-boat and sank. Of the 237 passengers, 136 died, among them 45 civilians. See Paul Collins, "Sinking of the *Caribou*," Heritage Newfoundland & Labrador, 2006, https://www.heritage.nf.ca/articles/politics/caribou-sinking.php, and Jennifer Morgan, *Almost Home: The Sinking of the S.S.* Caribou (St. John's: Breakwater, 2012).

Feb 2/1949

To Hon. J. R. Smallwood

Dear Sir I would be very glad indeed when you get things fixed up for Old age Pention will you kindly grant me Old age Pention as I been receiving widows allowance fifteen Dollars for three months Ever since my Husband Died my age will be 71 seventy one the 24th day of this month Feb and I taught it would be all Right to drop you a few lines I have my Birth certificate from the Church I am the Women wrote to you this past summer and you put it in your papers I am still doing my best for that Family of Boys and their Father as he is my son he is Feeling much better at present I did not get any answer of that Letter all my Families gave you their votes as I have five Daughters Married here and have three sons so I hope it will do good for them Please Oblige me by granting my Old age Pention when my Husband died he Leaved me pennyless I have had a hard struggle to get through that's over 6 years ago and those children is to much for me to look after in the condition they are in
I Remain yours Truly

I will be very glad when the time come for the Poor Children to get something to buy clothing as they are so Bad in need

April 6, 49

Dear Joe:
I am very greatful that you succeeded in bringing Newfoundland under confederation, to think that the poor succeeded in their vote, which is something to benefit them and to think that we overcome the merchants of the country which as been bringing us down to the depths of poverty.

I am a man of seventy six I have been seafaring since I was thirteen years old; that makes it sixty three years of sea experience. Out of them sixty three years I have been shipwreck five times.

Last year I was brought home sick, with high blood pressure and heart trouble and the doctor told me that my day was done regards to seafaring as any work. So if confederation had not won the day I would of had to resort to dole because no one could live on the old age pension that the Commission Government was paying.

Well I hope that every thing will go successful with you in making this country much better to live in.

I wish you much success in the future that lies ahead, and may God guard you.
I remain yours,

April 26, 1949

To Mr. Joseph R. Smallwood
St. John's

Dear Sir.

I am now taking pleasure to drop you a few lines. I no you will be surprised to get a letter from me. as I have only seen you once and that was when you were in [our community] on a visit. I congratulate you very much for winning confederation. as I were a confederate myself. So the reason I am writing to you now is because I am writing for a friend of mine. She has been left a widow now for 3 years and has now only herself as her husband was drowned 3 years ago and she never rec ~~any thing~~ cent money from the government yet as she had no one to write for her and has no one to support her there is only just she herself and has no children and no one to ~~look after~~ earn anything for her so I think it is right for the government to help her as she is intitled to it as she is a widow the same as other widows and they get it why not she get some help from the government as she as no one to earn anything for her atall as you said in your little speech you had in [our community] that the widows had to be looked after and anything the people wanted just drop you a letter and you would do all you could to help them so will you please & help this widow as I know you are the man to write to about things and I am sure you will do your best for her as I know it take quiet a bit of time to get things all straiten up so will you kindly answer this letter and let me no what you can do.

do your best to oblige me
yours truly

this widow I am trying for her

her name is

[name redacted]

May 19
1949

Dear Mr. Small wood,
I am asking you for to look out to me and gave me a job of work when the high road open up I gave my vote to you and I am going to vote for you again I know you will do your very best healp me out plase let me know as soon as you can. I am looking forward to the coming day to vote for you so good by and good luck to you trusting to hear from you. I haven't got any means to live I haven't got no fishing gare or that is not much good there is no fish around hear to get so I am trusting to you.

I remens yours,

June 13, 1949

Honourable J R Smallwood
Premier
Newfoundland

Dear Sir,
I am a little girl age 12 years, Mr. John R Courage[4] was here awhile ago, and he could only give one of your pictures So after he went away my little Sister age 7 years Saw it So She have been telling us to write to you to get your picture Would you please send me one for her, I am going to School and I enjoy it very much

The people of this little settlement Listens in to your addresses over the Radio. All congratulate you for Such wonderful Victorys. and are all praying you will get a larger victory on the 27 of June.

Mom and Dad Say them People that didnt support you did never know no hard times as they have had known. or else they certainly wouldnt of voted against you.

Have you any little boys and girls if so I know they must certainly be proud of you to hear what good you are doing for so many little boys and girls. I have receved the family allowance and of which I appreciated very much. as I am one of the little girls like many more have never had much of good clothes or good things to enjoy of coarse I have to thank you for the mony

And I would certainly appreciate your picture Mr. D Pinsent came to see us but he never got a very good reception.[5]
These are the words my mom gave him.

We chose Mr. Smallwood once and we will make no mistake if we choose him again.

and as I said before we are all praying that you will win all times.
by closing I wish you good health,
and may god bless you
yours truly,

---

4 John R. Courage, a Liberal, represented Fortune Bay & Hermitage in the House of Assembly from 1949 to 1962.

5 C.D. Pinsent, the Progressive Conservative candidate for Fortune Bay & Hermitage in the first provincial election of 1949, lost to the Liberal candidate, John R. Courage, by a large margin.

July 19th, 1949

The Honourable Joseph R. Smallwood,
Colonial Building,
City,

Dear Mr. Smallwood,

I have visited several city lawyers and asked them about obtaining a divorce.[6] *They all advise me that I have more than sufficient and that if I apply to the House of Commons at Ottawa I will obtain a divorce within a matter of monthes. They all add one further thing and that is it that it would cost me between $1000 and $1500. And further that I would have to travel to Ottawa to give evidence.*

Now Mr. Smallwood that does not seem fair as I cannot afford the money as I haven't got it and never expect to have it. I am just a plain ordinary person and why should I be kept from getting a divorce because I'm poor when some wealthy merchant can get one by just writing out his check.

I do not expect and would not ask that you make a law making it easy for anybody to get a divorce but I do ask that you make a law here that would allow me to get a divorce here on the same grounds as in Canada. As the law stands now it stands for the rich only and I do not think that it is right and I do not think that you think it is right, and I and thousands of other ordinary people are looking to you to straighten this out.

Very Truly Yours,

6 The accessibility of divorce upon Confederation with Canada was one of staunch anti-confederate Archbishop E.P. Roche's main concerns. For more on divorce in mid-twentieth-century Newfoundland and Labrador, see Sara Flaherty, "'Out of Date in a Good Many Respects': Newfoundland's Fight for Judicial Separation and Divorce in the 1940s," in Cullum, McGrath, and Porter, *Weather's Edge*, 222–33.

August 19/49
To Prime Minister Hon. J. R. Smallwood
St. John's

Dear Sir,

I know you are a busy Man, so won't take much of your time. I mainly wish to ask you a question. Is it possible for you to stop the manufacture of the A.C.M.E. products, made under the disguise of flavouring? It is pure alcohol and meant for drinking purposes only. Quite a lot of men from here are heavy drinkers of the same; not to mention the young men from twelve years up are drinking A.C.M.E. and ruining their lives, and making their parents lives miserable.

The people of [my community] are complaining and thing something should be done. Kindly oblige by doing your best,
Thank you,
Yours Truly

Oct 2th/49

Hon. J. R. Smallwood:
St. John's
Dear Sir,

As I was listening to your speech the other night I thought it was my duty to write you , I know I should look to Mr. L. Vardy, but seeing I have an important to discuss with you, I thought this letter would do for both.

Well Sir: The first thing I have to put before you is this, I am the teacher of this place and I am more or less as a leader here, and to my knowledge this place have been somewhat neglected in the past, and they have no one to intercede for them, into this matter, of which is very important.

The matter is this, for good many year the people of this community have to walk to [another community] a place about three miles from here to post all their mail even to a letter, everything in postal business they have to go to [that community] or [another community] which is a very difficult problem, for the people as this is a very isolated place and especially in winter, now sir: I would like for you to take this matter in the deepest consideration and see if you cant do something about it. They have a phone here which is of very little value, could it be possible of having a little place for the purpose of serving the people better, there are many men who would only be glad of having the purpose to bring the mail I'm sure the people would deeply appreciate your kindness if anything could be done about it.

As I was listening to you the other night, I think myself it was a wonderful thing, as there are around forty or forty five men here unemployed and theirs lots of work here to be done especially around the school and Church property, and above all the bridges of this community which one and all, old and young have to cross and if the matter is not looked into the majority of children will not be able to attend school on that purpose.

The fence around the Cemetry and Church need repairs badly and many other things. So sir, please let me know as quick as possible what can be done, I feel sure the men of this community are willing to do their part as well as I myself.

So sir please advise me by letter or wire your decision of the matter. Trusting you will oblige me in every respect.

Thank you,
yours faithfully
[Teacher]

Premier J. Smallwood
St. John's
Nfld

Dear Sir :-

My husband been sick for three years and we are living on $5 month each so that's not much. In fact we are nearly starved to death. As we have lost all our children and we got no support whatever. So I'm writing you to ask you could you help us in some way or other if you can't give us the old age pension my Husband will be 70 yrs old the 24 of December and I'm 63 in September coming We would be very glad if you could give us the old age pension as we are badly in need of it. I feel sure you will do your best & thanking you very much & hoping you every success & me & my husband wishes we could give 50 votes instead of one.

I remain
Yours faithfully,

GRAND FALLS

sugar, milk, butter[1]

Sonja Boon

YOU DIDN'T EVEN NOTICE. not at first.
but she gave you her handkerchief and then—
wet cheeks, a dribble, a stream
and your shoulders. aching.

shaking.

sugar.
milk.
butter.

simple things really. you could taste them, almost.

maybe?

1 In an April 1949 letter to Smallwood, a correspondent wrote of seeing a woman cry at a store as she paid for three simple ingredients—sugar, milk, and butter—with her Family Allowance cheque. This poem uses that encounter, in conjunction with a broader understanding of women's lives in mid-twentieth-century Newfoundland and Labrador, as revealed both in letters to Smallwood from across the province and in secondary literature, to consider possible reasons why this woman might have been crying.

maybe your husband was ill.
maybe he was away.
maybe he was gone.
maybe he was just
bad.

and maybe none of that mattered at all.

sugar.
milk.
butter.

feel their weight in your bag
in the bowl. in the oven. on the table—

sugar.
milk.
butter.

on your children's bones.

(they cried, you know. every night.
until they stopped, and the silence was worse.)

last Friday, you stood there and cried.

April 18th/1949

Hon J.R. Smallwood
Prime Minister
St John's

Dear Mr Smallwood

I have availed of this opportunity to inquire of you what are the plans, or line up for the forth coming Liberal Campaign.

Nobody seems to know anything here so far yet; and seeing that [my community], and the adjacent Settlements, namely [community] and [community] voted two to one in the late Referendum of July last year in favor of Confederation; our people deem it wise; that [our community] should have some say in the forth Coming political Campaign; and the Selecting of Candidate or Candidates for Grand Falls District for the Liberal Party.

I was in Conversation with … The Chairman of the Committee there; by phone a couple days ago; and he deemed it wise that I should write you; in fact he stressed the necessity of so doing.

There is a Rumor to the effect that [name redacted] was aspiring to be a Candidate for your Party in the forth Coming election for this District. "Confidentially Sir" should he be selected or accepted it would have an unpleasant effect for your party in this era; seeing how he opposed you and your cause during the Referendum.

I am willing to render you any assistance possible and would be quite willing to call a public meeting an arrange a good Strong working Committee, or any other assistance necessary; Therefore I would very greatly appreciate hearing from you; suggesting anything you deem necessary.

I may say that at any time in the Day or Night you can always get me by phone; either at the Employment /office of the A.N.D. Co … where I work; or at my Home, if you want to phone me for anything.

Wishing you every Success in your forth Coming Campaign; and trust you are keeping well

Yours sincerely

29 APR 1949

To
The Right Honourable J. Smallwood
St. John's

Dear Sir

Although this letter will only be one ore of the hundreds you must have already received from grateful Mothers all over Newfoundland, I feel I must say a personal 'Thank you" for fighting for Confederation, and all that it means, I don't think you can visualize what Family Allowance mean to some women, even though you have reached the top via the hard way – last Friday I was in a store, when a woman by my side bought some sugar, milk, butter etc. she offered her Family Allowance cheque as payment an on receiving the change, she just stood there and cried, how she must bless you. Fortunately I am one of the luckier ones, my husband works all year, but I felt I just had to let you know, how grateful we all are, to you.

I hope your Liberal Convention is a success, though I'm sure it will be, at least I know of one person who will enjoy it's proceedings – my husband he was just as excited as a kid with a new toy, when he found out he would be going.

Once again Sir, heartfelt thank – you, from one of the many Mothers in Canada's 10th Province, my I take this opportunity of wishing you every possible success in the future, you certainly deserve it. God Bless you.

Yours Faithfully,

May 6th 1949

Hon. J.R. Smallwood
St. John's

Dear Sir: -

First I must say Congratulations on your high promotion, which you rightly deserved after a long hard fight which you passed a joke to me one day, saying "you were like the Topsail blue berries couldn't be Jamed" which I'm coming to realize its something to it.

Now I hope you & your party comes out a Glorious Victory again this time. there is 6 in my house which you had the full benifit last time and will again this time.

Now when the last elections went off I was at that time on leave at my home in [community], and served as a traveling agent for you. received my ticket from [name redacted]. And which I received no money for same. they all got their money except myself. I went to [name redacted] and he advise me to write you, which I neglected in doing so untill now.

I've shifted my family on [this community] since. I also have a young man. … which he havn't received a days work since I came in with the family. Now Sir I wonder if you possibly do something in regards ot getting him a work of some nature.

he was studying Grade IX when he leaved school

I trust there is something you could do for him as you know what [my community] is like it takes all one's time to make ends meet.

Here's hoping I will hear from you in the near future.

Thanking you in anticipation
Your obedient servant

To Mr Joe Smallwood

With pleasure i rite you a letter concerning my condition wich i am placed in i am a man which cannot git a job for this last 40 years i have been working with they AND Co and now cant git a job 36 years ago I lost my left hand in a saw mill. i have been working with one hand since then now got turned down this spring and my right hand his gitting very Bad so what am I goining to with my family i have a wife and one child. And got no job. i Raised up a family of 5 all gone son them selfs excepted one girl and she his goining to school. I know what it his to find in hard to Bring them up with one hand i have Been usining they Buck saw and cutting with axe when no Buck saw was in use with one hand to use it with i have been fishining and could manage to git a livening off some how.

But now things his looking very dull with no help if you want to know what sort of man i and git in touch with they AND. Co and you will find it there so please will you kindely so some thing as soon as possible and answer this letter.

Your truly[2]

2 This letter and the next are both from the same correspondent and address the same concerns. However, as they differ in tone and style, it is likely that this man asked someone to write the second letter for him.

May11th/49

Hon J R Smallwood
St Johns

Dear Sir

I am writing you to know what can be done in regards the condition I am in. I have been working for Bowaters[3] *and the A.N.D. Co for a number of years in the lumber woods. I went to look for work and the companies have decided not to hire me any more and have considered me disabled. I have only one hand as I was unfortunate enough to lose my hand some fifteen years ago. I have a wife and one child to Support and I can tell you, Sir, I am in very poor circumstances. So I am writing you to know what you or your government can do for me in regard help of some kind.*

Hoping to hear from you soon,
I am yours faithfully,

3 Bowater's Newfoundland Pulp and Paper Mill Co., owned by Bowater-Lloyd (based in England), purchased a large paper mill in Corner Brook in 1938.

June 13/49

Dear Sir,

Just a word in explanation to a matter of which I would like your advice.

I served about three and a half years in the Nfld Forestry oversea, was discharged before the end of hostilities owing to suffering with rheumatic fever, I was laid up six months after arriving home after which I was employed with the Dept of public works for about three months. Since that time I have worked with the A.N.D. Co. about four months out of twelve the rest of the time I have not done much of anything I still am suffering from the rhuematic fever at times more than others.

Sir I am wondering if I comes under the War veterans compensation act and I would like to know if these benefits are meant for such as my case. Will you please let me know as soon as possible.

At present I am idle through an accident I received a short time ago but am receiving treatment for same.

Trusting to hear from you as soon as possible concerning this matter.

I remain
Cordially yours

Monday Aug 8th 1949
The Hon. J.R. Smallwood

Dear Sir

I am a man who served with the "Nfld forestry Unit" in Scotland for five 7 one half yrs. After being over there two years I tried to enlist into one of the Armed forces but wouldn't be admitted being told that the work being done by the foresters was too essential. I then joined the Home Guard, 7 gave all my spare tie into training to defend Britian if need be unlike the soldiers we weren't paid for our training.

It is my opinion that I have done my share for my King & Country during war yrs. So feel justified in demanding an explanation why we foresters do not qualify for the veterans benefit now being given to the Armed forces, as we were led to believe through booklets distributed to us before coming home that there was great advantages to be given us.

It took what small capital I possessed to establish me with a small house with one bedroom which my wife two children and I have been living in since returning home three & one half yrs ago. I haven't been in the position to better myself any as Ive had to take whatever odd job came along half the time being dole which I am now. I have even been compelled to take the dole.

Now I have to sit back and see some men who were in the armed forces a few yrs, but never left the country get all the privileges offered.

There is something wrong somewhere, it would seem the more you do the least you are appreciated.

I would like for you to give this matter its due consideration, as I feel we are not getting our rights.

Yours Very Truly

September 24th, 1949

Dear Mr. [name redacted]:

Thank you for your letter. I quite agree that you did your share in the War as did those who served with the Army, Navy or Air Force, but as I understand, The Forestry Corps in World War II was a civilian organization; its members were engaged on a civilian contract, (as is the case nowadays with civilian employees engaged by the U.S Forces to go to Greenland); they were paid at civilian rates and were entitled to resign and be repatriated to Newfoundland whilst the war was still in progress. Many members of the Forestry Unit availed themselves of the opportunity given them, on the expiry of this civilian contract, of enlisting in the combatant Forces of the United Kingdom. Those who did so naturally are treated as veterans of the Armed Forces because of this combatant status. Those who did not are, as civilians, not entitled to Veterans' benefits under the Veterans' Act.

I have contacted the Department of Veteran's Affairs, and they have given me this information.

Yours sincerely,

J.R. SMALLWOOD
PREMIER.

Aug 8th/49

To The Honorable.
J R Smallwood.
St. John's.

Dear Sir:

I am now working with [name redacted] doing carpenter work. & boarding with a friend for the time being & they say they are not allowed to take boarders; should I have to leave my boarding house: I will have to leave the gander.

So I am writing to you to know if you could place me in a Job with the Goverment carpenters with [another name redacted] or if you could place me in a job any where on the Gander. I should be very much obliged as I am a man who need a job.

I was working at Corner Brook last year on the Sanitorium, was layed of September 10th 1948. out of a job ever since; came hear July 28.

went to work August 1st – I would greatly appreciate any thing you would do for me; yours sincerely

PS. My home is at [community]

Mr Joseph R Smallwood
Premier of N.F.L.D.
St. John's, N.F.L.D.
Canada

Aug15/49

Your Hon:

May I have the pleasure of writing you. Will you please give this letter your kindness attention. I am writing Sir in connection with a job. I heard you say Sir if I Speak correctly there would be two jobs for every man in N.F.L.D. after you get in power. [name redacted] wrote you twice and you told him to keep in touch with you. And myself … wrote you once and I was told by your Second man my letter would be given your immediate attention. The both of us is working … at the present time (woods work) and this camp is finishing in a few days.[4] *And you can see Sir we will be out of work then. And we have no way to feed our families this winter. So Sir we are asking you to get a job for us. I … can take any kind of a job Mr Smallwood I have grade ten. It no good to go anywhere to look for a job the answer you get is "No Vacancy" or "Have you a father working here." I … and [name redacted] voted for you three times. And we'd vote again another three if we got the chance. Sir I am or shall I say we are depending on getting a job out of this letter would you please give this matter your considerate attention. Please reply.*

Your Servants

Please understand this is two addresses namely
[two names redacted]

4 For more on forestry in central Newfoundland, see Terry Bishop Stirling's essay, later in this volume.

Oct 8 1949

To Mr. J. Smallwood

Dear Sir

I am writing to you first explaining the way I am situated I am a married man with four children and my wife and self. That leaves six to feed. I first want to tell you how much work I have got since confederation came in force. I was in the wood last Summer. Finish in November. When my work was finish went to the other camp could not get another job, came Home took fifty dollars. Went away again could not get another job any where around in May. I got a moth and half work my camp close and I moved on to another one. Got a moth and half their and was in August so that is about three month work in a year. So the first of September I went to [a community] and signed up to get my unemployment did out the Papers. But never get any unemployment. I cant get in the union at [my community] and I am satisfied to work and feed my family if I could get anything of job But I am down and out nothing to eat and no money my mother and father died when I was twelve years old and I have been working every since so you see I am not afraid of work and I never eat a Bit of dole yet,. But when you cant get a job I cant take one.

trust that you will
do something for me.
Signed

GREEN BAY

Bringing History to Life: The Unique Illustrative Power of Primary Sources

Emily Murphy

IT IS ONE THING to learn about the poverty experienced by the residents of this province in the years leading up to Confederation. It is another thing entirely to hold a tangible, personal piece of that history in your hands. This was my experience as I read through the letters in the Smallwood collection. If my memory serves me correctly, in junior high school our Social Studies course focused on the history of Newfoundland and Labrador from the colonization of Indigenous peoples to the cod moratorium of 1992. We learned about how Newfoundland became a part of Canada through a referendum on Confederation and that widespread, abject poverty was one of the principal reasons why a majority of people voted for Confederation. I understood all of this as a series of rote facts, and as a part of our history, but it all felt very far removed from my eighth-grade classroom. Reading through the letters that people wrote to Smallwood has brought the material reality of pre-Confederation poverty into stark relief for me in a way that reading about poverty in a textbook could not.

In January of 1949, a man wrote the following to Smallwood:

> Dear Sir,
> As I writing to ask you please if you could send me pair Blankets as we are very old now I also Like to get one pair soft shoes or slippers

> size 7 for my wife and flat heels as My Wife Been cripple all the winter. I would be very thankful to you if you could to this Mutch for us.
> I like to here from you soon. Wishing you every success
> I remain yours

I imagined this man and his wife in a house near the ocean, trying to stay warm under blankets so threadbare as to be useless, as the winds off the North Atlantic Ocean howled around them. I imagined the bitter cold and the desperation he must have felt to write a letter to Mr. Smallwood, asking for two blankets and slippers so that he and his disabled wife could be warm during the winter. What had once existed as intellectual facts in my brain suddenly turned into a visceral understanding of what living in poverty in pre-Confederation Newfoundland looked and felt like. This letter brings the material reality of pre-Confederation poverty home in a way that few other sources could. Suddenly, with a letter to hold in my hands, the precarious situation lived by many became deeply personal. The time that has passed between then and now begins to feel smaller, and the space between this family's lived experiences and contemporary experience feels smaller, too. Living in poverty today might not look the same as writing a letter to a politician and asking for two blankets, but it is still prevalent in Newfoundland and Labrador, and while I fully appreciate the desperation that caused this man to request blankets and a pair of slippers, poverty needs a systemic solution.

I confess I have difficulty imagining how writing a letter to our current premier and asking him personally to keep my family warm during the winter would not be a waste of my time. I envy this correspondent's belief that his letter might be answered by Joey Smallwood, not because it was out of the realm of possibility at the time—though it might have been—but because the idea of merely feeling as though someone with power in this province might hear someone on a personal level feels foreign to me. I feel as though I have only ever known a political discourse rife with cynicism and distrust of politicians, so to see an earnest letter like this was shocking.

I would have loved to have had access to letters like this during my Social Studies lessons in junior high. They would have brought pre-Confederation Newfoundland to life and brought me closer to my own heritage as a Newfoundlander, as I feel the experience of reading these letters has done, fifteen years later. My roots in Newfoundland go back many generations on both sides of my family, but I didn't know three of my four grandparents, so I never got to hear stories about their lives. I feel as though these letters have given me a glimpse of what their lives might have looked like at that moment in Newfoundland's history and have thus given me a richer understanding of where I come from. The letters have allowed me to consider not only the differences between the past and the present but also what has remained the same, as well as what might be possible in the future.

Dear Mr .Smallwood,

Now that the greatest issue is at stake, I just wanted to drop you an encouraging word to carry on, always bearing in mind that you had over 63 thousand behind you in the first round and there is not a doubt about it but the number is increasing as more of the rottenness of the tactics used by the opponents of all that is fair and decent in life. Come to light. In this day and generation it is almost unbelievable that the people of our little country should take such an attitude towards affiliating themselves with the great Dominion of Canada At least if we are to believe the 69 thousand for their decision, which according to the reports reaching most everyone they are not to blame

If religion played any part in swinging the 69 thousand votes for Responsible Government it will go down in history as one of the vilest attempts of Religion to play its part in taking from mankind is very soul and making him nothing more than a piece of machinery such as Hitler and Stalin gained control over a great part of the Human race.

If NFLD was being lured into annexation by some unchristian country it would be the duty of all denominations to raise their voice in protest, but a country who is the very fountain head of Christian edeals common to all creeds in NFLD it is beyond me to understand what the motive would be for any church or religious society to use their influence against confederation with Canada, the bulk of the Christian literature that is read, that is cherish, that is honoured, by NFLDERS is printed in Canada, Would you sir go into any home in NFLD and if you saw The United Church Observer in that home would you tell them to take that filthy rag and burn it or The Salvation Army War Cry take that curse of the world and burn it or the Catholic Record and tell them it is not fit for a NFLDER to read then in this matter of voting if we bring forth excuses that Canada is dangerous to all that we hold dear in our Christian way of living, you would be justified in telling them that is now if religion played any part in the first election you would be justified I say, in telling people just that. I have a large family, but if it were announced from Ottawa tomorrow that some of Canadas social benefits are to be abolished I would still vote for Confederation, because the history of our advancement down through the centuries is tragic why even poor little Nova Scotia that our opponents show up so much has had her Universities for centuries, when we thought it a crime to have a railroad Canada even had her highroad from Sydney to Vancouver.

Oh I know we have many things to be proud of such as our endurance our bravery and our part played in the two great world conflicts our sons of NFLD did better than the best God bless them all but I shudder to think what would have happened if we had Responsible Government during the second world war.

I can picture our politicians nagging about this and that disagreeing even with the enemy at our doors and any sensible and rashionable human being in NFLD should know that but for Prime Minister Churchill and the late President Rossvelt arrangement for the joint defence of NFLD in a speedy manner was truly the only way out xxxxxxxxx even then Hitlers submarines came in and blew up ships in the harbour of Bell Island,, that is why I cannot agree with any who condemn the actions of our Commision of Government during those serious days, and even if they had allowed fifty bases on a 99 year lease to be built in NFLD they would have been justified in doing so.
Well Mr. Small I guess I had better quit, but it is something along these lines I would like to have letter printed in the Telegram,[1] but I just seem to be unable to use my wits brawn to put it together, I suppose after twenty five years pounding the old telegraph key this kind of work is out of my reach,

Best of luck anyway

Ps
I cannot remember what literature is printed in Canada for the use of people of the C of E faith.

June 18 ,1948.

Dear Mr. [name redacted]:

Many thanks for your letter which we were very glad to receive. I can see from what you say that you understand clearly how Responsible Government got the 69,000 votes it did. The old evil influence was brought to bear, but this time 'the boot will be on the other foot'. ' The tail will not wag the dog' on the 22nd of July.

1 *The Telegram*, a daily newspaper based in St. John's, was founded in 1879.

Again with many thanks for your letter.

Sincerely yours,

J.R. Smallwood, Campaign Manager,
Newfoundland Confederate Association.

Dec.29th

1948

Mr. J.R. Smallwood

Dear Sir I am wrighting you to see what you can do for me regarding a schooner for local coasting I will say local now as Canada is in with us or we are in with Canada thanks to our good fighters I had a schooner that I has for this past 6 years wrecked this summer I am a schooner master for over 26 years & I am use to most of the Nova Scoatia coast and I can get plenty of work on this coast & this vessel is only 6 or 7 years old & is equipped with 2 engines. new I can make a speed of 9 nots it is the [schooner name] capt [name redacted] at [community].

I was wondering if you could get one of the Canadian Banks to put up the money for her as I got none I think told you last Spring my circumstances at your office I got 3 sons all men [name redacted] I understand is coming in & he I think will tell you about me. I would like for you to do your best for me as I got confidance enough to think you can do a lot but perhaps not in this case as it is not on yor presen business lines.

Please try and do your best for me.

The price of the vessel is sixteen thousand with all her belongings.

I am sir yours truly

January 4, 1949

Dear Capt. [name redacted]

Your letter was handed to me by [name redacted]. I remember you well and I think you will believe me when I say that I would gladly help you in the matter of purchasing a schooner if it lay in my power to do so. I think you yourself have a good idea of whether I can do it, for I notice that you say in your letter that 'you have confidence enough to think that I can do it but perhaps not in this case as it is not in my business.' That is exactly the position. You doubtless know that the financing of a schooner is always done by business men, merchants, or other people of means. I am, as you know, neither of these.

It is always a hard thing to say no, and believe me I would a thousand times rather say yes. I just cannot do it.

I doubt very much that any Bank would put up the money without good security, and if you had almost anyone would put up the money.

I hope you will not take me wrong in this matter. I am simply not in a position to help you in this matter, and I am sorry that I am not.

If you are ever in the city, please be sure to drop in for a chat.

With all good wishes.

Sincerely yours,

J.R. SMALLWOOD

JR Smallwood ESQ,

St.John's *Jany 4/49*

Dear Sir:

The occasion of the signing at Ottawa some little time ago of the beginning of Confederation terms must have been a particularly happy event for you bringing as it did to near completion years of long and ardous work in behalf of our people . Though they are a little belated I offer you my sincere congratulations

It is regrettable that "Antis" in certain localities are still carrying on their lying propaganda and a particulary rotten example of this is the report being circulated that male children who are registered for family allowance will on attaining sixteenth birthday be removed to Canada for military training and that persons who refuse to accept the allowance will be exempt. While it is difficult to believe that people can be found who will believe this trash it is nevertheless a fact that in this vicinity some families are hesitant about registering their children because of this report. Its too bad that people who voted for union should be made the victims of unscrupulous propogandists who will stop at nothing in order to blacken the case for union. I am wondering if a public announcement from some authorative source contradicting such reports can be made.

It is rumoured that the C N R[2] *will take over the postal telegraph system and the dept of transport run the post office dept the two being thus separated. I imagine this would be rather difficult in a country such as ours. Whatever the setup I do hope that operators and postal officials in the isolated parts of the country will receive correspondingly as good treatment as these in the larger centres. This has not been the case in the past.*

You may recall that during the election campaigns I wrote you offering my active support and you were good enough to acknowledge my letter and thank me for same. This prompts me to take the liberty of asking to pass along any information you may be at liberty to divulge as to what form the proposed arrangements for the operation of the telegraph and postal services will take. With best wishes

Yours sincerely

(Pm and Opr)[3]

---

2 Canadian National Railway.

3 Postmaster and telegraph operator.

January 15,1949.

Dear Mr. [name redacted]:

I was glad to hear from you again. I appreciated your other letters to me, and I appreciate the good wishes you sent to me now.

There is no truth whatever in the report that male children receiving Family Allowance will, on reaching 16, be removed to Canada for military training. That is just one of the many lies circulated by the Responsible Government people. Tell the people for me, on my solemn word of honour, that they should fill out the Family Allowance forms to make sure of getting the Family Allowance on April 1. Let nothing stop them. Surely they should know by now that 99 per cent of what the anti-confederates said was downright lies.

With regard to Postal Telegraphs, my understanding is that they will be split, and that Canadian National Telegraphs will take over the telegraphs. You will not lose by this change.

I would be glad if you would keep in touch with me, especially after March 31.

Again, with kindest regards.

Sincerely yours,

J. R. Smallwood

Feb 1st

1949

Mr. J.R Smallwood

Dear Sir I take great Pleasure in your most welcome letter which I received on last mail. I am very glad to hear from you I am most delighted to know that you took time to reply to my letter you told me not to be put out because you could not help me in this matter of getting a schooner I know you cant or you would sir I have got confidance enough in you to think that you would do it if you could any way brother there is I am sure a better time coming for both you and me and God speed that day don't fail to carry on the good fight you will surely reach the target any way I expect I will be coming in St John's in April and if you are not to buisy I will be in to see you & have a chat as you mention on your letter.

I must thank you very much for your most kind invitation.

I am most delighted to know that we are going to have one man at least to represent us in the future or after March that we will be able to talk to and hear our request sometimes I know there is only a small amount one man can do.

Where there is going to be some will expect a lot but our countrys welfare is the most important and if the country is benefited then I as well as the rest will be benefited as well

thanking you again

I am sir your humble servent

March 9, 1949

Mr. J. R . Smallwood,

St Johns

Dear Sir:

First I wish you much congratulations on the victory well won, by yourself and Mr. Bradley, in behalf of Confederation. It seems to me as if your men raised by God, to free us poor Newfoundland slaves from the cruel yoke of Responsible Government. There has only been ten years of prosperity in the history of Newfoundland, four years in Kazer's war and six years in Hitler's war.[4] *apart from them there was years and years of poverty and starvation, my father worked for sixty cents a day in [my community] mine, Slavery. worked in lumbering woods for ten dollars a month, then when a man reached 75 years he could'nt get the old age pension until some other old man would die, that belonged to this place then they would pass the little mite belonging to the dead man over to the living man. Then strange to say that a lot of people was simple enough to vote for that again. I say, away with Responsible Government poverty, forever. The stink of it will rise up in the nostrils of the people for years to come. and sir there will need a man in every shop here at [my community], especially to govern the prices the merchants here,when they open their mouth to tell you the price of an article, they don't know how much to say. However they are charging a double price for everything and something's more.*

Price $17.50 a barrel for flour

50 c lb for beef

$1.20 lb for tea

plain biscuits per lb 40c

onions per lb 15c

sugar per lb 14c

raisins per lb 25c

fruit per tin 80c

apricots and peaches and pears and everything else according to this.

They are gone crazy with dry goods. Now sir here is another complaint. I wish to explain to you, I have a son 26 years old, who never earned five dollars in his life, he is

4 The correspondent references World Wars I and II. For more on war and the economy, see Jenny Higgins, "First World War and the Economy," Newfoundland & Labrador in the First World War, Heritage Newfoundland & Labrador, 2009, https://www.heritage.nf.ca/first-world-war/articles/first-world-war-economy.php and "Economic Impacts of WWII."

always a dead expense to me, he is simple, he dont know how to work, not even to cut up fire wood, for own home, burning. I have applied to the responsible Government twice, they said they could'nt do anything for him. So last summer, 1948, I took him along to [the doctor] for examination, so he gave me a certificate, concerning him addressed to the relieving officer [name redacted] I sent it to him.

He wrote me and told me that he sent it to the Department of Health and Welfare and would advise me when he would hear from them so I haven't heard a word about it since. So Sir do you think it right or should I support a young man at this age with a family besides, I am 53 years old, and have worked hard all my life and have injured a lot of hardship for that reason I worked in punishment now because I'm cripple with sciatic and rheumatic. So Sir I would ask you to please see what could be done for this fellow or for me his name is [name redacted]. I wish you Gods blessing and every success in a long and happy life.

April 12th, 1949

Mr. [name redacted]

Many thanks for your letter and your very encouraging words of good will, which I appreciate deeply, like you, I am keeping a close eye on the cost of prices. I have just appointed a committee of the Government to make a close survey of this question. With regard to your son, as soon as we are elected I will endeavour to provide a new law to give the Government authority to pay a pension to afflicted persons. We have no authority to pay such a pension now and that is why we will have to pass such a law.

With best wishes.

Sincerely yours,
Premier.

April 22,1949

Mr. J Smallwood

Dear Sir

Writing to you concerning the prices here . We voted for confederation at both times but it dont look like its going to bring down the prices here. the merchants here got their prices high then last year. So I taught I would write to you about it and let you know that the merchants is doing just what they like about the prices. Some of the thing we got to buy is gone up this spring. The prices are so high here that we got to send family allowances away to Canada. dry goods here we can't look at it. the prices are so high. not only dry goods but everything is gone past the mark altogether. and the merchants is not doing any thing about it till they are force to they say. and I suppose that means not before the law Canada has gets on them. but I guess they will have to come in person before they will put down their prices. there is no place around the Green Bay as high as the prices here. So I think you are the right man to know what the merchants are doing to the poor man here. if it was not for you we would not be united with Canada yet we are all so proud- that we got so good a man to run Newfoundland. I hope God will bless you in your work. duty is taken off and we get family allowances now. and if the prices goes down Newfoundland and its people will live in peace and plenty. were in if we got Responsibility Government. Newfoundland and its people .in less than a year would have been T.B. and starved to death.

Thanking you a thousand times for what you have already done.

Yours truly

giving you a few of the prices listed below. butter 37 cents lb beans $1.60 . gallon milk 18 tin baking powder 60 cents pound corn beef 50 tin. [illegible] 18 ct tomato soup 20 tin. sugar $14.00 sack cornflakes .20 & 23 pack.

new bologna just came in 50 cents lb.childrens stockings 80 & 90 pr. shoes childrens 5.50 pr 4.50 .common material for small childrens dress 1.95 yard coat material 4.80 yard. women stockings 1.10 pr .yard material coman 68 .70yd . cama & lux soaps 18 cents cake .washing soap .16 cents cake childrens underwear 6.20 boys suit .flour 8.70 sack. rice 22lb apricots 48 lb raisins 24 lb biscuits 32 lb 48 btl castoria 60 tea 1.10 lb onions 10 lb 14 lb and bread .75 cheese 70 lb molasses 1.50 gallon vinegar 22 pts broom 1.75 roats[5] 5 lb. beans 25 tin pk jelley 20 cents

---

5 Rolled oats.

June 1th

/49

To Hon J R Smallwood

Dear Sir

First of all I must congratulate you on the great victory that you and your candidates have won. Well sir I am a woman voter.[6] *Well in the first two elections I was a confederate and fought my way with all that was against us and so we won and thanks to you sir. We cannot praise you to highly for what you have done. and on May 27*[th] *I marked my x for Baxter Morgan and we also won. My husband is a fisherman. we have a family of ten 10 6 six receiving family allowance. 8 children myself and my husband. My husband is gone to [community] to go to the Straits of Belle Island fishing with [name redacted]. But I guess it will be a long time before they will get there as the coast is full of ice. And we have no supplies for the summer. we where getting releaf all winter but as you know it was cut off at the time of the elections. So I want to know if there could be any thing done for us as there will not be any returns from the fish untill November if they get any fish at all. And sir will you please let me know as we are in need. Also my husband's mother is living with us she is 77 years of age and haven't got a old age pension yet of any kind. and she as been in bed for 2 ½ years now. she gets the widows mite of$5.00 I have a son 18 years old he tried for work but could not get any.*

Yours truly

one of your supporters

ps. my husbands mothers name is [name redacted] as I know you will do something for her.

6 Women were granted partial suffrage in Newfoundland in 1925; however, the vote was suspended in 1933, while Newfoundland was governed by the Commission of Government. Many women who participated in the 1948 referenda and the election that followed had never previously voted.

June 10th, 1940

To The Hon J R Smallwood

St John's

My Dear Sir:-

First let me greet you with good wishes & congratulations. You have done a good job for us I have listened with profound interest to your speeches from the first Broadcast of the National Convention until the P election[7] *& I think you have opposed the bitterest attacks in a very magnificent & wonderful way & I think yes I know that you have won the respect, support & admiration of this place as well as many other places in [community]. With the exception of a few tories & we don't mind them.*

You are worthy of administration. The unclothed children alone blessed by your strenuous effort. May God bless you & give you the strength to carry on in the wonderful work that you are now doing. No doubt there has been many prayers gone up to God for you. I Sincerely hope that you will hold office as premier for many years to come.

While writing you honourable sir I would like to mention that there is no shed here on the P warf[8] *for the use of the public & no doubt I have a reason to be interested in this more than a good many.*

I am a widow & have a small grocery store. Two years ago I lost my dear husband & I have been trying as best I can to carry on try & support my family or to help I couldn't possibly exist in this alone my people have helped the children. However theres a privately owned shed on the warf owned by the two merchants here & my husband always used it & payed for it annually but one of them won't allow me to use it any more so my freight has to be exposed to all kinds of weather I have about $200 worth at one time sometimes I maybe less & if I have to loose probably three of four sacks of sugar & feeds & bis etc its better for me to give up & go on the dole. I certainly don't want that to happen.

My oldest son has been in the San[9] *in your city for 18 months he has arrived home just recently. I have two children depending on me yet & I am working very hard to try & educate them as well as support them.*

I see no possible way to carry on with my little business unless I could have protection for my freight. There is no possible way of pulling it from the warf immediately on landing as you already know freights are being landed all weathers & at all time from morning until morning again.

---

7 Provincial election.

8 Public wharf.

9 The Sanatorium, which was built in St. John's in 1917 to treat tuberculosis patients.

I will appreciate it very much Sir if you will have this very important matter looked into. I have written the Dept of P works[10] *on two occasions and they don't seem to have come to any decision about it.*

I know that you have to much already on your hands & mind but I feel sure you will do your best. [Illegible] & [my community] have no shed & our freight is sometimes exposed to sleet, rain & snow.

Respectfully yours

10 Department of Public Works.

To.

Mr.J.R. Smallwood

St.John's

Dear Sir:-

I am writing to you to see if the merchants here in [my community] have to put the price on their goods. I have heard from lots off other places and the goods are all gone down on price. But they are the same around here. here are the prices of a few things as now.

1 lb tin Baking Powder 60 ct tin

large pk Rinso 60ct small pk Rinso 25ct

Sun light Soap 18ct

and there is nothing taken off footwear of any kind. I would like to hear from you as soon as possible to know if they are compelled to do so.

Many thanks to you
for same.
I remain yours truly

HARBOUR GRACE

Reflections While Reading Letters to Joey Smallwood

Amy Sheppard

I CAME TO THIS PROJECT with an affection for Joey. Growing up, my Pop, my father's father, had a reverence for Joey Smallwood. Godlike might be taking it too far; a one-name celebrity in the vein of Madonna, Beyoncé, or Cher may be more accurate. I feel nostalgia for Joey Smallwood based on my Pop's holographic photo of Smallwood. The picture would move when I moved, and Joey was sort of standing out from the background. Placed in the TV cabinet, it held a place of prominence in the living room. As a child, I didn't have a really good idea of why this man was so revered. I heard vague comments about how he helped my Pop get work and how he helped Bell Island (where my father grew up), but nothing specific. I just knew that Joey Smallwood was a "Good Man."

So, I came to read letters from ordinary Newfoundlanders to Mr. Smallwood with that affection in my heart and mind. A number of the letters reflect my family's sense of reverence, but also familiarity and affection, for Joey. Many correspondents asked Joey to help with work, benefits, or money. In November of 1949, one woman asked for a loan so that she could start a candy shop! In May of the same year, another woman asked for an increase in her wages for her position as the mail courier. These correspondents believed that Joey would help them. Other seemed to feel as if they knew him. Their writing suggests a familiarity with the man, recounting times that they had met him personally, and asking for personal loans. I don't know if that belief was particular to their relationship to Joey Smallwood or if that's how things were at that time.

I can't help but compare these letters to Joey Smallwood with modern ways of communication with politicians. Politicians have social media accounts which lend a sense of accessibility, and some politicians—particularly at local levels—respond to their constituents frequently. But while it seems that politicians are available to us via instant means of communication, we also know that there may be a media team in charge of these accounts, particularly for higher-level politicians. But while there is some similarity between the two approaches, the familiarity via current iterations of social media is just not the same as the sincere familiarity in these letters to Smallwood. Evident to me is the way that we are more cynical today in communications with politicians, whereas the letter writers were sincere in their faith that Smallwood would help them and remember them. The correspondents referenced times they had met Joey and they stated they were Liberal. They mentioned their family connections. For example, two women mentioned their husbands and children, thus situating themselves in webs of kinship and community. These remarks signify attempts to connect with Smallwood on a personal level.

Reflecting on these letters to Smallwood, I was also struck by how often the voices of ordinary people get left out of history and, in particular, how the voices of women are often left out because they were rarely involved in public areas of life. However, this collection includes a number of letters from women, all of which demonstrate how they advocated for themselves and their families, and in this way participated actively in political life. For example, one woman (one of the few women to identify herself with her own name and not her husband's name) wrote a long letter to Smallwood about her husband's potential political career without his knowledge. She advocates that the Liberal Party provide more support to her husband in his political campaign. In her letter, she demonstrates a sound understanding of the political issues of the day, including anti-Confederation sentiment and concerns about the prices of goods.

Another woman offered to have her children vote for Smallwood if he would pay for their votes, as she had seen "a lot of money given out in the last election." She stated that she wanted to see Smallwood elected but could only guarantee votes for him if money was provided.

Both of these women engaged in the politics of the day. They used their roles as wives and mothers to influence and question the political process. Seeing these letters from women to a prominent politician challenges discourses that suggest that women in the past did not engage in public or political life. Rather, women used tools at their disposal to advocate for themselves and their families and to participate in the political process.

At first, I wanted to call these letters stories, but now I think that the word *story* misses that there are real people behind the letters. The letters are from real people with ancestors who were impacted by the outcomes of the problems detailed in the letters. I would like to know what happened to these people. Did the candy shop ever open? Did the woman's husband run for office? Newfoundlanders and Labradorians live in the legacy of Joey Smallwood and Confederation, and his story is written in bold. But we also live in the legacy of these ordinary people who tried to make their lives a little better by writing a letter. Reading the letters from ordinary citizens to Joey Smallwood has, for me, added more to the picture of the man who was revered by my father's family. Strangely, letters from other people humanize Joey Smallwood, in my view. They were, after all, just writing a letter to a politician for help with ordinary things that impacted daily life. However, my affection remains with that holographic image in the TV cabinet.

April 4th, 1949

Hon. J.R. Smallwood,
Prime Minister
St John's.

Dear Joey;

Again Congratulations.
A great personal triumph A
great personal responsibility A
great personal opportunity.

Yours very Sincerely

April 16 1949

Hon. J.R. Smallwood.
St John's, Nfld
Dear Sir;

For the first time in my married life I am not sure whether what I am doing for my husband is right or not. But after a phone call from my nephew [name redacted] it was agreed I should write you, restating the substance of a letter I wrote him. I told him in effect that [name redacted] was doubtful about going ahead and letting his name be submitted as a Liberal candidate for the Port de Grave district. He is so minded and I would do a good deal to keep him from withdrawing. So I am stating his objections and you can do as you see fit. Incidentally, this letter is entirely without his knowledge. But then you already knew that. He was anything but eager for a political career and had to be persuaded by [my nephew] and myself.

The first you can readily understand being well used to small farmers and fisherman, in a word those who live close to the margin. He feels he ought to have at least of couple of dollars in hand to scrape out on any campaign where taxis would be in cause and demand and no telling what other expenses. To have such expenses refunded later isn't enough. The spring is the hardest time of the year for farmers. Supplies low, outlay urgent. He would have to get a man to do the work for May month here on the farm. But then, I do not need to explain this to you- you know it once it is mentioned.

The other is the matter of canvassing the district. He feels strongly a house to house canvas here in his own field of [two communities] & to some extent, in [another community] and [another community] is his only bet. He is not a public speaker, but has a warm, winning personality in conversation. Everyone likes him. I noticed how many men spoke to him as were going out to [my community] Sunday and the crowd was coming from mass. But in these places the feeling was strong against Confederation and the problem now is disassociating people's minds linking Confederation & the Liberal Party. It will be hard. But in his quiet way I think he can. However, if there is a general stir-up as a public meeting and some bally-hoo might bring, I believe you will only stir up waters which have begun to settle. Have those farther down the Bay, but not here.

Two things he says will stick in people's minds – tobacco so high for the fisherman and the still high price of flour. There must be some convincing answer to those. Maybe the other party will promise a change in those items, a change they cant fulfill, but will catch on during an election. People say the present party if returned will keep the prices up, or why didn't they drop it before the election?

Now there might be a chance if one of your persuasive party members came over, say next week, Monday and talked to him and made these things clear. If it were someone who knew him before, so much the better.

I hope it can be pulled off, Incidentally, you had a letter from me long long ago, - I sent you some local holly one Xmas.

Yours very truly

April 21st 1949

Sir J.R. Smallwood

Dear Sir

Please excuse me if I annoy you by writing this note to you. I am not writing this myself as I have not got eyesight good enough to write. My daughter is writing this for me. I may say sir We as not education enough to state a letter to a man of your ability but I know you will excuse our letter. I certainly do Sir congratulate you and wish you ever success. I was the second last one to vote in this district which is called Hr Grace east. I certainly did mark my x for confederation my husband also.

Well Sir, I am going to ask you can you do me a favour and that is can your help me in any kind of way to get glasses. I have tried the NFLD Government several times but would not help me. Seven years ago Sir I drove a stick in my eye and had to go to the hospital. I really thought then I would get glasses but to no avail. Since then Sir trying to see out of one eye with no glasses my other eye is looking sight terrible. I as three small children and your may imagine how hard and I do find it trying to do for them with so bad eye sight. My husband is a cripple in his leg and as a terrible bad arm. All the help we get is from the government was thirty dollars per month. No other help whatever. So you see Sir what we are like. I myself Sir as not been out to a store or church this past four years for the want of a coat and clothing. You may believe me Sir but its as true as God in his heaven. Some day you may come to [my community] and can call to see for yourself.

I remain wishing I as not offend you in any way. Yours Sincerely

Please take this as a private letter

May 2/1949

Premier J. R. Smallwood

Dear Sir.

I have heard you speak over the radio many times and the things you have told us have come true. I am glad that you won and that you are premier over NFLD and I hope you will be elected again. I am a liberal and I know what Canada is like as I lived there for many years. The reason I am writing you as we are near election again. I have 5 in my own home and they say they are not going to vote unless they get paid for it. There was a lot of money given out in the last election. I am only a poor woman and cant afford to pay my boys for nothing and I no of to more wont vote unless they get paid. I am writing this and my own family don't know. I had the privilege to greet you in [my community] and I am the woman who told you I wish I could of cast a thousand votes for you. I would win my own family if I had the money. My wish is that you will go in flying when the final election comes ad that God will guard you to do what is right. It looks as if the poor is live. If you have any money to spare please do your best and I will try to win 7 for you.

I remain
Yours truly

A true Liberal

4th May

Prime Minster
J Smallwood
Government Bld
St John's

Dear Sir.

I wish to draw your attention to the prices of food, clothing and other dry goods sold in [my community] is dearer than in [another community].

Since we have joined Canada everyone thought, the prices would come down, but they haven't so far, at least, not in [my community].

We the people would like to know why.

Yours truly
A resident of
[my community]

May 30th /49

Hr. J.R. Smallwood
Prime Minister Newfoundland
St. John's

Dear Sir.

As I am a supportive for your Liberal Government and for you as Prime Minster of Newfoundland, I wonder if you would kindly give me an increase in my wages.

At the present moment I am mail courier from [community] to [community]. I have to use my own house as a post office and have to distribute the mail all for the paultry sum of ten dollars a month at which rate I am not intended to continue the service any longer than the 30th of June 1949.

Yours very truly

November 8th /49.

Hon.

J.R. Smallwood

Premier

St. John's

Dear Sir

Please Sir, grant me one special request. Help me out in some little way either financially or if you can see your way clear, I have a room in my house fixed up as sort of a Candy Shop so as to bring in a few cents as I have no means. My husband is in bed all the time suffering from a disease he developed at [community] "silieaocis."[1] *I would be very grateful if I could get a some little assistance so as I could get sine confectionary such as bars and all sorts of candy, gum etc. and put it in the window for display. I would like to get this little room ready by Xmas. Mr Smallwood, if I get a loan no doubt I would pay you back. You want capital to start and that I have no such. I would be very grateful for any donation to help me out with my little shop.*

I remain

---

1 Miners had been concerned about the health effects of inhaling dust since the mid-1930s. For more on silicosis and mining in Newfoundland and Labrador, see Rick Rennie, "Mining," Heritage Newfoundland & Labrador, 1998, https://www.heritage.nf.ca/articles/economy/mining.php and "Industrial Disease and the St. Lawrence Mines," Heritage Newfoundland & Labrador, 1998/2019, https://www.heritage.nf.ca/articles/economy/industrial-disease.php.

JAN 1. 1950
HON J RO SMALLWOOD, PREMIER
ST JOHNS NF.

YOUR RADIO ANALYSIS OF THE NEWFOUNDLAND ECONOMIC PLIGHT YOUR METHODS OF APPROACH AND CONDUCT OF ITS RE-HABILITATION ARE AFTER MY OWN HEART STOP I HEARTILY CONGRATULATE YOU AND YOUR CABINET.

Jan 26 1950

Mr Smallwood. Honorable Sir

This is indeed a wonderful pleasure for me to pen you these few lines. Since my last acquaintance with you in any way since you have been returned to power and become Premier of newfoundland as it appears to me you are going ahead by leaps and bounds surely no one can say they can stop you getting where you want to get after all you have done for the country in such short space of time that you have had and having done so much furthermore after hearing your toast to newfoundland at burns night dinner now mr Smallwood you and me know each other intimately in these four Elections I voted for you sir I foguth in a manner speaking like a beast in fact it wasnt safe for me to go down around the cove I am one that has to take care of a family if responsible government had been returned to power I would have no trouble writing letters I dont have any help from any source whatsoever in my home as regards family allowances old age pensions or any other way

I was in the poll boot last spring and never received one copper for my work this summer I made a very poor voyage this fall I applied for some help from the government and was turned away I am a fisherman and receive no unemployment insurance or assistance the landsmen can get some help but there nothing for me now mr smallwood I am asking you if you can help me in any form what ever I would like to get to work on this releif program I was on the road but when mr Pottle[2] *gave a speech over the radio, and said that he would be sending out forms for people to go and take oath that they didnt have enough to do until last of march to tell the truth Sir I wasnt able to do that a man have to be [illegible] very tight for anyone not to last until last of march now mr Smallwood I am not really destitute but I will need help before this spring I would like for you to do your best for me in this matter.*

Yours truly

2 Likely Herbert L. Pottle, the Liberal Member of the House of Assembly for Carbonear-Bay de Verde, and the first minister of public welfare. Pottle served from 1949 to 1956.

March 8, 1950

Hon. Joseph R. Smallwood
St. Johns.

Dear Sir:

No doubt you have received many letters like this one I now write you or maybe this is the first of its kind. I am not very good at writing letters to a premier or anyone who holds an office similar to yours, but you are the only one I feel sure who can now help me. I worked five months last summer on a tow boat with the polar whaling company here in [my community]. And received no stamps for the unemployment Insurance or assistance. When I came home last fall in October I had thirty stamps which I got last spring before I went on the tow boat to [a community]. I lost my unemployment Book and went to St. Johns. They would not give me any unemployment assistance because I never had stamps enough. I never drew any assistance last spring and I have only worked two weeks since I came home last fall in October.

I served in the Merchant Navy in World War II and I could not get any allotment from them

I have a wife and three small children under six years of age and I have no home. At present I am living with my father-in-Law. I voted confederate because I thought I was going to get work or some assistance in the winter months. You may wonder why I am writing you. Well Sir I have heard that you have done a lot of good for people in my circumstances and I know it to be true. Can you help me? I am willing to take a job but there is not much I can do because I have been a sailor most of my days.

Will you please give this letter your closest consideration and please help me.

I remain

Your most

Obedient Servant

To Hon J.R. Smallwood M.P.
Premier of NfLD *May 3rd 1950*
St Johns.

Hon. Sir: -

After trying on several occasions to see you in St Johns and to get you by Phone without success, I thought that I would write you before you go away to know if there is any job in sight that you could place me in.

It is nearly twelve months now that I have waited in hopes to get something to do. I am aware that you are a very busy man, but I did think that you would give me five minutes of you valuable time.

You will agree with me Sir that I have not bothered you very much since your Election. However, Sir, all I can say is to wish you well and a very pleasant trip and I trust that all your deliberations will be crowned with success.

I am in hopes of hearing from you soon, and knowing you as I do and the Benevolent Spirit which you possess I feel assured that you will give this your earnest consideration and find some job to place me in.

With Kind Regards
Yours Fraternally

HARBOUR MAIN-BELL ISLAND

"They have also opposed your party up to the present": Harbour Main-Bell Island

Shannon Lewis-Simpson

MY PATERNAL GRANDFATHER was a Lewis from the North Side of Holyrood. He was forty-one when Confederation occurred. He did not speak about Confederation, but neither did I ask him directly. My grandfather was a St. Bon's scholarship student,[1] a teacher in Holyrood, and had been a clerk in Gander during the war. I know that he was a friend or relative of some of those mentioned in Harbour Main-Bell Island letters. And so, I cannot imagine him being unaware or unopinionated. I do know that he supported the Boston Bruins, so perhaps that was his way of signalling political affiliation.

My paternal grandmother was a Fahey from Chapel's Cove. By 1949, her family had farmed the same piece of land for over 150 years, and they continue to do so in the present day.[2] Her unmarried brothers Uncle Pats and Uncle Eddie helped build the base at Argentia,[3] farmed, and fished, and their sister Mary kept

---

1 St. Bonaventure's College, an independent Catholic school in St. John's, opened in 1858.

2 "Fahey Farm Century Farm," Heritage Newfoundland & Labrador, https://heritagenl.ca/heritage-property/fahey-farm century-farm/.

3 The United States military constructed a large base in Argentia during World War II. See Jenny Higgins, "Argentia," Heritage Newfoundland & Labrador, July 2007,

a small store in the house. Uncle Eddie was a municipal councillor for many years. The Faheys and their friends were quietly pro-Confederation, and they could see the benefit of the union, particularly in terms of modernization of electricity and transportation.

In the Smallwood collection, 108 letters were written by people in the district of Harbour Main-Bell Island in 1949: 80 by men, and 28 by women. There were letters about the state of the roads, the fishery, trade union, higher wages, consumption of liquor, the mail system, the judicial system, the election, the Liberal Party, the social welfare system, the health system—many topics which continue to be top of mind for current constituents. But, as many people were impacted by or worried about bureaucratic changes resulting from Confederation, most letters were requests for employment assistance, the baby bonus, and pensions for veterans and the elderly.

Some writers stated their needs quite plainly; others embellished their requests with fervent declarations of loyalty to the Liberal Party. A simple note of congratulation was the third most common reason for men to write to Smallwood; the women congratulated him as part of a more urgent request, if at all.

In Harbour Main-Bell Island, it was customary for families to rely on multiple sources of income drawn from work in the fishery, railway, mining, construction, and/or agriculture. Men such as my grandfather found temporary well-paying work in the bases in Argentia and Gander as general labourers, clerks, and carpenters. Starting in the early 1900s, they also left home for the "Boston States," and many iron workers or "fish" from Newfoundland worked the high steel of New York, "Chicargo," and other major North American cities.[4] Women such as my grandmother left for service in New York, New England, or St. John's and if they returned, they did so with fancy clothes and high expectations of what was possible, as noted in the letters.

Close family ties with the Boston states meant that many district voters remained strongly in favour of responsible government and an economic union with the United States. In contrast to other districts—such as Burin and Burgeo-

---

https://www.heritage.nf.ca/articles/politics/argentia-base.php. See also Vicki S. Hallett's reflection on Placentia-St. Mary's, later in this volume.

4 D'Arcy Jenish, "Raising Steel," *Legion Magazine*, November 28, 2009, https://legionmagazine.com/en/raising-steel/; Hana Gartner, dir., "Ironworkers from Newfoundland: Walking Iron," *CBC The Fifth Estate*, May 13, 1986, YouTube, https://youtu.be/nIYdystZDJ4. (When the World Trade Centre fell, the men from the area felt this personally.)

La Poile, which voted strongly in favour of Confederation—only 17 per cent of Harbour Main-Bell Island voters cast a vote in favour of Confederation in the second referendum, the second lowest district confederate vote after Ferryland.[5] The district was 54 per cent Roman Catholic, 43 per cent Protestant, with the majority leaning Tory in political bent, and the letter writers were not shy to admit to that to Smallwood.

One can think of three separate areas within the Harbour Main-Bell Island district. The "Head of the Bay" (Marysvale to Holyrood) was overwhelmingly Roman Catholic and what was being proclaimed from the altar each Sunday surely impacted the referenda votes. "The Shore" (Seal Cove to Woodstock/Topsail) was a mixture of Catholic and Protestant. Bell Island, finally, was a diverse community with a Roman Catholic majority, with people settling to work in the iron ore mines hailing from across Newfoundland and, indeed, around the world. A large segment of the miners commuted to Bell Island from other parts of Conception Bay, only going home to their families on Saturday nights and Sundays.

Given the economic challenges faced by numerous constituent families, one can certainly understand the desperate tone of some letters when one considers the length of time it took for benefits to be approved. For example, applicants required a birth certificate to obtain an Old Age Pension. But acquiring a birth certificate was not necessarily an easy or straightforward process. In 1889, the Harbour Grace cathedral and all records burned to the ground, and this caused practical issues for many Roman Catholic pensioners hoping to receive benefits. My great-grandmother, Margaret Fahey (Crawley), for example, had her birth certificate reissued by the church on January 1, 1950. Her Old Age Pension of $40/month was approved almost a full year later on December 18, 1950, and backdated to August 1, 1950.

The letters to Smallwood from the Harbour Main-Bell Island district offer some insight as to the intersection between self-resilience and state reliance. Life was hard for many, and wealth not equally distributed. Concerning socio-economic status, my grandfather Lewis used to say that some people wore "elephant's trappings on the back of a mouse." But it could take only one crisis—a fire, a shipwreck, a death on a battlefield, a mine closure, tuberculosis, a bit of bad luck—for the resilience of a family to shatter. If there was no social network to rely upon from community, church, or government, then life was an unbearable

5 "Referendum Voting Trends by District."

misery. The letters in this collection remind us of the disparities which existed in a relatively proudly resilient district. The fact that Smallwood personally replied to many of these requests and letters meant that he knew the purpose of government was to raise everyone up, as best as possible. The people of Harbour Main-Bell Island were aware of that fact, but some only begrudgingly accepted it.

Dec 27/48[6]

Mr Smallwood.
Dear Sir,

From one Confederate to another one, I would like to ask a favour. Me and one other ex service man, had an arguement the arguement was about this, do wee exservice men of Newfoundland get the same as the Canadians meaning this, I said to him that wee would get around $8.00 Eigh hundred dollars for six years over seas she said no.

Next is, say I had six or seven children now. Well he said that I wouldent get the baby bonous, the children that are born on and after March will receive it, and now Mr. Smallwood there is anything I can do over here for you please let me know. I wish you and your family a Merry Christmas and a Happy New Year.

I remain,
Yours,

December 30, 1948

Dear Mr [name redacted]:

I was very glad to get your letter. With regard to Newfoundland War Veterans of World War I and/or II, the position is this: Every such veteran will be entitled to exactly the same payments and benefits as if he had served in the Canadian Forces.

Next, as to the Family Allowance: Every child in Newfoundland will receive the Family Allowance on April 1, 1949, and on the first of every month thereafter until that child passes the age of 16. We have in this country

6 Letters from this district were chosen by both Shannon Lewis-Simpson and Sarah Simpson.

today about 120,000 from a day old up to 16 years old. Every one of these children will receive the Family Allowance. There is no truth whatsoever in the statement that no children will get the Family Allowance except those born after March, 1949. That is a stupid lie put out by the anti-Confederate people during the campaign.

Again, my sincere thanks for your letter and offer of support, which I value very highly.

Yours sincerely,

J.R. SMALLWOOD

April 9th/49

Hon. J.R. Smallwood,
Premier
St. John's

Dear Hon Sir,

I congratulate you on having the hon of premier. I am relating to you of an occurrence came to me of a great loss two falls ago. Where I lost up to three thousand dollars worth of fishery equipment which put a damp on me not recovered yet. So I wrote to the Minister of Marines and everybody I could locate concerning the affairs, and to no avail. It took the wharf where my fishing property was attached and we fishermen of [our community] is a little fishing stand here. Due to this, we are in need of somewhere to land out catch. I myself and boys are engaged in the herring fishing and cod fish. So I took an advantage of addressing you asking if you could use your influence by making an efford to see what you could do in the matter. I am not familiar with the Departments now. So I am calling your attention to see if you could remedy this situation.

Please answer this if it is possible. I hear by the radio you are solving some urgent problems and I would like for you to be successful in this. We want to get it to work in April. As we have to haul our traps about 2 or 3 miles to get them in our transfer boats to set them. I have it sent in a long while to Mr [name redacted] of which I understanding is out of the Dept. So I would like for a personal reply. Pardon my long writing as I know and hear you have many letters and calls to attend to but this one is in great need.

Enclosing I wish you every success in the future.
Sincerely yours,

April 22/1949

Dear Sir,

I am writing you this letter to tell you of the unfair deal which the shop girls are given [in my community]. I am a young girl, 20 yrs old, and I am employed here as a Dry Goods Clerk. I have been working there for quite a few years. I am doing the hardest kind of work for I have to be on my legs for nine in the morning till 6 at evening, I also have to work Monday and Saturday nights. I have to ask for a raise and with great difficulty I get one after a while. I started with $22.50 a month. I am only getting $37.50 now. Don't you think Sir that is a bit on the skinny side for a girl to pay her board, buy clothes and pay unemployment insurance with.[7]

I also have two sisters getting the worst kind of a raw deal, Mr Smallwood they are getting a worse kind of a one even worse than the one I am getting. For they are not getting paid as much as I am getting. So Sir you can, I guess see very clearly how the girls at Bell Island are getting treated. The shop girls are working for nothing compared to the St. John's girls.

Mr Smallwood you did a grand thing for us poor Newfoundland creatures when you bought Confederation about. For it is going to be the best thing for Newfoundlanders. I don't know how to thank you Sir.

I hope Mr Smallwood you can do something for us Human Beings in bringing about a wage increase for us. And May God Bless you in your effort. In all things you do May Luck and Grace follow you.

I remain

Yours truly,

The girl given a raw deal

PS: there are many more girls the same way

---

7 For reference, the average per capita household income in Newfoundland was $498.20 in 1949, little more than half the national average (Canada: $982.50 per annum). Statistics Canada, "Long Run Provincial and Territorial Data," November 2, 2018, https://www150.statcan.gc.ca/t1/tbl1/en/tv.action?pid=3610022901&pickMembers%5B0%5D=2.1&pickMembers%5B1%5D=3.1&cubeTimeFrame.startYear=1949&cubeTimeFrame.endYear=1949&referencePeriods=19490101%2C19490101.

April 25/49

Hon JR Smallwood
Gentleman

Please pardon me for taking up your valuable time.

Hearing of your understanding and champion of the underprivileged, I am promoted to bring my case to your notice.

I am a x Postmistress of [my community]—April 1948 I was retired at age 63—by a change of CS Constitution by Commission Government—After 32 years of faithful work, full time, for little money, just as my salary was on the up, my superiors showed little appreciation for my years by not considering to keep me on for the extra two years, and so give me a chance to build up my pension to $25 as it was I was usured out with basic pay $15.55 + 2.05£. and which is inadequate for me to get along on and I cannot apply for old age pension nor should I have to, after 32 years, in His Majesties Service. I quite understand law is made to be kept. Still there is a way out for the privileged class and I am only looking for fair play not charity.

Sincerly,

April 26/49

Mr J.R. Smallwood
Prime Minister
St. John's

Dear Sir

The people of this small settlement would like to know if you will grant them a wharf at [community] to land their caplin for farm use. There is about one hundred (100) familys interested in this wharf and they have also opposed your party up to the present—but the tide is turning and if you grant this request you won't regret it.

Awaiting your reply
I remain sincerely yours

PS: one who fought hard against your party.

27-4-1949

Hon. J.R Smallwood.

Dear Sir,

I congratulate you on your new appointment as Acting Premier of Nfld and wish you every success in the forthcoming general election.

Sir, I am taking this opportunity of telling you this story as you may not be aware of what is going on in this Dist. I will not go into full details as I am sure you will do it yourself. It is concerning [my community], we have a very poor mail system here in regards to transportation of mails and passengers.

The people of this place would appreciate it very much if you would make arrangements to have the trains stop at this station and take mails and passengers and put them off there. It would be greatly appreciated by the people of this place as everyone is concerned about. We hope Sir you will make an announcement over the radio as soon as it is possible for you to do so.

Yours sincerely,

May 20th, 1949

Hon. J.R. Smallwood,
St. John's

Dear Sir,

This letter is merely to express my appreciation of your Government's attitude towards those of us who were unfortunate enough to purchase Streptomycin on our own.

I am not one of those who become blind to all the good a government does simply because he differs with it on some issue that affects him personally, but I do not believe anyone can defend on moral grounds, a government which demands its pound of flesh from an individual's efforts to save the life of some member of his family suffering from tuberculosis.

Only those who have been through months and years of that experience, know of the financial strain, the anxieties, the false hopes and the bitter disappointments that usually accompany this disease; but I think the government's demand of a 10% revenue tax on those financial sacrifices we made in our efforts to fight T.B. was the most unkindly cut of all.

No government should capitalize on the misfortunes or sufferings of its people.

Yours respectfully,

May 23/49

To Premier J.R. Smallwood

Dear Sir,

No doubt you get many letters from people all over Newfoundland asking several questions concerning things, and I am sure that you answer them some way or other.

I guess you are wondering why, what this letter is about.

Well Sir I am widow, and I wants to know about the widow's fees. I have been getting $10.00 a quarter, I was wondering if the widows are getting the same or if they are getting a raise, I have heard over the radio all the speeches concerning the Old Age Pension, Baby Bonus, etc, but I haven't heard about the widows. Is the widow's fees going to be taken away from us or is it going to continue the same as before $10.00 a quarter? I know I won't be bettering the old age pension because I am not old enough, many widows here on the Island are thinking the same thing, and wondering what's for the widows, I am very anxious to know.

"Thank you"

Yours sincerely,

Worried Widow.

June 4, 1949

Dear Mr Smallwood,

You cannot imagine how thrilled we were, when at the Memorial graduation ceremony today, you announced that in a short time you will be transforming Memorial College into a University![8] *I admire you greatly, sir, and there are many thousands who join me. This, I think, is a most wonderful gesture, and will leave for you in the pages of Newfoundland history a name that can never be erased. I attended Memorial College this year and I know that our country needs a university, and in the long run there will be a much higher number of professionals here who will be able to undertake the important matters of our province intelligently.*

Although there are still a paltry few who do not realize it, you are our benefactor—a born leader. Since you began your Confederation policy, we have been wholeheartedly with you and today we are fanatical Liberals.

This is the first time I've written a letter like this to any politician or newspaper, and I am deeply honoured that it is to you—our premier.

Thank you, Sir!

Yours for a continuous brilliant career,

I remain

Yours faithfully,

---

8 Memorial University College, founded in 1925 as a memorial to the Newfoundlanders and Labradorians who had died on the battlefront during World War I, became Memorial University in 1949, shortly after Confederation. So far as can be ascertained, this was the first time the idea of Memorial University was shared in public by Smallwood. It was given first airing in the House of Assembly July 13, 1949, with "An Act respecting the University of Newfoundland" receiving Royal Assent August 13, 1949. For more on the history of Memorial University, see Malcolm MacLeod, *A Bridge Built Halfway: A History of Memorial University College, 1925–1950* (Montreal & Kingston: McGill-Queen's University Press, 1990); Joseph R. Smallwood, "Memorial University of Newfoundland—'a live, dynamic centre of learning [and] culture,'" ed. Melvin Baker, n.d., http://www.ucs.mun.ca/~melbaker/jrs1949.htm#N_2_.

July 1, 1949

The Hon. J.R. Smallwood,

Dear Sir,

Please pardon my presumption in writing you, but I have been driven to it.

I am a widow. My husband has been dead almost two years. I have never received a cent from The Dept. of Public Health and Welfare, no chance of a pension, just because my son who was overseas, draws a war pension. He has been suffering from tuberculosis ever since his discharge, and I assure you can only keep himself going. My younger son who has been out of employment supports my youngest son. What am I supposed to live on?

The Relieving officer told me there's nothing for me. I ask you to please intercede for me.

I am my family, were ardent supporters of your party, I therefore ask your help. They say you are the poor person's friend, and now, We shall see. Please forgive me, and help A lonely widow,

July 25th, 1949

Dear Sir,

As I took my pen in hand to write you this note to say I am [name redacted] say that my Husband want away going on 10 years now and he left me one child and the child is going 11 years old now and we never hered from he sence I can't get nut for Him the only thing he getting 700 of Family awlenece. How can I get food and castle out of that for Him.

I can not do it.

I can't get nut out of [illegible] for him just write you if you please wood be able to help him out a bit for me that the only thing getting is the 700 dollars. What can I do with that I was getting 800 for him 4 years ago and Tom the lane cut him off and I never got after now I am asked you for to help him, and a bit if you please Sir and is my nat child. Please he harding have got any close to put on he to go school and you now he cant go

Sir we never got any thing from he father only 1 year after he going away that was nine years ago June gone he is in the forest.

Answer my letters please Sir.

Nov 9 1949

Dear Sir,

Rumours continue in spite of a statement made by letter to me by the Board of Liquor Control that no licences have been granted to [my community] (Oct 21), that licences have either been granted or will be granted shortly.

I am writing on behalf of my people to you that we view with dismay and alarm the possibility of licences for the sale of beer being granted here on the island.

Enough liquor (far too much) comes to [my community] now. It is a terrible curse and any government which increases opportunities for getting the vile stuff (in any form) will certainly pay the consequences. I cannot believe that you and your Government will be guilty of this.

Please use your influences, in the interests of our homes of families to make it impossible for any more licences to be granted, anywhere.

Assuring you of my support in anything you may do for the betterment of this land.

I am,

Very truly yours,

Nov. 17th, 1949

Dear Mr [name redacted]:

Many thanks for your letter which I have read carefully.

This whole business of liquor and beer sale in Newfoundland is a very vexacious one. Bootlegging has grown to very great proportions, and what is even worse is the fact that the consumption of the essences for purposes of becoming intoxicated as assumed very alarming proportions. I am personally a non-drinker. I have yet to taste my first drink of liquor. I expect that I shall never have that doubtful pleasure. I was once Secretary of the Vigilance Committee in St John's, a body launched to assist unofficially in the enforcement of the old Prohibition law.

I have always been, or I always was, a very strong Prohibitionist. However, I fear that the very logic of unpleasant facts has caused me to veer round from being an absolute Prohibitionist. I have seen too much bootlegging and drinking of essences to believe any more that Prohibition is the answer. It is, as I say, a most vexacious question.

I am going to make a very strong effort to clean up the beer taverns in Newfoundland. Most of them are low dives, a disgrace to Newfoundland. I fear, however, that the solution is not prohibition. I am still working on the questions, and as I write we have a new Act in draft which we will consider in Cabinet tomorrow with a view of presenting it to the House of Assembly next week.

Believe me, I deeply appreciate your interest, but I can only express the hope that though you and I share an abhorrence of drinking, yet we may in the end have to disagree as to the best means of coping with the practical problem which confronts us today in Newfoundland.

With kindest personal wishes,

Very sincerely yours,

J.R. SMALLWOOD
PREMIER

HUMBER

The Cost of Living (a Found Poem)

Sonja Boon

IN BEFOR TIMES we paid $20 cents per loaf for Bread
a can for 25 cents
hamburger steak for 65, 70—
          49¢ per pound in Sydney last week

so expensive

$11.75 ¢
98, 85, 70, 65, 49, 20, 18, 16
          20 cints

merchants fleecing the people
every cent
as they did for years

find me a job
a leg
a loan
a Tavern License

an independent living

some land
4 ¼ acres
three or four head of cattle
a bedroom suite at Eatons

could it be possible to get a telephone?

two years
three years
five years
ten years in sept

I voted for you twice.

a child
three children
five people
six more small ones
my grandchild

no home

twenty minutes' walk
around shore and over rocks

five miles
seven miles
ten to twelve miles

A person could die here in winter.[1]

---

1 This found poem has been constructed entirely from excerpts of letters from Humber district. Bringing these disparate voices together creates a polyphonic effect, with myriad voices jostling both together and against one another for attention. What struck me as I wrote this was the way writers mobilized quantifiable facts: prices, lot sizes, years, children, distance, and time, among others, to make their cases.

June 17th 48

Mr. J.R. Smallwood
St. John's

Dear Mr. Smallwood

to hear Some Propaganda concerning Government I think This island off ours is at The Most time when we Should go Confederation with Canada as My Self I did vote for Commission Just to Keep Responsible Government down But This time I will not loose my Vote I will Support confederation at The last Because I see now it's the only Thing for our People and The Country I am Confederate and I all ways will Be. I wish to Join the Great Democratic union by Confederation with Canada and I will do my utmost to Get all I can for That Great Cause.

Confederate

Jan 20th 1949

J R Smallwood Esq.
St. John's

Dear Sir
I am writing you to ask you if you would know of any Body that would lie to Buy 4 ¼ acres of land two acres under Hay. about 1000 feet From [redacted] to [redacted]. and about 1000 feet From [redacted] suitable for cabin's or any Body wanting to start chicken farm or anything else

as I am out of Employment I am Compelled to sell this nice spot of Land at a very low price this Block of land is granted and I am the oner and I would sell this land for the sum of Six Hundred Dollars for 4 acres 16 Perches 1 Rod. as per my grant I would Be very glad if you could Help me in this. this Land is twenty minutes walk From [community] four or five minutes By car.

Please advise and oblige

Yours Truly

January 27, 1949

Dear Mr. [name redacted]:

Thank you for your letter, which I have considered carefully, I must say that I have no idea at present time of anyone who would be interested in the land that you mention. I do know, however that there will be a very important tourist program on that coast after Confederation comes in. It seems to me that you should have no difficulty whatever in disposing of your property. If you will write me sometime after March 31, I may be in a position to be of some help to you.

Sincerely yours,

J.R. SMALLWOOD

TO THE HON JOSEPH SMALLWOOD

DO ANY OF OUR NFLD CITIZENS COME UNDER THE INDIAN ACT WOULD APPRECIATE HAVE ACT PUBLISHED REPLY[2]

505PM MAY 20, 1949

2. For more on Confederation and Indigenous peoples in Newfoundland and Labrador, see Grammond, "Equally Recognized?"; Hanrahan, "The Lasting Breach"; and MacKenzie, "The Indian Act."

June 27th 1949

To
The Hon Joseph R Smallwood
Prime Minister
St. John's

Dear Sir: -

I am writing you this letter concerning a road from [community to community] which is badly needed. And I hope you will give it your utmost consideration. I am a Maternity Nurse and have been for years. And the nearest Doctor is 30 miles away and in winter time there is no way to get back and forth only around shore and then you must travel around shore and over rocks.

Of course you know as you travelled it with my husband Some time ago when he was Mail Man [name redacted].

I know it would be a wonderful benefit to me and to the rest of the community if there was a road around [community]. Theres no trouble to get forth & back in Summer time but in Winter its neither open nor fast. it freezes up too much for a boat and not enough for a team. A person could die here in winter for need of a Doctor. And no way to get one here. So I think its time for something to be done about it.

I am expecting to hear from you in Short and I hope you will give my letter your consideration. And I am hoping that with your help we will have a road from [community] to [my community] in the near future.

I am
Yours sincerely

Maternity Nurse

July 23 – 49

Premeir JR Smallwood
St Johns

At present I am on government relief mean while I can get a loan to purchase three or four head of cattle which would enable me to support my family independent but Brookfield plant in Corner Brook refuses to buy my milk I have heard the schools are to have milk instead of cocomalt this coming winter could I get the chance to supply three school here in [my community] & [neighbouring community] with skim milk scalded I could go ahead and get these cows to freshen in august Ive tried every thing I know of to earn an honest living for my family twenty five dollars for a month for five people is very inadequate I have only one arm and cripple in my back. So hard work like farming vegetables is more than I am able to do. I have registered at the unemployment insurance office at [community] but they claim a person unphiscially fit dosent get any thing is there nothing we cripples come under for assistance could I secure Tavern License to sell controllers beer and wines at [neighbouring community]. I have been to health inspector & all [illegible] any authorities in [community] but no one seems to have any interest in a poor mans welfare so I hope to hear from you. Some thing satisfactory at your earliest convenience as the first time I wrote you I only got a reply from your Secretary as you were away on a Political campaign

Yours very Truly

9.12. /49

Mr. R. J. Smallwood

Premier of Newfoundland

Dear Sir

I am writing a few lines to ask you if could see about cutting down a bit on the flour and bread in the Humber District.

For instant when the flour was up to the price of $11.75 ¢ per sack in befor times we paid $20 cents per loaf for bread and now flour is dropped to $7.25 per sack we still pays ¢20 cents. And if the public should speak about [illegible] to a Baker he will only say write to Mr. Smallwood. So [illegible] as there is some one got to do it I think it might as well be me.

Now Sir for another thing if there were a union in this place for shops to be closed on Sundays & holidays is it right for a certain Merchant named [redacted] to open on such days & sell anything to any friend of his if so I don't see why all the Merchants cant do same. And he is always refuting to you as the person we should see about it well now Mr. Smallwood if you should write that person

Please. omit my name of the letter. But I do hope you do something about both things in the future.

I remain

Sept 14th, 1949

Premier J.R. Smallwood
St. John's.

Dear Sir

When stationed at [community] I discovered Manganese on Normans Cove head Trinity Bay. I had it staked. But having a large Family and a Small income I could not afford to do anything about it. Sir why I mention about manganese it may turn out to be of commercial value to your Government.

Wishing you the very best
Yours very Truly

Ex Sergt.

Oct. 6/49

Premier J.R. Smallwood

St. John's.

Dear Sir:-

I am writing to ask if all terms between Nfld. And Canada are settled yet.

My reason for asking you is I am a Blind widow of 59 years of age and so far I am only getting ten dollars every three months and using your own conclusions Mr. Smallwood that's quite a low figure it certainly isn't enough to feed and clothe anyone. I am after filling in a (Blind) application for the Blind, I was born blind in one eye. And the other is failing fast, this is certified by Dr. Authorities after being to the General Hospital at St. John's. from what I can understand the Blind Pension is $30.00 per month. As I heard over one of the Radio Broadcasts. Trusting you will look into the matter for me.

I Remain
Yours Respectifully

P.S. (I am one of your voters)

URGENT

OCT. 26, 1949

HON J R SMALLWOOD PREMIER
ST JOHNS NF

DUE TO THREATS OF A PROMINENT BUSINESS MAN HERE THE EDITOR OF THE WESTERN STAR[3] BERNARD GILL HAS BEEN DISMISSED DUE TO RECENT EDITORIALS RE THE COST OF LIVING THIS IN OUR OPINION IS ABSOLUTE MUZZELING OF THE FREEDOM OF THE PRESS AND WE ANTICIPATE YOUR IMMEDIATE ACTION THE LABOUR ORGINAZITIONS ARE LOUD IN THEIR PROTESTS AGAINST SUCH UNDEMOCRATIC PRINCIPALS

[NAMES OF FIVE UNION LEADERS REDACTED]

3 The *Western Star* was founded in Birchy Cove in 1900. F.B. Gill was its editor from December 1945 to October 31, 1949.

Nov. 4th

Mr. J R Smallwood
St. Johns

Dear Sir I am writing you concerning the Bus business here at Corner Brook as I am a Bus driver myself. There are about forty reglar Buses on the road here operating from 6 am to 12 pm and twenty or more part time Buses what I mean is men working in the Mill making from one dollar upwards to two $ and fifty cents per hour. which I think is enough for any man. then we have railroad and Garage men coming on the road after their day work with there cars running as a Bus. which I think isnt fair to the men who are depending on these Buses to feed there familys and run there cars. If something isnt done and done quick the regular Bus driver will be forced to leave the road as the part time man will run us off the road as we cant make enough money to pay expences and feed our family so I am expecting you to do something about this matter which is a serious thing, when a Bus driver got to work 18 hrs for a living and then cant make it

I remain yours Bus driver

Dear Mr Smallwood

There is a question I would like to ask you, and that is, are you going to force the Nfld merchants to sell at Canadian prices, or are they going to still be allowed to rob us as always? if we are going to have to pay taxes the first of July, where are people (who have no help coming in only what they earn daily) going to get the money? I don't know if you are aware of the way the merchants are fleecing the people in this town, but you could Easily find out. for instance, one store sells a can of something for 25 cts. the same thing is sold in another store for 20 cts. in another for 18 or 16 cts. Hamburger steak which I bought in Sydney last week was 49 cts per lb, here it's 65 & 70. the same price that it always was, Ham in some stores is one dollar, some others 98 & 85 cts. all the same brand. this is only an example of what's going on here. clothes in the stores here is twice the price as it is in other provinces. and we were told on confederation day we would have the same privileges as the old canadians.

I am not against paying our share of taxes, but we are getting old, our children are married and have large families, we have to pay Life, Fire & other insurance, Electric lights, water rates, fuel & Hospital Bills, we have no other help only what my husband earns as a labourer. so I would like to know how we are going to pay taxes, when we don't have any money left, when our bills are all paid up Every month, just because the merchants in this town take Every cent as they did for years.

you can put a stop to their Robbery. just as you got confederation for us, and if you were smart Enough to outwit that crafty George Drew in the Elections, you can put a stop to the highway Robbery by the merchants of this town. there is a good jail here, where some of them ought to spend a vacation in it.

I havent mentioned what they are still charging for their furniture, but I can buy a bedroom suite at Eatons at Moncton, NB and have Enough money to take me there to buy it, and it wouldn't cost as much as it would to buy one here in … Hoping you will do something about this and also send some of the mounties here to clean up on the Vice in this town as well.

yours truly

Hon. Jos. Smallwood

Dear Sir

I am a fisherman fishing in [a community] Labrador. I am married and have four children. In other years I took my wife and family there. My children went to school in [community]. This year the station agent ... advised me that children under fourteen years of age are not allowed to be taken to Labrador. As I have no home, I can't leave my wife and children here, where I was working this spring in various sherring plants. As the season here is now over and there is no work here, I would like to go back to Labrador. Is the information correct that I cannot take my wife and children with me? If so could you do something for me, as we have no home here.

Respectfully yours

P.S. I have my own place in [a Labrador community] and fish for myself. I have two shoremen fishing with me.

LABRADOR

The Only Voice They Were Familiar with Was Joey's on the Radio

Vicki S. Hallett with Patricia Way

IN JUNE OF 2008 Tshaukuesh Elizabeth Penashue wrote to then-premier Danny Williams asking him to visit her in Labrador. She suggested they take a canoe trip together up the Mista-shipu (Churchill River). This was not an invitation to a pleasure cruise but an offer to come and listen to the voice of the river, to the voices of the animals and the people of Labrador who depended on the river and who opposed the massive Muskrat Falls hydroelectric development.

In this letter, the Innu elder tries to make Williams understand the physical and spiritual importance of the river, one which has sustained life in Labrador since time immemorial. She writes about the river's beauty, its life-giving power, and its essential place in the lives of her people. She promises, "If you come, I can explain many more things about the river."[1]

Danny Williams never visited Elizabeth Penashue and never took that canoe trip. One wonders how things may have turned out differently if he had.

Writing a letter to the leader of the province takes courage and conviction. You have to summon your most persuasive attitude, use your strongest voice, and sustain a belief that it will make an impact. If you are writing in a language

1 Tshaukuesh Elizabeth Penashue, *Nitinikiau Innusi: I Keep the Land Alive*, ed. Elizabeth Yeoman (University of Manitoba Press, 2019), 172.

that is not your first, a language that was violently imposed upon you, then it takes a level of bravery unknown to most.

It is perhaps impossible to fully convey the meaning of a place in a letter, no matter how valiant the effort or how eloquent the voice. It is especially difficult if the people to whom you are writing have little to no experience of the place and seem to view it only through the lens of colonial resource extraction. If the people to whom you would write do not speak your language, do not know your traditions, and do not share your worldview—in short—if they cannot, or will not hear your voice. The great gulf those differences create may seem wider and colder than the Strait of Belle Isle.

Such chasms are difficult to span and letters perhaps not the most accessible means of doing so. For Labradorians in the late 1940s, St. John's and the politicians who resided there likely felt unreachable. Indeed, the brand of politics being practiced at that time was a novelty to most Labradorians, which helps to explain the dearth of letters in the Smallwood archive from Labrador from 1948 to 1952.

The first time Labradorians were given the option to vote was to elect a candidate (Reverend L.L. Burry) for the National Convention in 1946. Two years later they were voting to choose between Canada, Newfoundland, and the Commission of Government. The parameters of this choice, set out by colonial powers, and coupled with the sleight of hand known as enfranchisement, offered Labradorians little reassurance as they set forth into an unknown political future.

Of the many voices vying for Labradorian's attention in the Confederation debate cacophony, the only voice they were really familiar with was Joey's on the radio. Smallwood's program, *The Barrelman*, had been a familiar presence in homes from Nain to Mary's Harbour for six nights a week since 1937, and his "anti-mercantile theme" coupled with promises of a better standard of living for working people struck a chord with many.[2]

This is evident in the archived letters which speak to people's hopes for the future but also to their sense of trepidation. So much had been taken away. What would be given? How could it ever be enough? One voter wrote to J.R. Smallwood as an "Eskimo woman" who was concerned for the people of Labrador who had up until that time not been treated equitably with Newfoundlanders. Would

2 James K. Hiller, *Confederation, Deciding Newfoundland's Future 1934 to 1949* (Newfoundland Historical Society, 1998), 16–17, 51.

a new government ensure that her people would get the same opportunities as those on the island?

A nurse put pen to paper thanking Smallwood for his action that saved many people on the south coast from starvation in the winter of 1949. In addition to her gratitude, however, she was at pains to point out her frustration with the mercantile system that had left people so destitute and with the Newfoundland Rangers tasked with patrolling the Labrador Straits area, around whom she had to work "single handed" to get the food aid distributed to families.

Meanwhile, another resident of Labrador was concerned that necessary winter supplies would not be readily available to his community if the local store closed down. Could Mr. Smallwood ensure that Makkovik's winter provisions would be distributed through a local dealer? As someone "out to help the poor people," someone for whom the people of Labrador had voted time and again, surely Mr. Smallwood could understand that Family Allowance cheques would be useless if they had "to go fifty miles on dog team to haul our food."

Despite the presence of these heartfelt letters, it is the silence that rings most profoundly in this section of the Smallwood archive. It is not an empty silence, but one that is resonant with a multitude of voices. Voices of the people who would not or could not craft a letter, and voices of the beautiful land, of the water and ice. Voices that spoke in languages foreign to those in power. Much like the voice of the Mista-shipu, the Grand River, lately called the Churchill. As Elizabeth Penashue wrote to Williams in 1988, "The river is alive, just like a human being, and its voice is crying out, 'Don't kill me. I'm the water. I don't want to die. Hear my voice. Without water we cannot live.'"[3]

If only a river could write a letter to make its voice heard. But then again, what you hear depends on how you listen.

3 Penashue, *I Keep*, 185.

Labrador
October 28, 1948

J. R. Smallwood, Esq.
St. John's,

Dear Mr. Smallwood:

Congratulations on the victory & good luck to you for the next step. We are anxiously awaiting the developments in Ottawa now.

I know you are a busy man, & I would not take any of your time, but I should like to have some information as to your party's policy (Liberal) I resume. What the C.C.F. & Progressives are up to etc.[4] *Any information pamphlet form or otherwise you could send? I know nothing whatsoever as to what would be required of a member, but if Labrador is to be a district, and not included in some other district I may have the nerve to run. Should a member be required to live outside? What would the salary be approximately?*

There are several men whom I know to be on the job of canvassing as soon as things are ready. Why I mentioned salary above is, I have a fairly good job and a family (small) to look out for first & foremost, before I should make any move but its going to be a real temptation to be to see some upstart come out whose not interested in Labrador. I know Labrador fairly well from most angles, especially do I know the common Labradorian, and am expected by a lot of them to run. I'm sure that I can make a positive block against any that I know are coming out, whatever the platform. Whether I go or not anything I can do to further your cause up here I shall.

Yours Sincerely,

4 The Co-operative Commonwealth Federation, or CCF, was a political party established in Calgary in 1932. The precursor to the current New Democratic Party, the CCF was a social democratic party that sought co-operative economics. It was active at both provincial and federal levels.

December 28th 1948

J. Smallwood Esquire
Newfoundland Confederate Association
St. John's, Newfoundland

Dear Mr. Smallwood,

I am indeed sorry to trouble you at a time when you must be pressed for time with a great deal of work. First of all I would like to congratulate you upon the success of your Confederation campaign.

Could you possibly let me have copies of the White Book and the Black Book dealing with Confederation issues. What I am interested in is:-

(1) The possible reduction in the cost of living through Confederation.
(2) The possible help Mission Schools etc will obtain from the Canadian Government.

These questions vitally affect the finances of our Mission in Labrador and will help me in my discussions with my Mission Board while I am on furlough here in England

Trusting that you will be able to give me the information I require and with every good wish for the New Year.

I am
Yours faithfully

(Rev) F. W. Peacock
Superintendent of Moravian Missions
in Labrador

Labrador
April 5th 1949

Dear Mr. Smallwood

As now Honorable Premier of Newfoundland in which we are very glad to hear. We Belong to [our community] and are now at present working at Goose airport with our familys here at [community] 8 miles from the Base. I guess you will remember me as we were to see you often at your office last spring before going and coming from the ice fields Mr Smallwood to start with we and our familys are glad we are under Canada and want to thank you for the good work you have done to put her through We are glad to no that the duty are off and prices lower. I want to tell you about the prices of the Hudsons Bay Store here in which we are depending on. It dont look like its much duty taken of down hear We are going to give you the prices now at present with the duty taken of for we want to see what you can do about it. Because things are costing more down hear now than what it cost at St. Johns Before Canada too over. And now the prices are as follows Flour $17.00 per barrel Evaporated milk 21 cts pr tin Green label Butter 55 cts pr lb. Salt meet 40 cts pr lb dryed apricot 70 cts pr lb lowest price tea $1.10 pr lb Bologna 60 cts pr lb Coolstorage fresh meet 85 cts to $1.20 pr lb Sugar 14 cts pr lb Potatoes $14.00 pr barrel. Hd bread 20 cts pr lb Mens TY rubbers $12.50 pr pair and Everything Els according to the reason why we are Explaining those prices to you. We are sure you are going to do something about it. And if you would write we would be glad to hear from you. Or even if you could visit this place sometime as there are about one hundred familys living hear at Hamilton Village and we all are trusting to the Hudsons Bay Store and we are not satisfied with the prices We were listening to your Broadcast on Saturday night we gits all the news from St. John's down hear real good over the radio Except in the day we don't hear it very good. So as we are closing we are trusting to you to do your best for us Sincerely yours

[two names redacted]

The International Grenfell Association
INCORPORATED
SIR WILFRED GRENFELL, K. C. M. G., M.D., FOUNDER
CHARLES S. CURTIS, M.D., MEDICAL SUPERINTENDENT AND EXECUTIVE OFFICER ON THE COAST

SUPPORTING ASSOCIATIONS

GRENFELL ASSOCIATION OF AMERICA
NEW YORK, N. Y., U. S. A.
NEW ENGLAND GRENFELL ASSOCIATION
BOSTON, MASS., U. S. A.

GRENFELL LABRADOR MEDICAL MISSION
OTTAWA, CANADA

GRENFELL ASSOCIATION OF GREAT BRITAIN
AND IRELAND, LONDON, ENGLAND
GRENFELL ASSOCIATION OF NEWFOUNDLAND
ST. JOHN'S, NEWFOUNDLAND

Date: 13.4.49

The Right Honourable Joseph R. Smallwood
Prime Minister Province Newfoundland
St. John's.
Nfld.

Sir;
This is to confirm two telegrams sent to you by me about the shortage of food on Labrador.

I extend to you, Sir, my sincere thanks for your rapid action to get food brought to the Labrador. If it had not been for your intervention there would have been, without doubt, several deaths from starvation. I was very grieved, and not a little annoyed to hear, over Radio reports, that people were blaming the Government for the situation, there-fore for your information I send a report on the whole affair. I realise that I probably committed a breach of etiquete by contacting you, but I did so only as a last desperate measure, and I apologise for it.

As you probably know, in the Fall of the year Merchants on this, and other parts of the coast order their winter supplies to stock up their stores, and these are brought from St. John's. Last Fall (1948) I heard rumours about the order being sent to St. John's from Fox Harbour and Battle Harbour, and these reports said that the orders were the smallest on record. It was also said that the reason was that the Merchants did not want to "caught" with goods in the spring when Confederation took place.

Early in December Ranger [Grimes][5] came to see me on business, and , as is my custom I asked him how things were on the coast as he went around on his patrol. He answered my question, and then said voluntarily "I'll tell you one thing Nurse, there's going to be starvation next spring, you see now." Then he gave me the reason as above. Just before Christmas he went to [community], and Ranger [Smith] was left at [a second community]. On his patrol he also came in to see me, and told me the same thing.

From that time onward I had reports from widely scattered points about the sitation that was developing, and from independent sources, I heard about the empty stores.

On January 24th Ranger [Frank] came to see me about patients in [a third community], and I asked him if there was any truth in the reports. He said "That's what there is. There is nothing at [the fourth community] now, and the people have cleaned up [the third community]. Now they are cleaning up [the third community]. When that's finished there is nothing left." I asked him if he was going to do anything about it, and he just said "I don't know what to do."

Ranger [Smith] left [the second community] in December and Ranger [Fitzpatrick] took his place. Incidently I mention that Ranger [Frank] came here on his way to [the second community] to buy up all the soap there was there, as there was none in [the third community]. Ranger [Fitzpatrick] came here on February 7th to collect the Radio licence, and he told me that the food situation was getting serious, "the next dole orders would clean up the rest of the food." Again I asked him if he was going to do anything, and he too said "I don't know what to do."

At the end of February, [the doctor] came up on his annual visit, and he remarked to me that "he did not know what in the world the people on the shore were going to do, there was no more food to be had and some families were on their last sack of flour." The Doctor was around here three weeks, and left for the north on March 20th. From [the fifth community] he sent a message back to me in which he said "I have left a message at [the fourth community] for the Ranger to send to the Dept. of Public Health and Welfare when he send his, saying food must be flown in to avert a famine."

5 Because the correspondent names four different people, we have chosen to use pseudonyms for ease of reading.

Just after I received that message Ranger [Fitzpatrick] came through here on his way to [the second community], and again I discussed the question with him. He said "I will see what I can do." For two weeks after that I waited for him to do something, he said he would let me know if he decided on the best move, but I never heard from him. Things rapidly went from bad to worse, and babied began to die slowly from starvation, expectant mothers showed alarming signs of emaciation and listlessness and other men, women, and children were slowly starving; Day after day men came to me begging for food for the children, and I had none to give them. Finally in sheer desperation I threw all red tape and authority overboard, sent a note to the Ranger telling him that I was going to appeal to you, and went ahead.

Personally I think I was justified in my action; The people and I had waited for three months for the Rangers to do something about it. I held back because I did not consider that getting food was my business. The Rangers are supposed to look after the people who are down and out. My job is to look after their lives and health. When I saw that the lives and health of the people was being put in danger by the inactivity of the Rangers, I took matters into my own hands. Finally I inform you that not one of the Rangers in any way helped to distribute the food landed and dropped by plane. Ranger [Fitzpatrick] was here when the first plane came. He told me that I could not give out food until he had had "Instructions from St. John's as to what to do with it." I insisted that the milk, at least should be given out, and he gave way on that point on condition that I would give milk only to the babies that were sick. Here again I threw authority overboard; I gave out food to all who needed , and I am glad I did. I have not heard a word from the Ranger, and he has not been here to see if the people were alive or dead. Without wishing to boast, I can tell you that I have given out this food single handed, having the mission foreman haul the food over from the store for me. Finally, Sir I wish to say that I am prepared to take full responsibility for my actions; the Mission is in no way responsible.

I remain Sir,

Nurse in charge.

May 18, 1949

The Hon. Joseph R. Smallwood,
Premier of Newfoundland,
St. John's, Nfld.

Sir,

There is a problem facing the people of [my community] which I feel obliged to bring to your attention, and which I believe you will use your best influence to solve.

There are forty-seven families at [my community] who derive a livelihood by prosecuting the cod fishery. But if there is no effort made to solve the problem we feel sure that as a result the people will be forced to suffer.

Therefore I am enclosing a little sketch which will help to make plain the purpose of this letter to you. I know you will appreciate it.

From this sketch you will note the course of the ... river which really takes the shape of the letter S. This river will eventually change its course and break through the narrow sand bank at A, if not prevented. This will cause the people of [my community] much inconvenience. In fact many of the people here will be forced to abandon the fishery altogether.

Therefore we make an appeal to you. In doing so we think it advisable to inform you of our plan. If we can secure a little financial help we propose to change the course of the river, thus making it flow from B to C, and from thence on its usual course.

I shall be glad to give you any further information you desire.

Thanking you in anticipation,
I have the honour to be, Sir,
Your obedient servant,

May 30th/49

To. Hon. J.R. Smallwood
St. John's

Dear Sir,

You will be surprised to get a letter from me. I will introduce myself first. I am an Eskimo woman from lower part of Labrador. I came from Labrador seven years ago. I have been wondering if my people down Labrador will be treated like the Nfld people are treated, they never was treated like Newfoundlanders by their government, & I know that for a fact because I was down Labrador until I was 23 years old & came up here & found everything different, down there we do not know anything about "Widow's fee" or money for fatherless children, & I was wondering if my people down there are getting family allowances what I am lucky enough to get up here. There are lots down there, (like myself one time) never seen cheques in their life, & most of the time they cant even get relief like people can get it here. I am not claiming to be anybody important I am just a hard working woman with a hard working husband. We have listened to your speeches, over the radio & I have wondered many times& said many times I wonder what about my people down Labrador, I like to know what going to happen to them, I wonder is it going to be any better for them. I have heard lots of people say, what odds about Labrador think of ourselves & our country. Labrador is my country & they are my people although my father & mother is dead, I thinks of them as my family.

I hope you do not mind my writing it is the only way for me to find out & satisfy my mind. Thank you Sir.

Sincerely Yours,

June 1st 1949

To Hon. J. Smallwood
St. John's N.F.L.D

Dear Sir –

It's my desire to tell you about the wrong-doing in destroying common wealth Such as a crowd of men getting ready for a trip in back in the Country robbing Bird nests and killing muskrats. I think it is a very wrong thing and when we voted for a new form of Govt I think there should be some fair play and some protection for the welfare of the people they seldom got the gun off their shoulder as time rolls by there will be nothing too kill so please Sir I would like for you to give this statement the Earliest notice and give me advice so as I will be able to post it up and try and put it in force. I think its time for some one to see that the right things should be carried out. The Muskrats haves 3 broods a year and people is killing them with 10 and 14 young ones in them is anything like that fair Please let me know. I wrote to F.G. Bradley got no reply. Could I get this job as Game Warden

Yours Truly

July 17th 1949

Dear Friend

Just a few lines to let you know that we where to vote for confederation and have done so four other stations Beside [my community] and the stations are Hebron Nain Nutak also Makkovik we were interested in voting for confederation but now we are doubtfully amazed if we are going to be better off because we still continue in the same condition as before the confederation.

Before the voting started we were forced to vote for confederation for a Lower Cost of Living But every thing here what have Been in the shop for over a year are same price as the once that arrive during the summer also if [name redacted] still continue to be a manager over the clerks it will in no wise be better on the Labrador And it is true as they are printed in ink for we are por and hard up for a truth and helpless Please reply

From your sincerely

Friend

July 26th/49

Dear Sir,

My family and my fishing crew and I listened gratefully to the nice speech you made on the 23rd. We were right with you last year in each referendum, and again on Monday. We know you are out to help the poor people and, what you say, we pay great heed to.

We thank you sincerely for all that you have done and are still doing. We thank you for your interest in our country.

Sir, I want to put something in your hands. We tried merchants and also government, for a store of supplies at [our community], for winter purposes. No one seems to be interest except [one company]. I feel now with a little persuasion they would consider the matter. Most of the people of our district fishes for [this company], and during winter deals with Mr. [name redacted] at [community] who is backed by [the company]. This man gave me a small supply of goods last winter to see what kind of a success two stores would make in this district. It proved successful, but he is too small financially to back this without a great backing from [the company]. Now this same [man] is not staying on Labrador this winter for the sake of his invalid wife. So this means we will have to be without a store, and have to haul our supplies from [a community] which is fifty miles away. Unless you can have a talk with [this man] and see if he cant supply us winter and summer. There is always quite a lot of fur and cash and oils around here beside the cheques for fish which quite a few of our people received from Fishery Products during winter months. This with the additional Family Allowances will bring quite a bit of money into circulation, and its no good to us unless we go fifty miles on dog team to haul our food. [Our community] could dispose of 10 thousand dollars worth during winter even with a store at [another community] only eight miles away. Now even [that community] store will be closed this coming winter. We should have 25 thousand or at least 20 thousand. If [the company] would be satisfied to entrust me with the goods I will handle same on a small commission also no lading charges. And no storage charges. I would handle on my own premises. And would swear to do it to the nest of my ability. We the people of [our community] district puts great faith in you, and we know you will give it consideration, and do your best. We also know if we do not get a store of supplies this winter you will not be to blame for it. Thanking you again for all on behalf of our people.

I remain Yours
very Sincerely

PLACENTIA-ST. MARY'S

"Come Near at Your Peril, Canadian Wolf": On Lupine Threats and Enduring Legacies

Vicki S. Hallett

Men, hurrah for our own native isle, Newfoundland,
Not a stranger shall hold one inch of her strand;
Her face turns to Britain, her back to the Gulf,
Come near at your peril, Canadian Wolf[1]

HAD IT BEEN DECIDED by the residents of Placentia-St. Mary's, Newfoundland and Labrador would not have become Canada's tenth province. In the final referendum of 1948, they turned out in droves and voted 81.6 per cent in favour of responsible government. In fact, it was this district's second resounding repudiation of the "Canadian Wolf." The first had occurred in the 1869 election, when Newfoundland voters (male citizens of the colony, over twenty-one years of age) were deciding between their allegiance to Britain and the possibility of greater ties with the newly formed union of the British North American colonies and Upper Canada. The spectre of the wolf was raised in the "Anti-Confederation Song," penned sometime during the debates of the 1860s, which famously framed the issue as one of nationalistic self-defense.

The settler population envisioned themselves as natives, and their claim to

1 Fowke, "The Anti-Confederation Song."

the place was entrenched with "home rule, state-funded separate schools and a fair share of government patronage."[2] Losing such privileges was a frightful possibility, and few felt the fear more acutely than the predominantly Irish Catholic residents of small outport communities dotted along the shores of Placentia Bay and St. Mary's Bay. For them, union with a larger entity conjured up bitter ancestral memories of British rule in the homeland.

The lupine threat, and all it represented, still menaced during the Confederation debates of 1948.[3] So, when the Roman Catholic archdiocese in St. John's characterized Canada as a haven of divorce, inter-denominational marriages, and general immorality,[4] it was particularly impactful in districts such as Placentia-St. Mary's, where 92.1 per cent of the population was Catholic. Yet, while much has been made of the supposed sectarian divide in the referendum results, the truth is more complicated than such statistics would appear to support. Other districts with large Roman Catholic populations voted in favour of Confederation, while some with majority Protestant affiliations were not overwhelmingly in support of joining Canada. In the capital city, where religious affiliation was almost evenly divided among Catholic and Protestant denominations, the votes tallied almost 70 per cent in support of responsible government.[5] Nonetheless, we will never conclusively know whether the vote was split along sectarian lines, as voters were not questioned on such matters at the polling stations.

Indeed, even in such apparently clear cases as Placentia-St. Mary's, letters from constituents offer some insight as to the complex calculus they made when casting their ballots. One woman wrote to then-premier Smallwood on July 29, 1950, to reassure him that she had voted for Confederation and was pleased that, despite a grim economy, it would mean an end to the "extremity of miseries for our people." She was also keen to remind Mr. Smallwood of his commitment to retain the denominational system that kept Catholic and Protestant children separated in different schools. It "proves to all great moral Courage," she wrote, and prophesized that it would "be remembered longer than we realize." That denominational system would remain in place until 1999 and is still vividly recalled by any who passed through it. Whether those recollections are pleasant or horrific often depended upon how closely aligned one was to the structures of power the system upheld.

---

2 Hiller, "The Debate: Confederation Rejected, 1864–1869."

3 "The Anti-Confederation Song" was present in people's recent memory as it was featured in Gerald S. Doyle's popular publication *Old-Time Songs and Poetry of Newfoundland* (St. John's: Gerald S. Doyle, 1940).

4 Hiller, *Confederation*, 49.

5 All statistics from the 1948 referendum, "Referendum Voting Trends by District."

Equally memorable, and divisive, was the arrival of the Americans during World War II. Construction of the massive Fort McAndrew naval, air, and military base at Argentia changed the entire area irrevocably. The war brought an influx of US military and civilian personnel, demanded the expropriation of thousands of acres of family farmland, and displaced all the residents in the communities of Argentia and nearby Marquise. It also afforded jobs to thousands of local people, many of whom had never seen a paycheque before, much less a steady, and relatively handsome, one.[6] The maintenance of the base continued to provide significant employment in the area after the war, but everyone knew it would not last forever. One such employee wrote to Smallwood on January 6, 1949. Inquiring about job prospects in the civil service, he said, "I am at present time employed with the American Army ... My standard of education is grade XI, and through the recommendations I have received I am a good employee. My age is 21 years October past, and even though you may consider my age young, I think I would be capable of taking either one of these positions after a short while with the Department."

For those who had carried on fishing during the war years, the postwar slump in prices was devastating. "Poor relief" was not sufficient to support families, and people wanted to work. Many petitioned Smallwood directly. On September 10, 1949, one man sent a brief missive, part of which read, "A large percentage of the people here are depending on relief due to the poor fishery. I heard your suggestion to start working on the roads with pick and shovel and appeal to you to start the road here."

I do not know if this gentleman's request was granted, but I do know that someone out there *will* remember, and likely will get in touch after this piece is published to set me straight, and to share a story about Joey Smallwood's involvement with it. Smallwood's legacy, and Confederation, continue to inspire strong feelings, raucous debate, and occasional renditions of the famous "Anti-Confederation Song."[7] The lyrics may stir the latent embers of Newfoundland "nationalism" but should also remind us of how such sentiments mask the prejudices and power struggles that lurk behind them, along with the complex of intimate and existential reasons for fearing, or welcoming, the wolves at our doors.

---

6 Higgins, "Argentia."

7 The song was recorded and released by Newfoundland trad-music veterans Shanneygannock in 2013.

6th. January 1949.

Joseph R. Smallwood Esq.,
St. John's.

Dear Sir:-

As I have heard over the radio about your arrival back from Ottawa, it has been forecast that union with Canada will be consummated the 31st. day of March 1949.

Sir as I am aware that after union is consummated there will be quite a few changes made in the opening of new positions in the branch of civil service, therefore I have availed of the oppurunity to put an application in to you for a position in the civil service branch in St. John's. My application goes to you as Director of the Family Allowance Plan or Assistant Director, that is if the position is not already filled, or maybe through your understanding you would be able to place me at something else after I give you my qualifications.

I am at present time employed with the American Army, and I hold a position as Clerk in the cost section of the Head Office. My standard of education is grade X1, and through the recommendations I have received I am a good employee. My age is 21 years October past, and even though you may consider my age young, I think I would be capable of taking either one of these positions after a short while with the Department.

Sir if my application is accepted maybe I could go to St. John's this Spring for an interview with you. My home town is [community].

Wishing You A Happy New Year Sir; And Thrusting To Hear From You,
I Am Your Most Obedient Humble Servant,

Sgd

January 15, 1949

Dear Mr. [name redacted]:

Thank you for your letter, which I have read carefully. I expect that since you wrote this letter you have seen in our local papers, the advertisement of the Civil Service Commission of Canada to be stationed in Newfoundland. No doubt you have obtained one of the application forms and filled it in.

You will understand, of course, that I have nothing to do with the Federal Civil Service in Newfoundland. Before many weeks are over I may have something to do with the Civil Service of the Provincial Government of Newfoundland. After that date I would be glad to hear from you, and to do anything in my power to assist you.

Sincerely yours,

J.R. SMALLWOOD.

Jan 10/49

Mr J R Smallwood
Duckworth Street
St. John's

Dear Sir

I have been waiting for family allowance papers but up to now have not received them. They are not at our post office in [our community]. I would like to have sheet to fill in. I am more than proud that you have succeeded.

History will record your wonderful steps. You will keep a lot of children in Newfoundland from starvation.

Yours Truly
[married couple, names redacted]

January 15, 1949.

Dear Mr. & Mrs. [names redacted]:

Thank you for your letter. I am a little surprised that the Family Allowance forms have not arrived at your Post Office by January 10, the date of your letter. I have no doubt that they arrived by this time, in which case you will have no difficulty getting one. If not, I suggest that you obtain your form from the Post Office in some nearby place such as [community names redacted].

If you have any further difficulty in the matter please telegraph us collect and we will see that the matter is taken care of.

Again thanking you for writing.

Sincerely yours,

J.R. SMALLWOOD

4-17-49

Government House
St. John's

The Hon. Mr. Smallwood.

Dear Sir.

Being a Veteran of the first world's war, I am physically unfit for work. I am told that all veterans are now to receive a pension.

If such is the case would you please have my name and no. offered to at the war office; my regimental no. [redacted].

Thanking you

I am

Aug 12th/1949

Hon, J R Smallwood
Premier
Newfoundland

Dear Sir

I am writing to know if you there is yet any chance of me getting some help from your government, I am a cripple, & I wrote to you before elections, & you told me at that time, their was no pensions for cripples, so I never heard anything about it yet, I would like to know what can be done, if anything, I would like for you to let me know if I would have to write to anyone else in the government regarding it.

Yours truly

Sept 10, 1949

Hon. J. R. Smallwood,
St. John's

Dear Sir,

A large percentage of the people here are depending on relief due to the poor fishery. I heard your suggestion to start working on the roads with pick and shovel and appeal to you to start the road here. It would be very beneficial to the people here and is only a short distance ... from ... road to the head of the harbour.

Hoping you will give it your favorable consideration.

Yours very truly,

Mar. 2/50

Mr. Smallwood

Dear Sir

I understand there is a Fisherman lone bank Set up to help out the fishermen with equipment which they need as I need a new engine for my boat My engine is practurley worn out and I want to herring nets to secure bait in the Summer time two and three quarter mesh and also I would like to purchase a Macherl net for hauling Macherl as the macherl do be very plentiful in the summer time ground shores if I had a good Macherl net I wouldnt have to work on relief I would be able to earn a good living I dont know the right address so I am riting you I know you will send me the adress of the lone banks trusting you will do your best for me as I worked hard for you in Elections. Yours

---

March 9th, 1950

Dear Mr. [name redacted],

Thank you for your letter. The Government proposes to set up a Fishermans Assistance Loan Bank, but the Board has not yet been set up. Just as soon as it is you will know all about it, who to write, etc. However, do not hesitate to write me at any time.

Yours sincerely,

J.R. SMALLWOOD,
PREMIER.

April 2nd 1950

Hon - J.R. Smallwood
St. John's

Dear Sir.

Don't throw this in the waste paper Basket. read down a few lines, "I wrote you concerning Hired trucks with the highway. Dept, of public works, Now that department refuses to insure us for employment insurance.

I wrote the minister of labour But received very little Satisfaction if I was working on relief work or living on dole. I wouldent have any trouble to get assistance.

But as I can keep of the dole I am not given a chance to make my own living.

If your government, don't help those who try to help themselves, if we will all be living on dole. I never got dole in my life But I want to see a square deal. What I want to know is why the Dept refuses to unsure us.

Because, we are driving our own truck, when we are hired with them, Sorry to take up so much of your time

Yours Truly

April 25th, 1950.

Dear Mr. [name redacted] ,

Thank you for your letter. The Unemployment Insurance Department have certain rules and regulations which they must follow and they cannot change them for any individual person. If you were eligible to come under the Unemployment Insurance you would certainly be insured. Apparently you are not eligible and that is why you and others in the same position cannot be insured.

Yours sincerely,

J.R. SMALLWOOD
PREMIER.

July 22nd 1950

Premier J.R. Smallwood
St. John's
Nfld

Dear Sir.

I would appreciate if you could get me a job on the Highroads. I am looking for employment the whole summer and never got any.

Theres a truck working out this way and there are not all ex service men that are on her. They are a business man on her too. Could you please get me a job on her even if it is when she comes here I am a family man and have no way of earning anything. Thanking you
Please reply as soon as possible

Your truly

July 29/50

The Hon Prime Minister
J.R. Smallwood
St. John's

Dear Mr. Smallwood:

I wish to congratulate you on your splendidly inspiring address at the Burn's night, and comment your plans for the people of our Country.

Things may not look very bright but they are prosperous in comparison to what our position would have been under other leadership.

I am very pleased to have approved of it by vote so as there will never be this extremity of miseries for our people under Confederation.

I enclose a clipping from the Canadian "Ensign" on your decisions respecting our school system for the province and other matters relative to good morals.

These public pronouncements at this particular time can greatly alley the fears that were so often expressed during the early part of the year.

Your gesture proves to all great moral Courage, and will be remembered longer than we realize.

We wish you continued success in the new political year.

Yours Faithfully,

no reply necessary.

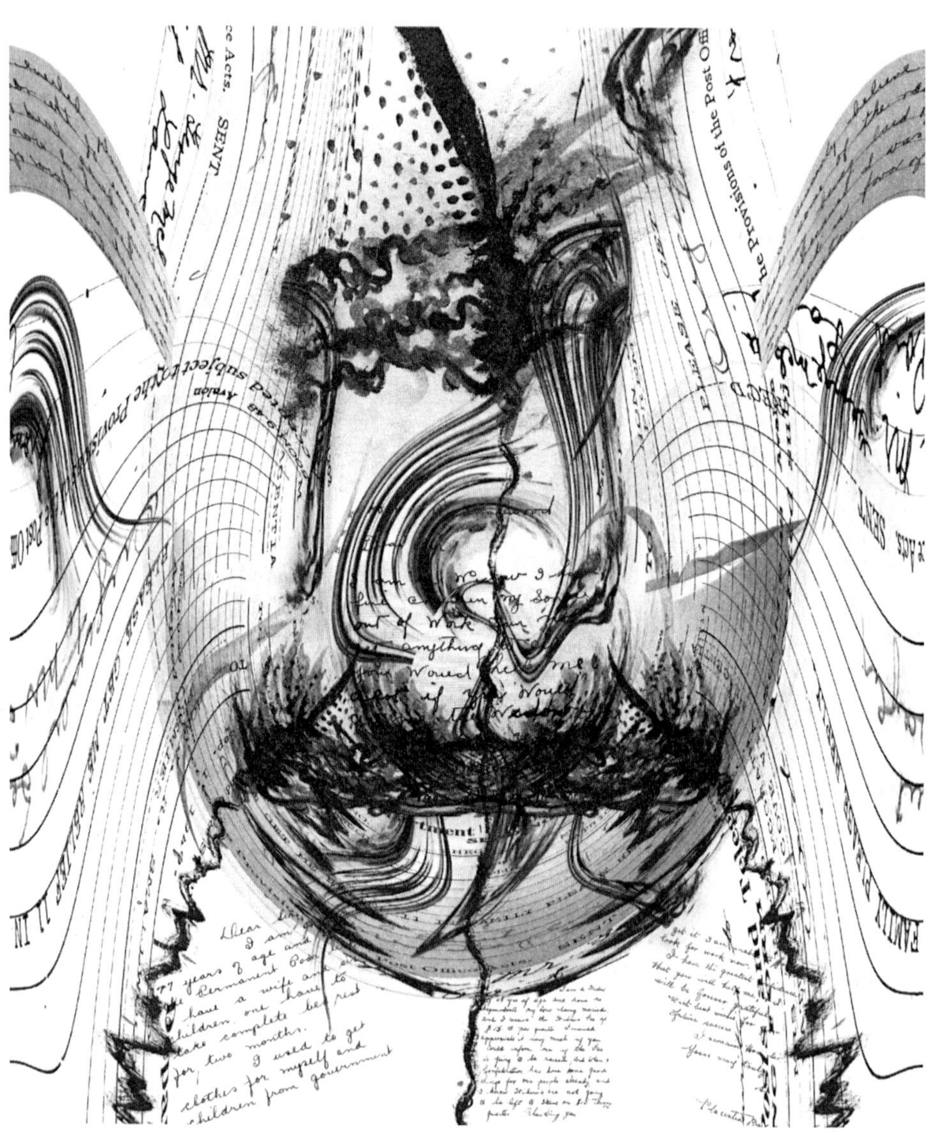
SENT.
the Provisions of the Post Of
77 years of age and
Permanent Post
have a wife and
take complete bed rest
for two months.
I used to get
clothes for myself and
children from government
look for work now.

PLACENTIA WEST

RELIEF REPLY

Violet Drake

AS I ENCOUNTERED THE LIVES of residents across Placentia West within these letters to Joey Smallwood, a collective voice of struggle and suffering emerged that is overwhelmingly present throughout their words. Paired alongside countless pleas was a specific trust in Smallwood, who was expected to have the best interest of the people in heart and mind. Whether this notion was strategic or naive, many held the undoubted belief that the new premier of Newfoundland would certainly take care of his people so that they weren't "going to be left to starve." Whether or not this hope was fulfilled can only be seen through further historical analysis, including diving further into the archive for more answers.

My response to this project, RELIEF REPLY, is a distorted multimedia cascade of ink, paper, and paint swirled and serrated together using both photos of the archival letters and original abstract visual art. It was crucial to me to find a form that reflected the reality that these letters were written by rural people whose words are just fragments of full lives that existed well beyond the few pages found within the archive. For me, the perfect form for this is an illustrative interplay between the words themselves, the paper holding them, and the ink used to inscribe the residents' voices coalescing into each other. Together, these elements anchor the residents' stories as central to not only the structural skeleton of the piece but also as the ultimate visual-poetic link between the archive and all of us.

RELIEF REPLY is my attempt to reconcile the historical subjugation the people of this place endured with contemporary archival desires to highlight pieces of our recorded history often overlooked or forgotten. The lived realities of Placentia West's residents detailed in these letters saw few supports for its disabled members, little government acknowledgement of children, the elderly, or widows, and even a large lack of compassion or opportunity for its most traditionally privileged: able working-class men whose role was to provide as much as they could for their families. This piercing desolation felt across many differing lives throughout these various communities, closely intertwined or seeming disconnected, is what I seek to highlight here. No matter whose words you find yourself pulled toward within my design, all of us touched by these letters today find ourselves reckoning with the ways those before us faced injustice. These are the voices and realities that reverberate into our present, echoing a reminder to us how much and how little of history changes as time moves.

Jan 28th
1948

Mr Joseph Smallwood.
St. John's

Dear Sir.

I recieved your letter last fall before elections. you wrote me to vote for you. I did so & a good many more as well as me.

You promised on your letter to rise my pension but you did not do so yet. I cannot live on 20 cts a day. my only son was a great help to me but he is married now at Hr. Grace. and he is not able to help me now he got enough to do for himself. I havent caught a fish this seven year because I am crippled up with rewematism you would'nt expect me to earn now up in eight years of age and no one to help me. You would'nt like to have to live on 20cts a day like me.

My next pension is due the last of march & if you are a man to your owrd it will be higher than what it is now. If now I cant live.
So Be a man to your word.
Write by next mail & let me know what you are going to do. I wants something to live on the rest of my days.
So Dear Sir my name & address is

please answer this quick.
Yours Sincerely

Apr. 21, 1949

Hon. J.R. Smallwood
Government House
St. John's.

Dear Sir,

I humbly beg your pardon for taking the liberty to write you this letter, but now that you are in a position to help me, I would like to bring to your attention the fact that I am a widow and was receiving my widows allowance up to about five years ago, when it was taken from me by our relieving Officer [name redacted].

I have only one son and he is my sole support, and at the time my order was taken he was barely seventeen, a mere school boy.

He has never had steady employment and only manages to get a few months work during the summer, mostly with the Highroads as a common labor man. I have no other income of any kind and I have missed the widow's allowance very much. In fact our circumstances were so poor this past winter that we were obliged to apply for relief which was also denied us. At present, my son is unemployed and has been since last October.

I would appreciate a reply from you at once and hoping you will do your best in my behalf

I am

Yours respectfully,

May 17th/49

Rt. Hon J.R. Smallwood:
Premier of NfLD

Dear Sir: -

We received our family Allowance for April. and like a great many more Newfoundland families we feel greatly indebted to you for your efforts in brining such a fine thing to our country. It is indeed a blessing to thousands of mothers, who like myself were having a hard time trying to make both ends meet. Naturally it is of great Benefit to all, but especially to us poorer class of people:
I am not a widow but unfortunately my husband and I are separated since October 1945. I am the sole support of my three children. I received $15 per month relief for them until the family Allowances were distributed but now it has been discontinued.
Is that how it is supposed to be? I understood that you could still get relief and your family allowance too. I thought the so-called "Baby Bonus" were separate from every thing else. I wrote our Relieving Officer [name redacted] at [community] but received no answer from him.
Please advise me about the matter as I don't think it should be cut off.
The family Allowances are supposed to be giving the children a higher standard of living, additional necessities and better Nourishment etc., but if cases like mine are the rule it is Just about the same as before. I got $15 relief for my three children before and now I lose my $15 to get $16 per month family Allowances for the same children, so there is not much to my advantage in that other people tell me that I should still get my relief. That the family Allowance is Canada's Gift to Newfoundland children so I decided the one and only thing to do was to write to you.

I know you are doing your very Best for all of us. and I hope that each and every one will give you their full support int eh forthcoming Elections.
There are only about 70 persons of Voting age in this harbour. but I am sure that at least 65 of them are in favor of the Smallwood Government
Hoping you can give me some light on this matter.
Wishing you all the Best of Luck & Success.

I am

Respectfully yours

June 2nd/49.

Somebody did a golden deed;
Somebody proved a friend in need;
Somebody thought "'Tis sweet to live;
Somebody said, "I'm glad to give;
Somebody fought a valiant fight;
Somebody lived to shield the night;
And that "somebody" was "You".

The Premier.
Hon. J. R. Smallwood
St. John's.

Dear Mr. Smallwood:

Please accept my heartiest congratulations and best wishes, for already you have indeed made our poor, miserable lives happier, easier and fuller.

We should treasure you as a precious Jewel because you are the only one in Your position that ever wanted to help the "down and out person". I would do anything in this world for you, 'cause I have seven small children and I tell you we have met difficult time.

Wishing you all kinds of cusses and thanking you a million times for all you are doing for us.

Respectfully yours,

June 6 1949.[1]

Honourable J.R. Smallwood
Colonial Building
St John's Nfld.

Dear Mr. Smallwood:
I have not
the shadow of a doubt as to the
fulfilment of your promise re.
finding employment for me. And
I am only writing now because
you asked me in your last letter
to keep in touch with you.
I know
that no one will understand better
than you. the problems involved
by a long period of unemployment.
For me this is developing into a
very serious financial difficulty
a short while ago I had some
Prestige with the merchants in and
around Burin. I forfeited that
prestige, gladly by supporting
Confederation and by backing the
F.W.P.U. of Burin.[2] *I would*
rather die than face those business
men now seeking Credit.
I would like work as a time-Keeper
for the Govt on the Burin Peninsula.
If this was impossible I would gladly

1 Three 1949 letters from the same correspondent (June 6, 1949, July 14, 1949, and August 17, 1949) have been transcribed following the lineation in the original letters, which matched the size of the letter paper used. This form of transcription can allow for a different reading of the letters.

2 The Fishermen's and Workmen's Protective Union, formed in one of the bigger fish plants in Burin in 1947, existed until the late 1960s.

work Anywhere in the Province and there are many jobs I think I could qualify for. I know you are a very busy man and I hate to bother you but just now I have no choice. I request you to try and place me in the very near future if Possible. And I beleive you will. I congratulate you on your election and I pray that God will help you and guide you to justify the great trust placed in You by such an overwhelming majority of your Countrymen.

Yours very sincerely

June 8th 1949

The Honorable Joseph R Smallwood,
St. John's.

Dear Mr. Smallwood;

I have heard about all your good work so as I need help I decided to write to you. I am a fisherman. I am now unable to endure the work of the fishery because I have a cripple hand I have 2 fingers cut off my left hand and one finger broken. I dont know any one in town so I thought that maybe you could help me. I wanted to see if you could please get me a job. I havent much education because when I was ten my father died and I had to go fishing. But I would be very thankful and Pleased with carpenter work or anything that do not require much education.

I have a wife and two children but thanks to the Family Allowance they do not need much help. If you can help you in any way, please let me know by return Bar Haven If Possible though I suppose this year is a busy one with you.

In closing I say

Congratulations on your Victory,

Thank I remain,

Yours truly,

June 11th/49

Hon J R Smallwood.

Premier St John's

Dear Mr. Smallwood

First of all, I send you hearty Congratulations on your recent success of being elected as the Premier of Nfld the 10th Province of Can.

We feel confident you are the man to fill that place as you understand ost about the people especially the poor

no doubt you have received many letters since you were elected

We need a friend now & I am writing you to see if you can arrange that we get a little help.

My husband is not well. He have had Berrie-Berrie[3] *for a long time he had been in the Hospital receiving electric treatment & other remedies but it has all failed to cure him this year. he is Just miserable all the time & have been trying to catch a few lobsters this spring in that condition to get a living this past three weeks he saw the Docter twice & he told him he is also suffering from a bad strain in the back.*

We only have one child home now & on the 19th day of May we had to take her from school & rush her to the [hospital] for a operation for Appendicitis We have her home now but the Docter says she cant go back to school any more this term but She may sit for exams as we live near the School.

She is taking grade IX this year. She is very thin & runed down and needs food to build her up.

Mr Smallwood that is why I am writing you as she is not getting the family Allowance <u>*as she was 16 Nov past*</u>

She is the only pupil in our school with the exception of one young man who is

3 Beriberi, a disease of malnutrition, results from a lack of thiamine, or Vitamin B1. For more on beriberi in Newfoundland and Labrador, see J.T.H. Connor, "Malnutrition Research in Newfoundland and Labrador in the 1900s to 1930s, Brown Flour, and the 'Dole Plague' of Beriberi, Part 1: The First Malnutrition Research Wave, 1900s–1930s," *Newfoundland Quarterly* 111, no. 4 (2019): 44–49; J.T.H. Connor, "Malnutrition Research in Newfoundland and Labrador in the 1900s to 1930s, Brown Flour, and the 'Dole Plague' of Beriberi, Part 2: The First Malnutrition Research Wave, 1900s–1930s," *Newfoundland Quarterly* 112, no. 1 (2019): 48–53; and James Overton, "Brown Flour and Beriberi: The Politics of Dietary and Health Reform in Newfoundland in the First Half of the Twentieth Century," *Newfoundland Studies* 14, no. 1 (1998): 1–27.

not getting the family Allowance. She is so mall you would only take her to be 14.

her intentions were to try & et a job in her Holidays to earn money to go back to school in sept but she can't do that now as she will need the two months rest to be fit to attend school in Sept. and unless we get help some way she wont be able to keep going to get her grades & she is really not strong enough to go out and work hard for a living.

Mr Smallwood we feel sure if anything can be done concerning our need you will do your best

both my Husband & I stood by you & your party in each elections by giving our vote's. Now we are going to trust you to stand by us.

And some how I feel confident that you will

May the Lord richly bless you & yours with good health and success in all your undertakings

Yours Very Sincerely

July 14/49

Hon J. R. Smallwood.
St. John's

Dear Mr Smallwood:
You asked me on a letter a long while ago to keep in touch with you. I wrote you after the provincial election but received no answer so I take it the letter was mislaid, or that you are too busy to answer it. I hate to bother you r take up your valuable time, but cercumstances force me to appeal to you again. As I told you, I forfeited whatever prestige I had with merchants in and around [community] and [community] by supporting Confed--ederation and cannot approach them Seeking credits. Long unemployment is confronting me with financial difficulties and I was hoping you could use me in some capacity in some of Your Departments or in some work around the Country. I have some experience in fisheries Roadbuilding, time keeping and Coal? work and beleive I could qualify in any of those capacities I would appreciate it if you could fit me in somewhere.

Yours very truly

August 17, 1949

Hon. J. R. Smallwood
Premiers Office, St John's.

Dear Mr Smallwood;

This will be the fourth letter I have written you, and received no answer. I am aware that you are a very busy man, and I am also aware that sometimes, letters never get beond secretaries. I cannot accept the beleif that you could forget so soon, or refuse to answer a letter, if you have received the letters I have written.

When, on last April 26th, you promised "to fit me in," in some Capacity, after the election, and failed to do so, you did me a great wrong. You hurt me, more than you can realize.

I depended on your promise, and made no other arrangements, consequently I am now unemployed, and in financial and economic difficulties the like of which I was never in before I cannot seek credit from Dealers as I lost my Prestige with them by supporting Confederation and later the Liberal Party. They know I am in difficulties, and they know that I was expecting a job with the new Govt.

I am not seeking a hand-out, I would rather die first. But I beleived that some of the new Depts. Could use my services, which I would gladly give to the best of my Ability.

I would like again to request your aid, and influence in trying to place me somewhere, I dont care where, but I would prefer to work for

the Fisheries Dept. I have written Canning[4]
twice in Connection with road work and rec. no
answer. Other Communities in our Dist are reporting
the same. If He Continues this attitude, we are
planning to ask for his resignation by organized
groups from all over the District
Expecting to hear from you by return mail and wishing
you the Best of Luck I am Yours truly,

---

4 Patrick Canning was the Liberal Member of the House of Assembly for Placentia West. First elected to the House of Assembly in 1949, he served as an MHA until 1972 and then again from 1975 until 1979, after which he retired from politics.

Aug 18 1949

Mr. Joseph
Small Wood
Dear Sir I receved your letter and thanks vary much for riting to me I know their do be a lot of people rit to you it must be hard for you to answer every one if their do be any work starts and you can see a place for me you plese let me know

Your vary
Truly

Jan 21st 1950

My Dear Hon. Premier

I have been listening attentively recently to your travels and proceedings , and your speech some time ago put a ray of future brightness in my heart and the hearts of many. And what do the future hold in store for us regards the fishery? enough I hope for every man engaged, to make a decent living for his family and himself. What about a chance Captain of some of the schooners you have at St Johns at present! I mean those Iceland schooners or should the fishery products be getting more dragers, would you kindly recommend me to them for Captain of one of them. I may be causing you some trouble, for which I beg of you to excuse me, butr I may be in the same anxious position about this affair of mine as you were about Confederation and we backed you in every way. If a chance arises you may contact my wife in due time for me to get the report and reach you at a convenient time. I am leaving [my community] tonight to take up work again at the fishery in Halifax. I am going mate with Captain [name], or if you wish to contact myself here is my address.

I am forty-four years of age and have been constantly engaged in the deep-sea fishery both in Nfld and Lunenburg. I took my best experience from that famous and well-known Captain .... So thanking you for your kind attention and hoping to hear from you at an early date.

I enclose

your sincere friend

The best of luck and success to you in all your undertakings for (1950)

PORT DE GRAVE

Letting in the Flood

Sharon King-Campbell

Champion of an island of the hungry,
their fingers frozen stiff, black underneath the nails—
you are their Hercules, at least along this shore
your portrait hangs in every kitchen (ninety
percent anyway), but the kingdom you've inherited
is broken, ravaged, ravenous, and their concerns
flow in with the tide, seep upward, soak your shoes—
the price of fish, sir, and the benefit come down
from Ottawa and we don't see a cent?
It's dangerous to shake too many hands, to glint your eye
or quirk the corner of your mouth at every voter
cause they know you now, they know you like a neighbour
and they'll call on you, each of them, for their
cup of sugar: sick relief and doctor's bills, or fare
for a grandchild's passage (sure your mother was that one's
mother's cousin, and would you turn down family?)
and what to do about the woman taking her husband
unsuccessfully to court, what are you to do with that?
Each one of them reaching for a piece of you,
their blackened fingernails on their cold hands seeking out
just a bit of scratch

April 9/49

Dear Mr. Smallwood,

I have been laid up for the pass five year with T.B. and have been receiving the sick relief for the pass three year up until February when I had to go to the hospital for a slight operation, while I was gone the children were cut off and I haven't been able to get it back since. Its no way one can see … the relieving officer or get him by phone because he is always drunk he is right out on it this pass week no one can see him. And if I can't get any help from the department theres nothing left for me and my family to do but starve of which the time is drawing near when we will be without food. Mr. Smallwood I am writing you as I don't know which department to write since the change over and trusting you will see that I get my sick ration back as well as the childrens of which I have four or some other relief which will give my wife, children and myself ample supply of food Trusting you will look into matter soon as possible and that you won't take this letter as an Insult

Yours Respectfully

May 7th 1949

Mr J.R. Smallwood

Dear Sir You will be surpprised to get a letter from me but seeing and believing your my only hope I said to my husband I would ask you what you could do to help me get my boy home. Sir he was overseas 5 years and 9 months 3 years of that time he was out to Madagaster when it was taken landing troops in Itley he was a first class Stoker much moore you can hear of him then when he came back he was given lefe home to see us during that time his father was sick and an old man and he our youngest boy our only support I only receive $6.20 from him monthly but when he came home I went to see [two names redacted] took me to see him and I showed him what I received he gave me 15 dollars more monthly and plased [name redacted] our boy in St Johns so he would be near us but after a little wile I received a letter from our boy telling us he was going to see it to a finish he said mother I feels I am letting my palls down who I stood shoulder to shoulder by so he went and seen it to a end. Sir when he came he brought his bride after he came he got a job as police at Argentia then his wife got discontented she went home last July 12 on the Newfoundlander took her 2 dear little boys so in October 18 [our boy] went taught he could get a job as he was promised before he came home but that he found very hard to get so she and him have decided to come home to take care of us as my husband have been in bead of and on sence December and yet in bead he will be 88 years of age the 8 of October it is manny years sence he could leave home to earn a dollar we got $350.00 dollars towards their passage but we needs 70 dollars moore for the other little boy half fair but we cannot get a passage for them until October so the girl in the office told she said there was no chance yet as the ships were all booked full Sir will you please try to get a chance home for him we as a family did our best for you no seckret we talked voted for Confederation as you asked us we cheered and waved for you as you passed perhaps you can remember the day you drove true we went out by the gate as you came up just a house above [name redacted] Shop Sir our 3 sons and 2 daughters and our 2 selves did our best that was 12 out of our family we raised 8 children all married we got 1 daughter married in [place] another in [community] and the other daughter in [another community]. All in [country] and we are hear all alone my husband in bead sick under the Docketer care my self with a verry bad leg the Docketer said it was a ulster so we needs our boy home and he told us they will come if we can arrange their passage with the [company]. So we sold our cow got $100.00 one hundred to-wards their passage then I went to the Bank and got a loan of 250 that made $ 3.50 dollars but we are told now the baby is a year old and that will be another 70 dollars he promises on the word of a man who ever pays he will see them paid as he gets home and gets work last *spring he voted and so did his wife sir if you can only get him home it will do us a wonderful good for I have and still having a verry hard time by night and day caring for my husband and a 10 dollars a month to live on only the help of our boy [name redacted] I cannot think what we would do Sir please pardon me if I am asking too much but as a mother I am asking your help for my he is a good man spent the prime of his life overseas and the other boy [name redacted] was in the Merchant Navey and our other boy [name redacted] offered for the Airforces we as a family are not afraid of work we were 25 years going to the fishery and taking all the children up and down every year we were stationed at Indian Harbour Labrador we rased them all and gave them very good learning now we are old and no help Sir if you can only see a way open to get our boy home you will brighten our last days more then words can tell yours truly*

May 28/49

To. Hon J R Smallwood
St. Johns

Dear Sir

First of all I must congratulate you on the many votes you got. Why wouldent any body vote for you especially the mothers. I am more than thankful for the family allowance myself. I would give you twenty votes if I could, altho some people thing I am on the other side. I felt so sore over something that happened yesterday I had to sit down and write you. A liberal car was going around here. I asked him what about taking me to the booth. He formed some excuse and did not take me. I suppose on account of my husband's people being Tory's they think we are all the same but my husband & I are out for our own selves and we are going to do what we think is best for our two children. Anyway Mr. Smallwood I went in what they call a Tory car but I can assure my vote was for you and I'm sure I can speak for my husband but he is away from home. Its not the car you go in tell your vote but its where you mark your X. I know my father was a liberal. I can remember a bit about it. I came from [community] and the most of the people there would not say Tory besides voting for it and I think they are the same now. I have a little business started now. I was wondering if you could give me a little donation towards getting a phone in. I have two small children my husband is away from home it's a job for me to get out and order my good. I hope its not asking you for too much.

Wishing you the best of luck in everything I know you will never let us down.
Yours very truly

June 8th 1949

To

Premier J.R. Smallwood

Dear Sir:-

Heartiest congratulations on the splendid liberal victory you won, and may the Great God abide with you to carry on.

Well Mr. Smallwood I am a fisherman and as we fishermen doesn't get much of a show in this country, I want to find out a few facts. First, there is the unemployment insurance, they say it's not for fishermen, well, who is it supposed to be for? I'm aware it's for the unemployed, and that they who are now receiving the unemployment insurance were supposed to work so long before they could receive the insurance. As far as I can learn, there are men who were fishing last summer fishing on the Labrador, came home, and worked two weeks, and now they can get the unemployment insurance, and still there is nothing set aside for the fishermen. Now there are men who work on the Whalers, at Hawkes Bay, Labrador, they get it and that's fishing![1] *Now if a fisherman goes to Labrador, when he is paid off in the fall, he may get two hundred dollars, sometimes more and sometimes less, a he has a family of six or seven, and he can't anything to do, he applys for the dole and he can't get it until every dime is gone. Maybe it's the first of April before he can get it. Now what is there to encourage fishermen to go through all kinds of hardship and when it's all over, he have'nt anything, and can't get anything, I think it's the fishermen who should be getting the unemployment insurance, and if they are not the toiling men of this country there are'nt any.*

Yours truly,

---

1 For more on whaling in Newfoundland and Labrador, see Anthony Bertram Dickinson and Chesley W. Sanger, *After the Basques: The Whaling Stations of Newfoundland and Labrador* (St. John's: DRC Publishing, 2018); A.B. Dickinson and C.W. Sanger, "Newfoundland and Labrador Shore-Station Whaling: The Third Major Phase, 1937–1951," *International Journal of Maritime History* 11, no. 1 (1999): 101–16; C.W. Sanger, A.B. Dickinson, and W.G. Handcock, "Commercial Whaling in Newfoundland and Labrador in the 20th Century," Heritage Newfoundland & Labrador, 1998, https://www.heritage.nf.ca/articles/environment/whaling-in-the-20th-century.php.

June 12. 49

Mr.J.R. Smallwood
Premier of Nfld.

Dear Mr. Smallwood.

I have been advised lately by Doctors since you are elected that I should write to you to know if there is any allowance for a Midwife.[2] *Which I have been doing a great number of years and have never received anything from any source except if there was a person who could pay me and very often nothing, as the people were unable to pay. In all my experience I've never refused to go to any person. I wrote to the Commission Govt. when it was in power and they replied there was nothing for "Midwifes".*

So I am appealing to you. I have been your supporter in all political activities, which helped to make Nfld. the province of Canada.

I am not old enough for the old age pension and am a widow for 11 years. It needs no telling what I receive quarterly. I have no children of my own, at present I live with an only stepchild. I fail to see why there is nothing for this midwife work. I register all babies at the Health and Welfare St. John's and look after the mothers until they are well. I was unable to talk with you when I saw you each time. So I thought I may write to you wishing you every success as I know you have and will continue so. Hoping for a favourable reply.

Midwife

2 For more on the history of midwifery in Newfoundland and Labrador, see Pearl Herbert and Association of Midwives of Newfoundland and Labrador, *History of Midwifery in Newfoundland and Labrador* (St. John's: Memorial University, 2014), and Esther Slaney Brown, *Labours of Love: Midwives of Newfoundland and Labrador* (St. John's: DRC Publishing, 2007).

July 25 1949

Premier Smallwood.

Dear Sir.

I am a poor sick woman suffering from heart trouble and skin disease and I am spitting blood all the time. And I have a husband who is beating me all the time. I have had him to law many a time but he tells a whole lot of lies and gets clear while I have to suffer. He is always making home brew drinks all he can drink then goes mad. I am living in a lonely place and my life is in danger all the time if there is no way that he can be stopped from beating me and making this stuff. Dr. [name] is treating me but he is away now on holiday. I have payed all the time for my treatment but my bit of money is nearly gone and I am writing you kind sir to know if you can do anything for me in this regard to a Dr or hospital for my husband is not earning. I was a widow when he married me and I sold my house so that is the bit of money I am spending. I have never got anything from the government. But what you have done for poor people I know you will do for me.

Your's truly,

Aug.8th 49

Hon. J.R. Smallwood
P.M. St Johns

Hon. Sir.

I have a crew of men on the Labrador coast cod-fishing and its very strongly rumoured that the price will be to fishermen around two dollars or two fifty per quintal less than last year.

We are all aware that rope lines and twines fishermen oil clothes and boots and other articles are more expensive to fishermen than last season. So please use you very strongest power to see that the fishermen get at least last seasons price for their fish.

Thanking you that you may be interested in this matter.

I remain
Yours truly

September 27th, 1949,

Dear Mr. [name redacted],

Thank you for your letter. The price of Labrador fish has not as yet been set, but I can assure you that the highest possible price will be paid for same.

Yours sincerely,

J.R. SMALLWOOD,
PREMIER.

November 3rd 49

Hon. J.R. Smallwood
Premier
St. Johns, Nfld

Hon Dear Sir:

In September I wrote you about Labrador Codfish shipped on the coast. Up to the present time we don't know what price per quintal the merchant is going to pay for same. When starting off this spring we expected to get last seasons prices namely $9.25 per quintal in fact I think it was broadcast in September that merchants should settle up the Labrador fishermen as last years price. Now Sir please use your influence and see that the Labrador shore fishermen are paid last seasons price. I imagine there was 60 or 70 fishermen from this place in the Labrador this past summer and if given last seasons price for their fish I would say that 80 per cent of these men wouldn't need assistance this winter. At any rate its time now to know what the price will be and get paid for our fish. Thanking you for your interest in this matter I remain

Yours truly

April 3th 1950

To the Honorable J R Smallwood I say honorable sir because you have done more for the poor of N F L D then all rest of the premears and politicans of the past eighty years You said when you made your final lecture in [my community] you were going to do something for [this community] well sir I think you have done a good lot for [our community] we don't forget it either if you were to visit every home in [this community] you would see your picture in almost every kitchen framed well ninety percent of the homes in [this community] so that is something that never happened in [this community] in all the responsible governments of the past the people here sir will never forget what you have done well sir for myself I and [my wife] did our best to bring about confederation if you took notice when you were in [our community] that big hill the south west side of [our community] I suspose it is three or four hundred feet from top to bottom well sir I climbed that hill and stuck a flag on it that day when we went in with Canada I like many others want to get something better then six cents a day to live on ... My mothers name was [name redacted] I often herd herd herd talking about Mrs. Smallwood I would like to have a little talk with you when I comes over when the roads is open if it were possible if I had the address of your house I heard there was quite a lot houses to be built in St Johns this somer I was thinking if you could get me a job I am not much of a carpenter but I could do rough carpenters work or if I could get a job carpenters helper I would be quite satisfied if it weren't to hard work I am sixty five years old the 19 of this month I haven't got either motor boat or engine to go fishing and it is to hard work for me now to go out in a row boat I want to earn a honest living if I could get work I am not old enough to get my old age pension and I suppose I am to old to get a job on the high road if I could get this chance it looks like the man that is 65 now is going to have it I hard I hope you will excuse me for taking up so much of your time as I know you are a very bissy man I am your humble servent

ST. BARBE

"DESTITUTE RECEIVED NO MONEY SINCE MARCH PLEASE ADVISE"[1]

Gina Snooks

IT WAS COLD, my grandmother's house. That's how I remember it. I remember the way the wind howled through the cracks of the old wood and how the curtains moved on a cold night. My grandmother's house (the one my grandfather built)—Nan's house with its tiny kitchen counters, fit just for her. The average height woman, like me, would get a backache bending over to wash dishes in that sink. My grandmother's house, the one with the most spectacular view of the harbour.

Although she did not write them, it was my Nan who I thought of when I first read these words: "DESTITUTE RECEIVED NO MONEY SINCE MARCH PLEASE ADVISE." The words—a brief but haunting message—constitute the entirety of a telegram sent on behalf of a woman in White Bay to J.R. Smallwood on September 7, 1949, just a few months after Newfoundland and Labrador joined Confederation with Canada.[2]

"The dead / do not like to be / forgotten."[3]

1 See COLL-075, ASC. I first explored this telegram in 2010 in Women's Studies 3000: Feminist Approaches to Research Methods taught by Dr. Sonja Boon.

2 This telegram is included among the White Bay letters, p. 409–23.

3 M. Jacqui Alexander, *Pedagogies of Crossing: Meditations on Feminism, Sexual Politics, Memory, and the Sacred* (Durham: Duke University Press, 2006), 289.

What could this brief but haunting telegram possibly tell me about the woman who had written it? The message was sent from the post office just a short walk from my grandmother's house, where my mother had been born just a few years previously. The telegram did not tell me that the woman who had written it was a widow or that she was seventy years old at the time—that information was in other archival records. Nor did the telegram tell me that this woman had lived with her daughter and that she was a quiet lady with grey hair—it was her former neighbour who told me that.[4] In fact, the telegram told me very little, either about the woman who had sent it or about the life that she had lived. Instead, the telegram left but a small trace of who the woman was, and maybe that is the reason I was—and remain—haunted by her words. When I try to imagine her life story, I think of all the women I know who have lived along this coastline—my mother, grandmothers, aunts, and neighbours—and I wonder how much of their life stories I can read between the lines of what isn't said in the telegram.

In 1949, my grandmother was a young married woman with two young daughters, but I wonder if Nan's life was all that different from that of the seventy-year-old. Perhaps the biggest difference between Nan's life and the life of the woman who had sent that telegram is that, in 1949, Nan was not yet a widow. But if Nan had been a widow, would she too have been a destitute woman in outport Newfoundland?

Before Newfoundland and Labrador joined Confederation with Canada, many outport communities were on the edge of survival and with limited resources many elderly folks were dependent upon Old Age Pension or widows' allowance for financial support, which was a meagre $72 per annum.[5] Hardly enough to survive on, I would think. With the support of federal monies, Old Age Pension increased to $40.62 per month beginning in May of 1949.[6] Although still a meagre amount, this increase likely improved the livelihood of many widows. Arguably it was the promise of federal monies that swayed the vote toward joining Canada among rural Newfoundlanders and Labradorians.[7]

4 [Name redacted], interview by Gina Snooks, La Scie, NL, November 6, 2010.

5 Marilyn Porter, "'She was skipper of the shore-crew': Notes on the History of the Sexual Division of Labour in Newfoundland," *Labour/Le Travail* 15 (1985): 112. Stuart R. Godfrey, *Human Rights and Social Policy in Newfoundland 1832–1982: Search for a Just Society* (St. John's: Harry Cuff Publications Ltd., 1985), 46.

6 Godfrey, *Human Rights*, 104.

7 Christine Elizabeth Abbott, "Exploring Women's Subjectivities: Women in a Newfoundland Outport" (master's thesis, Queens's University, 2004).

Was it Old Age Pension that this destitute woman had been inquiring about in her telegram to the premier of Canada's newest province? The truth is, I cannot know what prompted her to send that telegram to Smallwood. I can only imagine her life story. I can only imagine her walking along the same road near my grandmother's house that I myself have walked many times—and perhaps that is why her words haunt me still.

Jan 14, 1949.

J.R. Smallwood esq,
National Convention,
Government House,
St. John's

Dear Sir,

I am writing you in connection with my husbands illness. He is sixty six years old and was paralyzed July 20th 1948. He is a bed patient having no use of his right arm or leg. I his wife am also partially cripple owing to having my leg broken some years ago. My husband is a keen confederate.

We have one son twenty four years old. He cannot go away from home to work as we are entirely dependant on him for wood, water and the ordinary household chores. The money can make around home is not enough to maintain us. On the other hand our son is at the age when boys begin to look for homes of their own.

I want to know if you could possibly intercede to the proper authorites to gain some assistance or pension for my husband. Ive been to our local ranger and District nurse and they told me I couldn't get anything unless the patient was Tubercular. My husband is just as helpless and just as handicapped by his illness as any and I feel he deserves government aid.

Remembering one of your political speeches you said "that the sick and needy would receive help if confederation was voted in and before it came into effect officlally. I'm applying to you because my husband and I need help badly and quickly.

I feel confident that youll do something for us.

Yours Truly

I am a native of [community] but I want you to address all correspondence to [another community]

April 12/49

RT. Hon. J. R. Smallwood
Government Bldg
St Johns

Dear Sir: -

I would like to know if the Acetylene Lightkeepers of this Province are going to get any raise in salary, at the Present time I am getting the sum of ($17.00) per month and have to hire men + Boats to help Put the tanks to the station approximately 1 ½ miles away from the warf on which they are landed By the Costal Boats.

I would appreciate it very much if you would look into the matter and see if the Poor forgotten lightkeepers of this Province can get a living wage.

At the rate we are getting at Present we have got to seek elsewhere for employment and that is usualy when something goes wrong at the station, then you have to return home and loose a couple of days Pay which amts to approx. $6.80 per day whereas we get the approx. sum of 56c Per day as lightkeepers.

I cannot understand why we cant get the same rate of Pay as other Civil servants or at least a living rate.

Another thing when I have a mans Boat if it is damaged in any way I have to stand to the Cost my self and as the island is a Place where it is not always wise to land, there is a Boat here which belonged to the Custom department But which is not in use as we have no customs department here now could not this Boat be had for the work of the light station.

Mr. Smallwood I beg of you to give this every consideration and advise me the gross results.

I am a ex-serviceman having served in the Royal Canadian Air Force during the war, also I am a strong supporter of Confederation

Heres hoping for a Better slaray and living conditions with Confederation.

Your Obedient
Servant;

April 25/ 49

The right Hon

J.R. Smallwood

Dear Sir

It is indeed a great honour to sit down and write, such a noble and courageous leader, as you.

I congratulate you sir on a grand, and important job well done

you are all that we the toiling masses stand for in this country, an efficient, and fearless leader.

you are worshiped in these parts with a sincere reverence which I am at loss of words to describe.

Sir there are a few people who do not like you very well, but we don't mind them they are easily overcome.

I have seen people in the past fight for you, not with words alone, but also with muscles I have done my share of protecting your great, and Honourable name.

This past year or two we have seen exciting times, but thank God we have won the fight, and Confederation is now a reality.

I think Sir, and rightly so that only for your untiring attitude, and true conviction we would never have had Confederation.

The people here sir stand behind you all the way to them you are a symbol of all thats good, and pure. I dont mean to be flattering, for these are words which are very true indeed.

I hope the bulk of our people who have been oppressed so much in the past will get their just due in the future.

for myself sir I am a humble fisherman twenty seven years old I have had a scaling licence since 1943 but have been unable to secure a Job. Sir if you could or would use your influence to land me a Job then I would be grateful to you indeed I make this plea to you sir as a humble servant, and hope you will not fail me thank you very much please answer letter sir behind you all the way

Yours dutifully

June 1st/ 1949

Mr. J.R. Smallwood

Dear Sir

I am writing you to ask a few questions conserning a few things regarding family allowences and other things I cannot write very good as you can will see.

To being with I am a widow with seven children six girls and one Boy the oldest fifteen years old a girl she is working as a messanger girl in the telegraph office here at [our community] the three oldest of my children have not received any family allowance the reason is they were not going to school at the time we filled out our form But they have been going since I wrote and told the reason they were out of school sometimes we had nothing to eat other times they had no foot wear most of the time no fuel it's a hard life for widows and orphans here I have Been a widow for almost six years we have been sick hungry and cold a good many time all we ever got was thirty five Dollars a month you know what that could do for light people with cost of living so high, its still high a very little change we still have to pay 16 cents for milk 28 for tomatoes 18 for soup 6 cents for oranges 5 for apples 69 for flour 12 cents for sugar per pound this is only a few of the things 25 cents for S. Pork and Beef 48 cents for Shorting 40 for Blogna 75 for Ham + Bacon

Now Mr Smallwood are we going to have to pay that all the time if so what good will our family allowance Be to us none whatever I would like ot know if I am going to get any allowance for my three children [name redacted] 15 years old [name redacted] 14 years old [name redacted] 12 I have given my three [illegible] for the one thing confederation I would like to know if I voted in vain I go out to work every morning a nine come home a six in the evening for 1.50 a day we would Be starved long ago if god did not give me the health to work

one more thing I want to ask about that is fuel. how are we going to get fule this year the commission goverment gave us towo tons of coal for a year if we dont get any more than that you can send some one around with a gun and shoot us all that would Be a Blessing

I do hope you can Pick out and read what I have written Thank you

June 5 1949

Premier
Hon J R Smallwood

Something tell me that I should rite a letter to you conserning our Place where we lives how we are neglected not look after will this is it we havent no school no foan. No telegrham office. No Bridge to cross this Big river no Ferry. There are 35 children here in this little Place that's from a month old to the age up to 14 years old and there not one child here got education enough to rite a letter. we lives alongside a big river on the east side and there no Bridge across it no ferry. no school here. There a school in the cove. a mile from here. But as I say before there a river to cross. and in the spring he is dangerous to cross. it takes two men to roll the most to do it and late in the fawl. this river freezes up so far out and there is only a small stream in the middle. and some winters its in febuary before he is frozen across. and the road in the winter if children wants to go to school is two miles and a half or mor and there a big [illegible] to go. no one can forse a child to go there. you honour. we are supose to have [illegible] for education But this dont seem much like it. this is a beautifully river lots of salmon in it. there are lots of slamon caught out by sportsmen and local [illegible]. But there are no roads here nothing whatsoever. to interest people to come here. if this place were look after it would mean money to the people and the country. you Honour its not in St. Johns or Corner Brook or grand fawls. Mr George drew should come. its in St. Barbs distrect from Bonne Bay down to flowers cove and thats were he would fine out the plases were there is neglected and forgotten. we has done all we could give our votes for confederation and the liberl party in fast there are all liberls here and I hope you will do all in your power to help these neglected places little chidren no schools to go to. I think I has said all

I am yours truly

if we wants to send a message we got to go nine mile to send it.

Premier of N.F.L.D.
Hon Joseph R Smallwood

June 5/49

Dear Sir.

Congratulations to you I was so glad when I heard the count, to have you Our Premier of Newfoundland. You sertainly fought for us, you sertainly brought Heaven to Our children Already, and we the Poor People sertainly know what it means to them, I am a Poor man. I am a man 31 years of Age, I have a wife and Six children. I am a fisherman Probly you know what a Poor fisherman his, I am not lazey. and I have good Helth thank God. but this have been two failuers right after one another. I was to Bay of islands last fall come home the last of January Herring fishering, I work Hard and maid a failure. the Herring did not come, this Spring fitted up Bigger than ever for the Lobesters and they are just about half as good as last year. So you know what that means, Poor, my children are so much over Joyed over their money, they have Boots and cloths, I could not give them, it over-Joyed me as well as them, and I am sure it over-Joyed their mother, it does our Heart good to hear you Speak over the Radio, you talk like a father to the Poor, I done everything I could do in your favour from the first time I heard you in the Convencion, I know you was for a better country, I know who you was fiting against, I know what you was saying was true, their may be Smart Lawyers in Newfoundland but they got to Be Smarater to Beat Hon. Joseph R. Smallwood you faught the Battle, and you won. Thank God.)
Your Hon. Please dont dislike my litter because I am Poor, I love to get a advise from you, I am Honost, I am not lazy, I love to be able to make a living for my family, I got no learning I was in grade four when I finish school, I never had no chance, I had to go Bucksawing when I was 14 years of age. my father is a fisherman he always was, an he is a few months short of 75 years of age, he have seen some Poor times too, would you Please give me a Advice, could I, and how, get a truck through the Goverment to work out myself, I would be so glad on eny turns I know they can always fit a truck in to work out, I understand they are going to do a bit of road work around it would be a great time for me to work Her out, I know I can pay for her and give my family a bitter living than they got now, your Hon, I am sure you would never regreat it if you would help me out on this, I am wiling to work, I am honost, but I am poor it seems like when your are Poor, you are nothing, you Just got to sit and think about what the other man is making his money with. I got no money to Pay down on one, if the goverment would give me one to work out it would give me a chance to live, and I am sure they can always fit me in to work her out and I am sure they would not be any money out, Please your Hon, Please

Help me out on this, the people of St. Barbs are worth something according to their Vots the People of st. Barbs the most of them are Poor and they know the man who is fighting for the Poor. Please drop me a line and let me know if I can, or if I can't, take out a truck to work out. Please your Hon Exquse my writing and my mistakes. Please dont look down on me because I am Poor, give me a chance.

God Bless you and your family, long live our Premier, if you think I wozent honost you can fine out from the merchins of [my community] for one that's where I deals a good bit too.

Yours very Truly

August 22nd/1949

Dear Sir

I am just taking my pin to drop you a few lines to till you what employment are in Newfoundland the only employment are going a head now are just a few hundred cords of wood to cut to [community] and ther are not enough to employ the people but if we could get the employment to work at the roads fixed them up it would give the People a chance if there dont be something to get employment at the road are so bad the people can walk on them an the need repair on them so if you will give me the chance to go ahead an get those road fixed up it would be a good bit of employment to help out a lot of people because it are nothing to earn a dollar at nothing else So Please try and do something for us an let me know as soon as possible your healp will mean a lot to us.

Your Sincerely

Bonne Bay[8]
Sept 29th/49

The Hon. J. R. Smallwood
St. John's

Honorable Sire:

For Some time Now we have been corresponding with the Representative for our District, Mr. Sparks,[9] *Re. Road repairs undoubtedly You are aware that the present Highroad which terminates at the C of E Church, Woody Point, was promised to extend to Curzon Village, But so far Nothing has been done in that respect, But we have been advised (indirectly) that as the road is now is the end, If that is So, Then we have quiet a lot of traffic passing over our So Called local roads. In the Meantime, It was Suggested to us to repaire those Roads on a so-so Basis.*

Now Honorable Sir, We dont think it quiet fair to us as Tax payers to give our time repairing Roads to be used by motor traffic. and in the meantime The owners of said Vehicles not helping to defray one cent of the cost of such repairs.

and on the other Hand. Those Roads are proposed Highroads, and Traffic Cannot be debarred from using same.

Our Request to our Member did not wholly concern the completion of the Highroad. But, to get some Temporary Repairs to the Roads we already have, or I might go as for to say They are not Roads merely Gutters as Mr. Sparks can vouch for same

But Sir on the other Hand a few people dont like working for a lot without being Paid for it.

During the National Referendum, we listened to you with great Concern in your fight for Confederation and Better times and we Backed you at the Polls One Hundred per cent, and we still have that confidence in you That you are going to do the Job you begun, and

---

8 Our deepest thanks to the descendants of O. Parsons and O.E. Taylor for granting us permission to include their full letter and names in this book.

9 Reginald F. Sparkes represented St. Barbe as the first provincial Member of the House of Assembly, after winning an overwhelming majority of the vote in the 1949 election.

you also spoke with disgust on the Dole situation But sorry to say Sir, it's staring us in the face right now.

May I suggest a remedy to stave it off for a while at least in this Particular sechon and that is to give us a grant of money not to finish the Highroad, But to put our local roads in fit shape to walk on

There is at least two months yet before arrival of winter, and that would mean Two months Labor for at least 25 mn who are sorely in Need of employment, we earnestly pray Sir that you will take immediate action on this request of ours and grant us at least a small amount to help support our families, as I said before, You promised labor Not Dole, and we are quiet willing to get down to the pick and shovel to do a Hard days work for a Honest days pay.

We the undersigned are representing at least Twenty five eligible workers who are sorely in Need of employment

We are Sir
Very Truly Yours
O. Parsons
O.E. Taylor

October 17th, 1949.

Messrs. O. Parsons & O.E. Taylor,
Bonne Bay,
Newfoundland.

Gentlemen: -

I have read your letter carefully, and I am in complete sympathy with what you say. I have discussed the needs of your district with Mr. Sparkes, our Speaker, and we both agree that St. Barbe District has been more neglected in the past fifty years than any other District in Newfoundland. By the time our term of Office is over, that will not be said about St. Barbe District.

This is Sunday night, and before you receive this letter you will have heard on the radio of our big new policy of giving up the payment of dole and substituting work in its place. I have no doubt that the job you wish to have done in Bonne Bay will be done before this year is over, under our big new programme of work instead of dole.

Thank you once again for writing me, and I do wish you would keep in touch with me from time to time.

Sincerely yours,

J.R. SMALLWOOD.
PREMIER.

JRS/GC.

Nov. 2nd 1949.

Joe Smallwood
Premire

Dear Sir.

I have a wife and 3 small children. I need at least 3 sacks of flour and other food for the winter.
I havent any chance of getting any. will you Please give me a chance to work on the roads or at something so as I can get food for them.

From

ST. GEORGE'S-PORT AU PORT

"SOMETHING MUST BE DONE": Reflecting on Past and Present in the Letters to Smallwood

Lesley Derraugh

WHEN MY GRANDFATHER PASSED away in 2010, my family came across some letters that he had written to my grandmother while he was working around the province in road construction. They were not love letters in the traditional sense, yet for a man whose formal education ended by age eight, the writing of even seemingly banal notes updating his wife on his daily activities was an act of love. I find myself reflecting on those letters, and the question that comes to mind is always about motivation. My grandfather wrote out of a need to connect with his wife and out of love for her. How many letters are written with strong emotions attached, be it love, passion, anger, or, perhaps, desperation?

Shortly after finding my grandfather's letters, I completed an undergraduate research project that led me to again contemplate the act of letter writing and the emotions attached to this act. That project, much like this collection, asked me to examine and reflect on thousands of letters written to Premier Joey Smallwood by the people of Newfoundland and Labrador.

There is no denying that, in the years since Confederation, Smallwood has taken on an almost mythical status; there is a magnetism about the man who brought Newfoundland to Canada. Whether or not the citizens of this province (both then and now) agree with Confederation, it is hard to deny the tremendous impact that it has had on each and every resident.

As I return to the letters to Smallwood, I find myself once more considering the reasons people wrote to him. Their letters tell many stories, each one a unique, often vivid snapshot of their circumstances. For some, letters were an acknowledgement of their faith in Smallwood as an individual man and the Liberal Party as a political group, and in their letters they revealed what the promise of Confederation meant to them. A congratulatory telegram sent on April 4, 1949, was brief: "Many best wishes for your success." Yet while this missive is short, the act of sending that telegram, and in particular the expense of sending that simple message to a politician 1,000 kilometres away in St. John's, speaks to a sense of hope that positive changes will arise from Confederation. A letter, sent from the district on May 31, 1949, was also congratulatory. In this letter, the writer placed Smallwood on a pedestal, and it is almost as if joining with Canada in Confederation and being led by Premier Smallwood would transform the province and end all suffering. This correspondent appears to have idolized the new premier, and I find myself wondering if such messages would have buoyed Smallwood in his work, or, by contrast, if the weight of all that hope was crushing.

What speaks to me far more than the hope-filled congratulatory and supportive notes are those written out of desperation. I find myself struck by those who had nowhere else to turn. The (mostly) rural communities in which these citizens lived often offered few opportunities for employment or education, and in isolated regions of the province, there was little connection to the social resources promised by the newly formed government, such as Family Allowances, War Veterans' Allowance, Unemployment Insurance, and Old Age Pensions. Many of those who wrote to Smallwood wrote with a sense of despair, a despair born of the urgent need for help to better their circumstances and those of their families. It is for this reason, for example, that one woman, raising her niece, orphaned as a result of her father's death during the war, wrote to Smallwood. She urged him to connect her with the allowance for veterans' children, an allowance which would surely ease the financial burden of raising a child thrust upon her by difficult circumstances.

The two letters I found from one woman in particular reveal that her family was suffering. They struggled to get by, with the rising cost of basic food items draining the family budget and leaving little room for necessities such as clothing for the children. In her first letter (undated), the writer went so far as to ask that Smallwood have his wife send a parcel of items to assist the family. She wrote: "I know you have a family and well do you ask your wife to pick up some second hand clothes and send me as I have a big family and would appreciate a parcel very much you know ye people have thing we would appreciate." In her second letter, written on March 8, 1950, she requested support for her teenage daughter, a young woman who had achieved the highest education she could in her community and was now seeking to study shorthand typewriting. A shorthand typing course would offer new employment opportunities: the daughter would be well prepared to enter a workforce that increasingly valued that skill set.

How did such letters affect Smallwood? Was it difficult to hear the needs of the people of the province, to hear of all their struggles without being able to assist? While the social and economic changes that would shape the province over the nearly quarter century of Smallwood's premiership would go far to solve many of the issues raised in the public's letters, those changes would take time. The immediacy of need surely held great weight. The letters quoted here are just three of the thousands of letters that the new premier received; many others detailed similar requests in their own letters. How does one individual shoulder the burden of receiving all those appeals for aid?

I also came across many letters that revolved around health care. In one such letter, a man unable to access steady work sought benefits in the form of tuberculosis funding for his son, a boy stricken with the life-threatening illness and confined to bed for months. The doctor had highlighted the need to provide additional nourishing food for the boy, but the family could not shoulder the burden of those additional costs. In the father's words, "work is Very Scarce," and he had been without earnings since the previous fall. Another constituent, meanwhile, had a girl "in trouble." He could find no work and needed money to cover the expenses associated with her pregnancy. Both men struggled to find employment to support the situations in which they found themselves. While their letters date from 1949 and 1950, their correspondence to the premier illustrates a problem we still experience in this province today: medical care is expensive and, in remote communities, often difficult to access. Even with a public health care system and provincial programs that alleviate the expense of medications for the most vulnerable, there are always additional expenses associated with medical needs. The questions that underpinned these letters—How do we support the ill while maintaining employment? Can we afford to be sick for a prolonged period?—still resonate in the present day.

One gentleman sent a telegram that could just as easily have been a post on social media today. His message indicated that his stepson's mental health was in such an unstable position that he needed constant monitoring. This father's desperate attempts to get his stepson hospitalized for his mental health are reminiscent of the struggles current mental health advocates share. Despite the huge leaps and bounds we have made in our health care system since 1949, mental health treatment options are limited and still located primarily in St. John's. Writing from the other side of the province, this man was disempowered when it came to finding a place for his stepson. He had spent three weeks working toward hospitalization but was unable to get satisfaction. Meanwhile, the health of his stepson continued to decline. "Something must be done," he said, and this is the message we still hear repeatedly from mental health care advocates, patients, and their families.

The similarities between past and present stand out the most to me. Despite seventy-five years having now passed since Confederation and the writing of these letters, many of the issues constituents faced still ring true throughout the province. Many parents still struggle to access educational opportunities for their children in or near their home communities. We still suffer because of expenditures not covered by the provincial government, such as equipment, medication, and the time and lost work of caregivers. Advocates for better mental health care still work tirelessly for accessible treatment options for individuals in remote and rural communities. Many of the letters written by Newfoundlanders and Labradorians in 1949 could just as easily be written today and they offer a window through which we can look back, reflect, and connect with those who came before us.

July 6, 1948.

Mr. Joseph Smallwood,
Confederate Party Leader,
St. John's, Nfld.

Dear Mr. Smallwood:

Would you kindly foreward as soon as possible detailed information in pamphlet form about the following topics:

a. Canada's terms re. Confederation.

b. The economic and social benefits to be derived from Confederation.

c. The status of the Americain bases under Confederation

d. Any other strong evidence that can be used in intelligent discussion.

Very sincerely yours,

APRIL 4, 1949
MANY BEST WISHES FOR YOUR SUCCESS.
[NAME] & FAMILY

May 5th 1949

M J R Smallwood
Prime Minister
St. John's N.F.L.D

Dear Sir

I am sure you are very busy, and I will try and make this as short as possible. We all heard from your speach over Raido. We have near about one million fr of lumber to be shipped over the High road by trucks. we are operating on … this past 16 years. We are gone away backs on this … We are operating Sawmill at Present away in Across the High Road. All our lumber has to be trucked over High Road to-nearest-point-of Railway. We have over 300 ~~M~~BMfr order on hand now from the Buchans mining Md Buchans. We know these people are expecting their lumber.

I don't have to explain to you this important point. We want the use of the High Road right-away for this Purpose other orders from Port-aux-Basque. We want you to do this for us. A week or two from Now the Road will be O.K. to nearest Point-of Railway, say 15th. I shall be depending on this to be don in near future or we will loose our Orders.

(You can do anything) Well then do this for us please It's very important to keep our regular bunch of men employed and fill our lumber orders. Very <u>much</u> important. From your very [illegible]

May 31, 1949

Hon. J. R. Smallwood,

St. Johns.

Dear Mr. Smallwood,

Please accept my sincere congratulations on your personal victory + the victory of your party in the election just ended. It was I imagine the great political triumph ever achieved by any party and any leader in the history of this island. And I cannot tell you how greatly pleased I was with the result.

Up late the March 31st last to my mind the whole of Newfoundland was paralyzed – and to my mind it was yourself + the members of the District of St. Georges to the National Convention that cured the paralytic stroke – that relieved the sufferings of a great many poor children and aged people. At any time the province ~~would~~ might give you a knighthood – and to my mind this knighthood won't mean a thing to you – but when you close your eyes there'll be a knighthood prepared for you in the other world – because God likes prayers + there were many prayers said for you by people of all denominations + because you have done more for the children, + the poor + the suffering of this island than any other man ever has.

Yours Sincerely

June 10th/49

Mr. J. R. Smallwood

St. John's. N.F.L.D.

"Dear Sir"

Just a few lines in asking you a few Questions which I feel sure I will get Satisfaction which I haven't been able to Get Since Last fall. I understand that any one who is Sick with T.B. and Laid up by the Doctor are Due the Sum of $10.00 per month I have a Boy in bed now there is 9 nine months I have to buy Extra food for him according to the Doctor's rules and work is Very Scarce I haven't earned anything since Last fall I have already written to those who are looking after this in st. John's and haven't had an answer yet so far and I have been after the rangers for over two months and Cannot Get any Satisfaction I would like to know if I can Get that money for this Child. The Extra food which I bought is still owed for. Waiting for that Money to Come the Doctor told us that the Boy has to stay in bed for 3 months more before another X-ray that he is not Better yet. and besides that the Boy is 13 years old and we didn't Get any of his family allowances. We sent in his forms and we also wrote in about this since and didn't Get an answer so as you are the right Man in the right place I feel sure I will Get Satisfaction this time.

Your's Truly

Jan 29 .50

Dear Mr Small wood

I am writing you to say there no work to get around & I was very Glad to have that money out of the office. So I have aney more.

I have a Girl in truble & I have no money to pay the husptial Bills so would you pleas send me out $20.00 tell the works starts & I will Pay you Back. Please let me know <u>*answer*</u> *this soon,*

Your's truly

May 4th -50

Hon. Joseph R. Smallwood
Prime Minister ---
St. John's .

Dear Mr. Smallwood: – I would like to know if if my service and support would be acceptable to yourself and Party on a pay basis – as there isn't very much in newspaper correspondence and I need to make a little more money.

My idea is that I should oftener make comment on what I believe to be the good brought about by yourself and Government --- than I have been doing since the time of the National Convention and afterwards.

May say that I write for the Evening Telegram under the pen name of "Thistle" have been their correspondent for many years now and if you happen to read my notes and comments you will have noticed that I have been a strong supporter of yours all the time and a believer in the benefits in Confederation for the country and it's people.

May say, too, that I have acted in similar capacity for the late Government – when I found that I could do so conscientiously – as I can also do for your Administration.

Wishing you and your cabinet every success and trusting that I may have a word from you in the near future –

I am, Yours very Respectfully,

March 8 1950

Hon Jm Smallwood

Dear Sir

I am writing you to see if you can do me a favour. Well now Mr Small Wood I have a daughter here want to learn Short Hand Typle writing and I cannot afford to send her to learn as I have a large family and I am writing you to see if you can do any thing for here Hoping you will do your Best for her she is 16 ears old passed grade 10 Hoping to hear from you I Remain Yours truly

Hon Prime M J Smallwood

Dear sir

I am writing you to ask you if there cant be something here about the prices Well now for a start to tell you a poor person cant live with a large family like I have when I received the baby bonas This month I went to the store Here at [my community] and I paid 13.75 for 3 pairs of children boots and every thing according to that so you see 30 dollars dident go far so I would like if you would send out somebody here to Just see how we are treated I know you don't know thing are like They are here as The place is a little Backward The Think the can do what They like Beef is at present here 30 cts a lb. So I would like you could send somebody here and just see how we poor people are treated I am not a very good hand to state a letter so that's all so now I would like you do me a favour what it is I know you have a family and well do you ask your wife to pick up some second hand clothes and send me as I have a big family and would appreciate a parcel very much you know ye people have thing we would appreciate. So now I hope I am intruding on you by asking you to do this any way I would like you see things here and the prices would be better.

I remain yours truly

Premier.
Hon. Mr J. R. Smallwood.
St. John's
Newfoundland

Dear Hon. Sir –

Will you please give this letter your kind and valuable attention for which I extend my many humble thanks. I wish to explain that I have in my care a little girl age 13 years whom I have been looking after as my own child. This child is a daughter of my Brother who was accidentally killed while serving in the Newfoundland Forestry Unit in Scotland in 1941, July 5th. His name was [redacted]. His home was at [community] at the time of his death. He left 5 small children, who was all placed in homes of relatives + one in the orphanage at St. John's. Their Mother passed away a few years later and I took this child when she was only 3 years old. I am her lawful aunt.

My reason for writing your Hon. Sir is that I have been advised that this child is entitled to a certain allowance from the War Veterans Dept. But I do not know who to apply to for this allowance. So will you please advise me where I can apply to for what is due her.

Thanking you for prompt reply.

Yours truly.

ST. JOHN'S EAST

Joey Smallwood: Judas Iscariot, Betrayer of His People, or "a great man of vision and endurance"?

Sheila Hallett

MY MOTHER REFERRED TO JOEY as the little fellow from Gambo, and this was not meant as a compliment. My mother-in-law, meanwhile, was as avid a Joey supporter as my mother was anti-Joey.

My parents were East Enders from St. John's. They spent several years in Gander where Dad worked as a radio operator at the Gander airport. It was there that they met Joey. My in-laws, by contrast, were fishermen and -women from Flat Island in Bonavista Bay. Joey was a frequent visitor at my parents' home in Gander where he expounded his views on the benefits of Confederation, benefits my mother already enjoyed as a middle-class resident of St. John's. There were no doctors on Flat Island, no hospitals, no grocery stores, and education, while provided, was not readily available and was conducted in a one-room school. My mother and mother-in-law's opinions were so different that I often wished that I could go back in time to hear other voices of that time. Researching the letters written to Joey and stored in the Archives and Special Collections division at Memorial University's Queen Elizabeth II Library gave me that opportunity. I chose St. John's East as the district that I would research.

I was excited to find a letter written on April 1, 1949—some say the actual date of Confederation—which echoed my mother's opinion of Joey, and was possibly more virulent; according to one irate resident of St. John's East, Joey "acted the Judas Isacriot [sic] and sold Newfoundland for a mess of pottage." He called on the spirit of his beloved dead father to "haunt you in the years to come for having done this deed against the wishes of the people." I was equally excited to find another letter dated May 24, 1949, that praised Joey for his vision, comparing him to Abraham Lincoln and George Washington! This letter corresponded perfectly with the opinion held by my mother-in-law. That such diverse opinions could be held by so many about one person and issue spoke volumes. And I was looking only at one district, St. John's East.

The letters are fascinating. There are letters congratulating Smallwood and also letters asking for jobs and pensions, and help in finding adequate housing and paying medical bills, all issues that are as relevant today as they were in 1949. Many things impressed me about these letters: the belief held by all the letter writers that they could write directly to Joey, the premier; the belief that he would read the letters himself and respond to them personally (although there were few replies recorded in those files I accessed); and finally, the belief that Joey could—and more importantly *would*—fix each situation to everyone's satisfaction.

Some of the letters written to Joey were so personal they were heartbreaking. In one letter, a woman with six children and another on the way asked Joey if he could find a job for her husband, a "sober and reliable man" whose only drawback was his lack of education and the fact that he had only "what he stands in" for clothing, a situation which prevented him from even going to church. But there were also many letters that expressed a commitment to the future of Newfoundland. At first, from my cynical rear-view position, I scoffed at these letters because they seemed far-fetched and naive, offering business ideas such as knitting mills and Christmas tree farms. But the more I read, the prouder I became of the resilience of the people of Newfoundland. One letter, signed simply "a Mother," called on Joey, "the poor peoples champion for their rights," to help her daughter and the other young women working in the clothing factory in St. John's receive fair treatment from their newly formed union. Another was from one of Joey's supporters who, while supportive of Joey's new relief programme, thought the rate of pay under that programme was too low. This same writer also took Joey to task for the rising cost of living, especially the rising cost of tobacco, reminding Joey that one of his objectives as leader was a "better means of living for the working man." Joey's response to that letter was interesting. While he agreed that "times are not very good," and the rate of wages "is pretty low, but it is more than double the rate that is paid out in dole," he was "very much dissatisfied with the cost of living" and while he was trying to do something about it, "Rome was not built in a day."

From reading the letters, it seems obvious that the people of St. John's East had been listening to Joey's radio speeches and were paying attention to his campaign promises, and while many were willing to give him a chance, they were not going to sit quietly by. Such, for example, was the letter from a fisherman who challenged Joey to prove his claim that he was "a friend of the fisherman the farmer and in fact the country" by fixing the road in that area so that the fishermen from there and Paradise could access their traditional fishing grounds.

I was annoyed but at the same time admired the audacity of the letter writer who asked for a favour in obtaining a "Swill" contract with the new airport at Torbay. Just to ensure Joey's support, he was "tucking away a hundred dollars ($100.00) as a little inducement." And just as I was annoyed, I was also amazed by the letters from individual citizens and existing successful businesses. They outlined, in concrete ways, the creation of businesses and industries that could alleviate poverty, improve existing infrastructure, create employment, and, in some cases, improve food security in Newfoundland. There was a sense of hope and excitement in these letters. These business ideas included woollen and knitting mills that, if established, could, with plans for expansion, integrate sheep raising with wool production and provide food for the table and product for canning factories; a Navigational and Sea Engineering School that could become part of Memorial University's curriculum and, eventually, a separate department attracting students worldwide; improvements to the fisheries and to the roads network; and cement factories that could be funded by tapping into newly available federal government monies. All correspondents emphasized that small to medium businesses that utilized the skills and abilities of Newfoundlanders would, based on experience, be most successful.

As noted previously, although people wrote with the expectation of a reply, I found few. Those responses that I did read included one to an individual who had submitted a ten-point plan as an "endeavor to alleviate unemployment." Joey's response was "you are certainly brimful of ideas." Another acknowledged a letter from the Newfoundland Board of Trade and expressed, among other things, Joey's ambition to not only attach a thoroughly up to date Navigational School to the university but "one that will be the best in all of North America." In 1964, Joey opened the College of Fisheries, Navigation, Marine Engineering and Electronics, located on Parade Street in St. John's. In 1985, it was moved and renamed the Institute of Fisheries and Marine Technology, and in 1992, it was affiliated with Memorial University and renamed the Fisheries and Marine Institute of Memorial University of Newfoundland. Overall, the letters that I read made me sad, infuriated, and proud to be a Newfoundlander, because in spite of the hardships endured, people continued to have faith in each other and the future of Newfoundland and Labrador.

Both my mother and mother-in-law would lay claim to being right about Joey and in many ways they both were. Meanwhile, as the controversy still rages, those of us who call this place home live in hope and work hard for a better tomorrow.

Jan 22nd/49

J.R. Smallwood Esq.
St. John's

Dear Sir: –

I hope you will find time to read this note & I sincerely hope you wont resent my writing you.

First of all I feel that I should devote my time expressing our thanks to you for all you have done for us already also to thank kind providence for giving you strength to see it through most men would have cracked up under the strain long before this. Sir I'll make this as brief as possible.

Would it be fair I wonder if I were to ask you to do us a favour. I have a feeling that "Torbay Airport"[1] *might amount to something in the very near future if so there might be a chance of getting a Swill contract either with the Americans or Canadians.*

During the war I collected from the Army & Airforce I made a very good living & a honest one in other words I got along well with the Boys How Id like to get back there again if anything happens a lot Sir depends on you. I'm awfully serious about this Mr Smallwood and there will be a lot of people after it. I'm still in the pig business I'm teamed up with [name redacted] on a small scale. I collect from the "Nfld Hotel" through him on the halves we call it.

We have a Family of ten we have six little ones going to "Bishops Field & Spencer" colleges so you see Sir I have to be right on my toes in order to make a living. I'm tucking away a hundred dollars ($100.00) as a little inducement in case anything happens which is little enough for a favour of this size.

---

1 Construction of the Canadian Air Force base at Torbay began in 1941, with the first official landing taking place in October that same year. Bob Cole was prescient: Torbay Airport did, indeed, "amount to something." In 1964, Torbay Airport became St. John's airport: St. John's International Airport. Now the second-largest airport in the Atlantic provinces, some 1.6 million passengers move through the airport every year. For more on the history of Torbay Airport, see Jenny Higgins and Heather O'Brien, "Torbay," Heritage Newfoundland & Labrador, 2007, https://www.heritage.nf.ca/articles/politics/torbay-air-base.php, and "History," St. John's International Airport Authority, accessed November 16, 2023, https://stjohnsairport.com/about/corporate-information/history/.

We made several half hearted attempts to see you since you came back. But we will wait now trusting to hear from you in the event that something should happen between "Kennas Hill" & "Torbay Airport" in the near future. Closing now with the wish that March 31st/49 will see your fondest hopes & dreams realized & that you will be spared many long years to serve in the best interest of all.

With apologies for troubling you
Very Sincerely

April 1st/49

W.R. Smallwood

Dear Sir

Well you have completed your dastarly crime of Confederation against the wishes of half the population and you have acted the Judas Isacriot and sold Newfoundland for a mess of pottage. Today is the birthday of my beloved father and may his spirit haunt you in the years to come for having done this deed against the wishes of the people. We have not lost our spirit yet we are still able to do many things and I am afraid that the bed you have made for yourself and your wonderful government will be a hard one. It is hard to keep a good independent people down and we are not beaten yet. If the thing had been done in an openhanded manner we would not have minded but would my dear father have done such a transaction that you have been the leader of. That is the one thing he abhorred and any underhand was poison to him. His last words just before he died were. Do not go in for Confederation for if you do there will be blood and Riots. Vote against it to your last drop of blood. If you get Confederation the grass will grow on your peaceful streets because Canada will only take you for what she can gain from your union. Time will tell whether he was right or wrong. He was dead 10 minutes after he spoke those words to me and after 40 years they are still ringing in my ears. You were very hard in the Politicians of the past but what of the present setup. Wish to God we had them again with us but their spirits are there and may they haunt and dog your footsteps is the silent prayer of a staunch independent Newfoundlander.

Dear Sir

I have listened to your Radio speaches in wich you clamed to be a friend of the fishermen the farmer and in fact the country and you also stated that you were strong for roads well Sir here is your chance there is a road in [my community] leading to the beach were Padrice Topsail Road and [my community] people always fished now you cant get a horse on it as not been fixed this last 14 years the cliff slided down and filled the road if you could do something to help us out you know there are two or 3 hundred boats no one fishing there was about 90 salmon nets now there onely 9 people got to carry lobsters salmon fish herring on there backs and not any chance to haul caplin for the ground it is a wonderful draw back so sir if something cant be done and get this thing in working order its not good enough we are not working we are mulling when we could take our horses down like we always did. Now Mr Smallwood what about it yours truly

---

May 10th, 1949

Dear Mr. [name redacted]:

Thank you very, very much indeed. I can assure you that I appreciate your difficulty, and sympathize with the people of [your community] in the lack of attention they have received especially with regards to roads.

I can assure you that after the Liberal Party is elected, this state of affairs will not continue. Our party has a very strong platform in regards to roads, both highroads and local roads.

You understand, of course that no public works can be begun before the election, as all public works during the three weeks before an election are forbidden by law. This law was passed in 1913, and although we are not in favor of it, there is nothing we can do to alter it until the house meets this summer.

I can assure you that after the election, we will take action on the matter up in question. Thanking you again for writing.

Very truly yours

J.R. SMALLWOOD
PREMIER

May 24th/49

Hon. J.R.Smallwood
Premier of N.F.L.D.
St John's

Dear Sir:-

Just a big "Thank You" for what you have done for my family, and as a Newfoundlander for what Confederation will mean to Newfoundland.

I have meant to write you some months ago, to express my thanks to you, but neglected it. but was encouraged by [name redacted], who last year was a very strong supporter of Confederation, and who did not mind talking freely and openly to anyone, & urging them to vote for Confederation & who is today just as strongly in favour of the Liberal Party, I say this for [name redacted] because he was the only man who stood undauntless for your cause, and through his influence [my community] is 80% for the Liberal Party. Mr. Smallwood, America proudly remembers Abraham Lincoln, and George Washington, but the day will come when History will reveal that Providence did not pass us by but gave us two great men of vision & endurance when our country needed them most in the person of your good self, Mr. J.R. Smallwood, and Mr. F.G Bradley.[2]

Hope your candidates will be elected in St. John's East, to serve under your able leadership.

Kindest Regards.

2 F. Gordon Bradley, a Member of the House of Assembly in the former Dominion of Newfoundland, worked closely with Smallwood to promote Confederation. In 1949, he was elected as a federal Member of Parliament for Bonavista-Twillingate. He served as Secretary of State until 1953 and was then appointed to the Senate.

May 25 1949

Dear Mr Smallwood
I am the maturnity nurse
at Portugal Cove District I trained
at the Grace Hospital through
the Public Health and Welfare
and sense that time I have
Been Doing this work
my Reason for writing you is to ask
if you could do anything about
allowing me so much for this
work as most of the People here
are unable to Pay me when I
attend them many are on Relieft
and I make so little a year
as you [illegible] not a Enough to
keep me going I have to walk
three and four miles to my Patients Every
Day then in most cases the Patient
tells me she cannot pay me in
fact there are Women in this
Place to Day owe me for as
many as four or five Births I wrote
[the doctor] last year and he told
Me he would like to allow me
Something but he couldent but
the Public Health nurses are not
treated so and they Have a car
at there Disposal as a trained
Midwife Dont you think I am
Entitled to some help also
Mrs [illegible] thats [name redacted] mother
suggested I write [the doctor]
last year
I have no other way of living
as my Husbant is crippled

and Havent been able to
work for the Past Eight Years
I should like very much
if you would answer my
letter soon as Possible.
as in my family that is my
Husbant Sons and Daughters
And there Husbands and wives
There are about in all fifteen
votes and they Being telling
me to get your opinion in
this matter tanking you
and wishing you
the Best in your
Compaign
Yours truly[3]

3 This letter was written on a long, narrow scrap of paper, and its transcription follows the original lineation.

June 30/9 49

Mr. Joseph Smallwood

Dear Sir: I am [name redacted] a married woman with 6 children and a new arrival in November coming We are living on the relief this past year and my husband can't find employment. [illegible] he is Sober and reliable his only draw back is his education he can't read or write only sign his own name he is very quiet and his education makes him backward in finding work So I am writing this to you to see if you could possible find employment for him at anything or anywhere he will be grateful to you for it. He hasent got a bit of clothing to put on only what he stands in he cant go to his church or no where I heard from people that you are after doing a lot of good turns for men out of employment in getting work for them etc. My husband is not looking for money or help of no kind only want you to See if you could possible get him a job and get him of that cursed relief which is pure Starvation we get about enough of food to do us about half of the mnth, and the rest of the mnth Starved to death you certainly did a good turn when you got us the baby bonus my children where practely naked until I got it and both my husband and I were for you So if you could possible get him employment you would be doing another good turn long with the rest. You already done for a poor family that badly needs it.

Thank you

September,1st, 1949

Hon.J.R. Smallwood
Premier of Newfoundland,
Minster of Industrial Development,
Office of the Premier,
St.John's, NFLD

Dear Sir,

I am convinced that if woolen and knitting mills were established here in this Province, and with plans for expansion, this industry would develop a huge export trade and by producing superior quality products, outside business could be captured. Consequently, repeat orders would flow in.

Now I know that at present, we have not got wool enough for this project, but we could soon have plenty for all purposes.

While some of our local wool is of a fair quality, yet if a good breed of sheep were imported and as many of them as possible were given out to every co-operative society to supervise their breeding, it would help to establish and build up a supply of wool very quickly. Then too, reliable farmers could be induced to rear sheep and more sheep, if there were a sure market for their products. In fact, we could become, in time, as famous for our sheep ranches as is Australia, though possibly on a smaller scale.

Sheep are inexpensive to keep, and are always profitable. Speaking from experience, I have found that it is quite easy to rear sheep. They increase in numbers quickly and as we know, every sheep gives one or two lambs seasonally, and lambs well looked after soon become very sturdy. Results in six months: good fleece and choice mutton, very suitable for a canning factory.

I have always thought that goods manufactured from available local resources should have a very advantageous position in trade attended by a high degree of success.

At Truro, Nova Scotia, Stanfield's modern equipped plant and their large turnover should encourage us to start the wheels rolling.

Yours very truly,

Sept.8-49

Dear Mr. Smallwood.

I am a widow with three children. My oldest girl is working in a Clothing factory ... I want to bring to your attention the conditions that she works in. They makes some of the girls there work without any supper and they dont get paid for it.[4]

The supper is a Canadian and he told them not to vote for confederatione. I am writing this to you as I know you are the poor peoples champion for their rights My daughter paid five dollars entrance fee for a union that Jack White was forming I am after that isnt the first five dollars that he took and didnt anything for the people.

Please mr. Smallwood donot mention that you got a letter from anyone at that factory as they will fire my daughter.

I pray for your help and try and do something for those girls as Some are fed up with this small pay and the next thing they will be on the streets and then they are ruined for ever. please Sir give this your immediate attention.

your humble servant
a mother

4 For more on women's paid labour in St. John's during this era, see Nancy M. Forestell, "Times Were Hard: The Pattern of Women's Paid Labour in St. John's between the Two World Wars," in *Their Lives and Times: Women in Newfoundland and Labrador, A Collage*, ed. C. McGrath, B. Neis, and M. Porter (St. John's: Killick Press, 1995), 76–92.

Oct. 22/49

To the Hon. J.R. Smallwood

Dear Sir as I have lost all communication with you since moving into your new home By telephone. My only means at present to get in touch with you is by writing. Hence my reason for this letter to you. Well I have been listening to your Relief Program which I consider fairly good altho the rate of pay (I Know) is low I also Surmise that the returns for same will also be low. But there is quite a difference in (Say) 2.20 Per Day & 6 cts. as was paid to the Poor People in the very Bad times by the Commission Government which only meant Starvation Degradation & Misery. But I have some little thing to say to you. First of all I may say I was one of your Strong Supporters as you are well aware & did all in my power on your behalf, well what do I get now. Don't take wrong I am not asking favours. But my aim and object was better means of living for the working man, & I realy thought you were the same, I hope I am not mistaken. Altho apearently things are not working out that way. For instance take Beaver tobacco manufactured right here in this town as was the case before Confederation. Why I would like to ask is this item gone up at least 80%. Is it owing to the shareholders using their selfish ability to force people to buy this as a means of spite or what is the cause of it, Myself Personally I always smoked Beaver & always managed to get enough to smoke even in the bad times, & I might say have brought up nine children. Now in my last few years I have to give up smoking for I will not pay this price for Beaver & it looks as if we are not allowed tobacco made in U.S.A. as there is none to get as the business people will not import it. Now I dont have to tell you that things like this (which means cost of living)is keenly watched by people more especially men like myself that supported this government, as for myself I am not old enough to get Old Age Pension & am unable to work & am refused unemployment insurance What am I to do, there is Provision made for almost everyone even Civil Servants.

Trusting to hear from you at your earliest convenience I remain as ever yours

---

October 25th, 1949

Dear Mr. [name redacted],

I am very glad indeed to hear from you. In fact I wondered once or twice why you had not telephoned me from time to time as usual. Yes, I must admit that times are not very good. There are about ten thousand men in Newfoundland today who are on the dole. You know the reasons, namely, the bad failure of the fisheries in a good many places and the slowing down of the woods work. We have struck a pretty hard time in our first few months in power. One thing I am determined about, and that is to cut out the dole. You say that the rate of wages we are paying is low. Yes, it is pretty low, but it is more than double the rate that is paid out in dole. The average family of five in Newfoundland would get $25.00 a month for dole. By working on the fifty fifty basis the average family man will get over $57.00 per month under our new relief work programme. Surely that is a lot better than dole, although I know it is far from enough. However, there is a limit to the amount of money the Government has, and you can see for yourself that when we have to provide for ten thousand families, and probably more, it is going to run into a great deal of money. We had only about half as many in need of relief, then no doubt we could pay double the rate of wages. Like you, and very much dissatisfied with the cost of living. I am trying to do something about it, although it is not too easy to do, as you can understand. Do not forget that I am still in office only about six months. Rome was not built in a day, and I cannot be expected to do in six months what the Commission of Government were unable to do in fourteen years. Do not judge me yet, but give me another year before you make up your mind. I do not want to lose your support above all others. Please drop me a line from time to time, and keep in touch with me.

With very best wishes to you and Mrs. [name redacted], as always,

Sincerely yours,

J.R. SMALLWOOD,
PREMIER.

JRS/CC.

ST. JOHN'S WEST

No More Hooey: A Widow Writes the Premier

Jennifer Morgan

IN LATE SEPTEMBER 1949, Alice French[1] wrote the premier about her late husband's pension:

> I notice you said on your letter to me that there is really. Nothing whatever You can do about the question of my pension as the widow of a retired Civil Servant, more than to pass my letter's to you over to Mr. Carew who is head of the Civil Service. There seemed to be a whole lot you could do before the Country entered Confederation, as on a letter to me (Which I now have in my possession) you stated most emphatically that in case Nfld entered the Canadian Confederation I would most assurdely get my late husband's Civil pension and that is exactly what I have been writing to you about to make good your written promise to me

This was not Alice's first letter to Joseph Smallwood. The St. John's West (1949) file in the Smallwood collection contains seven letters and one letter fragment from her. Unlike some of the other letters in this file, Alice did not use a printed letterhead. She wrote on plain white stationery, in a fine copperplate hand, with elaborate swirls in India ink for the "H" in Honorable. When she was

1 Apart from the names of politicians, all names in this chapter have been changed.

unhappy with Mr. Smallwood—as she frequently was—Alice was liberal with underlined words.

Now that she has your attention, let me tell you what I've learned about Alice. She first appears in these letters as Mrs. George French, the widowed wife of a retired civil servant living in St. John's—a summary that is both true and devoid of essential details.

George's first wife, Elizabeth May, died in 1893, at a young age. Her tombstone bears the tender inscription: "In loving memory of Elizabeth May, beloved wife of George French. Also, her three children Elsie, Edward, and Tryphena. We shall meet again." Elizabeth May's tombstone raises more questions than answers. Why did she die so young? What tragedy caused the couple to lose three children? And why are the three children's names on Elizabeth May's tombstone? Did they die before her or at the same time? Why are the children listed in that order?

Elizabeth May could have been known by both names to distinguish her from the many Elizabeths in her family. Her daughter Elsie may have been named after Elizabeth May's mother and called Elsie because she was a child and because the original Elizabeth, possibly the child's maternal grandmother, was still living at the time. Did Elizabeth May die giving birth to Elsie or to Tryphena, the last named child on the tombstone? Or did all three children and the mother die of an infectious illness that George and their other offspring survived?

Without the marriage records of Elizabeth May or the baptismal records of Elsie, George, and Tryphena, it's difficult to know how old they were when they died. If Elizabeth May and George were teen sweethearts, their oldest child could have been fourteen or fifteen at her death. The record shows that Elizabeth May left at least two children when she died, one-year-old George Junior and a three-year-old named William.

At some point George moved to St. John's with his two sons and his second wife, Helen Mary. Helen Mary died, aged forty-six, in 1917. In November of that same year, George lost his namesake when twenty-five-year-old George Junior died. George Junior had not been living with his father but with his older brother, William and William's wife, Josephine, in the area around Quidi Vidi Road.

Alice French's name first shows up in the 1935 census. George was retired by then, drawing a pension from the Dominion of Newfoundland and renting a home. While George had been the same age as his first wife, Elizabeth May, he was ten years older than his second wife, Helen Mary. At seventy-five at the time of the 1935 census, George was twenty-five years older than his third wife, Alice. Indeed,

Alice, born in 1886, was closer in age to her stepson William, who was forty-five in 1935. Interestingly, although she was forty-nine at the time, the 1935 census incorrectly lists her as forty-five, the same age as William, a mistake repeated in the 1945 census. This makes me think that George, the pensioner, was the one who was interviewed by the census workers. His age is correct in both surveys.

Although George was a pensioner, the couple was not entirely dependent on his pension since, according to the census, Alice kept two boarders. I say that it was Alice who kept the boarders, because keeping boarders was one of the few ways a woman could earn money in the nineteenth and early twentieth centuries. It's possible that after Helen Mary died, George moved into Alice's boarding house and eventually married his landlady. Alice would have needed a marriage sanctioned by an ordained Anglican minister, since a landlady's social propriety was a required asset for attracting single lady boarders.

Alice had two ladies boarding with her in 1935: twenty-one-year-old Miss Joan F. Graham and a Miss Lily R. Gibson, aged forty-four. I couldn't learn anything more about Miss Graham, but I found a reference to Lily Gibson in the 1936 Business Directory and a reference to her employer (and possibly her brother-in-law) in *Who's Who in and from Newfoundland 1927*. Any landlady would have been proud to have a lodger as well born as Miss Gibson, from a community where the firm of J.G. Gibson was a prominent merchant house. Lily was a contemporary of William and Alice and worked as a saleslady at a store on Water Street. That store was owned by John Arthur Connor, who was a manager of the Fisherman's Union Trading Company, a previous employee of J.G. Gibson, and married to Sarah Gibson. A member of an influential outport family and an independent single woman, Lily Gibson was also, as further evidence will indicate, a valued friend of Alice French. Fourteen years later, Alice told Joseph Smallwood that she had been forced to borrow money to pay her rent, and this leads me to wonder if she might have borrowed that money from her former boarder, Miss Lily Gibson.

When George died in 1948, Alice was once again a single woman but, unlike Lily, she was not financially independent. Alice's first letter to Joseph Smallwood, then campaign manager for the Confederate side, penned during the heat of the Confederation campaign, explained that George's death had left her destitute. The file does not include her original letter, but it contains a carbon copy of Mr. Smallwood's reply, in which he indicates that she can expect a pension "under Confederation." He observes, "This is by far a more humane and civilized way of doing things than we have in our own little country."

This carbon copy has two sums written in pencil on the back:

$75
12
69.00

281
69
350

These calculations might show that Joseph Smallwood while thinking out loud to his secretary was costing out Alice's request. If that's the case, this is another hint that either as a campaign manager or as a premier, Smallwood once took her petition seriously.

Ten days after Newfoundland joined Canada, Mrs. George French wrote another letter, this time addressing the new premier: "To The Honourable J. R. Smallwood. Premier of Newfoundland. Canada." She congratulated him on his victory, reminded him about her previous letter, thanked him for his kind and courteous reply, and named the promise he had made her in his campaign. "P.S." Alice added, "Please pass along my Congratulations to Mrs. Smallwood on your great honour. [...] A.F."

But this seemingly buoyant letter did not lead to hoped-for results. Just a few months later, on July 5, Alice French wrote the premier again, "this is the fourth letter since I have written you on the subject ..." (indicating that there is a letter missing, perhaps the undated fragment that is in this file). In the July letter, Alice reiterated her point that she and George had no children and, she added, "I am not old enough by year's yet to receive the old age pension." Alice was losing her patience because Smallwood had shown "not even the common courtesy of an answer." But even in this fourth letter, she still demonstrated a naive faith in her premier: "if you say so I could come to your house some evening whenever it would suit you. And it would only take me five minutes to explain the whole situation to you, or," she offered generously, "you could drive up to my house any time."

This letter elicited a response. On July 25, J.R. Smallwood replied that he had passed her letter on to the Department of Home Affairs. And, sure enough, three days later a letter arrived in Alice's morning mail. Because of some misunderstanding, implying but not stating that the premier had directed her letter to the wrong department, Mr. Carew, the head of Newfoundland's Civil Service, indicated that he was passing her letter on to the Department of Finance.

"Whatever will I do," Alice asked Smallwood, in a letter she wrote the same day, "As I am physically unable to earn a living for myself (being totally deaf) And I have no one whatever to help me. There is so much money for other things like baby bonuses Old Age pensions (I am not for some year's eligible for the old Age pension) but I do feel that I am in the same class as a Blind person in that I am unable to earn a living for myself ..."

Thirteen days later, Alice wrote a follow-up, her sixth letter to Mr. Smallwood. By this point the Secretary of Finance, Mr. Marshall, had acquainted her with an Act passed in 1947 during the Commission of Government which stipulated that pensions terminated with the death of the pensioner. As Alice, the premier, the Deputy Minister of Home Affairs, and now the Secretary of Finance were all aware, Mr. George French died nine months before Confederation. "Mr. Smallwood do something about that Act ..." Alice pleaded, "I relied so much on what you told me." She begged him to "in this case, make your promise good." As she wrote, "I do not want to go on the Public Health & Welfare Dept to be classed as a pauper Oh God no. My late husband gave a life time Service to the Civil Service ... If you could only know how hard I am having it to exist at all," she concluded, asking the premier to respond "as soon as Convenient to you." Then Alice threw all caution to the wind with a postscript:

> P.S. Please Mr. Smallwood do not offer me Any Sympathy in my Circumstances As both the Home Affairs & Finance Dept have dished out a lot of that hooey to me And that do not feed my stomach pay my rent buy my food or fuel, So it's no good to me is it? A.F.

As evidenced by another letter, dated a month later, on August 24, "a lot of that hooey" did not get her very far. "Dear Hon. Premier," she began,

> This is about the 6th letter I have written you since our Island became the 10th Province of Canada ... Now Mr. Smallwood that Act is wrong and outdated now And you know it is wrong all wrong As the Widows of retired Civil Servants over on the Mainland do get their husbands' pension And I know it, And you know it also Mr. Smallwood we are all Canadians now isn't we so why the difference?
>
> ...

As in her previous letters, Alice summarized her case, adding "You only have to say so Mr. Smallwood and its done I know ..." Then Alice asked for a monthly pension of $40 to $45—which she pointed out was less than George was getting at $67.50. "Thanking you (for nothing yet but for what I am hoping to get) I am Sincerely Yours, Alice French."

Perhaps it is indicative of Alice's growing frustration that it was less than two weeks later (on September 5) that she penned her eighth letter: "Dear Mr. Smallwood, The months is still passing away And I am still without my pension ..."

Perhaps due to her complaint that he had not replied to her previous two letters, Smallwood finally wrote Alice on September 12. It seemed to me, when I was reading through this file, that Joey's answers to all his supplicants were growing increasingly formal and testy—but I will let you, dear reader, be the judge:

> There is really nothing that I can do about the question you have mentioned on your various letters to me. The matter is not in my Department, but comes under the Civil Service. I have passed your letters to Mr. Carew, the head of the Civil Service in Newfoundland, and there really is nothing else that I can do in the matter. I would be very happy if there was something I could do, but I am afraid there is not.

This letter was the context for Alice's forthright and spirited retort on September 29, 1949, that opens this reflection. At around the same time that she wrote that missive, Alice had visited Mr. H.J. Carew, the Deputy Minister of Home Affairs, in his office. As she reminded the deputy minister in her letter of November 28, she had shown Carew the letter in which Smallwood had promised her a pension: "you are the only person excepting my lawyer who have read it ..." Given Smallwood's promise "under his own signature," Alice was convinced that she had a legal case. Now, in her last letter in this file, Alice made Carew a promise of her own: "I have purposely refrained from writing you before so as to give you plenty of time, but I have no intention of letting the matter drop unless Mr. Smallwood is prepared to make it worth my while to do so ..." By this point Alice had assumed a larger mandate. She was no longer writing only on her own behalf, but for all the widows of other pensioners who, like her were left destitute at their husbands' deaths.

Just a few days later, Smallwood penned a response to Alice French. "I now understand from your letter that your late husband, being a Provincial civil servant, and not an employee of the Federal Government, would naturally come under our Provincial law," he stated. This, he asserted, was the cause of her problems: "our Provincial civil servants do not, and never did contribute any payment into a pension fund while they were working and receiving a salary. Federal Government civil servants do contribute to such a fund, which is why the Federal scheme is so much better than our own." While Smallwood suggested that it might be possible to change the provincial plan, this would be of no assistance to Alice.

That letter is the last of the correspondence between Alice French and Joseph Smallwood. There is no stationery with her familiar copperplate handwriting in the 1950 file. Alice was sixty-two in 1948, and the widow of a provincial employee, which meant that under then current law, she was ineligible for a pension, and Smallwood could not guarantee a change in provincial legislation. She was, however, not without resources. Three years earlier, the 1945 census, taken when George was eighty-four and Alice fifty, their house had one boarder, fifty-year-old Ralph Hart of Trinity North. She had four rooms, which meant that, if all else failed, she could sleep in the kitchen and rent out three rooms to lodgers. Mr. Hart may still have been boarding with Alice when she wrote these letters to Smallwood; however, if he was, she doesn't mention him.

Alice died in 1974, at the age of eighty-nine. William French, probably George's last surviving offspring, did not bury Alice in the family plot—even though there was room next to his wife Ethel's grave. Instead, Alice's grave is in another cemetery altogether.

William French lived almost a decade longer than Alice, dying in 1983 at ninety-three. He was buried next to his wife; his younger brother; his stepmother, Helen Mary; and his father. Alice spoke the truth when she told Smallwood she had no children to rely on. But thanks to old friendships, forty years after renting Lily a room, when she died Alice was buried next to Lily Gibson, who predeceased Alice by four years. Someone, maybe Alice, had "Rest in peace" inscribed on Lily's headstone. If their friendship was something more intimate, Alice would not have had the freedom to have "dearly beloved" inscribed on Lily's headstone, as George once wrote for his first wife. Alice's headstone is even more simple, listing her first and married name and her birth and death year. Here, where I won't be accused of vandalizing the graveyard, I add a postscript: "Alice French 1886–1975. Her letters struck fear in the hearts of powerful men."

June 17, 1948.

Mr. J.R. Smallwood,
St. John's.

Dear Sir,

I have heard discussion which went like this: Even if Confederation does get a few thousand more votes than Responsible Government we won't go in with Canada because there will be too many people against it; besides, Canada woulden't take us. Would you kindly tell me the truth about this – how many more votes we have to get before we can confederate. I realize how busy you must be so if you answer in only one sentence it will be Satisfactory.

I have enclosed a stamped, self-addressed envelope for your convenience in replying.

Thank you very much,
Yours sincerely,

P.S. I know quite a number of people, who voted for responsible government last time, who are voting for Confederation next time.

Dec 20/48

Mr. J R Smallwood
St. John's.

Dear Sir: -

It is somewhat difficult to express in words the admiration and appreciation we feel for you for the manner in which you have fought the terrific battle for Confederation. We may not know what power has so sustained you, but it is apparent to all that your victories now and to come, are all the more glorious because of the trying ordeals you have endured.

Suitable awards may not be your fortune, or even desired by you, but we believe by your abilities and unselfishness you have accomplished something that in future years will enshrine you among Newfoundland's Greatest.

Wishing you and Mrs Smallwood and children a very Merry Christmas and brightest future.

[married couple, names redacted]

Jan 24 1949

Mr J. R. Smallwood.

Dear Sir:-

Since seeing you last, I have been unsuccessful in finding a job, and although, while I was speaking to you at your house I had something special in mind, I did not see fit to bring it up.

I have been trying to find someone with influence enough to get me a berth to go to the seal-fishery.[2] *Unfortunately I dont have any friends close enough to the merchants or skippers to help me.*

I wonder if you could. It has occurred to me that you know quite a few Northern men and it may be possible for you to get me a berth, If it is at all possible I would be eternally grateful for such a favour.

Yours faithfully

January 27, 1949.

Dear Mr. [name redacted],

Thanks for your letter, they say it is better to be born lucky than right. It so happens that this is very true as an hour before reading your letter I have been offered a berth to the ice by Capt. [redacted], a close friend of mine. He is taking a three masted auxiliary vessel to the ice from Halifax this spring, I forget her name, but she was out to the ice last year. He will sail from Halifax but the men

2 The commercial seal fishery in Newfoundland and Labrador began in the eighteenth century. For more, see J.K. Hiller, "The Newfoundland and Labrador Seal Fishery," Heritage Newfoundland & Labrador, 2001, https://www.heritage.nf.ca/articles/economy/seal-fishery.php and "The Sailing Seal Fishery," Heritage Newfoundland & Labrador, 2001, https://www.heritage.nf.ca/articles/economy/sailing-seal-fishery.php; Shannon Ryan, Martha Drake, and Cater Andrews, *Seals and Sealers: A Pictorial History of the Newfoundland Seal Fishery Based on the Cater Andrews Collection* (St. John's: Breakwater, 1987); C.W. Sanger, "Seal Fishery in the 20th Century," Heritage Newfoundland & Labrador, 1998, https://www.heritage.nf.ca/articles/environment/sealing-fishery-in-the-20th-century.php.

will have their passages paid to Halifax and they will be delivered back to St. John's without any expense to you. If you would care to have this berth it is yours for the asking.

I am leaving tomorrow for Ottawa, and will be gone for about three weeks. See me sometime after I get back.

With best wishes,

Sincerely yours,

J.R. SMALLWOOD.

April 9th/49

To Hon J.R. Smallwood

Dear Sir: -

As I was a ardent supporter of responsible government and Lost; and now that we are a tenth Providence of Canada I sincerely believe that we should forget our difference's and try to make Newfoundland a good Providence, but owing to the fact that there are a great many mountains to climb I cannot see how it can be done before many of our People go to the mainland for to obtain decent wages & living. Personally I am just about fed up on the way things are going on here now I am a union man & worker & employed in local industry this last twelve years & see myself no farther ahead than first when I started, although I am still a young man of 33 years & married if things do not improve, as much as I hate to I will be forced for to go to a richer Providence now that there is nothing in my way for to stop me; I do not believe that I am wrong when I state that if I were Canada doing the same work that I do here I would be farther ahead that I am now: my occupation is spike makeing that is nails made for Wharves Ships etc & a man that as stood at his post for twelve years over a hot coke fire should have better treatment than trying to exist on a paltry $24.00 Per week which I am receiving now, I realise there are people a lot worst of than myself but that is beside the Point, at the moment I am interested in the form of government best for Newfoundland to my way of thinking the liberal govt, is best because you yourself has be a union man, therefor labour should back you to the fullest extent, it is high time that the working class forgot about the big money man for to run the country & give men like yourself a chance: Personally if I am still here in my beloved country which I sincerely hope that I am, you may rest assured that I will back you all I can because I believe you will do all in your Power for the working man, now that were going to have a money man opposing you in the first election;

Yours sincerely

(note) if you can find the time would you kindly favour me with a reply

owing to the fact that I am in the unfortunate Position with the money men who I guess do not like you to well as far as Nfld is concerned
Kindly keep this confidential

April 28th 49

Mr. J.R. Smallwood

Dear Sir

I hope you will excuse the liberty I take in writing you, but at the present time its a case of necessity. I am sixty six year old and have been idle over one year. am a baker by trade but althoug in good health Cannot procure work of any kind. am already listed with the unemployed. was overseas in world war one in Forestry work. have only my wife & what little I saved is gone no one to look for help. am sober & would take any light work Caretaker or Watchman. if I was eligible for old age pension it would help a lot I have never asked for any releif before but certianly need it now. hoping you will give this letter some consideration I reman

May 3rd/49

Hon

Mr. Joe R. Smallwood –

Dear Sir.

According to reports it would be useless to try and see you, so I am going to drop you a few words in the hope that you will find time to answer it.

What I want to know is are you able to get us some fertilizer we do not want you to give it to us but as a loan till the potatoes are ready to sell. As the herring fishery was a failure we are at a loss as to how to get it so we are going to ask you to try and help us. the fertilizer is namely 9 sacks Potatoe 5 sacks Cabbage and 5 sacks nitre of soda.[3] *hoping to hear from you as soon as possible.*

I remain

3 Sodium nitrate, typically used as fertilizer.

May 22, 1949

Dear Mr Smallwood

As polling day is drawing near I listened to your broadcast always. Everything seems to have been mentioned accept the Widow's Pension.[4] *I was surprised to see that you had forgotten them, as the sum they were receiving by The Commission Government was not enough for sweetening for their tea.*

For it is up to you to do your utmost on behalf of the Widows, and we'll do ours for you.

Yours Truly
A worker & Widow

P.S. Will be looking forward to your broadcast in reference to this.

4 For more on the widows' pension, see the reflection by Gina Snooks, earlier in this volume.

May 29th 1949

The Honorable J.R. Smallwood.
St. John's. City.

My Honorable Premier Friend "Joey"! –

I want to congratulate you in the way you have been used in brinig about the Great Victory on the side of True Liberalism and in the best intrests of our "Toiling Masses" The Victory is cimply wonderful. I feel the Good Lord has answered the cry of my heart! I have prayed much that our God would bless your efforts and He has Blest in such a marvelous way!

Will you bear with me as your friend, if I suggest to you the Christian like way of dealing with your "Tory Enemies"! The Good Lord has put you into the "Driver's Seat" of State. You are lifted above your Enemies and so need not even referr to them in a critical way! Eh? How do you feel over what you said last night (Saturday) about your Tory Enemies? Does it not Kick back? I feel you was not your normal self. You spoke as one who was over-wrought with the terrible strain of the past Day's. Will you not have enough Enemies without twisting the "Tory Enemies tail"? especially now since you are in the Victorious Drivers-Seat of State! I am going to continue to pray that wisdom may be given you in directing our shipt of State.

I am writing you as your true friend, not to criticize but to exhort you as a Spiritual Father in the Truly Christian way, God Bless You

Your devoted & faithful friend

June 21st 1949

Dear Sir

just a few lines regarding the windows pension.

There is so much work to fill out the form to the Child's welfar to the court house. and then the returning officer got to come and inspect you it is just putting you down on the dole. it is not enough to put all particulars on the form but you got to go all over with it to the returning officer anything you have to do is done right like the baby bonuses why not let us have it as the baby bonuses have it. I have not received any widows pensions as yet. the baby bonuses is alright but when they are able to buy bikes and put their cheques in the bank and the poor widow starving its up to you and I know you are the man can do it you ll get our vote and put you in and may (God) bless you and keep you in for 20 years. I am writing this on behalf of dozens of widows you have asked me to write you those few lines

Wishing you the best of luck and your men in the coming elections.

Widows of the West End.

Hon. J.R. Smallwood,
Prime Minister of N.f.l.d.
Prime Minister's Office.
St John's N.f.l.d.

"Hon Dear Sir: -

Having written to you a couple of years ago without receiving any answer to my Letter – I am now writing you again.

I have already told you that I was unjustly Placed in the Lunatic Asylum – I am still here. And I have now been here for Eighteen years this Past June.

I never in my Life committed the smallest of a Crime; and I was never inside of a Penatentiary in my Life. Neither did I ever in my Life-time have to pay a Fine in any way for any misdoing, and as well, I was never before Court for any Wrongdoing; and was never given notice to do so – not at any time.

I never took any medicine or Drugs of any kind since I came inside the Door of this Building. I was not sick when I came here I am not sick now., neither have I been sick for not even one day During all of these Eighteen years.

All the Doctor's who have come and gone from this Institution have admitted that they saw nothing mentally the matter with me.

Also, the Nurses and the Attendents, those who have gone from here as well as those who are here now have said they saw nothing mentally the matter with me, and that I should not be here; and the Doctors here now have admitted they don't see anything mentally the matter with me.
Still, I have been locked in over Fourteen yrs without being allowed outside of the Door – and in all I have been held here Eighteen years.

You are Prime Minister now Mr Smallwood!

Is this Just? And are you as Leader of the Liberal Government going to allow it to continue?

My Present condition Led up to what it is – because of the members of the Conservative side of the Old House of Assembly – they blamed me for Robbing money through a Note I got through Sir Richard Squires. I explained it (the cause of my getting the note) to you on my letter two years ago. It was because of the Fish Regulations of 1920; and because Sir Wm Coaker gave me wrong advice, which cost me excessive loss – and because the Prince of Fish was no better the following year, I could not pay it back. Then even though the Note was Discounted at the Bank according to what I was taught of Banking Laws – They held me up for the note, and took my Business and everything connected, and Gave my Premises to a [man] on the South Side. He was a strong Conservative at any rate.

I think he has since died.

If you are a man Sir, who want to see Justice done, and is bent upon having Justice done: you are in a Position to see that Justice in my case is carried out, or else brought about.

I have another Birthday due the [date redacted] this month. And wedding Annaversary Due on the [date redacted] which is only a few days later. I have also had to be contented in spending my wedding Jubilee Annaversary here a dozen years ago.

But I think Mr Smallwood you are in a Position now to see that I don't spend even another week in here.

I will be hoping Sir, to see something noticable in the next few days which will show something favorable through this Letter

Respectfully yours –

St. John's West
July 28, 1949.

The Hon. J. R. Smallwood,
Premier of Newfoundland,
St. John's

Dear Sir,

We, the undersigned, being academic students at the Summer Session of Memorial University College,[5] *have been informed by our respected Executive Officers that no subsidy will be granted to us married men this summer because we have not ten years' teaching experience.*

To us, this seems very unfair and we think that some consideration should be given to married students regardless of the number of years' experience, and especially when a subsidy is granted every student during the regular year, prospective teachers included.

In view of these facts, we, hereby, take the liberty of appealing to you and your cabinet to do your utmost to grant a subsidy payable to us as well as to any other married man.

Trusting that a favourable reply will be forwarded at your earliest convenience.

We are,
Yours truly,

[name redacted], 8 yrs experience + 2 yrs in college.
[name redacted] 9 yrs experience + 2 yrs in college.
[name redacted] 6 yrs Exp. 2 yrs in college

5 For more on the history of Memorial University College, see MacLeod, *A Bridge Built Halfway*.

TRINITY NORTH

Childhood Perspectives and Poignant Silences: A Study of Trinity North

Shruti Raheja

ON MAY 20, 2021, I entered the archives of Memorial's Queen Elizabeth II Library for the first time, equal parts nervous and eager to trace lives, hopes, and disenchantments through the collection of letters written to Smallwood by individuals in the district of Trinity North. Linda White and Paulette Noseworthy welcomed me with enthusiasm, offering me everything from historical anecdotes to advice on deciphering the loopy cursive handwriting scrawled across thin stationery—paper relics of tangible people whose vibrancy somehow leaked out through inky fervour. On that first day, Linda, Paulette, and I agreed to maintain weekly Thursday appointments, and I went home feeling encouraged.

Little did I know that precisely one week later, the tone of the summer would shift entirely. On May 27, 2021, headlines announced that the Tk'emlúps te Secwépemc First Nation had found 215 potential unmarked graves at the former site of Kamloops Indian Residential School. Two hundred and fifteen children buried haphazardly on these grounds, most of them far from their families and homes. Tk'emlúps te Secwépemc were the first to identify unmarked graves, but their announcement was soon followed by many others: Cowesses First Nation, Muskowekwan, Ktunaxa, Penelakut. Countless other sites are still being traced. Nameless faces never felt so vivid. Every few days for an entire summer, I heard about these children in the news. I wanted to ask if anyone had been there to hold those small hands during their last moments of life. Unsurprisingly, these children occupied my thoughts as I leafed through correspondence that marked the period when Newfoundland was joining Canada. I couldn't help but think about these other events that were taking place parallel to Confederation.

The letters I gathered to represent Trinity North reflect a range of experiences but, mostly, they focus on the children of the area: their needs, their desires, and their struggles, articulated through letters asking the government for everything from playgrounds to affordable groceries. Many of these young people faced poverty and illness; their lives were not easy, but while absorbing these stories, I simultaneously considered those children whose voices did not appear in letters to Smallwood. Among these were the youth attending institutions of assimilation in Nain, Makkovik, North West River, Cartwright, and St. Anthony. Why was it that certain citizens communicated—often repeatedly—with the premier, while others were far less connected to his presence? We know that many people in Labrador, including countless young Inuit, advocated against the residential schooling system in favour of more local, culture-based education. Yet, such protests took place painstakingly, often through negotiations with the school board, with government resistance every step of the way.[1] Would writing to Smallwood have been a helpful course of action? After all, when Newfoundland became part of Canada in 1949, the Terms of Union failed to acknowledge Indigenous peoples in the province.[2] There was no promise to protect or nurture these children.

A few months after completing my archival research, I found myself back in the foyer of the Queen Elizabeth II Library, where I'd returned to write this reflection. Red dresses were draped across the entrance,[3] and a miniscule maroon one caught my eye. The dress was sleeveless and trimmed with lace flowers. So tiny that I could fold it into my purse. It fluttered, almost imperceptibly, every time somebody opened the door. The province's last residential school closed in 1980, and the last Canadian one, in 1996, but systemic injustice lives on. Oji-Cree writer Joshua Whitehead recently wrote, "My home is full of hope and ghosts,"[4] and I believe this paradox captures our current moment remarkably:

1 Procter, *A Long Journey*, 373.

2 Procter, *A Long Journey*, 10.

3 Red Dress Day began in May of 2010 and has been observed annually as the National Day of Awareness for Missing and Murdered Indigenous Women, Girls, and Two-Spirit Individuals.

4 Joshua Whitehead, *Jonny Appleseed* (Arsenal Pulp, 2018), 20.

lives from the past surround us, ever-present in the pieces they have left behind for contemplation. Since beginning this project, I have started to see my world as a living archive, with truths to be found under every rock, inside every crevice, between the pages of every hardcover my fingers trace. I have been searching in unexpected places to find stories I might not see in ink or typeface, as well as ones that hide between the lines: stories etched in trees before these trees became paper, bearing witness to lives as vivid as sunlight hitting the northern snow. To listen to the voices that seek me out is my steadfast goal.

July 28/1948

To Mr. J R Smallwood
St. Johns

Dear Sir

First of all I must say congratulations on your victory to Confederation, I am a girl 16 years old and only wish I was old enough to vote for confederation, my mother and father voted for confederation on June the 3rd, and they also voted for it on July 22. and my grandmother which is nearly blind only can see out of half an eye mother lead her down to vote for confederation to. and my brother voted for it to, we have listened to your broadcast and know that you have well earned your victory, you are the one man out of a hundred could have carried on and won out, so please excuse my writing sir as I am not much good at writing letters, so heres wishing you luck sir in your good work, although we have no family to get the baby bonus, only one little boy who is seven years of age, and my aged grandmother, and they will be very glad with it.
So again I congradalate you.
Yours Truly

perhaps sir you would like to know my parents and Grandmothers name
my parents name is [names redacted]
my grandmothers name is
[name redacted],
and her husband also voted for confederation, [name redacted]

April 24th 1949

Dear sir:

I am writing you a few lines to see if there can be something done about the prices of some of our everyday needs the store keepers around here haven't dropped their prices any lower since we have come under confederation the majority here voted for the Canadian government with the understanding it would be better. I hope there will be something done about it in the near future. We are paying 14 cents per pound for sugar & 20 cents a pound for beans and around 18 dollars a barrel for salt beef more than it is at St. John's so I think it is about time for some authority to take action against them they are also selling without bills & trust this will do some good to us in the near future.

Yours faithfully,

P.S.

The Store Keepers are namely: [names redacted]

April 29/1949

Dear Sir

Well I am writing you these few lines to ask you to see if you would obliged me by doing me a favour I have a boy Born Dec 21st 1932 cristened April 28 1933 he was Babtized on dec 22nd 1932

he was born in Dec and he took sick and his eye run out and almost blind in the other on

So if you could do something for me I don't care how long

I like to get something for him he is a poor blind boy try and do something for him do it as soon has you can do it

I vote for you me and my husband, we vote for you two times I was sick the first time I vote posted up in bed

I said I was going to vote for you the 3rd June in walwyn cottage hospital I need a little help for him so I said I would write you these few lines I said, you would do something for me I will be expecting a answer next mail the boy name [name redacted] his mother is [name redacted] and now I am married now to Mr. [name redacted] so try and do your best for me.

Your truly

May 21st / 49

Hon. J. R. Smallwood

Dear premier:

I am taking the pleasure of presenting to you congratulations for having the honour of being the first premier of Newfoundland.

I was very interested in the accounts that came over the radio & was very happy when I heard that so many of the Liberal Candidates was being elected. I was more than over joyed when your accounts were read out & when I heard over the radio that you had been elected as the peoples leader as our first premier.

I am only ten years old but I am as interested in the elections as the ones that were old enough to vote. I was to the meeting that Mr. Hefferton had & I enjoyed it very much. I was trying to get a big picture of you but I didn't know where to get one. I asked Mr. Hefferton's brother for one but he had them all gone. I am asking you if you would be kind enough to send me one. I would like to get one to frame & keep so I would be able to have a picture of our first premier in years to come. I am getting my family allowance & I am thanking you for it, because only for you we would never be under confederation.

My father was in world war 1914-18 and he knows what Responsible Government & the Tory party are like. He was certainly glad that the merchants never got their own way this time. My Father mother & brother voted both times for you side because they taught it the best way.

All the family is sending you congratulations.

Yours truly

May 29th/49

Right Hon. Premier Joseph Smallwood

Dear Mr. Smallwood,

You don't know how happy I am to be able to send you our hearty congratulations from myself husband little girl 10 her last birthday, also my aged mother 84 her last Birthday, On becoming Nfld's first Premier under Confederation and no one has a better right to it than you, after fighting so hard the past three or four years yes and fought hard to,

We are a family with the many listeners who listen to all the convention meetings I heard all the talks etc thanks again to you for persevering to make the broadcasts possible, & sometimes it was very trying for you, still you fought on, and as I said & will always say God moves in mysterious ways & put into your mind to try & help bring about a better & happier Nfld for our toiling Masses, the Rich have plenty so they do not feel the wants of others or at least some don't, already it has done good by becoming a province of Canada by seeing lots of little children with shoes on their feet, clothes on their backs yes & better food for their stomach what they would'en have only for (Joe Smallwood) that old familiar name May the Good Lord prosperous you in your undertaking.

Well Mr. Smallwood I want to ask you if at your earliest convenience could you see that there was a telephone & a Post-Office put in [community], we have to walk between two and three miles to get our mail & for life or death have to go the same distance to reach a telephone.

We are a population of about 150 so if a Post Office could'en be got it would be a very important thing to have a telephone for all concerns, hope you will consider my asking and wishing you every pleasure in your duties.

I am Yours

Sincerely

May 30th/49

The Hon. Joseph R. Smallwood
St. John's

My Dear Sir:

I now take my pen and write to you in dire mud and anxiety. I am a youth of seventeen years, and owing to the present conditions, I am forced to write you, asking if you or some of your friends can help me in obtaining work.

I am the oldest of a family of nine children, and am naked of clothes, and a burning desire to fulfil my ambition. At the present I am studying Grade X, and as far as I can see, it is impossible to complete my Education without some financial assistance. But I do not want for someone to give it to me. I want to work during the summer months, and work I will supposing its the pick and shovel, if only I had the chance.

The summer is coming, I cannot go fishing, for some particular reasons, and I must walk about, if I cannot obtain work.

Mr. Smallwood, I think I can say with a contrite heart, that I am respectable, trustworthy, and obedient, I am a God fearing young man, and am capable of handling some kind of job, of some responsibility. I don't care what the job is, as long as it is a full time job.

Oh please, do something for me, help me, as you helped your country.

I Remain

Most Respectively yours,

P.S. Please reply as soon as possible.

May 31st/49

Premier J. R. Smallwood,

Dear Premier:

I had saw in your paper the Liberal sometime ago that your party would give some means of security for criples. I have my left leg off above my knee so you are a man of the type who understands what a man like me can do at hard work for depends I have a wife and 3 children my oldest being 10 yrs old, I do not receive any pension and if I had my two legs I would not be asking for help at this time this past winter these were young men able bodied getting relief while I had to sweat and work hard in the woods trying to get something for my family to eat. I voted & also my wife for your party the liberal party I hoped that life would become a little easier for me. My wife have recd the family allowance and very glad and grateful to receive it as the childrens were much in need at that time to keep them to school. I trusting you will be able to do something for me I had written you before but did not receive any answer trusting this will receive your best attention.

Sincerely yours

May 31st

Hon. J. R. Smallwood

St. John's

Dear Sir,

First of all I wish to congratulate you and your Liberal party on the sweeping victory in the Election. I am a School Teacher for the past two years. I intend to give it up for the teachers are not payed for their work. I think that you have done a lot of good for this country especially the past two months for I can see a great change in the clothing [illegible] the children lately. This Sunday there was a lot of new clothes around here. I have been very interested in Confederation ever since you spoke about it in the convention. I have worn my radio battery down this week listening to the counts, but I am not interested in the P.C. counts, only the Liberals.

I have been wondering if you could get a job for me the last of June, if so please let me know before I go to summer school. I would also like a picture of you to frame as the first Premier under Confederation. Please try and get a job for me. Once again, congratulations on your sweeping victory.

Please answer as soon as possible Yours truly,

[Teacher]

June 6th/49

Hon. J. R. Smallwood.

Dear Sir:

Just a few lines to explain to you, how I have to get along. I am not a widow, as my husband is living, but a patient at the mental hospital for 12 years, and in those years, I have seen hard times.

I was getting 5 dollars a month after he went to hospital and seeing I could not get along with that amount to buy food, clothes, & coal, as I have no body to earn for me. I couldn't stay home winter time because I was oftener cold than warm.

I went out in service winter time to try and earn something to help along.

After that my five dollars was cut off from me.

I am 50 years of age and not able to work at the hardest kind now. Mr. Smallwood, is there any way for me to help get a living as you know yourself 5 dollars was not much a month. I hope I am not asking you too much but I know you are the poor peoples friends.

Thanks for a reply.

Yours truly

July 11th 1949

Premier J. R. Smallwood
St. John's Newfoundland

Dear Sir:

I am writing you now concerning my daughter who is a cripple she have been to Come-By-Chance hospital and also the General hospital at St. John's, and nothing can be done for her. Dr. [name redacted] was her Dr. when at the General if you would see him no doubt you could get more information from him.

She is only eighteen years of age and sometimes (not very often) she gets the chance to earn a fifty cent or perhaps a dollar through knitting and as I am a widow myself it's a small lot I can do to help her so I am writing you to see if she is entitled to any allowance. It was her I had in mind each time I went to the polls to vote so please consider this over, and if there's anything can be done for her, I know you will do your best, hoping that you comes on top in your final trial.

I remain,

daughter's name [redacted]

Infirm in both legs name of disease angioneurotic edemu.

Sept 2/49

To the

Hon. J. R. Smallwood,

Premier for N.F.L.D.,

Hon. Dear Sir,

I am writing you to see if you would get in touch with the Dept. of Public Health and Welfare and see if a set of false teeth be granted me, I being an exservice man from World War II. I have spent one month in the merchant navy hospital. Owing to my stomach in fact I can't eat—owing to can't chew my food. It's two years now since I had my teeth out. I am unable to buy any owing to no work. So being a Confederate I drop you a line. Hoping by Dayrest- be given free attention and a reply given as hasty as possible.

I Remain

RNVR[5]

5 Royal Naval Volunteer Reserve.

To:
HON. J.R. SMALLWOOD
PREMIER
ST. JOHN'S.

BE IT RESOLVED THAT THIS MEETING OF ST PETERS CONGREGATION STRONGLY DISAPPROVE THE PROPOSED HIGHROAD PASSING NO NEAR ST PETERS SCHOOL THAT IT WILL PROVE A REAL DANGER TO THE EIGHTY FOUR CHILDREN NOW ATTENDING AND MANY MORE AS TIME PASSES AND REQUEST THE HIGHROADS DIVISION TO EXAMINE MORE CAREFULLY THE MATTER AND THAT A COPY OF THIS RESOLUTION BE SENT TO THEIR HONOURABLES THE PREMIER THE MINISTER OF EDUCATION AND THE MINISTER OF PUBLIC WORKS, [TWO NAMES REDACTED]

1040 AM SEP 6 1949

October 19-49

Mr. J. R. Smallwood,

Dear Sir:

Seeing that the government is spending money on public things, I wonder if [community] School would be able to get a play ground, for the children to play on. Down here at [our community] the children have to play on the marsh, and among big rocks.

I think it is time now for the government to do something down around here. You would want around five hundred dollars for to make a complete job. Hoping that this will be taken into consideration.

Your obedient servant,

To: J. R. SMALLWOOD

FEBRUARY 21, 1950.

WOULD YOU RUSH PLANE TAKE CHILD HOSPITAL BELIEVE SUFFERING PNEUMONIA.

[handwritten]: Phoned Dr. 9:30 am. Feb 22[6]

6 Some telegrams include handwritten commentary or stamped dates, likely added by a secretary. Wherever these occur, we note them with square brackets.

Hon. J.R. Smallwood,
Premier,
St. John's. *Aug. 15th, 1950.*

Dear Sir:

Some time ago at a meeting held at [community] United Church Board of Education that we needed a playground and we have in the community as in other people who do not want to work together for the good of the place then we wondered if we might write you and ask what help we could get this playground, it would be wise to know too that when the children come out of school they are on the public road and they have little or no playing around we want your support in this case hoping hear from you as soon as possible.

Fraternally Yours,

TRINITY SOUTH

"The Widows' Mite"

Angela Antle

THE PATERNAL SIDE of my family lived and fished out of the tiny Catholic enclave of Turk's Cove, just south of Winterton, from the 1800s to sometime in the early 1950s. Part of the electoral district of Trinity South, the residents there did not support Confederation. Indeed, as members of a Catholic community, my paternal forebears would've been advised against joining Canada from the pulpit even though they were as destitute as their neighbours. Once, on a visit to Turk's Cove, a Mrs. Conway told me that my grandfather could knock a seagull right out of the sky with a beach rock, a skill, she assured me, that kept the community from starving during the Great Depression.

Reading the Trinity South letters has given me a broader and more nuanced understanding of the deep and widespread hunger and poverty in this district, pre-Confederation. To quote a war bride's letter from May 11, 1949, "this is the poorest country I have ever come across." In particular, the following themes stand out in this collection of letters: rising food prices, poor access to health care, the injustice of the widows' allowance, lack of infrastructure, unemployment, and having to travel to obtain work. Interestingly, Newfoundlanders and Labradorians face many of the same concerns today.

The first time I sat with the letters, two items of ephemera caught my eye; grocery bills from April 1949: one from N. Smith's store for a total of $6.55 and another from the Heart's Content merchant Harold R. Martin for a total of

$16.62. The bills were sent with a letter to demonstrate what the correspondent considered unfairly high prices set by both merchants. In his words, "My Opinion Sir is that the mothers won't see any good of the family allowance cheques or anything else before their is some kind of a restriction put on these merchants. What hurts the most is when we go to the stores with a bit of hard earned money and have to pay the highest prices and know that we are soaked left and right."

Even without the letter, the two bills alone tell us about the economic reality of life in Trinity South at that time. At first glance, I thought each bill represented a single grocery trip to the merchants' stores. However, the repetition of the phrases "½ cup of baking powder," "carrots," and "1 C. of flakes," and on the Harold R. Martin bill, "big bens cig papers," indicates that each line was a separate visit to the store. As well, the Harold R. Martin bill states, "accounts collected monthly," and they are referred to in the letter as the April bills. The writer asks Mr. Smallwood to send the bills back so that he can pay them.

In addition to the many trips to the store for supplies, the bills also hint at the labour and time put into everyday meal preparation; no doubt there was baking daily or every few days in most households. There's no protein on one of the bills, but beef, sausages, and bacon appear on the other. The family was probably supplementing their diet with their own animals, wild meat, and fish. The foodstuffs are simple and the amounts small: "1 turnip," "½ cup of apricots," "a cabbage," "an apple," and such. It is difficult to imagine an individual, let alone "a family, and one horse" as they describe their household surviving on so little. And yet many families survived on less.

Another correspondent wrote that her husband earned $106 during his entire fishing season, while many others spoke of pre-Confederation government support of $10 or $15 a quarter. The merchant grocery bills illuminate clearly how challenging it would've been to survive on such a paltry amount of support.

Ill health is another common theme, and one only has to read a few letters to understand how an illness could derail a family's finances, and how little state support was available for those who were blind, "cripple," or found themselves ill at home or in the hospital. Others, meanwhile, shared concerns about the lack of health care in their communities, a theme which resonates strongly in the present day. The file contains a May 13, 1949, telegram from a woman that states: "WAITING FOR A BED AT GENERAL HOSPITAL TWO WEEKS CAN YOU ARRANGE FOR ADMISSION IMMEDIATELY PLEASE ADVISE."

Bad health, no doubt linked to the poor diet or, in the words of one correspondent, "made sick by hard work," left many destitute. Among them was a woman who wrote to Smallwood on May 8, 1949, stating that the doctor had diagnosed her with a "TB hip":

> I am a crippled woman, I have been cripple for seven years and I has five young children. My husband works in the lumber woods and as you can imagine the lumber woods does not employ him yearly, only a short while in the winter and a few summer months.

This woman requested better work for her husband, financial support for her family, and a better road to her house, because, as she observed, "Everytime I has to be taken to the hospital, I has to be carried from my home to the taxi on a stretcher or carried by two of three men in their arms so you also can imagine that's a hard way to be handled."

Another mother of thirteen children whose husband's leg was broken in an accident, wrote: "and owing to the leg being broke for so long before it was set, owing to being swelled so much, he will find that while he lives," she wrote, "the dr will tell you he is a cripple and he got three of his fingers gone by the inside of the middle joint, sir we gets $25 a month." She was worried that their relief would be cut off because she had additional cash in hand, having sold their only cow to buy food, make roof repairs, and purchase new cartwheels. Another woman shared concerns about the mental health of her teenage daughter. Her vivid language and the intimate descriptions of her daughter's symptoms stayed with me long after I read her letter. What caused her daughter's illness? Could the mother have misunderstood her daughter's condition? Did she find help and what kind of help was available at that time? How many other families were in similar situations?

From a contemporary vantage point, there's a naive quality to some of the requests for the simplest of items, among them seed potatoes, underwear, or shoes. The letters from widows often have a more pointed tone. Were the women emboldened, were they aware of themselves as a voting block? Smallwood often read letters aloud on his radio program. Did this practice build solidarity amongst widows? Or were they just so fed up with their meagre $10 a quarter and the sexist rules around their allowance that their letters became more combative? The rules were such that widows didn't qualify for an allowance if they had a living son, regardless of his health, age, or dependents. One mother of three, indicated that she didn't think her allowance of $10 every quarter "is a square deal. I cannot get clothes for myself." Another woman, meanwhile, referred to the allowance as her widow's mite, "which in the pass have been the $3.33 1/3 per month or $10 per quarter." Many letters in the Trinity South file agitate for a larger allowance and point out the injustice of the rules, but it's impossible to know if the widows were aware of their political clout.[1]

Another series of letters to Smallwood demonstrates both the tenacity and astute organizational skills of their authors. Two correspondents who signed their letters as "two confederates" made several pleas for electricity to be installed in their community, pleas not unlike current rural requests for high-speed internet and cell service. These women cited safety, darkness, and the isolation of the community during winter storms. In their first letter, on October 2, 1949, they asked why the "electric service" did not extend into their community when it existed just twelve miles away in nearby Whitbourne. Smallwood's lengthy response on October 17, 1949, suggested that they find out how many homes in the Chapel Arm area would be willing to pay for electricity from the United Towns Electric Company. The women took up his challenge, and less than a month later, after presumably going door to door to collect those names, they sent the premier a petition of over 200 names plus "5 schools, 4 churches, and one Orange Lodge," along with the note, "all of them are satisfied." Interestingly, the repetition of surnames on their petition functions as a sort of census, indicating the size of extended families, as well as the number of residents and public buildings in Chapel Arm at the time. What remains unclear is how many dwellings might have become future electricity customers.

The difficulty of finding employment and the need to travel far from home to attain wage work is another thread that runs through the Trinity South letters. One mother's son had returned home from six months in Greenland, married, and had to leave immediately to find work in Halifax. However, she wrote,

> It seemed that ill luck still followed him ... it seemed the wrong time of the year to get work so he left his wife living there with my other daughter that is married and living there and went on to Toronto he got work there in a steel plant but cannot get any rooms so he can have his wife, come live with him. He writes very little and I know he do not like his work.

---

1 A letter from St. John's West, signed "Widows of the West End," suggests that some widows, at least, were.

Other women wrote that their husbands hadn't been home in years or were home briefly before they had to leave again to go back to woods camps or away to work. The collection also includes letters and telegrams from men looking for the new government to hire them to build roads, bridges, and breakwaters, or from men in lumber camps requesting money just to get home.

The sense of urgency in all the letters and telegrams is acute. One gets the sense that some people had been making do while they waited for the change of government in hopes Confederation meant there would be more support. Others, however, were confused by or concerned about how new Canadian rules might impact the scanty support they already received.

It was during this post-Confederation era, in the early 1950s, that my grandmother, Gertrude Antle (Fisher) of New Perlican, closed up the family home in Turk's Cove and moved with her five children to Windsor. My grandfather was working as a labourer in the Buchans mine and like many of the families who wrote Smallwood, he did not have enough time off or money to travel back and forth to Trinity Bay from his post. But once the family relocated to Windsor, he would often walk 100 kilometres along the rail line to visit them on holidays. Neither he nor my grandmother romanticized life in Trinity Bay South; my grandfather gladly gave up fishing, sealing, and gull-hunting for wage work. Eventually, he landed a job as a labourer in the Grand Falls mill, where he worked alongside my electrician father and uncle. My aunts trained as nurses, accountants, and teachers, fulfilling my grandmother's dream. Her motivation for moving the family to Central Newfoundland from Trinity South was not only so the family could be together but she was determined that her children would attend and graduate high school, attain post-secondary training, and obtain wage-paying employment. She only returned to Turk's Cove once and often said life in Trinity Bay was "too difficult." Since reading these letters, I have a better appreciation of why.

Jan. 5th/ 49.

Mr. Joseph R. Smallwood
St John's

Dear Sir,

Hope you will please pardon the liberty I am taking in writing you as I realize you are kept busy, but feeling that you have a sincere interest in the welfare of others, I am writing you concerning a problem which for a long time has been affecting our family. Previous to my marriage I spent 11 ½ years in the Teaching profession in different Outports and at St John's and since coming here I have interested myself in all work for the betterment of our people such as being Pres. of Jubilee Guild,[2] *W.P.A.*[3] *church & school associations etc and although my efforts have not probably amounted to much I have tried to do my best. My problem is this, my husband was one of the crew of the A. B. Barteau which was lost off Cape Race in 1918. My husband lost part of each foot through frostbite and now as he gets older he finds it very difficult to get around especially in the winter time. We have a large family and he cannot go away to work owing to his disability, but during 2 months of the summer he works as patrolman on the … Road here. You can imagine how far two months pay will go towards supporting a family for the whole year! So I wondered if it were possible for him to get some assistance in the way of a small pension through some fund such as the Marine Disaster or*

---

2 For more on the Jubilee Guilds, see Linda Cullum's essay, later in this volume.

3 The Women's Patriotic Association (WPA) was a women's voluntary association established in 1914 to support the war effort. The WPA was also active during World War II. Additionally, the network enabled by this organization was vital to the suffrage movement. The WPA disbanded in 1948. For more on the Women's Patriotic Association, see Jennifer Flight, "'We are all in the front line this time': The Patriotic Association of the Women of Newfoundland during the Second World War" (master's research report, Memorial University, 2007); Gail Denise Warren, "Voluntarism and Patriotism: Newfoundland Women's War Work during the First World War" (master's research report, Memorial University, 2005); Margot I. Duley, "The Unquiet Knitters of Newfoundland: From Mothers of the Regiment to Mothers of the Nation," in *A Sisterhood of Suffering and Service: Women and Girls of Canada and Newfoundland during the First World War*, ed. Sarah Glassford and Amy Shaw (University of British Columbia Press, 2012), 51–74.

some fund that you may know of for that purpose. I would be glad indeed if you would give the matter your attention and kindly let me know what you think we could do. There is no chance of earning a dollar here unless by cutting logs which my husband finds to hard getting through the snow. I can assure you that your help in this way will be greatly appreciated.

Wishing you continued success in 1949 in your efforts for the benefit of our people for whom you have fought so hard and well!

Sincerely Yours,

P.S. An account of the Shipwreck of the A.B. Barteau was given by the Barrelman not so long ago and the story also appeared in the Newfoundlander.

March 7th/49

Mr. J R Smallwood.
St Johns.

Dear Sir,

Congratulations on your courageous and noble work in bringing Confederation for Nfld. You are the most remarkable and daring gentleman that can be found anywhere. We are proud of you as a citizen of Nfld. and the way you have stood up through all the slander and evil that others have fired at you. We feel a thrill of pride when we have listened to your name over the broadcasting corporation, and to know we as citizens of your native land to have such a worthy gentleman to fill such a position that should be yours on the 31st of March. It won't be long now!

I cannot express what I would like to say, but my husband and myself join with the many thousand who were who wish you the very best and may God bless you your labours of love and work for your fellow countrymen.

My husband was fishing last summer in a rodney, fishery was a failure.[4] *He earned around $106.00 (one hundred and six dollars) which wasn't much to live out of for very long. But for our son who is married and working we would have to get relief. I fell and broke my left arm on the 25th of February and as I am unable to knit or do any kind of work to help. My husband wished me to write you. If there was any possibility to get work after Confederation was proclaimed (31st of March) as a janitor or watchman or some other kind of work so that the necessities of life may be provided. Both ages are 60 years. If you come to [my community] my husband would like to see you or a reply to this letter. If this letter is not up to par please excuse. I hope you will do your very best in the way of work. Best of Luck and God be with you in all your undertakings for a better Newfoundland.*

Yours very Truly

4 Rodneys are traditional, small wooden boats in Newfoundland.

March 20/'49

Dear Mr. Smallwood

I am droping you a few words to ask you if you will intersead for me as I am badly in need as my wife was confinied this winter and there was know nurse in [a community] and I had to get the doctor from [another community] and he charged me $20.00 twenty dollars and the mid wife charged me $10. ten that was $30.00 thirty dollars I had to neighter cent belong to me I was I was living on the dole as I had to get aloned of the money to pay the doctor and the mid wife and put my poney up against it so I send my bill in to the department and I thought would get it because on account of know nurse in [a community] so I thought I would get in touch with you to see what you would do to help me out so as I wont have to sell my poney it is the only help I got and I would be very much obliged if you would do something to help me out.

Your. Truly

April 6, 1949

Hon. Joseph R. Smallwood,
Colonial Building,
St. John's.

Dear Sir,

Please forgive me for bothering you with my affairs but there is a matter about which I would like to gain some information.

Are merchants allowed to charge an eight cent tax on anything they sell when it is their old stock? That is what is already being done here in [my community].

I am one who voted for Confederation with the hope of having a better future but if merchants are allowed to continue thus, things will be much harder as we will have to pay our own taxes and theirs also.

I would prefer not to have this broadcast.

I remain,

Very truly yours,
A Confederate.

April 10. 1949

Mr. Smallwood
St John's

Dear Sir

I'm sending up to you to see if you can get me a bit of clothes for me and my 3 children to wear or some way of getting some.

I've been a widow for 2 yrs & have'nt had a bit of help from the goverment & they wouldn't give me none & I wrote to everybody I thought about so now I desided to try you I'm sick and can't work for to earn nothing I'm sending you a list of clothes that I wants for myself I wants 1 dress size 40 & 1 shiften of inside clothes & a pr shoes size 8 & for my oldest son. 14 yrs 1 shiften of inside clothes size 36 & 1 windbreaker size 36 & 1 pr pants size 36, 1 pr rubbers size 7

next son. 13 years 1 shiften of inside clothes size 28 & 1 windbreaker size 28 1 pr pants size 28 & 1 pr rubbers size 45

for my daughter 8 years, 1 dress size 12 1 shiften of inside clothes 1 pr shoes size 12 this is all for now hoping to hear from you soon

I remain
Sincerely yours

April 25th/49.

To Hon. J.R. Smalwood,
Premier,
St Johns

Dear Hon Sir: -

It is with great Pleasure that I wish you many congratulations on your Appointment as Premier, and I trust in coming election you will be elected as Premier of Newf'ld, and I wish you every success,
I am Strong Confederate and I was one of the four men who canvassed the Hr to get Confederation on the ballot paper.

I am writing for information and I am trusting you may be able to let me know, I am 40 yrs old, married and have two children,
On Mar. 23rd while shooting sea birds I had a gun accident and had to have left hand amputated, which means I am unable to go away to earn a living
My occupation is Carpenter and I am wondering if there is Cripple benefit given, hoping ot hear form you at your earliest convenience, I remain

Sinerely yours,

May 11, 1949

To Mr. J.R. Smallwood

Dear Sir, its a great Privilige for me to be able to write to you, or at least I think it so. I am a woman with a large family and my husband is out of work for the past year.

I know I receive the baby bonus, but I cannot spend that in any thing only for the children and then do the best I can for them. now I'm asking you to do me a favour could you give me 4 barrels of Potatoes for to set in the ground. and 2 sacks of fertilizer and 2 of soda or a check to buy them. as I can tell you Mr. small wood you are going to gain the day right here at Whitbourne if I know any thing about it well I will be expecting to hear from you soon. and also on that day. all members of my family and thats 6 to vote for you, I will thank you very much 4 same as I remain

P.S.

If I dont hear from you before Polling day I will vote for the other man.

June 3

1949

Mr. Smallwood

Dear Sir.

Since you won such great victory I thought I would write you. I an a little girl 10 years of age I an in grade 3 there is five of us 3 boys and 2 girls My Daddy was home for 5 years with bad lags and you may thing how glad we were to get the family Allowance the first money our Mother bought boots for the 3 boys and shoes for my sister and I and this month she bought us stockings and other things and thing to eat that we woult be able to get. and thanks to you Mr. Smallwood I belive every girl and boy should thank you – yours truley

Oct 2nd, 1949

To Pmr Smallwood
of Newfoundland.

Dear Mr. Smallwood,

Well seeing that you won Confederation & its about to come into force, we the people of [our community] would like to ask you to do us a favor. Mr. Smallwood you know we did you a favour & our utmost to get you in. As we knew you were the best man for it. And that you would do all you could to help us people.

Well Mr Smallwood were not very good at stating a Business letter like this; but anyway lets forward our request to you.

Well Mr Smallwood as you probably allready know we do not have any electric power running through here this settlment of [ours] but in the mean time its only 12 ml away from here, & we cant see why we cannot have the electric lights here, it sure would be a big help to us, but it seem like noone regarding goverment officials are worrying a bit about putting anything here.

Mr Smallwood as you know this is a very iselated Settlement especially in Winter time. There isent even a way to get an emergency message out of here, which is very important thing to all of us. Thers a telephone here in the post office, but after 6 o'clock it cant be used by anyone & its of no benefit whatsoever. It would be wonderful If you could do something about putting the electric light line connected from [community] to [our community] Im sure it wouldent cost the Company very much, it seem like the rest of the settlments are getting the rest of the brakes and we and we are not gaining anything by Confederation as we understood from you in your raido speeches, when & if you would get in, you woud give us all the most important things first, so now we would like to see something done regarding electric Power. Youd be surprised what a help it would be. In winter night if thers is an emergency to go out thers no way in this world to get it out except walk to [community] to get a Dr or nurse & the settlement could be dead before they would get to walk 12 miles & 12 miles more to walk back, as all the roads do closed once the snow comes. We really think & know something should be done to help get a Chance to live & overcome so much unessary hardship which the people go through. Mr. Smallwood would you please to something for us as we really need some ones help: Well Sir surely you will help us in our hour of need as you said you would: please ans as soon as possible.

Yours Truly,
[two names redacted]
2 Confedrates

11.5.49

Dear Mr. Smallwood

excuse me taking the Liberty to write you, but I feel I must have help of some sort if you can do so, I have served overseas, seven years. I came home too late to get anything from the Newfoundland government. I've tried to do my best to get a home, but we have had a hard time, the wife having a baby & have had to use up our money we had to rent a home, the Goverment is feeding us.

We also have wrote to the Department of Veterans Affairs to see about my pension, we received booklets. I read these through & it seems I have to put money out to get help from them, that is impossible for I don't have a cent, also I am going to try & get some sort of work the summer, to pay for bills, that we have had for food during the winter before we got help from the Goverment fifteen dollars a month, so sir, trusting you will reply & see if you can help us. by the way Mr. Smallwood, I am writing this on behalf of my husband & I am from the old country (Scotland), I served in the W.A.A.F.s[5] *was in Germany, but I can honestly say, this is the poorest country I have ever come across, the people are stung right & left, by the general dealers, they charge what they like for goods, it certainly would be a good idea if food prices was controlled, you certainly have done wonderful work for the something short time you have been in I know you can't do everything at once, so once again Good Luck sir.*

Sincerly yours

5 The Women's Auxiliary Air Force, the women's arm of the Royal Air Force, was established in the UK in 1939 and had 181,000 members by 1943.

Nov 11 1949.

To Prmr JR. Smallwood
" for Newfoundland.
Dear Sir

Here are a list of the names you requested to be satisified to have the Electric Power at [our community]: And us people would be Charmed if you would arrange to have them as soon as possible.

Thanking you from our hearts
Yours Truly,
[two names redacted][6]

all of these are satisfied.

[Petition signed by 203 individuals, five schools, four churches, and the I.O. Lodge]

6 These correspondents previously wrote to Smallwood on October 2, 1949.

TWILLINGATE

for another future seaforth

Daze Jefferies

DELICATELY SHIFTING MY FEELERS through a pile of time-worn letters from 1949, a torn paper fragment the size of my index fingernail releases itself from the assemblage. Utterance pressed between the unalike and yellowed sheets, it calls for encounter in the palm of my hand. With this, I witness the disappearing words:

harbor

please allow

sending them

will leave

+ I wonder how long and lonely it has waited there, ephemera embedded with exchanges of the nation-state. Noiseless at the archives, my body is silent. Still. I am listening to Cold World by SOPHIE, a soundscape of synths and distorted vocal samples that swell toward a vision of the surging yet-to-come. Forming a link between transfeminine techno and political crises in twentieth-century Newfoundland, my play with the past believes in reparation, a timeline within which Smallwood and his government are haunted by spirits of the sunken northeast. A chorus of rural voices living in the lyrics. A future unacknowledged.

Momentary gestures. Decoded vernacular. No need knowing how to spell to be a seaman. A letter from my hometown begs for a bridge to be built, connecting one island to the next. There are boats to make the crossing in the short summer months, but when the rough ice comes, that risky distance over the strait is walked and weakened. This was how grandfather Pelley got my nan and newborn mother ashore from the midwife. Following the markers of coastland by nightfall. Faith heavyhearted and fear unharboured. How and where the generation gone will wait for morningtide.

Blue-grey beach rocks are heated by the stove and bundled in a slew of blankets. Resting at the foot of a cold wooden bed while youngsters sleep away their hunger. Skin-and-bone girls in a salt fish world unmade by sickness and extraction. To romanticize living off the unforgiving ocean when the skipper of the house has drowned. No need. The wanting widow and her crippled child desperate for coins to buy fruit and milk. Settlers cry out for a gentle savior. History reckons with the violence of capital. All that has been withheld from the academy. An archipelagic community of loss.

I think about the little-known letters and their afterlives hidden and preserved inside the QEII Library instead of the aging Twillingate Museum. Filled with growing measures of worry, stories drift across a sea of hardened hope to meet me here. Sitting in the map room with my salty whorish hands all over the past. Touching the struggles of a weary people left to the water without promise.

Mr. Josesp Smallwood. Premier.

St Johns *April 9, 1949.*

Dear Sir,

I am writing this letter to you to see if you could help us in getting a bridge, which is needed badly.

In winter when the harbour is frozen over we can manage allright, but we it thaws out in the Spring, we got to risk our lives on this bad ice, to cross over & do some of our shopping also our post office work & also in order to go to church we have to cross over water.

When the ice is gone we have to cross over in boat, motor boats & row boats, & whatever we can get suitable to get in. Sometimes the situation looks grim. We may be half way across, & then it will blow a gale of wind & probably then lose some of our oars & then there is nothing to do but drift ashore.

I will tell you of two incidents which happened here last year. two little school girls left in boat to cross over to get the mail & on there way back a storm arose & it blew a storm & there boat filled full of water & both were almost drowned. But they got ashore after the storm abanded.

And this is a story concerning myself & our United School teacher and another young girl, we were crossing over one night & a storm came on & almost swamped our boat, we lost our oars, pins & wells, & there was nothing else to do but let her drift ashore, it came on to rain, & so dark, we were scared to pieces, anyway she drifted in ashore by a cliff & there happened to be a large rock out of the water & I jumped this rock & kept hold of the boat, so as she wouldn't beat to pieces & teacher jumped over into the icy water & we managed somehow to get out of her to the shore safely. it was a hard looking sight. So far yet no one has been drowned, but it would be a God Send for us people living here on [our island] to have a Bridge to cross over. Without of course, we had a office or church on our island.

There are twenty one families living on our Island & eighteen of these are confederates. So, Mr Smallwood we would be more than thankful if you could help us in our need for a bridge of some kind.

In case of sickness or whatever happens, we have to cross over in boat or walk on ice. For instance right now the ice is getting thawed out, & tomorow is Sunday. We just have to stay home or risk our lives on this bad ice. There are many mothers with aching hearts waiting for the return of their sons & daughters to return home after being over across the Harbour, probably shopping or attending a meeting of some kind. Our little Island consists of nice respectable Men & Women & children who have to stay in their homes, when they should be enjoying a church Service and etc.

I hope you will understand the circumstances, & do your best to help us people of [community] in getting our Bridge & thanking you.

Yours truly,

April 17 1949

Dear Mr Smallwood

I am just going to try to write you a few lines to let you know about my conditions and how I am living these days not living only starving on earth and I am not well and living on a bet of old Dole not fit to gave a dog I was too the Doctor yesterday and he to me I want good food where am I going to get it to. It is time for someone too drive that race out what have been starving us to death so long it time for us to get a change well Mr Smallwood I gave you my vote twice and I would voted twenty if I got the chance. So I am sending two you to see if you well send me a few dollars for to get a bet of nourishment I well be more than glad to get it we are all for you my Husband and son and daughter. My Husband was going away two work but he havent got any sence to go no money two pay his way along and I am not very well I hope you well answer this letter and do what you can for me and no one well know it so I wish you good health two carry on your work

From

April 22nd – 1949

To

Premire J.R Smallwood

St Johns

Dear Sir,

I am writing you to see what you can do to help me in regards to my support. I have been a widow for seven years, and have never got any keep as yet. I have one Son who went away seeking work. 4 or 5 diffrent places last fall and had to return home after Spending what little money he had unable to secure work. he wrote the Ranger in January asking for help to support me & himself and so far have got nothing. I would appricate it very much if you could secure the widows pension or help in some way for me

We are surely in need of help Will be looking forward to hearing from you real soon

Hon. J. R. Smallwood

St John's. *Apr 29th 19/49*

Dear Sir,

Am writing to inform you Mr Smallwood of a Bridge which is in a very poor condition here. I may say its complety gone, and has been like this since early last fall but not so bad as it is now. There has been several complaints put in concerning this Brigde and up to the present time nothing has been done about it.

This Bridge is built across a running brook (roughly) it maybe 8 or 10 ft across and you say only one plank to cross on. This Bridge is on the Public road and its our only means of crossing to get to the Church, Post offic or stores. But by wearing long Rubbers when the water isn't high you may step over the wood and wade across the Brook.

I'm sure this Bridge is not fit to walk on night time. and again its Very dangerous for old people to cross on. Then come the little children on their way to school one of the teachers said that she would have to close school unless something is done to fix the bridge. So I was wondering Mr. Small Wood if you could in some way make it possible to have this bridge fixed so as to cross over without any accident or probly someone drowned I'm sure if you could, that everyone at [our community] would appreciate it very much.

Thanking you Mr. Smallwood,

I remain yours truly,

[two names redacted]

To preimer J. Smallwood
St John's

May 18 / 49

Dear Sir –

I feel it my duty to write you Concerning the sick benifit.

I am a man that for the past four years have been turned down by my Dr unfit for work and have been forced to seek help from the Government which have been five dollars per head a month

We cannot exist on this. This is a thing that have been overlooked by the progressive party.

Will you do your best for us people that are physically handicaped, with a family to maintain

Will remember you on polling Day

Sincerely your

June 28th/1949

Dear Sir,

his there any Pensions for cripples. I have a cripple girl she cannot walk and can only eat food we can not afford to give her such has fruit milk etc. when she don't get these foods she gets sick. can we get any keep for her. please answer

July 4th – 1949

To Mr Joseph Smallwood,
premier of nfld,

Dear Mr Smallwood,

I would like to draw your attention for a moment and I would like or appreciate very much if you would kindly answer my question by mail or (personal letter)

I was very disappointed this mail when I received my widows allowance, Just 15.00 which you know is not enough to bye tea, sugar, & milk & meat only. For 3 months, I am 81 years of age and I never received any help from the Comission of Government until January past, and I have only rec'd 3 checques in all, which is only 45 dollars in all, and it is impossible to live on that 9 months. I filled out my papers applying for old age pensions for 30 dollars a month, and as yet received none, I am badly in need of it, could you tell me what time to expect this money. Or will i get it at all. I couldint purchase my birth certificate but my papers were signed by J. P. Witness, I do hope it dosent make any difference about my certificate please oblige me by answering by personal letter. if I will get my money and when, why should others get it in other places and more left out,

thanking you for your kindness

July 14th

1949

To

Premier J R Smallwood

St. Johns.

Dear Sir

I am writing you these few lines explaining to you my circumstances to see if you could help me out in any way.

My Husband been sick in ~~Hospital~~ House since March & went in Twillingate Hospital 6th of April had two operations and never recovered passed away. July 11th. Now I am left alone with no one or no help whatever. he havent done any work Since October 1948.

I am Stating you my circumstances to See if you could help me out as Soon as you possibly can. I have only one Girl no Sons. Whatever to Look Forward to.

Will you please Oblige.

Address

Please. Reply.

Feb 15, 1950

Dear Premier Smallwood,

As I am in need I thought I would write to you to give you understanding how I am situated I am a married woman and my husband is living he is a fisherman. He is a hard working man But still he dosent get the two ends to meet when there is no work. He havent got any money in the bank. There is nothing slack with neither one of us we realy work hard. The food is took care of in the home nothing wasted but still we have it hard to get along. When we got married he start all by himself and build us a fishing room. He has no help whatever we have a little house two bedrooms in it. So you see Mr Smallwood a mother bringing up children need a very good home. I have two children they have been sick ever since thier birth We have to take them to the doctor every Spring my oldest is 13 she go to school some days in school and some days home she is not well enough to attend school regular. And my youngest is 3 years old Now we have a chance to buy a nice little home it would cost us $400 or (four hundred dollars) But sorry we cannot buy it. So this is my idea of writing to you to see if you could help us out. We would be very glad if you would help us a little we get nothing from the government we get the family allowances and is very glad with that but we spend all that on our children. My husband tells me it is of no use to write you but I say "yes I think Mr Smallwood will help anyone that is in need". You can depend on every word is put down here it is true because I would not tell you any lies Hoping to recieve a little ceck from you later we give you all the praise for what you have already done Trusting you

Yours Sincerely

Mar 5 –
1950

Dear Premier,
I am With the greatest of pleasure riteing you this letter I am riteing you about A motorboat I had one all my life time But she came ashore in the gale last Fall and she Beat all to pices So I couldent afford to Buy neither one this Spring So I intended to go Fishing this Summer So I thought you would get one fore me I have Been Bucksawing every Summer But I was in the hospitable this Winter so I cant Bucksaw this Summer I have trawls myself so I thought you would help me out in Buying A boat fore me their his one here fore sale fore one hundred dollars So try and do your Best fore me I suppose their will Be lots of work here this Summer I herd the Keneal was going through from [one community] to [another] so if you Cant get A Boat fore me I would like to get A good job there likes of foreman I applied fore my unemployment A month ago and I havnt had meither Form Come yet I don't know What his the trouble
From [name redacted]
To HON J R Smallwood

yours sinsearly

WHITE BAY

"my dear baby was dead": A Family Tragedy in White Bay, 1951[1]

Heidi Coombs

THE LETTERS THAT NEWFOUNDLANDERS in the district of White Bay wrote to Smallwood in the early years of Confederation offer an intimate and revealing look into their lives, their hopes and dreams for the future, and their feelings of connection with a man they did not know.

People openly shared their life stories with Smallwood, often disclosing tragic personal circumstances and difficult living situations in their requests for Old Age Pensions, widows' allowances, and disability assistance. They sent urgent telegrams during medical emergencies asking for an air ambulance or a doctor to be sent by plane. They wrote complaining that there had been no change in the cost of food since Confederation, asking for seed potatoes and fishing equipment, reporting lost cod traps, and requesting radios, telephones, and weekly mail services for their communities. Some asked for juke boxes, licenses to sell homebrew, and permission to start hotel businesses.

However, there was one letter in the collection that stood out from all the others.

In February 1951, a mother by the name of Josephine Dempsey, from Canada

1 Our deepest thanks to the descendants of Josephine Dempsey for granting us permission to include her full letter and name in this book.

Harbour, wrote to Smallwood describing the circumstances around the death of her five-and-a-half-month-old baby boy.

I read the letter sitting in the reading room of Archives and Special Collections, surrounded by fellow researchers and archivists, amid a silence interrupted only by the whispers of rustling papers and hushed conversations. As I held the letter in my hand, I was transported back to the bleak midwinter of 1951, and Josephine's frantic journey across open water and through wooded paths by dog team in desperate search of help for her sick baby boy.

The letter left me speechless and with a lump in my throat.

After reading its contents, I laid the letter back down on the table and stared ahead in a daze. As the mother of a young son myself, my heart ached for Josephine and her little baby boy in what must have been the worst weeks of their lives.

Canada Harbour—now resettled—was located on the east side of the Northern Peninsula, four miles across the bay from Englee. In 1951, there was no doctor or nurse in the community. In cases of medical emergencies, residents had to travel to Roddickton, fifteen miles away, where the Grenfell Mission had a nursing station. The Grenfell Mission, or International Grenfell Association, was the only health care provider in northern Newfoundland and Labrador. It was established in 1892 by British physician Wilfred Grenfell in the absence of such government services. The Mission depended on nurses stationed in rural and remote communities to meet the health needs of the people and to handle medical emergencies.

The nurse in charge at Roddickton was Joan Cattell—an exceptionally capable British nurse and midwife. Cattell was adventurous and fearless in getting to people in need. But she was the only nurse from St. Anthony to Harbour Deep and she alone covered over 100 miles of rugged coast. There were few roads and most of the communities were accessible only by sea.

In addition, in 1951 these communities had no telephones or telegraphs. The only way to get help in a medical emergency was for someone to bring the sick or injured to the nursing station at Roddickton or else fetch the nurse and bring her back to the community.

By Monday, January 15, 1951, Josephine recognized that her baby had become seriously ill and required medical attention. But, the bay was blocked with ice, making it impossible to reach Englee, let alone Roddickton.

Three days later, on Thursday, January 18, the ice had moved off and the baby's father, together with several other men from Canada Harbour, managed to reach Roddickton. They had intended to bring Nurse Cattell back to Canada Harbour to treat the sick baby at home. However, when they arrived, Cattell was busy with a maternity case and unable to leave the station. The father was forced to return home without the nurse, equipped with some "tablets" for the baby.

Despite these tablets, over the next several days, the baby's condition did not improve. The family's only hope was to bring him to the station at Roddickton themselves. But it was winter and the bay had again become blocked with ice and was impassable for days.

Finally, on Friday, January 26, the wind changed and the bay opened up. Josephine set off with her sick baby, leaving her other six children at home. Her husband got her safely to Englee, and from there she secured a dog team over the road to Roddickton. By the time she arrived at the nursing station that Friday night, her baby was in critical condition.

Cattell tried the whole weekend to get the Grenfell Mission's air ambulance to bring the baby to St. Anthony, to no avail.

By Monday, January 29, a full two weeks after Josephine first recognized that her baby had become seriously ill, her baby's condition had worsened further and the situation was dire. Cattell decided that they could not continue to wait for an air ambulance. She would bring him to St. Anthony herself—by dog team to Main Brook and then snowmobile to St. Anthony—leaving first thing Tuesday morning.

But by the next morning, Tuesday, January 30, the baby was dead.

Josephine Dempsey found herself at Roddickton, grieving the death of her baby boy alone, without the comfort of her family back home in Canada Harbour. In the days following her baby's death, she wrote to Smallwood, "[t]he kindness and hospitality of Nurse Cattell and the people of Roddickton [could not] be excelled, they did all that could be done to make me feel comfortable and help me bear my never forgotten trouble of losing my baby."

And then, she faced the journey home with her dead baby boy.

She arrived at Englee via dog team on Wednesday, January 31. It was very cold: well below freezing.[2] The bay was again blocked with ice and she was forced to wait there until Saturday, February 3, before her husband could cross from Canada Harbour to pick her up. In her letter to Smallwood, she praised the kindness and sympathy of the people who hosted her at Englee during those difficult days.

2 Josephine Dempsey herself recorded the temperature as "17 degrees below zero." This was likely in Fahrenheit, which would have made for a chilly -28 degrees Celsius.

Josephine's letter to Smallwood recounting her ordeal and the death of her baby was at once personal, political, and poignant. It captured the anxiety and grief of parents who did everything they could to save their baby in very difficult circumstances. It captured the challenges of getting medical care in rural and remote areas of the province, where help was so far away and travel often complicated by difficult terrain and unpredictable weather. And it captured, too, the community and compassion of other people who came together to help the family reach Roddickton and to support Josephine as she travelled back home, in grief, with her dead baby.

After all the promises of Confederation, people living in rural Newfoundland and Labrador in 1951 continued to have limited access to medical services and were still vulnerable to painfully negative outcomes in cases of medical emergencies.

As a medical historian reading the White Bay letters, I was struck by several telegrams to Smallwood requesting immediate medical assistance, telegrams from people who would have had easier access to Grenfell services nearby than anything Smallwood could arrange from St. John's. Smallwood had clearly connected with people and raised their expectations to the point that they felt he could, and would, personally meet their needs, including sending a doctor by plane for an individual emergency. And, as several telegrams from May 1949 demonstrate, at first Smallwood met those requests.

However, by 1951, not even Joan Cattell could get a plane for Josephine Dempsey's dying baby boy.

Josephine Dempsey channelled her grief into advocating for better medical services for her community. Smallwood responded to her letter with sympathy and respect. He blamed past governments for years of neglect in White Bay and outlined his plan to work with the Grenfell Mission to expand medical services in the district, including the establishment of more nursing stations. And indeed, Grenfell services in White Bay expanded significantly after this period. A new nursing station was built at Englee later that same year, with a nurse posted there in 1952. Nursing stations were also built at Roddickton in 1957, Conche in 1961, and Harbour Deep in 1962. Smallwood was true to his word about increasing medical services in White Bay.

However, this all came too late for Josephine Dempsey and her baby boy. One can only hope that her tragic experience and advocacy hastened government action in expanding medical services in White Bay and saved other lives in the district.

Jan 4th 1948

Dear Sir:

I have been listening to your speeches over the radio and thought you was a good man to write and explain my statement to. I am turning toward's sixty five years old and have never had any help in any way. when I was able to work wages was only low, since wages went up I havent been able to work only at piddling jobs, fix a boat for a person or some thing that kind. I broke my leg six year ago a very bad brake I didnt get any help at the time I was laid up a twelve month and had a hard drag to get along, and you can imagine what money a person saved when he was getting the low wages two dollars a day and dollar fifty a day.

I had to go to hosipital when I broke my leg and pay my way and my wifes, but I struggle through. I never got a cent help from the goverment in my life.

When I had my leg broken I had to sell my gun and row boat, to buy some thing else that I needed worst at the time

Yours Truly,

Apr 5/49

Dear Sir

I am writing a few lines to wish you every success in your office. Sir will we gave you and Mr. Bradley a gun sulett and [illegible] was flying and shouting for every success in the future years So I must tell you that quite a lot of people Blames you for getting confederation in force and most all the Peopel Blames me for getting as many Votes for confederation on Poling day last But you dont mind the Peopel so you thinks its the Best for us all in the future so I am Justified in thinking that I dun Right in talking to the Peopel in your favor for confederation which I taught its Best and I hope so altho you and me are strangers But I worked for Responsivel & commision gov for 16 years in the Postol Service and I started on one dollr Pr month and I only Raised my salery up to 44 dollr a quarter in Telepown office + Post office and worked Besides at different Job to make enough to get along and Rais my family of Eleven But Tank god I did it and never add to get any dol

and I Hope and Trust to god that I well get By under confederation I congralat you on your Success I weill be at your service at any time if I can be of any use to you, you will have to exquise my letter Because I am not High qualified and not will Educated But I try to make the Best of what I have But I have been told that I have good Idias and great Idias and the main thing in my vieau is to be Honest as I was always taught in my Boy Hood days and I am Satisfied in life if I could get Plenty to Eat + drink and Keep my family deason and Edecate thim to Best of my abelety if I only could get a living wage out of my office work and Rais my own vigabetels I gess I would do it Some How

So my Idia for Riting you this letter is some of the Peopel have lost there potatoes that the had for seed Potatoes through frost and the ask me did I think I could get some so I tought I would write to you to see what you could do could you Boy and Ship 20 Barrels and send me the Bills and I would sell them for you or could you get in touch with agultur Dep and send some If so I will look after them for who ever send them all that I want is the Price the cost and freight and I well sell and collect the money and send to Hoom it may consern Personel or Deportment if you are sending we Peopel would need them on the first coastel Boat if the wer going to be Shiped to me Pleas wire me and state Shipping amount

also some thing else I want to ask you is if I still old fast to the Post office and cannot got enough to live on would you be enterested in starting me in a little Business if there would be any thing made on it. you would have a good Idia on the new Sistom because it is in your Presents but we are in the Icealated Part of this Island and we have to do without lots of food Requirements I alwas wanted to get some thing to work on for my own entrest so now I hope you may be abel to do some thing for me or Reckmend me to some

Canadian firm who would like to get a Business started in this Provedence try your Best I well do mind to get you elected again at the next elections Because you sertenley Deserve it I have had som Hard Talks with the Public and I had sum fun out of it some times againce Responcavel But we must forget the Past and carry on in the future with a good well I am and I am trying to talk to every Person that I come in contack with to do the Same in all Respects I have worked with Sivral of the Departments in the Past

Such as Dep Post + Telegraph

Dep Pub Works

Dep Naturel Resources

Also Different mining Companeys

Sops Arm mining co

Sops Arm gold claim co

Prospect + Sendagate Co.

Dep Public works the Pink Marbel quary Sops Arm

I super vised Jobs for all these

also I worked with the Topalgraphal Servay for the [illegible] in the Past I have worked Hard for my living and old Post office for the Past 16 years Part time and connect with the coastel Steamer every trip 2 miles from office I wonder if there could be any thing dun to have coastel Steamer call at [a community] in Stead of [the other community] 2 miles from the office if it could be arranged for the Steamer to call at [community] there is a worf that could be used on tell we could get one Belt as [Mr. Jones][3] Sugested a Plan to Belt at [community] on the main land for the future out look of the contery Because Boolwater[4] have a large Timber clame on [community] it Istemates 50 years cut cutting 100 thousand cords a year so its Istemated from some servayers some years ago would you kindely Reply and gave me some out lind of some of the questins I have ask you and a few linds of the out look so I could dwell and Talk to the Public in your behalf I hope you will under stand my noat Because I could talk and gave you lot more of Ideas But I now you may not be enterested as yet But let us work together for the Best I well I am Shore if I can make a living thats all I Expect because there is not much Indurested here to gave Imployment O yes I spoke of the worf was here that the Steamer could call to is a one that [Mr. Arthur] + [Mr. Snow] use for a Shipping worf for lumbr to load Schooners like Teasue and Mariam Richards Etc there is lots of [illegible] near it it would be much Better then taking freight in Boat

Wishing you the Riches Blessings and successful upertunety you have taken upon you

Your truly [name redacted].

---

3 Because the correspondent names four different people, we have chosen to use pseudonyms for ease of reading.

4 Likely Bowater's Newfoundland Pulp and Paper Mill.

April 19 1949

Mr J Small Wood Dear Sir
I am Droping you a few lines Hoping this will Reach you Safe I am asking You I want to know whats the Reason there cant Be something Don toward us I am 67 years old and I cant get any work Because I am to old to get Ensurance and I cant work Lik a yound man and I Have a wife 61 years old I suppose we will Have to Starve it is Right that I should get something to Help me out in Living I cant go fishing Because I Havent got a Boat or Engine we cant get anything from them without the money it is all Because we voted for you I talked and did my Best for you see to this for me and try and get something for me I should think that a man when He is 65 should get is old age Penchen I am Not lame or Blind I Been Listen to your talking on Radio good for you I would like to Here you often I Havent got No money to Live with sometimes make a Dollar at something for someone Else we Just Drages along Dry Enough Sometimes I Have made Lots of money in my time and got Non We Have to Pay a Big Price for Stuff Down Here you Know when a person gets 67 year old He is going the other way you may look at this and thow it aside I voted for you Both times But I Had a lot said to me so try and Do something for me Excuse my Riting for my Hand chakes a wonderful Lot sometimes

answer this letter

Do your Best for me

Yours truly

APRIL 30 – 1949.

HONORABLE J.R. SMALLWOOD,
ST. JOHN'S.

DEAR SIR: -

FIRST EXCUSE MY WRITING AND SPELLING I AM LACK OF EDUCATION. BECAUSE I WAS IN THE FISHING BOAT AND THE LUMBERING WOODS, WHEN I SHOULD OF BEEN IN SCHOOL. BROUGHT AROUND BY LEADERS OF THIS COUNTRY, IN RESPONSIBLE GOV'T DAYS, I TRUST MY CHILDREN WILL BE EDUCATED BETTER NOW, UNDER WHAT YOU FAUGHT HARD FOR, YOUR AMAN OF STEEL, I WAS STRUCK TWICE IN THE FACE TALKING FOR CONFEDERATION BUT WE GOT IT TANK GOD, AND YOU.:

MY LETTER TO YOU ITS FOR TO TRY AND GET AN ANSWER ON WHAT I BEEN WRITING ABOUT FOR TWO YEARS, SO HERE IT IS.
YOU NO ALL ABOUT THIS COAST, AND THE MAIL SERVICE WE GET SUMMER TIME FROM THE S.S NORTHERN RANGER, ONCE EVERY THREE AND FOUR WEEKS I HAVE KNOWEN IT FOR THIRTY DAYS WIHTOUT A MAIL, THATS NOT GOOD ENOUGH FOR SUMMER MONTHS, WE DONT EXPECT GOOD SERVICE WINTER TIME, IF WE HAD A FEW ERIC BLACK-WOODS
WE WOULD HAVE BETTER SERVICES WINTER TIME, HE IS AMAN WORTH ALL PRAISE.[5]

I OFFIERED THE POST AND TELEGRAPHS TO PUT A BOAT ON TO TAKE MAIL AND PASSANGERS, FROM LEWISPORTE TO HAMPDEN CALLING AT 12 MAIN PORTS IN THE WHITE BAY, FROM LEWISPORTE TO LA SCIE FIRST PORT AND THERE ON TO HAMPDEN, THIS WOULD SATIFIDY A GOOD MANY PEOPLE IN WHITE BAY AND SERVIE THEM, WHICH HAVE NOT BEEN LOOK AFTER, FOR MAIL AND MOVEING FROM PLACE TO PLACE, THIS BOAT WOULD BE OF GOOD SERVICE AND VERY LITTLE COST TO THE POST AND TELEGRAPHS.,
LAST SUMMER WHEN I WAS IN ST JOHNS I TOOK THE MATTER UP WITH

5 Likely Eric Blackwood, an aviator who was instrumental in establishing Newfoundland Aero Sales and Service and, later, Eastern Provincial Airlines.

MANAGER OF THE RAIL WAY [NAMES REDACTED]. THEY WERE VERY ENTERESTED, AND GIVE ME ALL I WANT FROM THEM [NAME REDACTED] GAVE ME A LETTER TO TAKE DOWN TO RODDIS WHEN I LEFT HIM THE DEAL WAS MADE, BUT AFTER I GOT HOME AND SPEND AN HUNDRED DOLLARDS ON MY BOAT ETC., I GETS A LETTER FROM STATEING THIS COULD NOT BE DONE AT PRESENT TO WAITE, SO I BEEN WAITING EVERY SENCE, I WANT YOU TO SEE IN TO THIS MATTER, SERVIC E FROM LEWIS-PORT TO HAMPDEN CALLING LA-SCIE FIRST PORT. THIS WOULD MEAN ALOT TO THIS BAY, AND PEOPLE. THIS WILL BE DONE AT A LOW COST. THIS BOAT COULD DO IT WEEKLY CHEPAER THEN A STEAMER COULD DO IT, IF THEY CONSIDER ME RUNNING TO ST ANTHONY I COULD GIVE A WEEKLY SERVICE THERE TOO.

SO NOW I THINK YOU WILL SEE WHAT I AM AFTER, I JUST WANT TO GIVE MYSELF AND THE PEOPLE OF WHITE BAY A WEEKLY MAIL SERVICE WHAT WE ARE NOT USE TOO, WE CANT TAKE A PAPER DOWN HERE ITS OLD NEWS WHEN WE GET IT, IF THIS BOAT WAS MAKING WEEKLY TRIPS TO THE MAINE LINE, , THE GOVT WOULD EN BE GETTING SO MANY MES-SAGES FOR PLANES TO TAKE SICK PEOPLE OUT OF THIS BAY BECAUSE THIS BOAT COULD TAKE THEM TO HOSPITAL IN THE SAME LENGTH OF TIME WHILE GETTING MESSAGE THROUGH, AND IN LOTS OF CASES POOR PEOPLE GETS A PLANE TO TAKE SOME OF THERE PEOPLE TO H OSPITAL, AND THE PLANE COST SO MUCH TH GOVT GOT TO FOOT THE BILL, SAME TIME THEY COULD GO BY THIS SERVICE BOAT FOR LITTLE COST AND PAY TE BILL THEM SELFS SO YOU UNDER STAND WHAT I AM TRYING TO SAY, YOU WILL HAVE TO EXCUSE THIS LENGTHY LETTER, MY EDUCATION MAKES IT LONG. NOW MR SMALLWOOD I DID MY BEST FOR YOU PAST, I HOLD THE BOOTH HERE PURPOSE TO SEE FAIR PLAY TO FOR CONFEDER-ATION. NOW IN 1933 THOSE LETTERS FROM MEN LIKE ME WOULD BE THROW IN THE WASTE BASKET AND BURNED. SO THE LEAST YOU CAN DO SIR TO ANSWER IT, AND I WILL NO THE WHITE BAY IS CONSIDER. EXCUSE LONG LETTER. I AM A FOREMAN WITH THE BOWATERS HERE, AND I GOT A NUMBER SIX SIXS.,

HOPEING TO HERE FROM YOU AN EARLY DATE,
RESPECTFULLY YOURS.

URGENT

HON J R SMALLWOOD
PREMIER STJOHNS.

WIFE SERIOUSLY ILL CAN YOU ARRANGE PLANE WITH DOCTOR SEA PLANE LANDING OK

344P.

[handwritten: Plane Arranged]

A series of three telegrams between a man and the premier's office, May 1949

URGENT

HON J R SMALLWOOD
PREMIER OF NFLD STJOHNS

WIFE PREGNANT FIVE MONTHS FELL AND HURT HERSELF STILL UNBORN BUT LOSING ALL BLOOD NEED DOCTOR IMMEDIATELY COULD YOU SEND BOAT OR PLANE TAKE TO HOSPITAL

[stamped: May 7 – 1949.]

PRIORITY

SENDER J.R. SMALLWOOD
PREMIER.

MAY 7, 1949.

PLANE LEAVING AROUND FOUR OCLOCK TAKE YOUR WIFE GANDER HOSPITAL STOP MAY OR MAY NOT REACH THERE TODAY STOP WILL ARRIVE FIRST CHANCE.

J.R. SMALLWOOD
PREMIER.

[handwritten: Phone 3 05]

PRIORITY

PLEASE ANNOUNCE OVER DOYLES NEW BULLETIN IF PLANE CIRCLES AND DOES NOT LAND *[handwritten: it is because]* CONSIDER WATER TOO ROUGH FOR LANDING BRING PATIENT TO PACQUET BY BOAT.

June 28th

49

Mr J R Smallwood.

Dear Sir.

I wish to congratulate you for what goodness you have done for our country no longer then you has started.

I am just writing to say I am a fisherman and has had it hard to get along but hope to see a brighter future.

and will you please do me a favour I have heard rumored that There is some class will help fisherman in what I mean. I want a boat now and cannot afford to get it. So people tell me There is a place in St Johns where people can get money for This purpose and they will give you so many years to pay it back. If This is so and you know anything about it will you please send me the Adress has I can do that by paying it back yearly but I cannot afford to pay right down.

My home is at [community] but I come here to … for the pass twenty Summers fishing and go back to or home Again in the fall. So please do your very best and help me in some way and I am willing to do my best when ever possible

I remain yours

MR J R SMALLWOOD
ST. JOHN'S

DESTITUTE RECEIVED NO MONEY SINCE MARCH PLEASE ADVISE

[stamped: Sep 7 1949]

To [name redacted]
Sender J.R. SMALLWOOD

SEPTEMBER 8, 1949

HAVE INSTRUCTED WELFARE DEPARTMENT TO LOOK INTO YOUR CASE

J.R. SMALLWOOD

[handwritten: phoned 4:45]

To Primer
J R. Smallwood *Sept 8th 1949*
St. John's

Dear Sir:- I am taking the oprunity to write you again to see if I can get any help. I am cripple & cannot Work. so I think you should be able to do something for me. to get a living
Would you be able to get me a licine to sell. Home brew beer. Or control beer. because I ado not except for the goverment to feed I want to make a living my self because the world know I can work any other way but if I could get a licines to sell beer I would make my own living. Please try and do something for me because I only got one arm no & this is my left one. You know I am not able to work to get a living if I can not get any thing for to make a living for to support my family I am entend to make beer. if you do not give me a license to see Home Made beer
I havent got any boy old enough to work for me. Try to do something for me. answer.

I remain

your truly

Canada Hr[6]
Feb 22/51

TO
Hon J.R. Smallwood M.H.A.
St. John's
Nfld

Dear Sir: -

I shall just let you know briefly of an experience of the most trying conditions one has to contend with in this White Bay Dist. of our Island. Perhaps you'll ignore my letter, and you'll just put it in the waste paper basket, but I'll ask you Hon. Premier to read the contents please, and when you have done this, compare it with your way of living and ours; -

Well, on January 15th 1951, my baby boy 5½ mos old took seriously ill and at that time there was no way to wire for a nurse or get one, without going around Canada Bay taking at least two days for probably half dozen men and dogs. On January 18th the ice moved off and my husband with some others launched a small motor boat, proceeded to edge of ice with Komatic & dogs went from there to the Grenfell Station at Roddickton, where one nurse is stationed there to give medical aid from Hr Deep to Conche.

(Now please take the map of Newfoundland and just see the ship of Coast line from Hr Deep, Williamsport, Hooping Hr, Canada Hr, Roddickton, Hare Bay, Englee & Conche. And see how many nurses do this south, with the means of [illegible] as we have here no telephone from Hr Deep to Roddickton.) When my husband arrived at Roddickton the nurse had a maternity case at the Station and impossible for her to leave. She gave my husband some tablets and he came home. Well from Jan 18th until Jan 25th no improvement and the place was all filled with slob all through those day. The wind change on Friday Jan 26th and my husband with others took the baby and I and tried to get to Englee by boat. We succeeded in doing so, and as the slob was running in very fast, they got safely back. I left 6 small children at Canada Hr and secured a dogteam at Englee and arrived Roddickton by one night. But with the condition of that road it's a wonder that my poor baby ever lived to get to Roddickton. However, when I got Roddickton Nurse Cattell said that he would have to go to St. Anthony for treatment by plane, but when one got to wait for a plane you can be dead;-

6 Our deepest thanks to the descendants of Josephine Dempsey for granting us permission to include this letter in full in this book.

But as I can see it only the rich and some one with a big name can get a plane when they need it. When Monday came the nurse decided to go by snow-mobile as far as Main-Brook and there by dog-team to St. Anthony. She would leave on Tuesday morning. But on Tuesday morning, sad to say my dear baby was dead, and passed on to a place where he shall need no planes or snow-mobiles, where all of us will pass some day, needless to say the rich as well as poor. Well here I was at Roddickton, my family at Canada Hr, they could hear from me broadcast but I could not hear from them. The kindness and hospitality of Nurse Cattell and the people of Roddickton cannot be excelled, they did all that could be done to make me feel comfortable and help me bear my never forgotten trouble of losing my baby.

Well, on January 31st I came by dog-team out to Englee 17 degrees below zero and had to wait for a chance to get home to Canada Hr by boat again. And on February 3rd my husband got a chance to get by row boat to Englee for me and my dead baby. I got home that evening. The kindness and sympathy of the people at Englee were the same as of Roddickton. Now, if you think this is a lie contact Nurse Cattell at Roddickton and people and those of Englee including [name redacted]. This is one question of great importance. We hear every day of so many nurses graduating in St. John's. Why don't you, as Premier of Newfoundland send a nurse to help the nurse at Roddickton? Was it for a good time and [illegible] that they trained for a nurse or was it to save lives? And why don't these small places be supplied with ship to shore telephone for to help the people to survive. Yes its time Confederation promised us a lot but I can safely say that very little has been accomplished in White Bay Dist especially at Canada Hr, Hooping Hr, and Williamsport. Nothing as I can see when Mr S. Drover[7] told you and your colleagues the truth about White Bay Dist as every living person in the district knew it was the truth, he was put out of the house. But if we had more men like Mr. Drover in the Govt House I think White Bay Dist would share in the booty but all would not be put up south. Could you blame me with the experience I've had, and there are hundreds of others that go through the same ordeal as I did. We don't ask you for anu big thing but we need a telephone and we need another nurse so as when one go for her, she can come. You know one nurse at Roddickton cannot do all this work with two woods companies there Bo-waters & Saunders & Howell. Besides, those nurses will come from England far ahead of New-foundland and give their all in White Bay Dist to help the people and our own Nfld nurses cannot come north (because I suppose [illegible] no cars, no movies and countless other advantages) to save life;-

7 Samuel Drover was the Liberal MHA for White Bay from 1949 to 1956.

Well, Mr. Smallwood, you have it. As I went through it and with the loss of my baby, makes life lonesome hard for some time to come.

I am,

Very Respectfully Yours

Mrs. Josephine M. Dempsey

Canada Hr

CONTEXTUAL ESSAYS

Everyday Life in Mid-Twentieth-Century Newfoundland and Labrador

Sonja Boon and Vicki S. Hallett

WHEN WE INVITED SCHOLARS, activists, and community leaders to contribute short contextual essays, we had a simple question: What was life like in the mid-twentieth century for Newfoundlanders and Labradorians? Not the broad sweep of politics writ large, but rather, everyday life. The letters themselves can give us a sense of those lives, but in some instances, they leave us with more questions than answers.

Why was one correspondent—a disappointed confederate—so concerned about the price of apples in Carbonear? Why did another identify herself as a leader and member of numerous community organizations, including the Jubilee Guild? What were the Jubilee Guilds, and why were they so important, not just to her identity but to questions of Newfoundland identity? In a province whose identity is bound up with the fishery, what about forestry workers—and one in particular who didn't finish school because he "WAS IN THE FISHING BOAT AND THE LUMBERING WOODS, WHEN [HE] SHOULD OF BEEN IN SCHOOL"?[1] What roles did women such as an outport maternity nurse or a Grenfell Mission nurse play in the communities for which they were responsible? And what about all the Newfoundlanders and Labradorians suffering from tuberculosis: what kinds of promises did Smallwood make to them? And finally, what about the lives of those who don't appear to have written to Smallwood at all? How might we understand them? The short essays in this section address some aspects of everyday life at mid-century—health care, food security, work, and community building. They also point to erasures, silences, and resistance, not just in the archival record but also in relation to the popular imaginary of Newfoundland and Labrador.

1 Letter to J.R. Smallwood, April 30, 1949, 413–14, this volume.

This section of contextual essays opens with archivist Colleen Quigley's overview of the Smallwood collection, which is held at Archives and Special Collections, Queen Elizabeth II Library, Memorial University. In it, Quigley gives insight into the scope and nature of the collection as a whole, as well as the correspondence more specifically. The essays that follow deal with a broad range of aspects of daily life in mid-twentieth-century Newfoundland and Labrador.

J.T.H. Connor offers an overview of the state of medical care at Confederation, considering the tensions between self-congratulatory statements made by the Smallwood government and the longer history of medical care for Newfoundlanders and Labradorians. In particular, he points to the strength and innovation of the cottage hospital system and other hospitals, most of which were in place well before Confederation. In his "medico-historical checkup," Connor notes that "the claims of Smallwood and others about the later [post-1949] 'revolution' and 'improvements' in health, among other things, ought to be tempered," as they were not always based securely in evidence.[2]

Terry Bishop Stirling, meanwhile, focuses on the lives and working conditions of forestry workers in Grand Falls-Windsor. Noting the seasonal nature of the work, and the many men who came from other areas of the island to work in lumber camps in the winter, Bishop Stirling writes that in letters to Smallwood "[m]any loggers expressed their desire for steady work, while others looked for less physically demanding jobs as the hard manual labour and rough living conditions took their toll."[3] Some, who had been part of the Newfoundland Overseas Forestry Unit, returned to find that they did not qualify for veterans' benefits, and had little hope of finding steady employment. Bishop Stirling notes that logging employed men across the island from the late nineteenth century onward. Despite this, their lives and experiences have remained under-examined.

Heidi Coombs and Linda Cullum observe the role of women as community leaders and advocates. Coombs, who takes up the issue of food insecurity at mid-century, looks at the important role nurses played in advocating for the needs of local communities. As she writes about nurses of the Grenfell Mission, "[i]n addition to nursing, midwifery, and public health, they administered the stations, diagnosed patients, prescribed medications, and performed duties that

2 p. 438, this volume.

3 p. 441, this volume.

were traditionally beyond their scope of practice."[4] By focusing on one nurse's response to starvation on the South Coast of Labrador, Coombs highlights the dangers of political inattention to Newfoundland and Labrador's precarious food systems, both past and present.

Linda Cullum, meanwhile, considers the Jubilee Guilds, a network of women's groups established in the 1930s by privileged Anglo-Newfoundland women, mostly in St. John's, to support what they saw as the necessary rehabilitation of impoverished rural communities. While the Guilds were active across Newfoundland and concerned with the social uplift of rural women and their communities through distaff work, Cullum observes that "rural women saw in the Jubilee Guilds an opportunity to come together, gain access to work materials, learn new skills, and have a social time of their own."[5] The Guilds were foundational not just for community building but also as a way for women in rural Newfoundland to forge collective social and, indeed, political identities and to work toward the improvement of both their local communities and the larger province of which they were a part, even as Guild goals and objectives sometimes challenged prevailing political visions. Coombs's and Cullum's essays point to the important—if often underconsidered—role of women as community builders, leaders, and advocates.

And yet, as we noted in the Introduction, some Newfoundlanders and Labradorians do not appear to have written to the premier at all. Miriam Wright and Robert Hong give insight into the lives of Chinese Newfoundlanders who saw in Confederation the opportunity to become Canadian citizens. While many of these men had long called Newfoundland home, they did not share the rights of citizenship. As Wright and Hong recount, by September 1949 over forty of these men had applied for citizenship, with the first ten receiving their citizenship certificates in February 1951. The silences and struggles of Chinese Newfoundlanders invite consideration of the many peoples who were prohibited from full participation in mainstream social and political life in Newfoundland and Labrador.

In a similar vein, Dave Lough, Andrea Procter, Mi'sel Joe, Sheila O'Neill, Jessica Bound, and Jocelyn Thorpe all point to the exclusion of Indigenous peoples from both the terms of Confederation and the larger story of Newfoundland and Labrador itself.

---

4 p. 459, this volume.

5 p. 467, this volume.

Letters from Labrador in the years surrounding Confederation are few, certainly far fewer in total number than in other districts. While it might be tempting to attribute this to a smaller population in Labrador, that wasn't the case at mid-century: Dave Lough notes that the population in Labrador was just over 5,000. And so, we should look elsewhere for insight. It is likely that many people may have felt too distant from, or ill-equipped to communicate with, the halls of power. As Thorwald Perrault, quoted in Lough's essay, states, "In those days it didn't seem like the people of Labrador had any say at all."[6] Indeed, Lough observes that Innu and Inuit were not consulted prior to discussions about their possible future. As is abundantly evident, that lack of consultation and consideration has continued into the present day.

And yet, while Innu and Inuit people may not have written Smallwood directly, they nevertheless found ways to make their voices heard. Andrea Procter discusses an important resistance effort by the people of Hopedale in 1949. According to Procter, as new federal and provincial authorities arrived in their community, Inuit there were able to solicit "these new sources of authority to challenge the local Moravian missionaries and pursue their own goals"[7] of community education and governance, in this way asserting their right to self-determination.

Finally, we close this book with an excerpt from a larger essay by Mi'sel Joe, Sheila O'Neill, Jessica Bound, and Jocelyn Thorpe that asks readers to think about the erasure and silencing of Mi'kmaw lives, voices, experiences, and history in the colonial archival record and about how reading this record in conversation with and alongside Indigenous knowledge can reveal new insights.

Together these essays offer a window into life in mid-twentieth-century Newfoundland and Labrador. Read in conjunction with the correspondence, they offer vital insight into a remarkable period in the life and times of Newfoundlanders and Labradorians.

---

6 p. 451, this volume.

7 p. 483, this volume.

A Contextual Note from the Archivist

Colleen Quigley

MEMORIAL UNIVERSITY LIBRARIES' Archives and Special Collections (ASC) serves as the archival repository for the papers of Premier Joseph R. Smallwood. The letters to Smallwood that are so thoughtfully reflected upon in this book represent the tip of the iceberg of the archival material that Smallwood amassed and created during his ninety-year life. And yet, even this small part of the Smallwood collection is vast: researchers have the opportunity to pore over more than 10,000 letters sent to Smallwood spanning his entire political career. During the research process of this book, we hosted the book's contributors. As is evidenced in this book, the letters reflect the concerns, hopes, and dreams of Newfoundlanders and Labradorians.

My job as archivist is to safely house and provide access, in the physical and digital worlds, to our unique holdings that testify to the province's rich history and culture. In addition to such a lofty task, our responsibility is to provide context. The archivist's goal is to provide information regarding who, how, when, where, and why the items were created and curated. These insights can confirm, counter, or inspire further exploration. This book illustrates how profound meaning and surprising connections can be found within the archive.

Smallwood Archival Fonds

The archive safeguards material, and archivists provide the access to and context around these historical items. Although ASC is part of the Memorial University Libraries system, we define ourselves as a community-based archive within an academic-research environment. To many we are known as "Centre for Newfoundland Studies Archives," despite our name change in the early 2000s to "Archives and Manuscripts," which was then followed by a change a few years later to "Archives and Special Collections" when we merged with the rare and special book collection. Our archival holdings consist of a wide breadth of materials, including the province's largest performing arts archival materials relating to venues, festivals, troupes/groups, as well as individual artists/creators/patrons in addition to oral histories. ASC also houses literary and scholars' papers, the papers of community advocacy groups, nursing and health care collections as well as family and individual papers/fonds.[1] Our robust archive of political papers has been described by many, including the Honourable Edward Roberts, as the most important collection of post-confederacy archives in the province.

Smallwood Letters

The bulk of the Smallwood fonds arrived at ASC in two donations in 1974 (COLL-075) and 1992 (COLL-285). The fonds consists of

- 83 metres of textual material (83 shelves)
- 2,000+ photographs
- 500+ blueprints, maps, and other oversized items

This book's eloquent ruminations draw from the 10,000+ letters held within 101 acid-free boxes of Series 1.0 "District Files" of COLL-075. These files retain Smallwood's original order, in which the letters are filed chronologically by year (and alphabetically within each file), and sorted alphabetically by electoral district.[2] This filing choice is revealing. Does this illustrate that Smallwood viewed these interactions as important enough to organize and preserve because they were letters from voters regarding election issues specific to their electoral district? How might these letters have served Smallwood in his re-election campaigns?

1 Fonds: Canadian archival terminology: "The whole of the documents, regardless of form or medium, automatically or organically created and/or accumulated and used by a particular individual, family, or corporate body in the course of that creator's activities or functions." Bureau of Canadian Archivists, *Rules for Archival Description*, rev. ed. (Ottawa: Bureau of Canadian Archivists, 2008), D5. https://archivescanada.ca/wp-content/uploads/2022/08/RADComplete_July2008.pdf.

2 The transcriptions in this volume are organized alphabetically by district, and chronologically within each district, with undated letters placed at the end.

What is unfortunate is that not all the replies are included with each letter. However, even without replies, many of the letters include annotations that provide a variety of insights. Many of the letters include names of one or several government departments or ministers. In some instances, the draft responses are written on the top of the letter in pencil. The responses copy or refer to government departments, resources, programs, politicians, and/or contacts for follow-up. The evidence included on and with the letters suggests that Smallwood read every letter he received.[3]

Did Smallwood read these letters in solitude? Again, the annotations on the letters offer evidence that this was not the case. On many letters, in addition to draft responses (perhaps dictated?), there is secretarial shorthand. Muriel Templeman served as Smallwood's personal assistant during his career as premier (1949–72). As the years passed, the letters indicate that Templeman's imprint increases. Thus, not only are these letters indicators of the immediate concerns, issues, and/or passions consuming the people of this province at a given time, they are also, possibly, presented through Templeman's lens.

Templeman was profiled in Iris Power's 1954 *Atlantic Guardian* article entitled "Joey's 'Girl Friday,'" where she is described as "the resourceful person who routes the endless complaints and requests to their proper channels …"[4] A woman who "[had] to have all the answers," Templeman is described as being possessed of an "unruffled air. She is steady as a rock and waits unhurriedly while a caller states his business."[5] In this profile, Templeman is heralded for her "long experience and sure knowledge."[6] Her status is almost hero-level with claims that "The Premier's 'girl Friday' somehow finds the answer to the people's problems" and "sees them all."[7] It is worth considering the level of influence Templeman had on the content of the district files. Was she the one who arranged them all chronologically and alphabetically by district? Did she draft the responses herself or was she was taking dictation directly from Smallwood?

Many of the letters to Smallwood were written by women. These women often reached out to Smallwood as a last resort in order to deal with issues relating

---

3 However, as is clear from numerous letters included in this volume, correspondents did not aways receive responses to the letters they sent.

4 Iris Power, "Joey's 'Girl Friday,'" *Atlantic Guardian*, June 1954, 23.

5 Power, "Joey's 'Girl Friday,'" 23.

6 Power, "Joey's 'Girl Friday,'" 23.

7 Power, "Joey's 'Girl Friday,'" 24, 23.

to medical care, financial support for widows/veterans, education, food security, unemployment, labour rights, resettlement, and more.

Finally, as mentioned in the Introduction to this volume, it is also important to note that the archive may not be complete. We have no way of knowing if any letters have been destroyed, discarded, or stolen. We can only interpret the letters that we do have.

With more than 10,000 letters in J.R. Smallwood COLL-075's District Files (Series 1.0) to pore over, the *Atlantic Guardian*'s statement that "nearly everyone in Newfoundland writes 'Joey' on just about everything under the sun" seems apt.[8] In some ways, ASC is like the Smallwood government, in that we are also dedicated to routing every single person to their proper channel! We welcome a variety of researchers to interpret these letters, including scholars in feminist and gender theory, historians, linguists, writers, genealogists, and community members interested in the histories of their communities. We encourage you to make an appointment with ASC to embark on your own research adventure with our archival treasures.

8 Power, "Joey's 'Girl Friday,'" 23.

Medicine and Health Care in Pre- and Post-Confederation Newfoundland: Results of a Preliminary Medico-historical Checkup

J.T.H. Connor

IN 1945, the *Canadian Medical Association Journal* (*CMAJ*) published a report authored by a blue-ribbon medical team from the US, Britain, and Canada that depicted the population of Newfoundland as uniformly malnourished, physically stunted, and "slow in mental reactions."[1] Immediately, this assessment became front-page news; Newfoundlanders were outraged. The Wayfarer (journalist Albert B. Perlin) wrote one of the many rejoinders in which he railed at the report's "grave and gratuitous insults," the "infamous insults to the people of this country," and the negative "sweeping characterization of the whole population." In brief, the only resolution to this whole issue, he continued, was for a "complete and unequivocal denial" of the report that would go out to all Newfoundlanders and be communicated across Canada and "wherever else the reports have gone." The Wayfarer also raised possible untoward economic consequences that might arise due to the bad publicity from all the "false and damaging statements." Why would any industrialist wish to invest in Newfoundland if he believed the poor labour picture described in the *CMAJ*? And wouldn't tourists be diverted from visiting the island to avoid encountering a "land peopled by diseased morons"?[2] On April 1, 1949—the first day after Newfoundland's Confederation with Canada—the *CMAJ* published a follow-up report modelled on the previous one, and which was written by almost the identical research

1 J.D. Adamson, N. Jolliffe, H.D. Kruse, O.H. Lowry, P.E. Moore, B.S. Platt, W.H. Sebrell, J.W. Tice, F.F. Tisdall, R.M. Wilder, and P.C. Zamecnik, "Medical Survey of Nutrition in Newfoundland," *Canadian Medical Association Journal* 52 (1945): 227–50.

2 The Wayfarer, "In the News," *The Daily News* (St. John's), March 8, 1945, 8.

team, that concluded in the intervening lustrum that the health and well-being of Newfoundlanders had greatly improved.[3]

Critical in-depth analysis of both *CMAJ* articles reveals research flaws and bias owing to their arbitrary sampling techniques and inconsistency and difficulty in applying clinical and laboratory standards that, while it does not render them nugatory, requires them to be understood as being impressionistic rather than representing an objective reality.[4] Yet, there can be no denying that, due to the friendly massive invasion of Newfoundland by Allied troops who brought cash and infrastructure investment, many local residents and communities began to enjoy the fruits of a much-improved economy.[5] And there was, of course, the later injection of large amounts of federal dollars from Ottawa (by way of Old Age Pension benefits and baby bonuses, for example).[6] Characteristically, Joseph R. Smallwood, along with other commentators, trumpeted how a "revolution has swept Newfoundland since confederation [with Canada] in 1949." He further declared that "[s]wift improvements in our education, health, transportation and communication facilities have set the stage for further economic growth. . . . If the progress since confederation might be counted as considerable . . . this progress will nevertheless seem puny in comparison with the growth I envisage for Newfoundland over the coming decades."[7]

In the same vein, S.J. Colman of Memorial University also invoked the

---

3 W.R. Aykroyd, N. Jolliffe, O.H. Lowry, P.E. Moore, W.H. Sebrell, R.E. Shank, F.F. Tisdall, R.M. Wilder, and P.C. Zamecnik, "Medical Resurvey of Nutrition in Newfoundland 1948," *Canadian Medical Association Journal* 60 (1949): 329–52.

4 For context on malnutrition in pre-Confederation Newfoundland, see Eric Strikwerda, "Newfoundland and Labrador Maligned: Taking Stock of Nutritional Health in Rural Newfoundland and Labrador, 1912–1949," *Acadiensis* 47, no. 1 (2018): 118–39; and Connor, "Malnutrition Research in Newfoundland and Labrador ... Part 1" and "Malnutrition Research in Newfoundland and Labrador ... Part 2."

5 Steven High, *Base Colonies in the Western Hemisphere, 1940–1967* (New York: Palgrave Macmillan, 2009), see especially ch. 3 "Working for Uncle Sam in Newfoundland"; High, *Occupied St. John's*; High, "From Outport to Outport Base: The American Occupation of Stephenville 1940–1945," *Newfoundland Studies* 18 (2002): 84–113; and Peter Neary, "'A Mortgaged Property': The Impact of the United States on Newfoundland, 1940–49," in *Twentieth-Century Newfoundland: Explorations*, ed. James Hiller and Peter Neary (St. John's: Breakwater, 1994), 179–94.

6 Blake, *Canadians at Last.*

7 Joseph Smallwood, foreword to *Newfoundland and Labrador: The First Fifteen Years of Confederation*, ed. R.I. McAllister (St. John's: Dicks, 1966), n.p.

concept of revolution and indicated that progress meant Newfoundlanders "no longer [had] to take their sick in small boats to seek medical assistance at a sometimes distant cottage hospital."[8] The overarching theme of inexorable progress in these commentaries was echoed by Albert Perlin, still writing as a journalist, who noted that "great modern hospitals" had sprung up in the 1950s and 1960s, which was "all very much to the good." But he also cautioned that modernity seemed to become almost an "obsession" and that the "province has been precipitated like a rocket into a more sophisticated age and perhaps Newfoundlanders have been trying to adapt too quickly."[9]

Perlin's more cautious assessment is a necessary antidote to Smallwood's smug pontification, especially in the matters of hospital construction and health care. It has been widely held that health care in pre-Confederation Newfoundland was dismal—a view often promulgated by Smallwood for his own self-serving purposes. Noted Newfoundland journalist, political commentator, and satirist Ray Guy once quipped:

> After Confederation and before it, there was an inferiority complex in Newfoundland—especially when the Yanks marched in here, and they all had teeth and were plump. After Confederation, Joey [Smallwood] and his crowd harped on it for their own aggrandizement. The world started in 1949 (according to Smallwood)—before that, there was only depravity, poverty and corruption.[10]

Recent medical historiography suggests that whatever shortcomings there were, health care in Newfoundland before 1949 had its high points, much to recommend it, and made good inroads in treating the population—assessments

8 S.J. Colman (and members of the Extension Department, Memorial University), "Social Changes since Confederation," in McAllister, *Newfoundland and Labrador*, 8–13.

9 A.B. Perlin, "History and Health in Newfoundland," *Canadian Journal of Public Health* 61 (1970): 313–16.

10 Mark Paddeck, "The Guy Philosophy," *The Express* (St. John's), February 3, 1993, 9–10. Much of Guy's oeuvre is anthologized in Ray Guy, *Ray Guy: The Smallwood Years* (Portugal Cove-St. Philip's, NL: Boulder Publications, 2008). See also Robert Paine, "Smallwood: Political Strategy, and a 'Career' of Rhetoric," *Newfoundland Studies* 3 (1987): 217–26. Smallwood's penchant for embellishing and stretching facts to the point of telling "tall tales" is explored in Paine, "The Persuasiveness of Smallwood: Rhetoric of *Cuffer* and *Scoff*, of Metonym and Metaphor," *Newfoundland Studies* 1 (1985): 57–75.

that both contemporary American and English commentators agreed on.[11] More apposite is the use of hospital construction as a metric in this medico-historical checkup. Of the eighteen cottage hospitals that were eventually built, the majority (fourteen) were constructed before Confederation; indeed, the entire cottage hospital system, which was one of the earliest national health schemes in North America and the British empire, was a spectacular innovation created in the 1930s by the much-maligned Commission of Government.[12] Add to these the several general and specialized hospitals operating in St. John's and Twillingate, along with the network of hospitals, nursing stations, and floating ship clinics working under the auspices of the International Grenfell Association—all of which were long-standing institutions founded well before 1949.[13]

Further, the claims of Smallwood and others about the later "revolution" and "improvements" in health, among other things, ought to be tempered. The case study of the West Coast Sanatorium is salutary. The official opening in June 1952 of the new Corner Brook facility for the treatment of tuberculosis was a gala affair with numerous dignitaries in attendance, but, curiously, *sans* Smallwood himself. It was touted in the local newspaper as "up-to-date and as modern an institution as there is almost anywhere in the world."[14] But the problem was that the whole concept of a sanatorium, modern or not, was out of date! Across the Western world at this time, sanatoria were winding down and closing beds because older methods of treatments such as the rest cure (lasting years), cold fresh air, and invasive surgical operations, all of which had underpinned the

11 J.T.H. Connor, "'... medicine is here to stay': Rural Medical Practice, Frontier Life, and Modernization in 1930s' Newfoundland," in *Medicine in the Remote and Rural North, 1800–2000*, ed. J.T.H. Connor and Stephan Curtis (London: Pickering & Chatto, 2011), 129–51, 260–65; Connor, Connor, Kidd, and Mathews, "Conceptualizing Health Care"; J.T.H. Connor, "American Aid, the International Grenfell Association, and Health Care in Newfoundland, 1920s–1930s," in *The Grenfell Medical Mission and American Support in Newfoundland and Labrador, 1890s–1940s*, ed. Jennifer J. Connor and Katherine Side (McGill-Queen's University Press, 2019), 245–66; and J.T.H. Connor, "'for her own safety and the good of society at large': Eugenics, Sterilization, and Anglo-American Transnationalism in Newfoundland, 1928–1934," *Acadiensis* 48, no. 1 (2019): 32–59.

12 Lawson and Noseworthy, "Newfoundland's Cottage Hospital System: 1920–1970"; and Lake, *Capturing an Era*.

13 Leonard A. Miller, "The Newfoundland Department of Health," *Canadian Journal of Public Health* 50 (June 1959): 228–39.

14 "Sanatorium Officially Opened," *The Western Star* (Corner Brook), June 6, 1952, 1.

raison d'être of the sanatorium, were being fast supplanted by more convenient and effective chemotherapy. Pharmaceuticals such as the antibiotic streptomycin (dating from the late 1940s), along with other chemotherapeutic drugs (e.g., para-amino salicylic acid [PAS] and isonicotinic acid hydrazine [INH]), shortened treatment from years to months, and they did not need to be administered in expensive and highly staffed institutional settings. Tellingly, months before the opening of the West Coast Sanatorium the same newspaper ran a story under the headline "Tests of New Anti-T.B. Drug Lead to Optimism," which reported how Dr. Peters, sanatorium superintendent, had travelled to the US to acquire quantities of INH for use in both St. John's and Corner Brook.[15]

Results of this preliminary medico-historical checkup of medicine and health care in pre- and post-Confederation Newfoundland are far from being definitive, but they suggest that the former era was perhaps not as bleak all the time and the latter era was not as modern and progressive as Smallwood et al. might have had us believe.[16]

15 "Tests of New Anti-T.B. Drug Lead to Optimism," *The Western Star* (Corner Brook), April 8, 1952, 3.

16 The content of this brief essay is one component of a much larger, more comprehensive discussion of health care past and present in Newfoundland and Labrador; see J.T.H. Connor, "Newfoundland and Labrador: The Paradoxical 'Sick Man' of Canada," *Newfoundland and Labrador Studies* 37, no. 1 (2022), https://journals.lib.unb.ca/index.php/NFLDS/article/view/33490.

"isn't much work to get beside the Bucksaw": Grand Falls Workers and Their Hopes for Confederation

Terry Bishop Stirling

THE DISTRICT OF GRAND FALLS was a large and varied one. As elsewhere in the province, people fished and farmed, ran small and large businesses, and did clerical and retail work. Others worked at the mill in Grand Falls, the mine at Buchans, or the airport in Gander. But thousands of men made their living "on the Gander," using bucksaws to cut pulpwood for the Anglo-Newfoundland Development Company. Loggers included men who lived full time in the district but also hundreds who regularly moved in and out, combining logging with fishing in their home communities in Trinity or Conception Bays.[1] Many loggers expressed their desire for steady work, while others looked for less physically demanding jobs as the hard manual labour and rough living conditions took their toll. Letters frequently expressed appreciation for Family Allowances, but they still needed work to support their families, and jobs remained the priority.

"depending on getting a job out of this letter"

Loggers who wrote to Smallwood did not complain about wages, but the work was irregular, with men employed for a few weeks on a particular site and then left to find their next camp. Letter writers hoped for steadier work after Confederation and expected Smallwood to reward their support with jobs. One man outlined his work history in 1949, writing:

1 Background information on the logging industry is from Dufferin Sutherland, "'We are only Loggers': Loggers and the Struggle for Development in Newfoundland, 1929–59" (PhD diss., Simon Fraser University, 1995). Proquest NN17130.

> I was in the wood last Summer. Finish in November. When my work was finish went to the other camp could not get another job, came Home took fifty dollars. Went away again could not get another job any where around in May. I got a moth and half work my camp close and I moved on to another one. Got a moth and half their and was in August so that is about three month work in a year.[2]

He had worked since he lost his parents at the age of twelve and proudly concluded his letter, "I am not afraid of work and I never eat a Bit of dole yet, But when you cant get a job I cant take one."

Two men wrote to Smallwood several times. In a joint letter in August 1949, they reported that their present camp was about to finish and there was no sign of further work: "We have no way to feed our families this winter." They assured Smallwood that they had voted for him three times and then quoted him as promising that "there would be two jobs for every man in N.F.L.D. after you get in power." They concluded assertively that they were "depending on getting a job out of this letter."[3]

"it is hard for me to do any hard work"

Men typically had to walk six miles a day to their camps. They laboured all day with bucksaws and then endured drafty, dirty, and uncomfortable bunkhouses. Joint problems, accidents, and illness made it hard for many men to keep up the pace required by camp bosses anxious to meet their quotas. As a result of their working conditions, loggers were often old before their time and wrote to Smallwood asking about pensions, or more often, alternate work. A veteran had his arm "broken up" in World War I and by 1949 was not able to work in the woods. He told Smallwood that "it is hard for me to do any hard work, in fact i cant do it. i have been turned down by doctors, not to use the Bucksaw, they have told me if I keep using her i would loose my arm some day." He hoped to get a job as a ferry operator since there "isn't much work to get beside the Bucksaw."[4] Another man, meanwhile,

2 [Name redacted] to J.R. Smallwood, October 8, 1949, COLL-075, Box 37, 1.14.003, ASC. All letters cited in this essay are from this source and cited only by file number.

3 [Names redacted] to J.R. Smallwood, August 15, 1949, 1.14.002.

4 [Name redacted] to J.R. Smallwood, June 12, 1949, 1.14.002.

wrote Smallwood at least twice. He had supported his family of five despite losing a hand in the mill some fifteen years years earlier. In his first letter, he wrote:

> i Raised up a family of 5 all gone for them selfs excepted one girl and she his goining to school. I know what it his to find it hard to Bring them up with one hand i have Been usining they Buck saw and cutting with axe when no Buck saw was in use with one hand to use it with i have been fishining and could manage to git a livening off some how.[5]

He wrote Smallwood again in the spring of 1949 to see what the government could do for him because the company now considered him disabled and would not offer him any more work.

"I have done my share for my King & Country"

Many loggers from Grand Falls district had joined the Newfoundland Overseas Forestry Unit, which spent World War II logging in Scotland. Their work, cutting timber for essential industries, including pit props for Britain's mines, was advertised as essential war work, and recruiters pushed hard to enlist experienced Newfoundland loggers.[6] A veteran of the Forestry Unit struggled with illness which began during his service and wrote Smallwood about possible veterans' benefits. Whether as a result of his poor health or the general job shortage in 1949, he found it hard to keep regular employment:

5 The files contain two back-to-back letters from the same man, one dated and the other undated. The dated one is slightly shorter and, interestingly, has perfect spelling and grammar; the undated one has many spelling and punctuation/grammar errors. Perhaps this was an earlier version and he sought help with the second one, believing a "better" written letter might get more results. He had lost an arm but the date of his accident is unclear; the longer letter says he lost it thirty-nine years previously, while the more formal one dates it to fifteen years. [Name redacted] to J.R. Smallwood, May 11, 1949, and [name redacted] to Smallwood, undated, 1.14.003.

6 For a brief introduction to the Newfoundland Overseas Forestry Unit, see Jenny Higgins, "Newfoundland Overseas Forestry Unit," Newfoundland & Labrador Heritage, 2006, https://www.heritage.nf.ca/articles/politics/overseas-forestry-unit-wwii.php.

> I served about three and a half years in the Nfld Forestry overseas, was discharged before the end of hostilities owing to suffering with rheumatic fever, I was laid up six months after arriving home after which I was employed with the Dept of public works for about three months. Since that time I have worked with the A.N.D. Co. about four months out of twelve the rest of the time I have not done much of anything I still am suffering from the rhuematic fever at times more than others.[7]

Another veteran of the Forestry Unit questioned why he was not eligible for veterans' benefits:

> I am a man who served with the "Nfld forestry Unit" in Scotland for five & one half yrs. After being over there two yrs I tried to enlist into one of the Armed forces but wouldn't be admitted being told that the work being done by the foresters was too essential. I then joined the Home Guard, & gave all my spare time into training to defend Britian if need be unlike the soldiers we weren't paid for our training.[8]

He questioned why "we foresters do not qualify for the veterans' benefit now being given to the Armed forces, as we were led to believe through booklets distributed to us before coming home that there was great advantages to be given us." After consulting with Veterans' Affairs, Smallwood replied that while he agreed that the Overseas Forestry men had played an important role, they were considered civilian war workers, paid accordingly and able to return home or transfer to fighting forces at the end of their initial contract. This response did not correspond to the experience of the forestry vets and these letters foreshadow a more organized fight for recognition which began in the 1960s. In 1962, men of the Newfoundland Overseas Forestry Unit were recognized under the Civilian War Allowance Act, but they had to wait until 2000 to be fully eligible for veterans' benefits. It is unlikely that these late reforms helped men such as those letter writers.

7 [Name redacted] to J.R. Smallwood, June 13, 1949, 1.14.003.

8 [Name redacted] to J.R. Smallwood, August 8, 1949, 1.14.003.

Conclusion

Logging employed large numbers of Newfoundland men from the late nineteenth century onward, expanding significantly with the growth of the pulp and paper industry in the early twentieth century. The story of these labourers, as well as loggers' contribution to the war efforts, deserves attention. What struck me most about loggers' letters was the extreme conditions under which they lived and worked. Men endured the stress of uncertain employment as well as frequent injuries and long-term physical strains, resulting in constant pain and the inability to continue in logging or the other labour-intensive jobs available to them. Loggers hoped that Confederation would provide more job security and more options for those who could no longer endure woods work. But political change provided no quick fix. Loggers' working conditions did not improve in the decade following Confederation, ultimately leading to the 1959 International Woodworkers of America (IWA) strike, one of the most violent and bitter labour actions in the province's history.

Confederation: Labrador Gets the Right to Vote but Not a Voice

Dave Lough

Labrador Pre-1940s

IN 1713, the Treaty of Utrecht assigned the island of Newfoundland to Britain, while Labrador was assigned to France. However, in 1763, by virtue of the Treaty of Paris, France ceded to Great Britain all possessions and rights in North America, including Labrador. King George III immediately placed Labrador under the authority of the governor of Newfoundland.

In 1765, the governor of Newfoundland, Hugh Palliser, issued an "Order for Establishing Communication and Trade with the Esquimaux Savages on the coast of Labrador," requiring in part to "banish all disorderly people who cant be depended upon for preserving good order and peace with the savages (upon which the success of his Majesty's intentions for opening this extensive field of commerce to his subjects wholly depends)" and that the Inuit population be treated "in the most civil and friendly manner."[1] He also offered land in Labrador to Moravian missionaries, who were already established in Greenland, believing that the missionaries would maintain the European presence while limiting destructive contact between Inuit and Europeans.

In effect, as soon as Newfoundland itself became an operati[...]ntity, the feeling in Labrador was that it became a colony, a summer home f[...]onception

1 Hugh Pallister et al., "Order for Establishing Communicati[...]d Trade with the Esquimaux Savages on the Coast of Labrador, 1765," in La[...] *Boundary Dispute Extracts from Charters, Acts Etc.* (ca. 1915), Labrador Inuit t[...] Moravian Eyes, [...]8. https://collections.mun.ca/digital/collection/moraviar

Bay and its fishing fleets, a place from which to take things.[2] Sir Wilfred Grenfell estimated the annual summer migration to Labrador at approximately 20,000 persons, and historian H.A. Innis cited the number of schooners in 1908 as 1,432.[3] For two centuries, the Labrador floater fishery made a significant contribution to the economic growth of Newfoundland, accounting for one-quarter to one-half of the entire production of salt codfish.[4]

Politically, the boundary of Labrador remained an issue on many occasions from 1765 to the 1927 Privy Council decision which awarded Labrador to Newfoundland. Immediately following the Privy Council decision, Labrador was the subject of a massive amount of attention, especially in Newfoundland. The St. John's *Evening Telegram* engaged in an orgy of congratulation for several weeks after the boundary decision, hailing Labrador as the economic saviour of Newfoundland because of its limitless resource wealth.[5] However, the extent of official Newfoundland presence in the vast Labrador territory up to Confederation was minimal. At the turn of the twentieth century, historian W.G. Gosling echoed pioneering doctor Wilfred Grenfell's complaint that such a vast territory was still without a regular police presence.[6]

The issues of health and well-being were not addressed in an organized way until the creation in 1914 of the International Grenfell Association by British doctor Wilfred Grenfell. Hospitals had been built in Battle Harbour in 1893 and Indian Harbour in 1894. In 1915, Dr. Harry L. Paddon established a hospital in North West River which would eventually serve the entire coast of Labrador health care before Confederation. It was through the fundraising efforts of the International Grenfell Association in the UK and USA that Labrador had access t[illegible] health care, but it was not until the 1980s that the province took full responsi[illegible]lity for health care in Labrador. Newfoundland chose not to allocate its limite[illegible]financial resources to provide services in Labrador.

[illegible] 1924, while Newfoundland and Quebec were preparing their case for review [illegible]y the judicial committee of the Privy Council, Newfoundland prime

2 Lynn [illegible]itzhugh, *The Labradorians: Voices from the Land of Cain* (Breakwater Books, 1999), [illegible]

3 S.J.R. N[illegible] *Politics in Newfoundland* (Toronto: University of Toronto Press, 1971), 91.

4 Black, "L[illegible]dor Floater Cod Fishery," 267.

5 R. Budgel[illegible] M. Staveley, *The Labrador Boundary* (Labrador Institute of Northern Studies, M[illegible]l University, 1987), 10.

6 Keith Merce[illegible]h *Justice: Policing, Crime, and the Origins of the Newfoundland Constabulary,* [illegible]71 (St. John's: Flanker Press, 2021), 344.

minister Walter S. Moore proposed to sell Labrador to Quebec for $15 million, provided that Newfoundland would retain rights to a three-mile coastal zone for the use of fishermen. Quebec's premier Louis-Alexandre Taschereau declined the offer. After the 1927 Privy Council decision awarding Labrador to Newfoundland, Sir Richard Squires turned to Ottawa in 1931 to sell Labrador for $110 million, but Ottawa rejected the offer.[7] Desperate for funds, Newfoundland needed to sell Labrador or find developers of its rich resources.

Labrador in the 1940s

While there was much talk in St. John's about the mineral and hydro riches of Labrador, the economy of Labrador was based on traditional hunting, fishing, and trapping. It was not until the 1940s that significant economic changes began to happen in Labrador. World War II and the entry of the United States and Canada suddenly made Labrador a critical strategic location for support to the North American war effort. The wage economy opportunities attracted some coastal residents to take employment constructing the Goose Bay air force base and create the new community of Happy Valley.

The final specifications of the 1941 agreement by the Government of Canada approved the building of an air base for 5,000 officers and men and 3,000 civilians on a large flat plateau in central Labrador with the largest runway in the world at the time enabling air access from North America to Europe.[8] Labrador was suddenly a strategic place in North America defence. The huge and sudden military investment in what became known as Goose Bay Airport quickly changed the small communities in the Lake Melville region and introduced the wage economy to Labrador.

Change was also happening on the north coast. The 1942 withdrawal of the Hudson's Bay Company from northern Labrador meant immediate action was required by the Newfoundland government. The Northern Labrador Trading Operations (NLTO) was established as a branch of the Department of Natural Resources. Trapping was encouraged, as well as cod, char, and seal fisheries. An

---

7 Larry Dohey, "Newfoundland Proposed to Sell Labrador to Quebec," *Archival Moments* (blog), March 4, 2018, http://archivalmoments.ca/2018/03/04/newfoundland-proposed-to-sell-labrador-to-quebec-2/.

8 William Guy Carr, *Checkmate in the North: The Axis Planned to Invade America* (Toronto: MacMillan Company, 1944), 86.

agreement which was implemented in 1942 provided funds for Indigenous peoples and some money from Canada flowed into what were then called the Indian and Eskimo communities.[9]

In Labrador, there was little Newfoundland government involvement except through limited educational efforts, wireless, mail, and passenger services and the Newfoundland Rangers, who represented every department. Newfoundland Ranger stations were established between 1935 and 1949 and the Rangers were particularly important, as they were often the only liaison between the people and their government.[10] Battle Harbour was the key communications point and the de facto capital of Labrador until 1930, when a fire destroyed the hospital and school and replacement buildings were built in Mary's Harbour.

Reverend Lester Burry, a Methodist-United Church clergyman who devoted his ministry to working in Labrador with the encouragement of Dr. Wilfred Grenfell, was a key figure in Labrador at this time. Burry's mission was to take care of the physical and spiritual needs of Labradorians. To further this mission, in 1937 Burry built his own radio broadcast station in North West River to improve the lives of isolated people by providing news, weather, and public announcements.[11] It was his desire to improve the standard of living that caused him to decide that confederation with Canada would help the average person in Labrador.

By the 1940s, Labrador's total population hovered just over 5,000 people scattered in small communities along the coast and in the Lake Melville area. Reverend Burry's ham operating station Vo6B allowed communications to small communities and to trappers who gathered on Sundays in remote Labrador with a small receiver to hear the weekly church service and news. In 1950, *Maclean's* published the article "The Mechanized Missionary of North West River," which showed that Burry had a 35-foot cabin cruiser, *Glad Tidings*, and in 1946 he went from dog team to a motorized snow machine.[12]

In the spring of 1946, letters from Labrador to the governor of Newfoundland requested the appointment of Reverend Lester Burry to the National

---

9 Royal Commission on Labrador, "Report of the Royal Commission on Labrador" (St. John's: The Commission, 1974), 1294.

10 Higgins, "Newfoundland Ranger Force."

11 "Rev. Dr. Lester Leeland Burry," Heritage Newfoundland & Labrador, https://heritagenl.ca/discover/provincial-historic-commemorations-program-designations/rev-dr-lester-leeland-burry/.

12 Gerald Anglin, "The Mechanized Missionary of North West River," *Maclean's*, August 1, 1950.

Convention. Ranger C. Gilbert and Jack Watts from North West River, W.S. Moores on behalf of the Sandwich Bay Committee, and Jacques Thevenet on behalf of the Labrador Citizens at Goose Air Base cited Burry's knowledge of Labrador and commitment to its people.[13] Joe Goudie of Happy Valley, who was ten years old in 1949, remembers his mother, Elizabeth Goudie, talking of Reverend Burry fondly and how he was viewed with respect by many in Labrador.[14] Burry was selected to represent Labrador in the National Convention and elected in February 1947 to the seven-member Ottawa delegation to negotiate terms of union with Canada. Labrador had representation at the table by a resident who knew the territory and was trusted by Labradorians. Burry would play a key role in promoting Confederation as the best option for Labrador.

Labrador Votes for the First Time

Prior to Confederation with Canada, the people of Labrador had never had the right to vote, although on the island of Newfoundland the right to vote was granted to most men in 1833. The first opportunity to vote for Labradorians was in 1948 when two referenda on the future of the province were conducted. Thorwald Perrault, originally from Makkovik, who settled in Happy Valley, said, "In those days it didn't seem like the people of Labrador had any say at all. It seems as though as long as they came across the Straits, across the water to Labrador. Anybody such as a schoolteacher or a minister, 'You go ask them.' It didn't seem as though we had the rights to go and talk for ourselves."[15]

The referenda results in the electoral district of Labrador were conclusive. In the first referendum, on June 3, 1948, Commission of Government got 162 votes, responsible government 263, and Confederation with Canada 1,858. In the second referendum, on July 22, 1948, 766 voted for responsible government and 2,681 for Confederation with Canada. Labrador had voted decisively in the first opportunity for its residents to have the democratic right to vote. It was a small beginning

13 "Commission of Government, Natural Resources General Administration 1940–1947," File 3, File # GN38-S-2-1-22, The Rooms Provincial Archives (RPA), St. John's, NL.

14 Joe Goudie, interview by Dave Lough, 2022.

15 David J. Whalen, *Just One Interloper after Another: An Unabridged, Unofficial, Unauthorized History of the Labrador Straits* (Forteau, NL: Labrador Straits Historical Development Corporation, 1990), 140.

of greater recognition of Labrador people as citizens in the new province.

Labrador Straits native Doug Letto remembered his father talking about the older people being eager to get a Canadian Old Age Pension, a much richer payment than the Newfoundland pension of $15 every three months. Families were eager, as well, to receive the Family Allowance. It gave families a guaranteed cash allowance, something unheard of in previous times.[16]

In 1946, discussions in St. John's on making the case for Confederation considered the idea that "[a]s part of the deal for union, Labrador might be sold to Canada for $200 million, payable in fifty installments of $4 million each with fishing rights being reserved."[17] While the idea was not pursued, it does clearly indicate that Labrador again was considered a commodity of value to Newfoundland. However, Joey Smallwood, as the new province's economic saviour, had a vision for Labrador.

The 1949 Newfoundland general election was held on May 27, 1949, to elect members of the 29th General Assembly of Newfoundland. It was the first general election held since Newfoundland joined the Canadian Confederation on March 31, 1949, and the first Newfoundland-wide election of any kind since the suspension of responsible government and the creation of Commission of Government in 1934. The election was held under the House of Assembly Act of 1932, with the same twenty-seven seats, plus a new seat for Labrador, although the election in the Labrador seat was deferred until July 25 because of logistics of transportation on the coast.[18]

Harold Horwood, a young journalist and supporter of Smallwood from St. John's, was elected to represent Labrador in the 1949 general election. Horwood, like many other candidates for election in rural and remote areas, was appointed from St. John's. The priority of the new government seemed to be the development of hydroelectric and iron ore resources in Labrador, not the well-being of the residents. Isolation, a scattered population, and political inexperience combined to frustrate the hopes of Labrador residents for community-based economic development and a role in provincial affairs.[19] It would be 1972 before a Labrador

---

16 Douglas Mervyn Letto, *In Cain's Footsteps: [People of the Labrador Straits]* (Paradise, NL: Blue Hill Publishing, 2000), 108.

17 Melvin Baker and Peter Neary, *Joseph Roberts Smallwood: Masthead Newfoundlander, 1900–1949* (Montreal: McGill-Queen's University Press, 2021), 127.

18 "Labrador," accessed December 10, 2022, https://www.wikiwand.com/en/Labrador.

19 W. Flowers, A. Fowler, L. Jackson, D. Lough, and N. Markham, *As If People Mattered* (Labrador Resources Advisory Council, 1977), 3.

resident would be elected to the House of Assembly, when Mike Martin from Cartwright was elected to represent Labrador South for the New Labrador Party.

Recognition of the Indigenous Population of Labrador

During the discussions between Canada and Newfoundland in 1948 leading to Confederation, the matter of governmental responsibility for Inuit and Innu peoples was considered by the negotiators. It is some indication of the state of local politics that neither Inuit nor the Innu were consulted about their disposition. A joint Canada-Newfoundland special committee concluded that both Aboriginal peoples should become a direct federal responsibility, as in the rest of Canada. The special committee identified eleven conditions that would apply to Aboriginal peoples if union occurred. In the end, however, the 1949 Terms of Union with Canada contained no reference to Aboriginal peoples. The Terms of Union failed to recognize the Indigenous peoples of Labrador and Newfoundland. In 1949, a Federal Interdepartmental Committee on Newfoundland Indians and Eskimos decided not to exercise Canada's fiduciary responsibility to Indigenous populations in the province.[20]

It was five years later, after some discussion of the legal dimensions of this arrangement, a 1954 agreement, outside the Terms of Union, provided for federal funding to be transferred to the Newfoundland government for the administration of programs for the Indigenous peoples of Newfoundland and Labrador. In practice, funding provided under the federal-provincial agreements had not been directed specifically to Indigenous peoples but to "designated communities": the agreements funded persons according to where they lived. This arrangement avoided the necessity of registration under the Indian Act. The Innu and Inuit of Labrador were granted full Canadian citizenship instead of status. They had voting rights and paid taxes; however, the Newfoundland government denied them hunting privileges and fined them for infractions of game laws from which, as First Peoples, they were entitled to exemption.[21] The Innu population remained nomadic until long after Confederation and the only service extended to them was in the form of welfare and limited medical aid, while the Inuit received some support for those living in designated communities on the north coast.

20 Hanrahan, "The Lasting Breach," 235.

21 Fitzhugh, *The Labradorians*, 372.

Without access to adequate funds from Canada to improve housing, health, education, and economic development, the Indigenous communities in Labrador would continue to struggle. Labrador was one of the last regions in Canada to get the right to vote. However, the right to vote without a voice was not enough to bring real change. It would be left to Labrador and its leaders through strong community-based organizations, created in the 1970s, to strongly present the case for fair and equal treatment, which was denied at Confederation. Real democracy came to Labrador decades after Confederation and then it was clear Labrador would no longer be offered for sale, ignored, or exploited under the careful watch of its residents. Finally, Labrador would begin to have a voice in its own future.

For Labrador Inuit leader Johannes Lampe, the failure to recognize Labrador's Indigenous population in the Terms of Union remains an outstanding reconciliation issue for Labrador Inuit. Lampe raised the issue with Premier Andrew Furey in a meeting in 2021, hoping that the Government of Newfoundland and Labrador would acknowledge the injustice committed on Indigenous peoples in Labrador.[22]

22 Johannes Lampe, interview by Dave Lough, September 2022.

"There is a serious shortage of food on this coast"[1]: Food Security, Agriculture, and Advocacy in Northern Newfoundland and Labrador

Heidi Coombs

ON APRIL 7, 1949, just one week after Newfoundland became the tenth province of Canada, the *Evening Telegram* in St. John's published an alarming headline:

> Starvation in Labrador
>
> ----------
>
> Serious Shortage of Food in Labrador,
> To Avert Starvation Immediate Aid Must be Sent to St. Mary's River
>
> ----------
>
> Only Seven Bags of Flour on Coast, Babies Being
> Fed on Flour, Water and Molasses-Water—
> There is No Milk and No Rolled Oats Available.
>
> ----------
>
> International Grenfell Association Nurse in Area Sends Appeal for Help—
> Attempt Will Be Made to Fly Supplies in, Fog Causing Delay.[2]

The International Grenfell Association (or Grenfell Mission) nurse at St. Mary's River,[3] Dorothy Jupp, and doctor at Cartwright, Dr. Garth Forsyth, had both wired urgent appeals for food directly to the new province's premier, Joseph R. Smallwood. Their appeals garnered considerable public attention and threatened

1 "Starvation in Labrador," *Evening Telegram*, April 7, 1949, 3.

2 "Starvation in Labrador."

3 More commonly known today as Mary's Harbour.

to become a political crisis at a time of heightened political awareness. Newfoundlanders and Labradorians had spent the previous two and a half years debating their constitutional future and the merits of Confederation with Canada. The results of the second referendum (July 22, 1948) exposed a nation deeply divided, with Confederation (52.3 per cent) narrowly winning over responsible government (47.7 per cent). At this time, proponents of Confederation would have been eager to prove the wisdom of joining Canada, while opponents would have exploited potential failings of the new government—such as starvation in Labrador. The food shortage also reflected poorly on the Grenfell Mission which, with limited government presence in northern Newfoundland and Labrador, had established itself as the medical and social authority in the region. The fact that starvation was happening on the Labrador Coast under their "watch," and that one of their own nurses sounded the alarm directly to the premier, created an embarrassing public relations situation for an organization eager for favour from their wealthy international benefactors and from the new federal and provincial governments.[4]

Food security had been a longstanding issue in northern Newfoundland and Labrador.[5] Many of the communities were isolated and depended to a significant degree on the importation of food—either by merchants through the "truck" or credit system or by the Hudson's Bay Company (HBC) and other European traders in Labrador. These were capitalist arrangements established through the processes of colonization—arrangements that were imposed on Indigenous peoples in the region, which disrupted and undermined their traditional foodways and subsistence practices.[6] They were also arrangements

4 For a critical interpretation of this incident and the tension between Jupp and the Grenfell Mission over her assertiveness in calling public attention to the matter, see Iona L. Bulgin, "Mapping the Self in the 'Utmost Purple Rim': Published Labrador Memoirs of Four Grenfell Nurses" (PhD diss., Memorial University, 2001). See also Gordon W. Thomas, "Winter Plane Trips," *Among the Deep Sea Fishers* 47, no. 2 (July 1949): 35–36.

5 On food security, see Linda Kealey, "Historical Perspectives on Nutrition and Food Security in Newfoundland and Labrador," in *Resetting the Kitchen Table: Food Security, Culture, Health and Resilience in Coastal Communities*, ed. Christopher C. Parrish, Nancy J. Turner, and Shirley M. Solberg (New York: Nova Science Publishers, 2007), 177–90.

6 For more on the impact of colonialism on food acquisition, consumption, and meaning in Labrador Inuit society, see Maura Hanrahan, "Tracing Social Change among the Labrador Inuit: What Does the Nutrition Literature Tell Us?" in *Settlement, Subsistence, and Change among the Labrador Inuit: The Nunatsiavummuit*

that settlers depended upon for survival. The truck system was especially dominant in the region until the mid-1960s: merchants supplied local fish producers with goods and supplies on credit and tabulated the cost of those supplies at the end of the fishing season, after deciding what they would pay for the fish. A cashless system of exchange based on the commodity of fish, the truck system often trapped families in perpetual cycles of debt. Historians have traditionally interpreted this "fishocracy" as not only exploitative toward fishing families but also as detrimental to the local accumulation of capital and to the development and diversification of the economy.[7] There was little exchange of currency and fishing families often functioned at subsistence levels, vulnerable to merchant prerogative and to the precariousness of primary resources in fluctuating global markets.[8]

Shortly after arriving in Labrador, British physician Dr. Wilfred Grenfell, founder of the Grenfell Mission, recognized the power of the merchants over the local people through the truck system and the related challenges that people faced in acquiring fresh produce and foodstuffs on the Coast.[9] He attempted to break the hold of the merchants by establishing co-operatives, with limited success—the first and most successful being the Red Bay Cooperative Store in

---

Experience, ed. D.C. Natcher, L. Felt, and A. Procter (Winnipeg: University of Manitoba Press, 2012), 121–38. On the activities of the HBC in Labrador, see Kurt Korneski, "Planters, Eskimos, and Indians: Race and the Organization of Trade under the Hudson's Bay Company in Labrador, 1830–50," *Journal of Social History* 50, no. 2 (2016): 307–35.

7 John C. Kennedy, "The Impact of the Grenfell Mission on Southeastern Labrador Communities," *Polar Record* 24, no. 150 (1988): 199.

8 While the truck system has traditionally been criticized for causing impoverishment, Sean Cadigan has argued that it was a mutually beneficial accommodation. See Sean Cadigan, *Hope and Deception in Conception Bay: Merchant-Settler Relations in Newfoundland, 1785–1855* (Toronto: University of Toronto Press, 1995), viii, and "Truck, Paternalism and Ecology: The Struggle between Fishers and Merchants in the 19th and Early 20th Centuries," in *Amulree's Legacy: Truth, Lies and Consequences*, ed. Garfield Fizzard (St. John's: Newfoundland Historical Society, 2001), 29–37.

9 The Grenfell Mission was a philanthropic medical organization with a "civilizing" agenda, affiliated with the British Mission to Deep Sea Fishermen. For more on the early history of the Mission, see Heidi Coombs-Thorne, "To Prevent 'the Otherwise Inevitable Catastrophe': American Philanthropy and the Creation of the International Grenfell Association, 1905–1914," in Connor and Side, *The Grenfell Medical Mission and American Support*, 77–99.

1896.[10] He also introduced an agricultural program at the Mission[11] as an alternate source of food and an attempt to combat the widespread deficiency diseases identified in the region.[12] To supplement their limited external access to fresh produce, many families participated in subsistence agriculture if possible, by maintaining their own vegetable gardens and keeping farmyard animals.[13] However, agriculture as an industry remained underdeveloped in the area due to the acidic nature of the soil, the short growing season, and the labour-intensive demands of the primary industry—the fishery. Grenfell's program was intended to expand agriculture in northern Newfoundland and Labrador.[14]

Nurses were integral to this program. Nursing with the Grenfell Mission was, as Jill Perry has argued, an "exceptional female work experience."[15] Perry

---

10 For an analysis of Grenfell's co-operative movement, see Rafico Ruiz, "Sites of Communication: The Grenfell Mission of Newfoundland and Labrador" (PhD diss., McGill University, 2014).

11 Maura Hanrahan argues that the Mission's agricultural activities and nutrition interventions were based on an institutionalized patron-client relationship and persistent European food ways. The Mission did not incorporate, or even consider, Indigenous nutritional knowledge even though there were few deficiency diseases among Inuit. See Maura Hanrahan, "'Through their own efforts': Nutrition Studies and Interventions in Early 20th-Century Northern Newfoundland and Southern Labrador," *Cuizine: The Journal of Canadian Food Cultures* 7, no. 1 (2016), https://doi.org/10.7202/1037390ar.

12 On the various nutrition studies, see Connor, "Malnutrition Research in Newfoundland and Labrador ... Part 1," and "Malnutrition Research in Newfoundland and Labrador in the 1900s to 1930s ... Part 2"; Eric Strikwerda, "Newfoundland and Labrador Maligned"; and Anaïs, "(Mal)Nutrition and the 'Informal Economy' Bootstrap."

13 Women participated in a significant amount of subsistence agriculture. See Hilda Chaulk Murray, *More Than Fifty Percent: Woman's Life in a Newfoundland Outport, 1900–1950* (St. John's: Flanker Press, 2010).

14 In 1928, Grenfell placed the agricultural program under the direction of Fred C. Sears, an American horticulturalist and orchard pioneer at Massachusetts State College. See Ronald Rompkey, *Grenfell of Labrador: A Biography* (Toronto: University of Toronto Press, 1991), 243, and Fred C. Sears, "The 1933 Labrador Garden Campaign," *Among the Deep Sea Fishers* 32, no. 1 (April 1934): 8–12. On the Mission's attempt at nutrition and dietary reform, see Gail Ruby Shirlene Lush, "Nutrition, Health Education, and Dietary Reform: Gendering the 'New Science' in Northern Newfoundland and Labrador, 1893–1928" (master's thesis, Memorial University, 2008). On Newfoundland's larger health reform movement, see Overton, "Brown Flour and Beriberi."

15 Jill Samfya Perry, "Nursing for the Grenfell Mission: Maternalism and Moral

and others have been careful to point out that this work experience was limited by established gendered parameters appropriate to the dictates of the paternalistic medical hierarchy of the Grenfell Mission and that the messaging around the nurses' professional independence was constructed to appease the Mission's middle-class benefactors.[16] However, as the only medically trained individuals in their communities, and in their large districts, Grenfell nurses held a significant amount of professional independence and authority. In addition to nursing, midwifery, and public health, they administered the stations, diagnosed patients, prescribed medications, and performed duties that were traditionally beyond their scope of practice.[17] They handled every medical emergency in their communities and surrounding areas and most often had no one to turn to for help. Indeed, for the vast array of duties they performed and the importance of their services, superintendent Dr. Charles Curtis referred to nurses as "the backbone of this Mission."[18]

In addition to their medical and administrative duties, nurses were expected to advance the agricultural programs at their stations. They regularly maintained vegetable gardens, root cellars, and farmyards, and for many nurses, "[b]eing a farmer was just another new experience."[19] These were activities that nurses had to fit into their already busy schedules.[20] At Happy Valley, after completing her list of nursing- and station-related duties, Barbara Watson

---

Reform in Northern Newfoundland and Labrador, 1894–1938" (master's thesis, Memorial University, 1997), 61.

16 See Perry, "Nursing for the Grenfell Mission"; Bulgin, "Mapping the Self"; and Heidi Coombs-Thorne, "Nursing with the Grenfell Mission in Northern Newfoundland and Labrador, 1939–81" (PhD diss., University of New Brunswick, 2010).

17 Heidi Coombs-Thorne, "'Such a Many-Purpose Job': Nursing, Identity, and Place with the Grenfell Mission, 1939–1960," *Nursing History Review* 32 (2012): 89–96, and "Conflict and Resistance to Paternalism: Nursing with the Grenfell Mission in Newfoundland and Labrador," in *Caregiving on the Periphery*, ed. Myra Rutherdale (Kingston & Montreal: McGill-Queen's University Press, 2010), 210–42.

18 Charles S. Curtis, "Note of Thanks," *Among the Deep Sea Fishers* 46, no. 4 (January 1949): 117.

19 RPA, MG 63, File 1295 "Murdoch, Wilhemina," Murdoch to Spalding, December 6, 1932; Jean Smith, "Flowers Cove," *Among the Deep Sea Fishers* 45, no. 2 (July 1947): 36.

20 The Mission recruited volunteers (workers without pay, or WOPs) in various capacities, who assisted with the agricultural program. On Grenfell's American volunteers, see Jennifer J. Connor, "'We Are Anglo-Saxons': Grenfell, Race, and Mission Movements," in Connor and Side, *The Grenfell Medical Mission and American Support*, 45–68.

would sometimes spend the remainder of a day "persuading plants & vegetables to get on and grow."[21] Ethel Currant, meanwhile, was well known for her gardening prowess. At Flowers Cove, she frequently received high praise for the abundance of vegetables at the station and for bottling local produce for the winter. In keeping with the middle-class gospel of self-help and the Mission's fear of "pauperizing" the local people, she required families to pay for her services by having women help in the garden: "On certain days a week they came and weeded and hoed it, and in the fall they came and got in the crops."[22]

Due to the nature of their positions, Grenfell nurses interacted on some level with every person in their communities and surrounding areas. They therefore held a significant amount of knowledge about their patients, their families, and the communities in general. They knew the circumstances of everyone in the community and the challenges that every family faced. They also knew the circumstances of the employers in their districts, since employment directly impacted people's welfare and their survival. In December 1947—over a year before the headlines of starvation in Labrador—a lumber company in Jupp's district crashed and she reported that

> the people were left without food. Two thirds of the population of the District had to go on the "dole" ($5.00 per month). Dogs died in scores, and men had to walk to Fox Harbour [St. Lewis], 25 miles over the ice and drag their supplies back by hand or on their backs. People look very thin and haggard, and the children seem to be listless. Several horses, belonging to the Co. were brought to St. Mary's for shelter and food—two of them dropped dead from starvation. Needless to say, no wood was cut—except for the Mission. Now no merchant will give any supplies *until* they get the salmon or fish.[23]

The situation in Jupp's district did not improve over the next year. By the first week of December 1948, it became evident that a food shortage was looming in the district, and "things came to a head when babies started dying from starvation, and pregnant women and nursing mothers became emaciated and weak."[24]

21 RPA, MG 63, File 1145 "Lumsden (Watson), Barbara," Watson to Seabrook, July 17, 1953.

22 Charles Curtis, "Heroines," *Among the Deep Sea Fishers* 43, no. 2 (July 1945): 46.

23 RPA, MG 63, File 1057, "Jupp, Dorothy," Dorothy Jupp to Betty Seabrook, June 17, 1948.

24 RPA, MG 63, File 1057, Jupp to Seabrook, April 17, 1949.

Jupp spent two months warning the Newfoundland Rangers of the situation, but no action was taken until she and Forsyth sent their wires to the premier. Smallwood likely saw a political opportunity in this crisis. In addition to publishing Jupp's and Forsyth's appeals in the newspaper, he broadcast them via radio on the *Gerald S. Doyle News Bulletin.* This broadcast ensured that everyone across the province would know about the crisis in Labrador. In effect, Smallwood set the stage for a grand rescue. According to Jupp, the government quickly "swung into action. A plane came over loaded with food supplies next day. The following day an R.C.A.F. plane flew over and dropped 40 packages by parachute. The icebreaker *Sorell* [sic] loaded up with food and came down...."[25] With the assistance of the federal government, Smallwood saved the day and in this way appeared to prove the wisdom of choosing Confederation for the people of Newfoundland and Labrador.

The food shortage of 1949 highlights both the longstanding issue of food security in Newfoundland and Labrador and also the central role of nurses in ensuring the well-being of a community. Dorothy Jupp anticipated a food crisis in her district, began advocating for government assistance, and finally sounded the alarm directly to the premier, thereby averting a catastrophe. In March 1950, reflecting on the incident and the circumstances under which people made a living in the region, Jupp noted: "I do think ... that people everywhere had the idea that Confederation would change Newfoundland and Labrador overnight—falls in prices, lots of work, plenty of money and food, and a sense of being looked after...."[26] However, she concluded that "[i]f there were no family allowances and no 'Dole' stocks on the Labrador the conditions would be nothing short of disastrous for the people. My personal and frank opinion is that there is more poverty and distress and unemployment on the Labrador than there was two years ago."[27]

Jupp's reflections demonstrate her intimate knowledge of the circumstances in which families in her district lived, the high expectations that Smallwood had set for Confederation, and the reality that Canada's recently developed social security programs had limited immediate impact on many families. In the long run, access to these programs increased people's standards of living in northern Newfoundland and Labrador. However, change did not occur overnight

25 RPA, MG 63, File 1057, Jupp to Seabrook, April 17, 1949.

26 RPA, MG 63, File 1057, Jupp to Seabrook, March 10, 1950.

27 RPA, MG 63, File 1057, Jupp to Seabrook, March 10, 1950.

and Confederation could not remedy the structural, geographic, and logistical challenges of communities dependent on primary-resource industries in rural and remote regions. With an underdeveloped agricultural industry, the province remains heavily dependent on the importation of food today; and food security continues to be a matter of concern for Newfoundland and Labrador.

Surviving Confederation in the Jubilee Guilds

Linda Cullum

THROUGHOUT MUCH OF THE FIRST half of the twentieth century, economic and political instability plagued the country of Newfoundland. World War I debt, merchant profiteering, poor salt cod production, and high unemployment eventually led to public unrest, marches, and riots in St. John's. In the 1930s, the dole of six cents a day did little to relieve struggling rural and urban families.[1]

Prominent members of the St. John's elite proposed disenfranchisement of the poor as a solution to problems of civil unrest and disruptions in the community.[2] Even temporary relief to able-bodied workers and their families was not well supported; concern was widespread among the upper classes that so-called indiscriminate charitable giving would undermine working-class independence and induce pauperization of the poor, a condition seen as both a moral and economic failing in Newfoundland.[3] Ultimately, the Amulree

1 For correspondence on relief efforts, see Colonial Secretary's Office, Special Files, Box 63, #424.B, Charity Organization Bureau (COB); relief in St. John's, January 8, 1925–October 20, 1932, RPA.

2 Charles A. Magrath Papers, Microfilm H1419-20-21, 1933, Library and Archives Canada (LAC). The first president of the Charity Organization Bureau, Sir Leonard Outerbridge, supported disenfranchisement. See James Overton, "Self-Help, Charity, and Individual Responsibility: The Political Economy of Social Policy in Newfoundland in the 1920s," in *Twentieth-Century Newfoundland: Explorations*, ed. James K. Hiller (St. John's: Breakwater Books, 1994), 97.

3 For discussion of this in Canada, see Mariana Valverde, *The Age of Light, Soap, and Water: Moral Reform in English Canada, 1885–1925* (Toronto: McClelland & Stewart, 1991), 20. See Overton, "Moral Education of the Poor: Adult Education and Land Settlement Schemes in Newfoundland in the 1930s," *Newfoundland Studies* 11, no. 2 (1995): 250–82 and "Public Relief and Social Unrest in Newfoundland in the 1930s:

Commission of 1933[4] condemned the social and economic conditions in the country, which led to the loss of responsible government and the establishment of Commission of Government in 1934 in Newfoundland.[5]

According to some, the character of the people of Newfoundland was "the biggest problem."[6] Rural Newfoundlanders were seen as the "undeserving" poor, as lazy and unmotivated workers. A letter in the *Evening Telegram* characterized women as either "idle" and having "no means of using their talents," or at the other extreme, as "good industrious women who by their enterprise are helping their menfolk to ward off the 'big bad wolf' and keeping their dependents well and warmly clad."[7] The latter group was seen as the "backbone"—the moral and productive force—in rural communities.[8]

In the midst of these calls, the Jubilee Guilds of Newfoundland was created in 1935 by prominent Anglo-Newfoundland women, most living in St. John's, and closely interconnected through ties of social class, business, political, marital, and familial relations. They emphasized self-help rather than public charity for the destitute and unemployed and aimed to rehabilitate what they saw as socially and economically depressed rural communities. Jubilee Guilds' programs established a refined, middle-class urban ideal for the domestic and community labour of

---

An Evaluation of the Ideas of Piven and Cloward," *Canadian Journal of Sociology* 13, no. 1/2 (1988): 143–69; and the essay by Heidi Coombs, earlier in this volume.

4 Also called Newfoundland Royal Commission, 1933, it was established by Britain and Canada to examine the financial situation and future of Newfoundland. See Peter Neary, *Newfoundland in the North Atlantic World, 1929–1949* (Montreal: McGill-Queen's University Press, 1988), 16.

5 Following the Amulree Report and the suspension of the country's constitution and democracy, the Commission of Government was established in 1934 to run the country of Newfoundland. Six appointed commissioners, three British and three Newfoundlanders, held posts. See Neary, *Newfoundland*, 361–62. For general information, see Terry Bishop Stirling and Jeff A. Webb, "The Twentieth Century," in *A Short History of Newfoundland and Labrador*, ed. Newfoundland Historical Society (St. John's: Boulder Publications, 2008), 115–17, and Cadigan, *Newfoundland and Labrador*, 209–33.

6 Peter Neary, ed., *White Tie and Decorations: Sir John and Lady Hope Simpson in Newfoundland, 1934–1936* (Toronto: University of Toronto Press, 1996), 64. See Letter, Q.H.S. to Greta, April 6, 1934, 64. Lady Quita Hope Simpson was the wife of Sir John Hope-Simpson, British Commissioner of Natural Resources in the Commission of Government from 1934 to 1936. See also the essay by J.T.H Connor, earlier in this volume.

7 "Launch of the Jubilee Guilds," *Evening Telegram*, October 18, 1935, 19. See also "Lady Anderson Outlines Jubilee Guilds of Newfoundland," *Evening Telegram*, May 31, 1935, 5.

8 "Can It Be Done? A Timely Jubilee Guild Proposal," *Evening Telegram*, January 9, 1936, 9.

rural women. Through learning specific skills and knowledges, rural women would be trained for "better" motherhood and care of their families and their homes. Improved household production skills and labour would sustain and revive the family and, by extension, communities. The Guilds' main aim was a stronger nation of Newfoundland, through the "uplift" of its rural women.[9]

Over the next two decades, Jubilee Guilds' goals and programming clashed repeatedly with the economic and social goals of the Commission of Government and, post-Confederation with Canada in 1949, the new province of Newfoundland. Who would determine the content, and undertake delivery, of women's educational programs in Newfoundland?

Getting off the Ground

Lady Muriel Anderson, first president of the Jubilee Guilds, launched the organization. Following the model of the Women's Institutes (WI) in Canada and England, she aimed to form Guild branches throughout Newfoundland.[10] She envisioned a non-political, financially independent, education-oriented organization like the WI, but unlike the WI, a non-sectarian one.

Anderson described the Guilds as an organization to "help the people of the outports to provide themselves with clothing, make their homes more comfortable, and develop their own local resources to these ends,"[11] all through self-reliance and self-help approaches. The official launch of the Guilds was a public event attended by many important social, political, and economic leaders, and points to the embedding of the Guilds in the traditional fabric of power in Newfoundland.[12]

9 Jubilee Guilds-Newfoundland and Labrador Women's Institute (JG-NLWI), COLL-166, 1.14.001, President's Report, ASC.

10 Anderson was the Australian wife of the British governor Sir David Murray Anderson. Agnes M. Richard, *Threads of Gold: Newfoundland and Labrador Jubilee Guilds Women's Institutes* (St. John's: Creative Publishers, 1989), 155–56.

11 "Can It Be Done?"

12 Leaders of the Methodist, Church of England, Salvation Army, and Catholic religions and educational institutions, the Commission of Government, Women's Patriotic Association and the suffrage movement, prominent business owners and newspaper editors attended. See Linda Cullum, "Under Construction: Women, The Jubilee Guilds and Commission Government in Newfoundland and Labrador, 1935–41" (master's thesis, Ontario Institute for Studies in Education/University of Toronto, 1993), and "Lady Anderson Outlines Jubilee Guilds."

Newspaper coverage references outside expertise and imperial connections supporting the Jubilee Guilds as well.[13]

Long-established community class and economic power structures, such as the local merchants, were not to be challenged. Jubilee Guilds' work would not affect fishery and household fish production, except insofar as the "betterment" of home and family contributed to increased labour power and productivity, and thus, more fish for sale to merchants.[14]

The Jubilee Guilds relied on paid female workers. The organizing secretary was usually a single, university-trained home economist, and field workers were drawn largely from outport communities.[15] The Guilds' educational programs operated along traditional gender lines; "cooking, better bread-making and household economy, so as to get the best value out of the materials at their command ... instruction in Weaving and Dyeing; Home Handicrafts; First Aid in accidents; Infant Welfare; Care of Health; and Home Nursing; Poultry Keeping;

---

13 "Launch of the Jubilee Guilds." The Carnegie Corporation, an influential New York City group active in social reform across North America, the Antigonish Movement in Nova Scotia, and agriculture specialists who argued for channelling government work through one pre-existing community organization for efficiency and minimum cost contributed to the debate. W.W. Baird provided a report on the social, economic, and agricultural conditions in outport communities. See Commission Government (CG), GN 38.8.1, October 2, 1934, 108, #695, RPA. The Carnegie Corporation donated $4,000 to the Jubilee Guilds to finance start-up costs for the organization. See Richard, *Threads*, 14.

14 "Launch of the Jubilee Guilds."

15 Jones, "He Was a Student Minister and I Was a Jubilee Guilds Fieldworker," *Decks Awash* 7, no. 2 (1978): 26–27. Elizabeth MacMillan from Prince Edward Island was hired in 1936 as the first organizing secretary (OS) for the Jubilee Guilds. Anna Templeton replaced her in 1939. Templeton, a Newfoundlander, was a home economics graduate of MacDonald College, Quebec, who joined the Guilds in June 1938 as a field worker for weaving, sewing, and domestic science. Templeton, TS 1991a, Memorial University of Newfoundland Folklore and Language Archive (MUNFLA). See also *Evening Telegram*, Woman of the Week, Templeton, www.web.archive.org/web/20150614171258/http://staff.library.mun.ca/~ebrowne/nf_history/Templeton19451229.php. Field workers were hired for their expert skills in weaving, dressmaking, cooking and home nursing, and an aptitude for working with other women in Guilds' activities in rural communities. OS Anna Templeton posted field workers in communities largely irrespective of their personal religious affiliation, but she also pointedly dispatched Roman Catholic field workers to Roman Catholic communities in response to accepted norms. See Templeton, TS 1991a, MUNFLA.

Fruit Growing; and Jam Making" were to be delivered.[16] Women would learn to "turn collars and cuffs," use technologically advanced preserving, canning, and bottling methods, and know and use ingredients not typically found in rural Newfoundland to improve their cooking. Weaving and knitting patterns were imported from other parts of the world. Women were urged to create new colour schemes for their kitchens and plant flowers around their homes.[17] All of these activities were offered in a time of desperate economic conditions.

Between 1935 and 1945, 107 Guild branches were established across the island, more in the years to come. Branches organized in various ways, but the Guilds' leadership conducted moral investigations of communities for their "industry" level before they consented to branch formation: independent community formation was strongly discouraged.[18]

Nonetheless, rather than passively waiting for sanction, rural women saw in the Jubilee Guilds an opportunity to come together, gain access to work materials, learn new skills, and have a social time of their own.[19] Jubilee Guilds' halls or rooms were created where books, magazines, and other women might be found.[20] Links between rural women developed through branch meetings, district conventions, handicraft courses, and special projects, and those living in isolated rural communities called upon these connections for assistance and support. Women also gained materially through access to goods and services: patterns for sewing, bottles for preserving, carding machines for processing raw wool into homespun for socks, mitts, and caps, looms for weaving, boxes of books for reading, advice in the purchase of sheep and sale of chickens.[21]

---

16 "Lady Anderson Outlines Jubilee Guilds."

17 For example, JG-NLWI, COLL-166, 1.14.001, OS Report, ASC.

18 "Launch of the Jubilee Guilds." Sometimes the merchant's wife started a branch, or the priest or minister wrote on behalf of the community. See JG-NLWI, COLL-166, 1.05.001, April 7, 1936, ASC. Rural women also wrote directly to the Guilds to request formal organization. See JG-NLWI, COLL-166, 1.05.001–1.05.004, 1936, ASC.

19 Templeton TS 1991b, MUNFLA.

20 JG-NLWI, COLL-166, 1.14.005, OS Report, ASC. The Burnt Islands branch, on the southwest coast, records that their hall was "the means of uniting the women of our community and of giving us a chance to work together in harmony and good feeling."

21 In 1937, the Red Island Guild, Placentia Bay, reported the members produced 47 pairs of gloves, 12 knitted sweaters, 21 suits of knitted underwear, 30 pairs of socks, 33 yards of homespun cloth, 10 men's shirts, 6 dozen ladies dresses, 8 smocks, 26 aprons. They preserved 60 jars blueberries, 12 jars of salmon, 80 jars carrot

Who's in Charge?

The relationship between the Jubilee Guilds and the Commission of Government was complex and often contested, with individual departments in conflict with the Guilds to manage women's work in rural Newfoundland.[22] In a sign of significant conflicts to come, Guilds' branch formation was quickly challenged in 1935 by Public Health and Welfare.[23]

The Department of Natural Resources, especially the Rural Reconstruction section with its emphasis on agricultural development, land settlements, and formation of co-operatives, had different education and economic goals for women. In 1937, new Jubilee Guilds president Lady Eileen Walwyn[24] wrote to Robert Ewbank, Commissioner for Natural Resources, seeking assurance that "cottage industries and other homemaking subjects would not be introduced in the Rural Reconstruction program for a period of one year," leaving space for Guilds branch formation and programs.[25] Little changed, but by 1938, the Commission provided the Guilds an annual operating grant of $9,000, later increased to $12,000, and thus drew them into a closer, more dependent relationship with the state structure and goals. The Guilds had to restrict workers' salaries, administrative costs and auditing practices, maintain a "nothing for nothing" policy, distributing nothing for free, and field workers were to "maintain a strictly noncommittal attitude on all questions of public policy."[26] This final demand suggests that Guilds' workers were developing a critique of government policies and expressing it publicly.

marmalade, 18 jars of bakeapples, 200 jars of pickles, 12 jars of peas, several jars of marshberries and strawberries. JG-NLWI, COLL-166, 1.05.003, ASC. When the Jubilee Guilds received requests beyond the scope of Guilds' work, they were passed along to the Commissioner for Natural Resource. JG-NLWI, COLL-166, 1.05.001, ASC. See also Templeton, TS 1989, MUNFLA.

22 Commission Departments of Natural Resources, Education, and Public Health and Welfare were represented on the Guilds' Board of Trustees.

23 JG-NLWI, COLL-166, 1.04.001, September 19, 1935; December 2, 1935, ASC.

24 Lady Eileen Walwyn was the wife of the incoming British governor, Sir Humphrey Walwyn. She assumed the presidency of the Jubilee Guilds in 1936 with the departure for Australia of Lady Anderson. For biography, see Richard, *Threads*, 156–57.

25 JG-NLWI, COLL-166, 1.05.002, April 26, 1937, ASC.

26 JG-NLWI, COLL-166, 1.04.001, May 4, 1938, and 1.05.003, May 16, 1938, ASC; Cullum, "'A Woman's Place.'"

The Commission-Guilds relationship became more contested when John Gorvin, Commissioner of Natural Resources, 1939–41, concluded that the Jubilee Guilds were not the place for building co-operative societies, credit unions, or efforts to increase cash in rural homes.[27] Gorvin and the Co-operative section leadership believed the Guilds had a clear, vested interest in the merchant class and were not receptive to education work that challenged traditional merchant control in rural communities.[28] When the Co-operative Division initiated the Co-operative Women's Guilds in 1939 to draw women into economic reconstruction through production and sale of goods, something the Jubilee Guilds had resisted for their own members, further strains appeared.[29] Walwyn saw the Co-op Guilds as competition and accused them of being "state-assisted" and "a medium for the distribution of charity" through the provision of raw materials.[30]

---

27 In 1939, J.G. Howell, Acting Secretary for Rural Reconstruction, stated, "It must be recognized that the Jubilee Guilds have not the machinery or the technique to deal with Co-operative problems." Howell to Commissioner for Rural Reconstruction, CG, DNR, GN 31/3A, Box 56, File R166, Jubilee Guilds, February 2, 1939, RPA.

28 See MacNeil to Commissioner for Natural Resources, August 26, 1939, CG, DNR, GN 31/3A, Box 56, R166, RPA. Neil MacNeil argues that the Guilds' leadership had close marital and business ties to merchants and businessmen in communities, and that field workers often stayed in local merchants' homes when visiting a Guilds' branch. MacNeil's handwritten notes on a copy of Jubilee Guild Executive Committee Minutes, December 1, 1939, state "This is Water Street" when the Executive is concerned about loans with "no security and no interest rates." Excerpts from Jubilee Guild Executive Committee Meeting, December 1, 1939, CG, DNR, GN 31/2, Box 77, File 318, Jubilee Guilds of Newfoundland and Labrador (JGNL), Vol. I, 1939–1945, RPA. See also MacNeil, Asst. Director of Co-operation to Commissioner for Natural Resources, January 12, 1940, CG, DNR, GN 31/2, Box 77, File #318, JGNL, Vol. I, 1939–1945, RPA.

29 MacNeil to Commissioner for Natural Resources, CG, DNR, GN 31/3A, Box 56, File R166, Jubilee Guilds, RPA. MacNeil states that women are indispensable to economic development in Newfoundland and must be given "an important place in its structure." See also Jubilee Guilds policy statement, Letter, Turner to Gorvin, February 24, 1940, CG, DNR, GN 31/2, Box 77, File #318, JGNL, Vol. I, 1939–1945, RPA. Cullum, "Under Construction."

30 JG-NLWI, COLL-166, 1.01.03, Letter, Walwyn to Ewbank, February 27, 1939, ASC. See also Cullum, "'A Woman's Place,'" 105–6. The Jubilee Guilds objected to the Commission efforts on many grounds: perceived duplication of Guilds' work, use of the word "Guild" on the part of the Co-operative Women's Guild, and Commission policy of supplying materials to support the production of goods for sale, to name a few.

Tension increased in 1944 when a new Commissioner of Natural Resources, Peter Dunn, proposed the creation of a Handicrafts and Home Industries program.[31] The Jubilee Guilds Executive feared the loss of their identity and maintained "that any instruction in women's work should remain under the jurisdiction of the Jubilee Guilds."[32] From July 1945 to January 1946, art, dressmaking, cooking, woodworking, and wood carving instructors were hired by the Commission to teach at the new Handicrafts Centre established in St. John's.[33] Then, in April 1946, Anna Templeton and field workers were hired on a part-time basis, so their work was divided between the two organizations.[34] This created further problems in November 1946 when the Jubilee Guilds argued that there was "duplication of the aims of the National Handicraft Centre and the Guilds' work" and sought to know the Commission's future commitments to the Guilds.[35] Mrs. Evangeline Winter,[36] then-president of the Jubilee Guilds, pushed forward the Guilds' agenda for independence and autonomy in women's programming, staff, and funding from the Commission. But the Commission of Government resisted, fearing that, "under the Guilds, the women's work might develop in a manner which would not be entirely acceptable to Government."[37]

Commission-Guilds discussions dragged on into mid-1947 when the Guilds' Executive decided the political future of the country was too uncertain and that Commission-controlled schemes might well lead to decline in the

---

31 CG, GN 38.8.4, May 11, 1945, 1565, #394, RPA. This initiative was led by Oscar Beriau of Quebec.

32 JG-NLWI, COLL-166, 1.05.004, October 28, 1944, ASC.

33 CG, GN 38.8.4, September 29, 1945, 1621, #839; 1622, #846; January 18, 1946, 1663–64, #29, RPA.

34 CG, GN 38.8.4, April 30, 1946, 1702, #338, RPA. Field worker Iris Jones was assigned as weaving instructor, and Ann McLennan, Gertrude White, Clara Roberts, Agatha Ryan, and Hattie Simmons were to be district workers.

35 JG-NLWI, COLL-166, 1.05.004, November 19, 1946, ASC. The constant review of Commission-Guilds relations was due, in part, to the turnover in commissioners; there were five Commissioners of Natural Resources between 1936 and 1949.

36 Winter was a Charter member of the Jubilee Guilds, first vice-president (1935–45), then president (1945–53). For biography, see Richard, *Threads*, 157–58.

37 CG, GN 38, Box S2 119, Memoranda 1937, 1940, 1947, File #1, Relations between the Jubilee Guilds and the National Handicrafts Centre, Confidential Memo, April 22, 1947, 3, RPA.

Guilds.[38] Outport Guilds were advised of the efforts to "keep the organization in existence" and to solicit dues paying "towards the upkeep of the organization."[39]

As Confederation with Canada arrived in April 1949, a Jubilee Guilds' committee[40] examined the problematic relationship between the Guilds and the Handicrafts Centre. They met with the new provincial ministers of education and natural resources and provided the new premier, J.R. Smallwood, who was also minister of economic development, "first hand knowledge of the situation."[41] Winter emphasized the economy of the province and unemployment and argued that women could be part of the solution.[42] Following an October 1949 meeting with the new provincial Cabinet,[43] and an inconclusive meeting with Premier Smallwood, Winter wrote to him in February 1950. This finally resulted in a meeting between Smallwood, Minister Ted Russell of Natural Resources, and the Jubilee Guilds, where the Guilds argued for a three-pronged approach to their work: maintaining a training school in St. John's; outport work around education and service; commercial production, especially weaving, and a showroom for sales.[44] Money earned from weaving sales was to go to the weavers, increasing income for some rural families. The Guilds consistently stressed this economic impact in both their annual reports and their arguments for government support.[45]

The Executive noted that, at this meeting, "Mr. Smallwood showed great insight into the problems concerning the Jubilee Guilds and the Handicraft

---

38 JG-NLWI, COLL-166, 1.05.004, July 17, 1947.

39 JG-NLWI, COLL-166, 1.05.004, November 14, 1947, and May 14, 1948, ASC. Despite this uncertainty, and the postponing of the 1947 AGM, new Guilds continued to be formed. JG-NLWI, COLL-166, 1.14.012, OS Report.

40 This committee included prominent members of the Guilds' Executive and Trustee Committees, including Sir Leonard Outerbridge, a well-known businessman and Confederation supporter who would become lieutenant-governor of the new province in 1949. In 1947, the committee also included Mr. K.J. Carter of the Department of Natural Resources.

41 JG-NLWI, COLL-166, 1.05.004, June 13, 1949, ASC.

42 JG-NLWI, COLL-166, 1.01.013, Letter, Winter to Smallwood, October 17, 1949, ASC.

43 JG-NLWI, COLL-166, 1.05.004, October 14, 1949, ASC. This meeting was deemed "satisfactory but nothing new undertaken."

44 Richard, *Threads*, 37.

45 JG-NLWI, COLL-166, 1.14.001–1.14.007, ASC. In JG-NLWI, COLL-166, 1.14.012, March 1948, Templeton reports that in 1947, "48 Guilds had woven a total of 4305 yards of material" for a value of "$8,610.00 ... a substantial contribution to the economy of Newfoundland."

Centre. He asked many questions about the policy of the Jubilee Guilds" and requested "in writing the grant that would be necessary to carry on a greatly expanded program of Jubilee Guild work." The Guilds requested $30,000 a year, more than doubling their yearly grant and began considering changes to the Executive and Trustee Committees and the Constitution. With this, they realigned the Jubilee Guilds' structure to fit the new post-Confederation world.[46]

Realignment was taking place in the new provincial government too; the minister of education, Samuel J. Hefferton, closed the Handicraft Centre on May 31, 1950, and responsibility for the Jubilee Guilds was taken over by the Ministry of Education.[47] The field was now open to expand Guilds' work in rural communities. Activities ramped up quickly, with equipment, stock, and staff from the Handicraft Centre acquired[48] and commercial weaving production increased, settling a long-standing struggle within the Guilds over recognizing women as economic subjects, interested in earning money for their work. "Earn and Learn" became the Guilds' motto of the early 1950s, and the economic value of handicraft production and sale continued to be emphasized to government.[49] This fit comfortably with Smallwood's education and economic goals to "develop or perish" in the fishery, new industries, and natural resources.[50]

But not for long, as subsequent actions by the Guilds' executive bore little fruit for the Guilds through the 1950s. A multi-year plan for Guild work was submitted at Smallwood's request in 1951, but was turned down. In 1955, the Guilds sought a grant increase to $50,000 to expand their work. Like previous applications for supplementary grants and increases, this was denied and Smallwood was never available for a meeting with the Guilds.[51] It appears that with the

46 JG-NLWI, COLL-166, 1.05.004, February 17, 1950; March 14, 1950, ASC. With a new constitution in March 1955, a Board of Managers replaced the Executive Committee and Board of Trustees. JG-NLWI, COLL-166, 1.06.001, April 22, 1955, ASC.

47 See Letter, Winter to Carter, May 23, 1950. CG, DNR, GN 31/2, Box 77, File #318, Vol. II, JGNL, 1945–1961, RPA; Richard, *Threads*, 38.

48 JG-NLWI, COLL-166, 1.05.005, May 10, 1950, ASC.

49 Richard, *Threads*, 41–42. In the first year, sales amounted to over $11,000 and steadily increased throughout the decade.

50 James Hiller and Melanie Martin, "Develop or Perish," Heritage Newfoundland & Labrador, 2006, www.heritage.nf.ca/articles/politics/develop-or-perish.php.

51 JG-NLWI, COLL-166, 1.14.016, OS Report, May 10, 1954, 1, ASC; 1.14.017, OS Report, April 19, 1955, and President's Report, 1955; 1.01.019, Letter, Carnell (president 1955–57) to Smallwood, November 2, 1955, ASC. See Richard, *Threads*, 159, for Carnell biography.

shift to the new political realities of Confederation, the Jubilee Guilds leadership lost much of their personal influence and connections to government.

Finally, the minister of education, James R. Chalker, advised the Jubilee Guilds that they would "eventually become an integral part of the extension program of the Memorial University of Newfoundland and it is the policy of the Government to keep the Guilds going during that interim period with a fixed grant."[52] Nothing seems to come of this idea, as in 1957 records show a detailed plan for amalgamation with Newfoundland Outport Nursing and Industrial Association (NONIA) and also an informal meeting with Dr. Florence O'Neill of the Department of Education to discuss co-operation between Adult Education and the Jubilee Guilds.[53] Little came from these meetings either, and the bumpy road to firm control of women's education work persisted well into the 1950s despite the significant change in government.

Post-Confederation life for the Jubilee Guilds brought a renewed focus on branch formation, training workers, teaching, and grappling with rapidly changing community life, all on a limited budget. The Jubilee Guilds joined the Associated Country Women of the World (ACWW) in 1945 and the Federated Women's Institutes of Canada (FWIC) in 1951. Provincial Conventions, linking women and branches, began in 1954. Eventually, improved access to cash and jobs away for young people, store-bought goods and foods, increased urbanization, and resettlement programs that reduced communities, brought a decline in Jubilee Guilds branches.[54] The Jubilee Guilds' name was changed to Women's Institutes in 1968, and affiliated programs targeting both rural and urban women developed. While today branch numbers are fewer, they extend into Labrador and urban centres and remain an important part of community life for many women across the province.[55]

52 JG-NLWI, COLL-166, 1.14.018, OS Report, April 9, 1956, ASC.

53 JG-NLWI, COLL-166, 1.01.021, ASC. NONIA, the Newfoundland Outport Nursing and Industrial Association, founded in 1920, raised money from the sale of hand-knit garments to pay the salaries of public health nurses. In 1934, the health care portion of NONIA's operation was taken over by the government, but the industrial side continues today. See www.https://nonia.com.

54 See JG-NLWI COLL-166, 1.03.005, Branch Histories, Change Islands and Carmanville, ASC.

55 See https://www.nlwi.ca/about.html. Accessed January 27, 2022.

Family Reunification and Citizenship: The Meaning of Confederation for Chinese Immigrants in Newfoundland

Miriam Wright and Robert Hong

MARCH 31, 1949, the day that Newfoundland became a Canadian province, was the beginning of potentially life-altering changes for the more than 100 Chinese immigrant men then living on the island. Chinese immigrants, part of a larger diaspora seeking economic and political stability, had been coming to Newfoundland since the late nineteenth century. Largely shut out of other forms of employment, they opened hand laundries, and later cafés and restaurants, to earn a living. Racism marked their daily experiences, from encounters with hostile locals on the streetcorners, to politicians expounding on the threat they believed the newcomers posed to the social, cultural, and economic well-being of the white population. In 1906, following the leads of Canada and the United States, the Newfoundland government enacted the Chinese Immigration Act, which imposed a $300 tax on every Chinese national entering the country.[1]

1 Robert Hong, "'To take action without delay': Newfoundland's Chinese Immigration Act of 1906" (honours essay, Memorial University, 1987). For other work on the early history of Chinese immigration to Newfoundland, see the documentary film *The Last Chinese Laundry*, directed by Charles Callanan (St. John's: School of Continuing Studies and Extension, Memorial University, 1987); Margaret Ann Chang, "Chinese Pioneers in Newfoundland," *The Asianadian* 3, no. 4 (1981): 3–7; Miriam Wright, "'The most modern dining hall in the city': Chinese Immigrants, Restaurants, and Social Spaces in St. John's, Newfoundland, 1918–1945," *Acadiensis* 50, no. 1 (2021): 5–33. For background on the experiences of people of Chinese heritage in Canada in this period, see Lisa Mar, *Brokering Belonging: Chinese in Canada's Exclusion Era, 1885–1945* (New York: Oxford University Press, 2010).

Newfoundland never repealed its racist legislation, but Canada had abolished its own specific restrictions on Chinese immigration two years earlier, in 1947. On March 31, 1949, then, the Chinese men living in Newfoundland gained a path to becoming Canadian, and an opportunity to bring family members from China to live with them.

The Chinese head tax affected the lives of the over 400 Chinese men who came to Newfoundland before 1949 in specific ways.[2] First, the tax meant that new immigrants had to rely on other family members or fellow immigrants living in Newfoundland to cover their fees. Once in Newfoundland, the newcomers would work at their sponsor's laundry or café to pay off the debt. As wages were low generally in the Atlantic region, and even lower in the service sector, most new Chinese immigrants would spend years paying off the $300.[3] Only then was it possible to leave for new employment or to start a new business of their own. Second, the head tax ensured that the Chinese immigrant community in Newfoundland would remain largely male. Paying head tax fees for wives or children who were not working for wages was not feasible for most. Instead, those who were already married before they came to Newfoundland left their wives and children in China, sending money when they could and returning occasionally for visits. Others who had left China as single men got married on subsequent visits home. In the 1935 Newfoundland census, nearly one-third of Chinese immigrant men indicated that they were married.[4] As their sons and

---

2 Library and Archives Canada, RG 76-D-2-d-v, R1206-174-2-E, Government of Newfoundland, "Newfoundland Register: Arrivals and Outward Registration—Registration of Persons of Chinese Race Admitted into the Colony of Newfoundland Under the Provisions of the Chinese Immigration Act 6 EDW VII CAP2. June 4, 1910 to March 26, 1949." When Newfoundland imposed the Chinese Head Tax in 1906, government sources estimated there were 127 Chinese nationals in the Dominion: "House of Assembly Debates for Tuesday, April 17, 1906," *Evening Telegram*, April 21, 1906, 2.

3 Statistics Canada, Series E 248, "Hourly Wage Rates in Select Building Trades by City, 1901 to 1974," July 17, 2014, https://www150.statcan.gc.ca/n1/pub/11-516-x/sectione/E248_267a-eng.csv. For example, hourly wage rates for general building labourers in Halifax in 1910 was 20 cents an hour.

4 *Tenth Census of Newfoundland and Labrador, 1935*, vol. 1 (St. John's: Department of Health and Welfare, 1937), 27. Taken from Table 18, Birthplaces of the Population; RPA, MG 364 Margaret Chang Papers, Box 1, file on Newfoundland censuses. These papers are from research Margaret (Chang) Deaville did on the history of the Chinese community in Newfoundland. This file contained transcriptions of the entries for people with Chinese names found in the Newfoundland censuses of

grandsons came of age, the Chinese immigrant men already living in Newfoundland brought them to the island, paying their head tax fees and getting them work in laundries or cafés. William (Seto) Ping, from Kaiping, Guangdong, who arrived in St. John's in 1931, had his head tax paid by an uncle, and he worked for years to pay it back.[5] Another Kaiping native, Jack Chow, arrived in St. John's in 1935, where his father paid his head tax.[6] He later opened a restaurant in Grand Falls. In the head tax era, family reunifications in Newfoundland were primarily between fathers, sons, and grandsons.

While the high cost of bringing their wives may have deterred them, there is evidence that the Chinese men in Newfoundland believed that female relatives were not allowed to enter the Dominion. The Chinese Immigration Act did not bar Chinese women from entering Newfoundland if the head tax was paid, but the Canadian legislation, with which many of the Chinese immigrants living in Newfoundland would have been familiar, did restrict some Chinese women's entry. The Chinese men may have assumed Newfoundland had those same restrictions. A letter to the editor of a St. John's newspaper in 1920 by Chinese immigrant Charlie Dean suggested that he believed they could not bring their wives. In his letter, Dean explained, "We would really appreciate it if the government of Newfoundland would give us permission to bring our own womenfolk here. Should this be done we would be most thankful."[7] How he and others came to believe that is unknown, but no Chinese women immigrated to Newfoundland until after 1949.

Not all Chinese immigrants married women in China. Some remained single in their sojourning years, while others formed relationships with local white women. As scholars have noted about Chinese immigrant populations in North America in the late nineteenth and early twentieth century, it was not uncommon for Chinese male sojourners to marry or have relationships with

---

1921, 1935, and 1945. Along with the notes from the census, someone (likely a member of the Chinese community) added more notes beside the names, making corrections, writing the names in Chinese characters, and adding other comments about the individuals.

5 Bill Ping, "William Ping, 1909–1939," in *Reflections of the Chinese Community on the Occasion of the 30th Anniversary of the Chinese Association of Newfoundland and Labrador* (St. John's: Chinese Association of Newfoundland and Labrador, 2006), 49.

6 May Soo, "The Four Generations of the Tom Family," in *Reflections of the Chinese Community*, 54–55.

7 Chas. Dean, letter to the editor, *St. John's Daily Star*, January 21, 1921, 10.

non-Chinese women.[8] While these relationships never comprised the majority, they were nevertheless significant. In Newfoundland, the 1935 and 1945 census records suggest at least fifteen Chinese men had been married to white, Newfoundland women, at a time when the Chinese immigrant male population was around 135.[9] Nearly all these couples had children, who grew up in their parents' laundry and restaurant businesses.

When Newfoundland joined Canada in 1949, the door opened for Chinese men in the former Dominion to apply for citizenship and bring relatives from home. The St. John's *Evening Telegram* reported in late September 1949 that forty Chinese men had applied for Canadian citizenship, noting that some had been in Newfoundland for as long as thirty-six years.[10] While some Chinese immigrants had become naturalized British subjects before 1949 and would not have needed to apply, the majority of immigrants would have had to go through the formal application process.[11]

At a ceremony in St. John's in February 1951, the first ten Chinese men in the post-Confederation era received their Canadian citizenship certificates.[12] They included Charlie Hong, who had run a St. John's restaurant during World War II, and Charlie Wing, who owned a confectionary on Bell Island. Two more Chinese men living on Bell Island, Peter Chon and Samuel Hong, received

---

8 For works that address relationships between people of Chinese heritage and non-Chinese, see John Kuo Wei Tchen, *New York before Chinatown: Orientalism and the Shaping of American Culture 1776–1882* (Baltimore: Johns Hopkins University Press, 1999), and Elise Chenier, "Sex, Intimacy, and Desire among Men of Chinese Heritage and Women of Non-Chinese Heritage in Toronto, 1910–1950," *Urban History Review* 17, no. 2 (2014): 29–43.

9 *Tenth Census of Newfoundland and Labrador, 1935*, 27. Taken from Table 18, Birthplaces of the Population; *Census of Newfoundland and Labrador, 1945, vol. 1* (Ottawa: Dominion Bureau of Statistics, 1945), 105. Taken from Table 28, Population of Newfoundland by Ethnic Origin. The total number of people designated "Chinese" was 164, but this included the Newfoundland-born children of Chinese men and local white, Newfoundland-born women. We subtracted the number of those children identified in the manuscript census, and arrived at 135 Chinese-born adult men; RPA, MG 364 Margaret Chang Papers, Box 1, file on Newfoundland censuses.

10 "Chinese Seek to Become Canadian Citizens," *Evening Telegram*, September 23, 1949.

11 RPA, MG 364 Margaret Chang Papers, Box 1, file on Newfoundland censuses. In the manuscript census for 1935, it asked for both arrival date and naturalization date. At least ten Chinese immigrants were granted naturalized British subject status several years after arriving. The 1945 census did not ask for date of naturalization.

12 "Chinese Residents Become Citizens," *St. John's Daily News*, February 14, 1941, 3.

their citizenship a few months later.[13] Chon, it was reported, had been in Newfoundland since 1922 and had lived and worked in several communities, including Corner Brook, St. John's, and Grand Falls. Years earlier, he had married a white, Newfoundland woman, and they had a daughter. Samuel Hong, who was then managing a Bell Island grocery store, had a wife and three children still living in China (all of whom he eventually brought to Newfoundland).

Wives and children of Chinese immigrants began arriving from China in the early 1950s, but several years earlier, some Chinese men had tried unsuccessfully to bring female family members to Newfoundland. In 1946, St. John's lawyer Gordon Higgins had contacted the Chief Commissioner for Immigration on behalf of several Chinese men who were naturalized British subjects, who wanted to bring their wives to Newfoundland.[14] The Chief Commissioner for Immigration and the Secretary for Justice exchanged several letters, trying to determine if they could deny these Chinese women entry.[15] After reviewing the legislation and consulting with officials in the Dominion Office in London, they concluded that they could not. Indeed, they admitted that as wives of naturalized British subjects, the women were technically British subjects themselves, despite never having lived in a British territory. The government officials, however, were reluctant to tell Higgins. The Secretary for Justice remarked in a letter that "I notice from Mr. Higgins' letter that he assumes that you have the power to prohibit the landing of Chinese women and if you wish to exercise this supposed power he may not question your right to do so."[16] This exchange provides an example of the more subtle ways government officials discouraged Chinese immigration and perhaps underscores the nature of systemic racism in Newfoundland's immigration policy.

By 1950, however, members of the Chinese community could navigate the immigration system more easily. The timing was critical too, as the Sino-Japanese War/World War II had put some of the Chinese immigrant men's families in immediate danger. The *Evening Telegram* had reported in early 1947 that at least six members of the Chinese community in Newfoundland had returned to China to "re-organize their families who had been bombed, killed, and scattered in the war-torn land."[17] As well, the Chinese Communist Revolution in 1949 created

13 "Chinese Become Citizens of Canada," *St. John's Daily News*, June 13, 1951, 5.

14 RPA, GN 13, Box 106, file 85, "Chinese Women Entering Newfoundland."

15 RPA, GN 13, Box 106, file 85, "Chinese Women Entering Newfoundland."

16 RPA, GN 13, Box 106, file 85, "Chinese Women Entering Newfoundland."

17 "Chinese Leaving to Return to Hong Kong," *Evening Telegram*, January 22, 1947, 3.

uncertainty for those with family members remaining in China. Whether or not Chinese men in Newfoundland could continue to visit or send money to China under the new regime was uncertain.

Among the Chinese men who brought their families to Newfoundland in the early 1950s was James Yick, who had come to St. John's from Taishan County, Guangdong, in 1932.[18] After Confederation, his wife, Helen, and daughter joined him on Bell Island. After the family was reunited, the couple had two sons, both born in Newfoundland. Yick ran a general store on Bell Island until his retirement in his nineties, and he lived to be 100 years old. Gene (Mon Jin) Hong, who had married a white woman, Edna Mansfield from Trinity Bay in the early 1950s, brought his five younger brothers to Newfoundland in the years following Confederation.[19] Dr. Kim Hong, a long-time and well-known physician in St. John's, arrived in Newfoundland as a thirteen-year-old in 1950, less than a year after the former Dominion joined Canada.[20] His father and grandfather had been in St. John's for decades, working at a Gower Street laundry.

While that Gower Street laundry where Kim Hong's father and grandfather worked continued operating into the 1960s, hand laundries were becoming out of fashion with the advent of modern laundromats and home washing machines. In the two decades following Confederation, the food service industry (confectionaries, snack bars, and restaurants) became the main avenue to make a living for the Chinese immigrants and their families. Earlier generations of Chinese immigrants had built the restaurant sector on the island, dating to the latter years of World War I.[21] As rising incomes and an expanding service sector created new opportunities in the 1950s and 1960s, Chinese families opened convenience stores, snack bars, and restaurants across Newfoundland. A 1955 directory of businesses owned by people of Chinese heritage in Atlantic Canada documents sixty-five such establishments in Newfoundland, in eleven different communities.[22] As most families lived in apartments either above or behind their restaurants or stores, children grew up in the businesses, helping out after school when they were old enough. In the restaurants, younger family members washed dishes or peeled potatoes in between doing homework, while others tended cash or made milkshakes and sundaes.

---

18 Robin Levinson, "Bell Island Icon Dies at 100," *The Telegram*, July 14, 2012, A13.

19 Gene Hong was the father of this essay's co-author, Robert Hong.

20 Kim Hong, "My Life in Newfoundland," in *Reflections of the Chinese Community*, 32–33.

21 See Wright, "'The most modern dining hall.'"

22 *Eastern Canada Chinese Directory* (Vancouver: Chinese Publicity Bureau Ltd., 1955).

As William Ping (grandson of the William [Seto] Ping who arrived in Newfoundland in the 1930s) observes in his radio documentary "Chicken Balls and Baymen," the cafés and restaurants owned by people of Chinese heritage had become part of the fabric of Newfoundland society.[23] Often, in many smaller communities, the "Chinese restaurants" were the only places to buy a meal. The Star Café in Carbonear, for example, had started serving fish and chips in the 1930s; it was still operating in the 1950s. Other long-standing restaurants in St. John's, such as the London Café and the White Lily, continued into the post-Confederation era, run by families of the men who had founded them in the 1930s.[24] Some were even starting to offer Chinese cuisine, a difference from the fare served before the 1950s.[25] Such places were also sites of cultural interaction, where ethnic stereotypes would begin to break down.

Still, questions remain about the challenges these families faced in the decades after Confederation—both the newly reunited Chinese families and those who were born of Chinese men and white, Newfoundland-born women. How did decades of separation affect the families who were reunited after 1949? What was it like for the families with older siblings born in China and younger ones born and raised in Newfoundland? How did the children born of Chinese fathers and white, Newfoundland-born women identify and relate to their parents' diverse cultures? And finally, at a time when the dominant Newfoundland cultural identity was decidedly "white," how were these families accepted into the wider society? Despite these lingering questions about identity and acceptance, however, with Confederation, the racist head tax died, opening up new possibilities for the Chinese immigrants who had come to Newfoundland, looking for a better life for themselves and their families.

---

23 William Ping, "Chicken Balls and Baymen" (CBC Atlantic Voice radio documentary, 2020), https://www.cbc.ca/player/play/1997282883583. Also see Ann Hui, *Chop Suey Nation: The Legion Café and Other Stories from Canada's Chinese Restaurants* (Madeira Park, BC: Douglas & McIntyre, 2019).

24 Wright, "'The most modern dining hall,'" 16, 32.

25 Exhibit Guide, "Taking Root: Chinese Immigrants and their Families in Newfoundland, 1895–1970s—Work, Family, and Community" (Newfoundland and Labrador Headtax Redress Organization Inc. in conjunction with Centre for Newfoundland Studies, Queen Elizabeth II Library, Memorial University, St. John's, 2012). This exhibit included menus from St. John's restaurants in the 1950s and 1960s, all of which served "Canadian" and "Chinese Food."

"Democracy before they are ready for it": The Hopedale Protest of 1949 and Inuit Political Autonomy

Andrea Procter

IN NORTHERN LABRADOR, Confederation launched a wave of provincial and federal policies that eroded Inuit political authority for years afterwards. The RCMP and Social Services replaced the Inuit Elders' councils in mediating family and community problems, and, in the late 1950s, provincial officials orchestrated the massive and devastating eviction of Inuit from the northern communities of Hebron and Nutâk.[1] But for a brief period in 1949, Inuit in Hopedale skilfully leveraged the new political structure to their own advantage. As they recognized, the governance situation was changing rapidly. Provincial and federal interest in Labrador was suddenly surfacing, and Hopedale Inuit enlisted these new sources of authority to challenge the local Moravian missionaries and pursue their own goals.

Since the 1770s, when the Moravian Mission arrived in northern Labrador, Inuit leaders and missionaries had struggled over control of Inuit society.[2] The missionaries had assumed the role of liaison between Inuit and outside agencies and had attempted to dominate life at the mission stations,

1 Rosina Pamack-Jeddore, "What Confederation Has Meant for the Labrador Eskimo," *Decks Awash* 3, no. 5 (October 1974): 6–7; Adrian Tanner, "The Aboriginal Peoples of Newfoundland and Labrador and Confederation," *Newfoundland Studies* 14, no. 2 (1998): 238–52; Carol Brice-Bennett, *Dispossessed: The Eviction of Inuit from Hebron, Labrador* (Montréal: Imaginaire/Nord, 2017).

2 Peter Evans, "Transformations of Inuit Resistance and Identity in Northern Labrador, 1771–1959" (PhD diss., Cambridge University, 2013); Nigel Markham, "'Murmuring Against God': Inuit-Moravian Confrontations in Late Nineteenth-Century Labrador," *Newfoundland and Labrador Studies* 36, no. 1 (2021): 87–115.

but by the late 1940s they were losing their grip on power. They no longer had economic clout, having sold the Mission's exclusive trading rights to the Hudson's Bay Company in the 1920s, and they were quickly losing social influence, as World War II had introduced Inuit to new work opportunities and new social interactions at the American military base in Goose Bay.[3] Tensions were rising, and Inuit and missionaries clashed over how Inuit families should face the changing world.

Education was a common area of conflict. The Mission provided seasonal day schools for Inuit children to learn religious subjects and how to read and write in the Inuktitut language.[4] In Makkovik, where families of mixed ancestry spoke English, missionaries built an English-language boarding school in the early 1900s. About thirty children lived at the dormitory each year, and the Mission oversaw all aspects of the school, from curriculum and staffing to food and supplies; the Newfoundland government was not involved.[5] Parents had to pay school fees and missionaries struggled to enforce school attendance.[6]

By the 1940s, many of the children at the boarding school came from the large Inuit population in the Hopedale region. Neither Inuit families nor the Moravian missionaries were satisfied with the school. Missionaries complained when parents failed to pay school fees or refused to send their children to school.[7] Parents, on the other hand, were unhappy with the quality of education offered and with the treatment of their children.[8] Hopedale's elected Inuit leaders, the community Elders, brought these complaints to the Moravian Mission superintendent, Rev. William Peacock, in 1944. They "asked if they might not have a boarding school in Hopedale"; all agreed that a day school was not feasible because most families lived at homesteads outside of Hopedale during the winter.[9] The Elders confirmed that the community would be willing to supply

3 Carol Brice-Bennett, "Renewable Resource Use and Wage Employment in the Economy of Northern Labrador" (St. John's: Background Report for the Royal Commission on Employment and Unemployment, 1986).

4 Procter, *A Long Journey*, 45–49.

5 Procter, *A Long Journey*, 63–69, 74–78.

6 Procter, *A Long Journey*, 84–90.

7 Rev. Sach to Connor, February 24, 1944, Muswell Hill Moravian Church Archives.

8 Rev. Harp to Peacock, n.d. [ca. 1945], Moravian Mission Box 37, *Them Days* Archive.

9 Superintendent's report on annual visit to Mission stations, May 20, 1944, Moravian Mission Box 5, *Them Days* Archive.

the school with firewood without charge and emphasized widespread Inuit support. Regardless, the superintendent refused the idea.[10]

But the Hopedale families continued to push for a local school. In February 1948, after the Makkovik church and mission building burned to the ground, more than twenty boarding school students from Hopedale returned home. One of the Makkovik teachers moved to Hopedale and held classes for them there.[11] The families again proposed the idea of a community school. Calling it a "Hopedale protest," the local missionary described their proposal: "As the main portion of the boarders in Makkovik are Hopedale children, it would save them the journey to Makkovik and back, especially on ice in the cold weather.... There have been some complaints about the way that the children have been looked after this winter ..."[12]

In early 1949, the conflict escalated. Increasingly frustrated with the boarding school situation, Hopedale parents decided to withdraw their children from Makkovik en masse. A Newfoundland Ranger reported that parents said that "the children were hungry, Eskimo[13] children were not treated on a line with the White children, and work other than ordinary school work was put upon the school children to do."[14] Despite pressure from the missionaries, many families in Hopedale refused to send their children back. When the newly elected Member of Parliament for Labrador, Harold Horwood, visited Hopedale in the summer of 1949—a novel event—Inuit leaders enlisted his support in organizing a school at home.

The Elders, under the leadership of Natan Frieda, met with the federal politician.[15] They outlined their frustrations with the Makkovik boarding school and presented their plan for a school in their own community. Horwood agreed and promised government support for the idea.[16] Already critical of the Moravian Mission, he remarked that the missionaries and the Newfoundland government

10 Superintendent's report on annual visit to Mission stations, May 20, 1944, Moravian Mission Box 5, *Them Days* Archive.

11 Annual report for Hopedale, 1948, S. Hettasch, Moravian Mission Box 2, *Them Days* Archive.

12 Fred Grubb to Peacock, March 19, 1948, Moravian Mission Box 37, *Them Days* Archive.

13 I have retained this offensive term in the chapter's historical quotes in order to illustrate the derogatory attitudes of colonial figures.

14 W. Mullaly, Ranger report re: School attendance in Hopedale, March 1949, PRC 9 Box 7433 File 75 Vol V: Moravian Mission, RPA.

15 Peacock to Harp, September 15, 1949, Moravian Mission Box 2, *Them Days* Archive.

16 S. Hettasch to Birtill, October 30, 1949, Moravian Mission Box 2, *Them Days* Archive.

were "all assimilationists of one stripe or another."[17] The missionaries were irate to see their authority undermined. "I do not know what Mr. Horwood promised them," fumed Rev. Peacock, "but one thing was definite that the people did not intend to send their children to Makkovik to board.... These people have been agitating for a school here and it would appear that they are likely to get one and if we do not take the initiative, we shall find that we have no influence at all in Hopedale."[18] Under pressure, Peacock agreed to open a day school in Hopedale in the fall, with loose plans for a boarding school the following year. The Mission would supply a teacher if local Inuit supplied the firewood.

Once the dominant colonial authority in northern Inuit communities, the Moravian Mission now found both the Newfoundland and Canadian governments encroaching on its domain. The new provincial government had jurisdiction over many fields, including education, and the federal government, although initially reluctant to accept responsibility for Indigenous affairs, had deep pockets and significant influence.[19] The Moravian superintendent expressed frustration at the people's successful leverage of the new political field. He scolded them for airing their grievances to Horwood:

> I told them that in future, I expected them to bring their complaints about school to the missionary in charge and that I expected their loyal co-operation in all things.... We are once more faced with the innate ingratitude of the Eskimos and I can only reiterate that I am certain that they have no sense of loyalty.[20]

The missionaries attributed the Inuit leaders' defiance of Mission rule to their recent experiences at the Goose Bay military base. In the early 1940s, many people from Hopedale had travelled to central Labrador to work at the new air base and had experienced life away from strict Moravian control. Peacock blamed the "Hopedale protest" on this strengthened sense of Inuit autonomy: "I am sorry that this situation has arisen, but I fear that it is the natural outcome of the Eskimos' contact with the White Man and is the result of giving them

17 Evans, "Transformations of Inuit Resistance," 297.

18 Peacock to Harp, September 15, 1949, Moravian Mission Box 2, *Them Days* Archive.

19 Tanner, "Aboriginal Peoples."

20 Memorandum on the visits of Father Cyr and Mr. Horwood, MP, to Labrador, September 14, 1949, Moravian Mission Box 5, *Them Days* Archive.

democracy before they are ready for it."[21] As for Horwood, Peacock wrote, he was "undoubtedly a Socialist and according to many ... a Communist."[22]

When the day school opened in the Hopedale Mission House on September 26, 1949, twenty-five children attended.[23] The teacher, Margaret Fountain, reported that "there is much voluntary labour given, and eagerness on the part of the children to learn, and on the part of the parents to get their children to school."[24] Horwood's promised support arrived later that fall, consisting merely of a shipment of lumber for making desks.[25] Although a boarding school was never established in the community, the day school grew. Over the next two years, school attendance rose as more families moved into Hopedale to work on the construction of a new American military radar site.[26] At the same time, the number of children in the Makkovik dormitory steadily fell. In 1955, with only a few boarding students, the Moravian Mission decided to close it and to run only day schools at Makkovik and Hopedale.[27] The Mission also transferred all responsibility for schools at its stations to the provincial Department of Education.[28]

By deftly mobilizing Confederation politics, Hopedale Inuit had successfully destabilized the Moravian establishment in northern Labrador. Playing one authority off another, they forced the Mission to face its increasingly tenuous position in community governance and to be more responsive to Inuit demands. In pressuring the missionaries to modify the education system to better reflect Inuit interests, the Hopedale families asserted their autonomy in governing their own lives.

---

21 Peacock to Harp, September 15, 1949, Moravian Mission Box 2, *Them Days* Archive.

22 Memorandum on the visits of Father Cyr and Mr. Horwood, MP, to Labrador, September 14, 1949, Moravian Mission Box 5, *Them Days* Archive.

23 Teacher's notice of opening school in Hopedale, September 26, 1949; Peacock to Birtill, October 15, 1949, Moravian Mission Box 2, *Them Days* Archive.

24 British Minute Book #13, November 23, 1949: 34, Muswell Hill Moravian Church Archives.

25 S. Hettasch to Peacock, November 6, 1949, Moravian Mission Box 2, *Them Days* Archive.

26 Carol Brice-Bennett, *Hopedale: Three Ages of a Community in Northern Labrador* (St. John's: Historic Sites Association of Newfoundland and Labrador, 2003), 111.

27 Inge Vollprecht and G.J. Vollprecht, "Makkovik," *Periodical Accounts of the Work of the Moravian Mission*, no. 164 (1956): 48–52, https://collections.mun.ca/digital/collection/cns_permorv/id/16696/rec/1.

28 J.R. Chalker, Minister of Education, Memorandum to Executive Council: Northern Labrador Education, August 11, 1955, PRC 9, Box 7433, File 75, Vol. XIII: Moravian Mission, RPA.

Excerpt from "Newfoundland Mi'kmaw Resistance and Vibrancy in a History of Erasure"[1]

Mi'sel Joe, Sheila O'Neill, Jessica Bound, and Jocelyn Thorpe

THE ABSENCE OF Indigenous perspectives in the history of Newfoundland is striking. In the most well-known historical account, William Cormack, a white man born in St. John's, writes of his 1822 journey across the island. His story, first published in 1829 in the *Edinburgh Philosophical Journal*, has been told and retold ever since. In the one hundredth anniversary edition, editor F. A. Bruton calls Cormack's tale "one of the classics of the literature of Newfoundland, and a priceless heritage for the children of the Island." He refers to Cormack as an "intrepid explorer and accomplished naturalist."[2] Bruton prepared the anniversary edition "at the request of the Educational Authorities of Newfoundland, for use in the schools of the Island."[3] Cormack's account has not only been told, but has also been taught and celebrated for generations.

While the story of Cormack is relatively well known, much less known is the reality that Cormack was able to complete his journey only because of the efforts of his Mi'kmaw guide, a man Cormack refers to as "my Indian."[4] George Story, former president of the Newfoundland Historical Society, notes that it is "curiously hard to get a clear and firm portrait" of the guide from the story that

1 For the full text of this essay, see *Canadian Historical Review* 104, no. 3 (2023): 315–42.

2 F.A. Bruton, introduction, *Narrative of a Journey across the Island of Newfoundland in 1822*, by W.E. Cormack, ed. F.A. Bruton (London and New York: Longmans, Green and Co., 1928), vii, ix.

3 Bruton, introduction, viii.

4 In 2002, Cormack's guide was recognized by Parks Canada as a "National Historic Person." By 2002, Cormack's story had been told for almost 200 years. See "Joe, Sylvester: National Historic Person," *Parks Canada Directory of Federal Heritage Designations*, https://www.pc.gc.ca/apps/dfhd/page_nhs_eng.aspx?id=1971.

Cormack tells.[5] Story adds that he does not know where one might turn to learn more about the guide, but asserts that he would rather have "a novel or a play about the famous journey" from the perspective of the guide than from Cormack's point of view.[6]

In noting both his desire to learn more about the guide and his doubt about how to do that, Story gestures to a larger challenge of history: how to tell stories about the past when the record we rely on to do so is partial in both senses of the word.[7] The partiality of Cormack's account, which describes lands available for settlement and marginalizes the work of his guide, is a product of the colonial history that also produced him and that his story's retelling reproduces. Historical research is important for what it has to teach us about how we got to the current moment, but it is not easy or apolitical work. The report of the Truth and Reconciliation Commission of Canada (TRC), for example, demonstrates both the significance of undertaking research from the perspective of underrepresented groups and the degree to which the previously existing record is embedded in the colonial history responsible in the first place for the

---

5 George M. Story, "Guides to Newfoundland," *Aspects: A Publication of the Newfoundland Historical Society* 2, no. 2 (1980): 18. The Parks Canada plaque does not add much detail, stating, "Thanks to his knowledge and understanding of the natural world, Sylvester Joe, a Mi'kmaw, ensured the success of William Eppes Cormack's expedition across Newfoundland in 1822. Their mapping and exploration efforts in the rugged interior, traversing a landscape not yet explored by Europeans, formed the basis for subsequent work by the Geological Survey of Newfoundland. With Sylvester Joe's invaluable aid, the expedition amassed a great deal of information for future students of the island's natural history." "Joe, Sylvester: National Historic Person."

6 Story, "Guides to Newfoundland," 18, 19.

7 This is not a new insight, of course. William Cronon articulates many of the challenges of telling stories about the past in his 1992 article, "A Place for Stories." See William Cronon, "A Place for Stories: Nature, History, and Narrative," *Journal of American History* 78, no. 4 (1992): 1347–76. Indigenous historians have been working to challenge Eurocentric historical accounts, with non-Indigenous historians also contributing to this effort. See, for example: Dimitry Anastakis, Mary-Ellen Kelm, and Suzanne Morton, eds., special issue of the *Canadian Historical Review—Indigenous Historical Perspectives: New Approaches to Indigenous History* 98, no. 1 (2017); Aimée Craft, *Breathing Life into the Stone Fort Treaty: An Anishinabe Understanding of Treaty One* (Saskatoon: Purich Pub., 2013); Susan M. Hill, *The Clay We Are Made Of: Haudenosaunee Land Tenure on the Grand River* (Winnipeg: University of Manitoba Press, 2017); Lianne C. Leddy, *Serpent River Resurgence: Confronting Uranium Mining at Elliot Lake* (Toronto: University of Toronto Press, 2022); Brittany Luby, *Dammed: The Politics of Loss and Survival in Anishinaabe Territory* (Winnipeg: University of Manitoba Press, 2020).

establishment and maintenance of the residential school system.[8] The *United Nations Declaration on the Rights of Indigenous Peoples Act*, which came into force in Canada in 2021, includes the provision that "Indigenous peoples have the right to the dignity and diversity of their cultures, traditions, histories and aspirations which shall be appropriately reflected in education and public information."[9] There is a need to tell stories that are respectful of Indigenous peoples in their diversity, and a role for historians in this process.[10] But there is an equally pressing need to examine the partiality of the specific records we rely on to tell stories so that we may make it clear that omissions as well as inclusions shape what stories it is possible to tell.[11]

....

The record created by and for white people inadvertently portrays a rich Mi'kmaw history on the island of Newfoundland, which has been largely overlooked.[12] His-

8 Truth and Reconciliation Commission of Canada, *Honouring the Truth, Reconciling for the Future: Summary of the Final Report of the Truth and Reconciliation Commission of Canada* (Truth and Reconciliation Commission of Canada, 2015), https://ehprnh2mwo3.exactdn.com/wp-content/uploads/2021/01/Executive_Summary_English_Web.pdf.

9 "The United Nations Declaration on the Rights of Indigenous Peoples," *Government of Canada*, https://www.justice.gc.ca/eng/declaration/decl_doc.html.

10 Raymond Frogner, Head of Archives at the National Centre for Truth and Reconciliation, has written about implementing the United Nations Declaration on the Rights of Indigenous Peoples (UNDRIP) in public archives in Canada. He shows that there is an important role also for archives and archivists in promoting Indigenous cultures and identities. See Raymond O. Frogner, "The Train from Dunvegan: Implementing the United Nations Declaration on the Rights of Indigenous Peoples (UNDRIP) in Public Archives in Canada," *Archival Science* 22, no. 2 (2022): 209–38.

11 See Jennifer S.H. Brown and Elizabeth Vibert, eds., *Reading beyond Words: Contexts for Native History*, 2nd ed. (Peterborough: Broadview Press, 2003); Antoinette M. Burton, ed., *Archive Stories: Facts, Fictions, and the Writing of History* (Durham: Duke University Press, 2005); Donna Haraway, "Situated Knowledges: The Science Question in Feminism and the Privilege of Partial Perspective," *Feminist Studies* 14, no. 3 (1988): 575–99; Ann Laura Stoler, *Along the Archival Grain: Epistemic Anxieties and Colonial Common Sense* (Princeton: Princeton University Press, 2009); David Thomas, Simon Fowler, and Valerie Johnson, *The Silence of the Archive* (London: Facet, 2017); Michel-Rolph Trouillot, *Silencing the Past: Power and the Production of History* (Boston: Beacon Press, 1995); Kirsten Weld, *Paper Cadavers: The Archives of Dictatorship in Guatemala* (Durham: Duke University Press, 2014).

12 This history has not been entirely overlooked, however. See, for example, Dorothy

torian Adele Perry reminds us that, while history is about the past, "we research, write, and discuss it in the present."[13] Her history of the Winnipeg Aqueduct explains that the City of Winnipeg's access to clean drinking water came at the expense of the Indigenous community living at the other end of the pipe. History enters the present through infrastructure set up in the past, infrastructure that is in turn built upon the ideas that made it possible. Just as history creates the present, so too do ideas create reality....

Scholars who conduct anti-colonial research recognize as a starting point that the written record is partial. As Qwul'sih'yah'maht (Robina Thomas), who is a member of Lyackson First Nation and a professor of social work, puts it, "stories from Indigenous people tell a counter-story to that of the documented history of Indigenous people in Canada." A mentor of hers once said, "it is such a shame that every time someone who went to residential school dies without telling their stories, our government and the churches look more innocent." Telling counter-stories, then, "is a form of resistance to colonization."[14] Such narratives

---

Anger, *Nogcswa'mkisk (Where the Sand Blows): Vignettes of Bay St. George Micmacs* (Port au Port, NL: Bay St. George Regional Indian Band Council, 1988); Dennis Bartels and Alice Bartels, "Mi'gmaq Lives: Aboriginal Identity in Newfoundland," in *Walking a Tightrope: Aboriginal People and Their Representations*, ed. David McNab and Ute Lischke (Waterloo, ON: Wilfrid Laurier University Press, 2005): 249–80; Doug Jackson, *On the Country: The Micmac of Newfoundland*, ed. Gerald Penney (St. John's: Harry Cuff Publications Limited, 1993); Charles Martijn, "Early Mi'kmaq Presence in Southern Newfoundland: An Ethnohistorical Perspective, c. 1500–1763," *Newfoundland Studies* 19, no. 1 (2003): 44–102; Michelle Matthews and Angela Robinson, "Newfoundland Mi'kmaq Place Names; Ktaqmkuk: Across the Waters," Qalipu First Nation, https://qalipu.ca/qalipu/wp-content/uploads/2018/11/Ktaqmkuk%20Handbook.pdf; Adrian Tanner, "The Aboriginal People of Newfoundland and Labrador, and Confederation," *Newfoundland Studies* 14, no. 2 (1998): 238–52; Jerry Wetzel, Pat Anderson, and Douglas Sanders, *Freedom to Live Our Own Way in Our Own Land*, ed. Peter J. Usher (Conne River, NL: Ktaqamkuk Ilnui Saqimawoutie and the Conne River Indian Band Council, 1980).

13 Adele Perry, *Aqueduct: Colonialism, Resources, and the Histories We Remember* (Winnipeg: ARP Books, 2016), 18. Anishinaabe historian Lianne Leddy similarly observes that it is "important to remember that stories of dispossession and environmental disruption are not only of the past but also continue in the present day." See Lianne C. Leddy, "Intersections of Indigenous and Environmental History in Canada," *Canadian Historical Review* 98, no. 1 (2017): 86.

14 Qwul'sih'yah'maht (Robina Anne Thomas), "Honouring the Oral Traditions of the Ta't Mustimuxw (Ancestors) through Storytelling," in *Research as Resistance: Revisiting Critical, Indigenous, and Anti-Oppressive Approaches*, 2nd ed., ed. Susan Strega

can alter dominant accounts by revealing those accounts as partial.[15] The Truth and Reconciliation Commission, by adding Indigenous perspectives on residential schools to the "official" historical record, challenges and changes the record itself.[16] This process of challenging and changing the record to include Indigenous perspectives is itself resistance to the erasure of Indigenous peoples, histories, and worldviews.

Yet resistance alone is not enough to counter the injustices embedded in dominant accounts of the past. Critical accounts that "reveal how colonial relationships operate and become naturalized" risk centering "the very histories and power relations they mean to challenge," while leaving "nothing in their place."[17] Métis scholar of political thought and treaty history Adam Gaudry argues that while it is necessary to "critique and undermine colonialism by deconstructing its misleading and disingenuous claims," critique cannot be the main work of what he calls insurgent research.[18] Instead, insurgent research must attend to the "pressing need for the construction of alternative Indigenous accounts: the reclamations of Indigenous histories, perspectives and worldviews."[19] By putting forward an "empowering and decolonized view of the people with whom they conduct research," engaged researchers "work toward

---

and Leslie Brown (Toronto: Canadian Scholars' Press, 2015), 183.

15 See Dian Million, "Felt Theory," *American Quarterly* 60, no. 2 (2008): 267–72.

16 Historian Greg Bak describes the TRC testimony of residential school Survivors as a "corrective and counterweight" to the colonial records created by the government and churches. See Greg Bak, "Counterweight: Helen Samuels, Archival Decolonization, and Social License," *The American Archivist* 84, no. 2 (2021): 425.

17 Jocelyn Thorpe, "It Matters Where You Begin: A (Continuing) Journey toward Decolonizing Research," in *Methodological Challenges in Nature-Culture and Environmental History Research*, ed. Jocelyn Thorpe, Stephanie Rutherford, and L. Anders Sandberg (London and New York: Routledge, 2017), 135.

18 Adam Gaudry, "Researching the Resurgence: Insurgent Research and Community-Engaged Methodologies in 21st-Century Academic Inquiry," in Strega and Brown, *Research as Resistance*, 256. Gaudry defines insurgent research as an approach to community-engaged academic research that relies on four main principles: "1. Research is grounded in, respects, and validates Indigenous worldviews; 2. Research output is intended for use by Indigenous communities; 3. Researchers are responsible to Indigenous communities for the decisions they make, and communities are the final judges of the validity and effectiveness of research projects; 4. Research is action oriented and inspires direct action in Indigenous communities." Gaudry, "Researching the Resurgence," 248.

19 Gaudry, "Researching the Resurgence," 256.

something new and positive," clarifying what Indigenous cultures "offer in terms of creative and anticolonial alternatives."[20]

As more sites of potential unmarked graves of Indigenous children are investigated, the consequences of a history of official indifference and cruelty toward Indigenous peoples become increasingly clear.[21] We cannot change what happened, but we can go back to the past differently, recognizing that the perspectives of those reflected in the written record tell only a fraction of the story. Indigenous peoples endured through generations of genocidal policies and practices. Their stories of how people survived and thrived elucidate the strength, determination, knowledge, skills, and indeed humanity of Indigenous peoples. These are stories we need in order to move toward respectful relationships in a world indelibly marked by the arrogance and greed of colonialism. We hope that our article offers such stories, stories that counter and go beyond the narrative of Indigenous absence on the island of Newfoundland, an island full of Indigenous pasts, presents, and futures.

20 Gaudry, "Researching the Resurgence," 244, 256.

21 "Dozens More Graves Found at Former Residential School Sites," *BBC News*, February 16, 2022, https://www.bbc.com/news/world-us-canada-60395242.

REFERENCES AND FURTHER READING

Archival Materials

Archives and Special Collections, Queen Elizabeth II Library, Memorial University of Newfoundland (ASC)

The Barrelman Radio Program papers, COLL-028

Jubilee Guilds of Newfoundland-Newfoundland and Labrador Women's Institutes (JG-NLWI) COLL-166

1.01 Board of Managers, 1937–71

1.01.003 Letter, Walwyn to Ewbank, February 27, 1939

1.01.013, Letter, Winter to Smallwood, October 17, 1949

1.01.019, Letter, Carnell to Smallwood, November 2, 1955

1.03.005 Branch Histories

1.04.001 Trustee Minutes, 1935–47

1.05 Executive Committee Minute Book, 1936–1974

1.05.001 Book I, January 1936–July 1936

1.05.002 Book II, August 1936–April 1938

1.05.003 Book III, May 1938–February 1942

1.05.004 Book IV, March 1942–November 1949

1.05.005 Book V, January 1950–December 1950, Box 2

1.06.001 Annual General Meeting Minutes, 1937–64

1.14.001–1.14.050 Annual Reports, 1936–1988

J.R. Smallwood Collection, COLL-075

1.1.01–1.1.50 District Files

4.01.007 Joseph R. Smallwood: Confederation Speeches

Memorial University of Newfoundland Folklore and Language Archives (MUN FLA), MUN

Interview Transcripts (TS)

A. Templeton (1989) November 2. Accession #: 90-350, Shelf List #: C1160 and C1161

A. Templeton (1991a) October 24. Accession #: 92-098, Shelf List #: C14739 and C14740

A. Templeton (1991b) December 5. Accession #: 92-098, Shelf List #: C14747 and C14748

Library and Archives Canada (LAC)

Government of Newfoundland, RG 76-D-2-d-v, R1206-174-2-E

McGrath, Charles A. Papers. Microfilm H1419-20-21, 1933

The Rooms Provincial Archives of Newfoundland and Labrador (RPA)

Colonial Secretary's Office, Special Files, Box 63, #424.B, Charity Organization Bureau (COB); relief in St. John's, January 8, 1925–October 20, 1932

Commission of Government Records (CG)

Certified Minutes GN 38, Series GN 38.8, 1934–1949

Jubilee Guild File, GN 31/2, Box 77, File #318, Jubilee Guilds of Newfoundland and Labrador, Volume I and Volume II

Jubilee Guilds of Newfoundland and Jubilee Guilds of Newfoundland, Organization of the Guilds, Department of Natural Resources (DNR), GN 31/3A, Box 56, File R166

Memoranda, GN 38, Box S2 119

Natural Resources General Administration, 1940–1947, File #3, GN 38-S-2-1-22, File #3

Department of Justice, Box 106, File 85

Margaret Chang Papers, MG364, Box 1

Secondary Materials

Abbott, Christine Elizabeth. "Exploring Women's Subjectivities: Women in a Newfoundland Outport." Master of Arts thesis, Queen's University, 2004.

Adamson, J.D., N. Jolliffe, H.D. Kruse, O.H. Lowry, P.E. Moore, B.S. Platt, W.H. Sebrell, J.W. Tice, F.F. Tisdall, R.M. Wilder, and P.C. Zamecnik. "Medical Survey of Nutrition in Newfoundland." *Canadian Medical Association Journal* 52 (1945): 227–50.

Alexander, M. Jacqui. *Pedagogies of Crossing: Meditations on Feminism, Sexual Politics, Memory, and the Sacred.* Durham: Duke University Press, 2006.

Anaïs, Seantel. "(Mal)Nutrition, and the 'Informal Economy' Bootstrap: The Politics of Poverty, Food Relief, and Self Help." *Newfoundland and Labrador Studies* 24, no. 2 (2009): 239–60.

Anastakis, Dimitry, Mary-Ellen Kelm, and Suzanne Morton, eds. Special issue of the *Canadian Historical Review—Indigenous Historical Perspectives: New Approaches to Indigenous History* 98, no. 1 (2017).

Andrieux, J.P. *Rumrunners: The Smugglers from St. Pierre and Miquelon and the Burin Peninsula from Prohibition to Present Day.* Paradise, NL: Flanker Press, 2009.

Anger, Dorothy. *Nogcswa'mkisk (Where the Sand Blows): Vignettes of Bay St. George Micmacs.* Port au Port, NL: Bay St. George Regional Indian Band Council, 1988.

Anglin, Gerald. "The Mechanized Missionary of North West River." *Maclean's,* August 1, 1950.

Argyle, Ray. *Joey Smallwood: Schemer and Dreamer.* Toronto: Dundurn, 2012.

Aykroyd, W.R., N. Jolliffe, O.H. Lowry, P.E. Moore, W.H. Sebrell, R.E. Shank, F.F. Tisdall, R.M. Wilder, and P.C. Zamecnik. "Medical Resurvey of Nutrition in Newfoundland 1948." *Canadian Medical Association Journal* 60 (1949): 329–52.

Bak, Greg. "Counterweight: Helen Samuels, Archival Decolonization, and Social License." *The American Archivist* 84, no. 2 (2021): 420–44.

Baker, Melvin and Peter Neary. *Joseph Roberts Smallwood: Masthead Newfoundlander, 1900–1949.* Montreal: McGill-Queen's University Press, 2021.

Baker, Melvin and Peter Neary. "Joseph Roberts Smallwood: A Biographical Sketch, 1900–1934." *Newfoundland and Labrador Studies* 33, no. 2 (2018): 354–412.

Baker, Melvin and Peter Neary. "Negotiating Final Terms of Union with Canada: The Memorandum Submitted by the Newfoundland Delegation, Ottawa, 13 October, 1948." *Newfoundland and Labrador Studies* 33, no. 2 (2018): 459–506.

Bartels, Dennis and Alice Bartels. "Mi'gmaq Lives: Aboriginal Identity in Newfoundland." In *Walking a Tightrope: Aboriginal People and their Representations,* edited by David McNab and Ute Lischke, 249–80. Waterloo, ON: Wilfrid Laurier University Press, 2005.

Bishop Stirling, Terry and Jeff A. Webb. "The Twentieth Century." In *A Short History of Newfoundland and Labrador,* edited by Newfoundland Historical Society, 103–40. Portugal Cove-St. Philip's, NL: Boulder Publications, 2008.

Black, W.A. "The Labrador Floater Codfishery." *Annals of the Association of American Geographers* 50, no. 3 (1960): 267–95.

Blake, Raymond Benjamin. *Canadians at Last: The Integration of Newfoundland as Province.* Toronto: University of Toronto Press, 1994.

Blake, Raymond and Melvin Baker. *Where Once They Stood: Newfoundland's Rocky Road towards Confederation.* Regina: University of Regina Press, 2019.

Boon, Sonja. "'I Am Very Badly in Need of Help': Promises and Promissory Notes in Women's Letters to J.R. Smallwood." In Cullum and Porter, *Creating This Place*, 221–42.

Brice-Bennett, Carol. *Dispossessed: The Eviction of Inuit from Hebron, Labrador.* Montréal: Imaginaire/Nord, 2017.

Brice-Bennett, Carol. *Hopedale: Three Ages of a Community in Northern Labrador.* St. John's: Historic Sites Association of Newfoundland and Labrador, 2003.

Brice-Bennett, Carol. "Renewable Resource Use and Wage Employment in the Economy of Northern Labrador." Background Report for the Royal Commission on Employment and Unemployment, 1986.

Brown, Cassie, *Death on the Ice: The Great Newfoundland Sealing Disaster of 1914.* Toronto: Doubleday, 1988.

Brown, Esther Slaney. *Labours of Love: Midwives of Newfoundland and Labrador.* St. John's: DRC Publishing, 2007.

Brown, Jennifer S.H. and Elizabeth Vibert, eds. *Reading beyond Words: Contexts for Native History.* 2nd ed. Peterborough: Broadview Press, 2003.

Bruton, F.A. Introduction to *Narrative of a Journey across the Island of Newfoundland in 1822*, by W.E. Cormack, vii–xi. Edited by F.A. Bruton. London and New York: Longmans, Green and Co., 1928.

Budgell, R. and M. Staveley. *The Labrador Boundary.* Labrador Institute of Northern Studies, Memorial University, 1987.

Bulgin, Iona L. "Mapping the Self in the 'Utmost Purple Rim': Published Labrador Memoirs of Four Grenfell Nurses." PhD diss., Memorial University, 2001.

Bureau of Canadian Archivists. *Rules for Archival Description.* Rev. ed. Ottawa: Bureau of Canadian Archivists, 2008. https://archivescanada.ca/wp-content/uploads/2022/08/RADComplete_July2008.pdf.

Burton, Antoinette M., ed. *Archive Stories: Facts, Fictions, and the Writing of History.* Durham: Duke University Press, 2005.

Butt, Jeff. "Labrador Fishery." Heritage Newfoundland & Labrador, 1998. https://www.heritage.nf.ca/articles/exploration/labrador-fishery.php.

Cadigan, Sean. *Hope and Deception in Conception Bay: Merchant-Settler Relations in Newfoundland, 1785–1855.* Toronto: University of Toronto Press, 2016. https://doi.org/10.3138/9781442675858.

Cadigan, Sean. *Newfoundland and Labrador: A History*. Toronto: University of Toronto Press, 2009.

Cadigan, Sean. "Truck, Paternalism and Ecology: The Struggle between Fishers and Merchants in the 19th and early 20th Centuries." In *Amulree's Legacy: Truth, Lies and Consequences*, edited by Garfield Fizzard, 29–37. St. John's: Newfoundland Historical Society, 2001.

Callanan, Andreae. "This project changed me. Thank you for welcoming me into it! I can't wait to see everyone's work." Twitter, 8:14 p.m., January 13, 2023.

Callanan, Charles, dir. *The Last Chinese Laundry*. St. John's: School of Continuing Studies and Extension, Memorial University, 1987.

Canada Dominion Bureau of Statistics. "Census of Newfoundland and Labrador, 1945, Vol. 1." Ottawa: Dominion Bureau of Statistics, 1945.

Cardell, Kylie and Jane Haggis. "Contemporary Perspectives on Epistolarity." *Life Writing* 8, no. 2 (2011): 129–33. https://doi.org/10.1080/14484528.2011.559731.

Carr, William Guy. *Checkmate in the North: The Axis Planned to Invade America*. Toronto: The Macmillan Co., 1944.

Cashin, Peter. *My Fight for Newfoundland*. Edited by Edward Roberts. Paradise, NL: Flanker Press, 2012.

Chang, Margaret Ann. "Chinese Pioneers in Newfoundland." *The Asianadian* 3, no. 4 (1981): 3–7.

Chenier, Elise. "Sex, Intimacy, and Desire among Men of Chinese Heritage and Women of Non-Asian Heritage in Toronto, 1910–1950." *Urban History Review* 42, no. 2 (2014): 29–43. https://doi.org/10.3138/uhr.42.02.04.

Chinese Association of Newfoundland and Labrador. *Reflections of the Chinese Community on the Occasion of the 30th Anniversary of the Chinese Association of Newfoundland and Labrador 1976–2006*. 2nd printing with minor revisions. St. John's: Chinese Association of Newfoundland and Labrador, 2007.

Chinese Publicity Bureau. *Eastern Canada Chinese Directory*. Vancouver: Chinese Publicity Bureau, 1955.

Collier, Keith. "Cottage Hospitals and Health Care in Newfoundland." Heritage Newfoundland & Labrador, 2011. https://www.heritage.nf.ca/articles/society/cottage-hospitals.php.

Collier, Keith. "Fighting Tuberculosis in Newfoundland and Labrador." Heritage Newfoundland & Labrador, 2011. https://www.heritage.nf.ca/articles/society/fighting-tuberculosis.php.

Collier, Keith. "History of Tuberculosis and Its Presence in Newfoundland." Heritage Newfoundland & Labrador, 2011. https://www.heritage.nf.ca/

articles/society/tuberculosis-newfoundland.php.

Collins, Paul. "Sinking of the *Caribou*." Heritage Newfoundland & Labrador, 2006. https://www.heritage.nf.ca/articles/politics/caribou-sinking.php.

Colman, S.J. (and members of the Extension Department, Memorial University). "Social Changes since Confederation." In McAllister, *Newfoundland and Labrador*, 8–13.

Connor, Jennifer J. "'We Are Anglo-Saxons': Grenfell, Race, and Mission Movements." In Connor and Side, *The Grenfell Medical Mission and American Support*, 45–68.

Connor, Jennifer J. and Katherine Side, eds. *The Grenfell Medical Mission and American Support in Newfoundland and Labrador, 1890s–1940s*. Montreal and Kingston: McGill-Queen's University Press, 2019.

Connor, J.T.H. "Newfoundland and Labrador: The Paradoxical 'Sick Man' of Canada." *Newfoundland and Labrador Studies* 37, no. 1 (2022). https://journals.lib.unb.ca/index.php/NFLDS/article/view/33490.

Connor, J.T.H. "American Aid, the International Grenfell Association, and Health Care in Newfoundland, 1920s–1930s." In Connor and Side, *The Grenfell Mission and American Support*, 245–66.

Connor, J.T.H. "'For her own safety and the good of society at large': Eugenics, Sterilization, and Anglo-American Transnationalism in Newfoundland, 1928–1934." *Acadiensis* 48, no. 1 (2019): 32–59.

Connor, J.T.H. "Malnutrition Research in Newfoundland and Labrador in the 1900s to 1930s, Brown Flour, and the 'Dole Plague' of Beriberi, Part 2: The First Malnutrition Research Wave, 1900s–1930s." *Newfoundland Quarterly* 112, no. 1 (2019): 48–53.

Connor, J.T.H. "Malnutrition Research in Newfoundland and Labrador in the 1900s to 1930s, Brown Flour, and the 'Dole Plague' of Beriberi, Part 1: The First Malnutrition Research Wave, 1900s–1930s." *Newfoundland Quarterly* 111, no. 4 (2019): 44–49.

Connor, J.T.H. "'... medicine is here to stay': Rural Medical Practice, Frontier Life, and Modernization in 1930s' Newfoundland." In *Medicine in the Remote and Rural North, 1800–2000*, edited by J.T.H. Connor and Stephan Curtis, 129–51, 260–65. London: Pickering & Chatto, 2011.

Connor, J.T.H., Jennifer J. Connor, Monica G. Kidd, and Maria Mathews. "Conceptualizing Health Care in Rural and Remote Pre-Confederation Newfoundland as Ecosystem." *Newfoundland and Labrador Studies* 30, no. 1 (2015): 115–40.

Cook, Clayton D. *The Bonavista Peninsula of Days Gone By*. St. John's: Jeff Blackwood & Associates, 1999.

Coombs-Thorne, Heidi. "To Prevent 'the Otherwise Inevitable Catastrophe': American Philanthropy and the Creation of the International Grenfell Association, 1905–1914." In Connor and Side, *The Grenfell Medical Mission and American Support*, 77–99.

Coombs-Thorne, Heidi. "'Such a Many-Purpose Job': Nursing, Identity, and Place with the Grenfell Mission, 1939–1960." *Nursing History Review* 32 (2012): 89–96.

Coombs-Thorne, Heidi. "Conflict and Resistance to Paternalism: Nursing with the Grenfell Mission in Newfoundland and Labrador." In *Caregiving on the Periphery*, edited by Myra Rutherdale, 210–42. Montreal and Kingston: McGill-Queen's University Press, 2010.

Coombs-Thorne, Heidi. "Nursing with the Grenfell Mission in Northern Newfoundland and Labrador, 1939–81." PhD diss., University of New Brunswick, 2010.

Craft, Aimée. *Breathing Life into the Stone Fort Treaty: An Anishinabe Understanding of Treaty One*. Saskatoon: Purich Pub., 2013.

Cronon, William. "A Place for Stories: Nature, History, and Narrative." *Journal of American History* 78, no. 4 (1992): 1347–76.

Cuff, Robert. "Telegraphy." Heritage Newfoundland & Labrador, 2001. https://www.heritage.nf.ca/articles/economy/railway-telegraph.php.

Cullum, Linda. "Below Stairs: Domestic Service in Twentieth-Century St. John's." In Cullum and Porter, *Creating This Place*, 89–113.

Cullum, Linda. "'It's Up to the Women': Gender, Class and Nation Building in Newfoundland." In Cullum and Porter, *Creating This Place*, 179–201.

Cullum, Linda. "'A Woman's Place': The Work of Two Women's Voluntary Organizations in Newfoundland, 1934–1941." In *Their Lives and Times: Women in Newfoundland and Labrador, A Collage*, edited by Carmelita McGrath, Barbara Neis, and Marilyn Porter, 93–108. St. John's: Killick Press, 1995.

Cullum, Linda. "Under Construction: Women, The Jubilee Guilds and Commission Government in Newfoundland and Labrador, 1935–41." Master of Arts thesis, Ontario Institute for Studies in Education/University of Toronto, 1993.

Cullum, Linda and Marilyn Porter, eds. *Creating This Place: Women, Family, and Class in St. John's, 1900–1950*. Montreal, Quebec: McGill-Queen's University Press, 2014.

Cullum, Linda, Carmelita McGrath, and Marilyn Porter, eds. *Weather's Edge: Women in Newfoundland and Labrador*. St. John's: Killick Press, 2006.

Curtis, Charles S. "Note of Thanks." *Among the Deep Sea Fishers* 46, no. 4 (January 1949): 117.

Curtis, Charles. "Heroines." *Among the Deep Sea Fishers* 43, no. 2 (July 1945): 46.

"Develop or Perish: Smallwood's Development Approach." Heritage Newfoundland & Labrador. https://www.heritage.nf.ca/articles/politics/develop-or-perish.php.

Dickinson, A.B. and C.W. Sanger. "Newfoundland and Labrador Shore-Station Whaling: The Third Major Phase, 1937–1951." *International Journal of Maritime History* 11, no. 1 (1999): 101–16.

Dickinson, Anthony Bertram and Chesley W. Sanger. *After the Basques: The Whaling Stations of Newfoundland and Labrador*. St. John's: DRC Publishing, 2018.

Dohey, Larry. "Newfoundland Proposed to Sell Labrador to Quebec." *Archival Moments* (blog), March 4, 2018. http://archivalmoments.ca/2018/03/04/newfoundland-proposed-to-sell-labrador-to-quebec-2/.

Doyle, Gerald S. *The Old-Time Songs and Poetry of Newfoundland*. St. John's: Gerald S. Doyle, 1940.

"Dozens More Graves Found at Former Residential School Sites." *BBC News*, February 16, 2022. https://www.bbc.com/news/world-us-canada-60395242.

Duley, Margot I. "The Unquiet Knitters of Newfoundland: From Mothers of the Regiment to Mothers of the Nation." In *A Sisterhood of Suffering and Service: Women and Girls of Canada and Newfoundland During the First World War*, edited by Sarah Glassford and Amy Shaw, 51–74. University of British Columbia Press, 2012.

Evans, Peter. "Transformations of Inuit Resistance and Identity in Northern Labrador, 1771–1959." PhD diss., Cambridge University, 2013.

Evening Telegram. "Chinese Seek to Become Canadian Citizens." September 23, 1949.

Evening Telegram. "Starvation in Labrador." April 7, 1949.

Evening Telegram. "Chinese Leaving to Return to Hong Kong." January 22, 1947.

Evening Telegram. "Can It Be Done? A Timely Jubilee Guild Proposal." January 9, 1936.

Evening Telegram. "Launch of the Jubilee Guilds." October 18, 1935.

Evening Telegram. "Lady Anderson Outlines Jubilee Guilds of Newfoundland." May 31, 1935.

Evening Telegram. "House of Assembly Debates for Tuesday, April 17, 1906." April 21, 1906.

Fitzhugh, Lynne. *The Labradorians: Voices from the Land of Cain*. St. John's: Breakwater Books, 1999.

Fizzard, Garfield, ed. *Amulree's Legacy: Truth, Lies and Consequences Symposium: March 2000. Papers and Presentations*. St. John's: Newfoundland Historical Society, 2001.

Flaherty, Sara. "'Out of Date in a Good Many Respects': Newfoundland's Fight for Judicial Separation and Divorce in the 1940s." In Cullum, McGrath, and Porter, *Weather's Edge*, 222–33.

Flight, Jennifer. "'We are all in the front line this time': The Patriotic Association of the Women of Newfoundland during the Second World War." Master of Arts research report, Memorial University, 2007.

Flowers, W., A. Fowler, L. Jackson, D. Lough, and N. Markham. *As If People Mattered*. Labrador Resources Advisory Council, 1977.

Forestell, Nancy M. "Times Were Hard: The Pattern of Women's Paid Labour in St. John's between the Two World Wars." In *Their Lives and Times: Women in Newfoundland and Labrador, A Collage*, edited by C. McGrath, B. Neis, and M. Porter, 76–92. St. John's: Killick Books, 1995.

Fowke, Edith. "The Anti-Confederation Song." In *The Canadian Encyclopedia*, August 11, 2014. https://www.thecanadianencyclopedia.ca/en/article/quotthe-anti-confederation-songquot-emc.

Frogner, Raymond O. "The Train from Dunvegan: Implementing the United Nations Declaration on the Rights of Indigenous Peoples (UNDRIP) in Public Archives in Canada." *Archival Science* 22, no. 2 (2022): 209–38.

Gartner, Hana, dir. "Ironworkers from Newfoundland: Walking Iron." *CBC The Fifth Estate*, May 13, 1986. https://youtu.be/nIYdystZDJ4.

Gaudry, Adam. "Researching the Resurgence: Insurgent Research and Community-Engaged Methodologies in 21st-Century Academic Inquiry." In Strega and Brown, *Research as Resistance*, 243–66.

Godfrey, Stuart R. *Human Rights and Social Policy in Newfoundland, 1832–1982: Search for a Just Society*. St. John's: Harry Cuff Publications Ltd., 1985.

Grammond, Sébastien. "Equally Reocognized? The Indigenous Peoples of Newfoundland and Labrador." *Osgoode Hall Law Journal* 51, no. 2 (1960): 469–99.

Guy, Ray. *Ray Guy: The Smallwood Years*. Portugal Cove-St. Philip's, NL: Boulder Publications, 2008.

Gwyn, Richard J. *Smallwood: The Unlikely Revolutionary.* Toronto: McClelland & Stewart, 1999.

Hanrahan, Maura. "'Through their own efforts': Nutrition Studies and Interventions in Early 20th-Century Northern Newfoundland and Southern Labrador." *Cuizine: The Journal of Canadian Food Cultures* 7, no. 1 (2016). https://doi.org/10.7202/1037390ar.

Hanrahan, Maura. "Tracing Social Change among the Labrador Inuit: What Does the Nutrition Literature Tell Us?" In *Settlement, Subsistence, and Change Among the Labrador Inuit: The Nunatsiavummuit Experience,* edited by D.C. Natcher, L. Felt, and A. Procter, 121–38. Winnipeg: University of Manitoba Press, 2012.

Hanrahan, Maura. "The Lasting Breach: The Omission of Aboriginal People from the Terms of Union between Newfoundland and Canada and Its Ongoing Impacts." In *Royal Commission on Renewing and Strengthening Our Place in Canada,* 207–78. St. John's: The Royal Commission, 2003.

Haraway, Donna. "Situated Knowledges: The Science Question in Feminism and the Privilege of Partial Perspective." *Feminist Studies* 14, no. 3 (1988): 575–99.

Herbert, Pearl and Association of Midwives of Newfoundland and Labrador. *History of Midwifery in Newfoundland and Labrador.* St. John's: Memorial University, 2014.

Heritage Newfoundland & Labrador. "Fahey Farm Century Farm." https://heritagenl.ca/heritage-property/fahey-farm-century-farm/.

Heritage Newfoundland & Labrador. "Referendum Voting Trends by District." https://www.heritage.nf.ca/articles/politics/denominational-percentages-statistics.php.

Heritage Newfoundland & Labrador. "Rev. Dr. Lester Leeland Burry." https://heritagenl.ca/discover/provincial-historic-commemorations-program-designations/rev-dr-lester-leeland-burry/.

Higgins, Jenny. "Women's Patriotic Association." Heritage Newfoundland & Labrador, April 2015. https://www.heritage.nf.ca/first-world-war/articles/womens-patriotic-association-en.php.

Higgins, Jenny. *Perished: The 1914 Newfoundland Sealing Disaster.* Portugal Cove-St. Philip's, NL: Boulder Publications, 2013.

Higgins, Jenny. "Education 1949–1968." Heritage Newfoundland & Labrador, 2011. https://www.heritage.nf.ca/articles/society/education-1949-1968.php.

Higgins, Jenny. "The Peckford Government: 1979–1989." Heritage Newfoundland & Labrador, 2011. https://www.heritage.nf.ca/articles/politics/peckford-government.php.

Higgins, Jenny. "First World War and the Economy." Heritage Newfoundland & Labrador, 2009. https://www.heritage.nf.ca/first-world-war/articles/first-world-war-economy.php.

Higgins, Jenny. "Argentia." Heritage Newfoundland & Labrador, July 2007. https://www.heritage.nf.ca/articles/politics/argentia-base.php.

Higgins, Jenny. "Economic Impacts of WWII." Heritage Newfoundland & Labrador, 2007. https://www.heritage.nf.ca/articles/politics/economic-impacts-wwii.php.

Higgins, Jenny. "Great Depression—Impacts on the Working Class." Heritage Newfoundland & Labrador, 2007. https://www.heritage.nf.ca/articles/politics/depression-impacts.php.

Higgins, Jenny. "Newfoundland Ranger Force." Heritage Newfoundland & Labrador, 2007, 2015. https://www.heritage.nf.ca/articles/politics/newfoundland-rangers.php.

Higgins, Jenny. "The 1914 Sealing Disaster." Heritage Newfoundland & Labrador, 2007. https://www.heritage.nf.ca/articles/politics/sealing-disaster-1914.php.

Higgins, Jenny. "Harmon Field, Stephenville." Heritage Newfoundland & Labrador, 2006. https://www.heritage.nf.ca/articles/politics/stephenville-base.php.

Higgins, Jenny. "Newfoundland Overseas Forestry Unit." Heritage Newfoundland & Labrador, 2006. https://www.heritage.nf.ca/articles/politics/overseas-forestry-unit-wwii.php.

Higgins, Jenny and Heather O'Brien. "Torbay." Heritage Newfoundland & Labrador, 2007. https://www.heritage.nf.ca/articles/politics/torbay-air-base.php.

Higgins, Jenny and Luke Callanan. "Post-1949 Communications and Transportation." Heritage Newfoundland & Labrador, 2008/2019. https://www.heritage.nf.ca/articles/society/post-1949-communication.php.

High, Steven. *Occupied St. John's: A Social History of a City at War, 1939–1945*. Montreal: McGill-Queen's University Press, 2010.

High, Steven C. *Base Colonies in the Western Hemisphere, 1940–1967*. 1st ed. Studies of the Americas. New York: Palgrave Macmillan, 2009.

High, Steven. "From Outport to Outport Base: The American Occupation of Stephenville, 1940–1945." *Newfoundland Studies* 18 (2002): 84–113.

Hill, Susan M. *The Clay We Are Made Of: Haudenosaunee Land Tenure on the Grand River*. Winnipeg: University of Manitoba Press, 2017.

Hiller, James K. *Confederation: Deciding Newfoundland's Future 1934 to 1949*. St. John's: Newfoundland Historical Society, 1998.

Hiller, James K. "The Debate: Confederation Rejected, 1864–1869." Heritage Newfoundland & Labrador, 1997. https://www.heritage.nf.ca/articles/politics/confederation-rejected-1864-1869.php.

Hiller, J.K. "The Newfoundland and Labrador Seal Fishery." Heritage Newfoundland & Labrador, 2001. https://www.heritage.nf.ca/articles/economy/seal-fishery.php.

Hiller, J.K. "The Sailing Seal Fishery." Heritage Newfoundland & Labrador, 2001. https://www.heritage.nf.ca/articles/economy/sailing-seal-fishery.php.

Hiller, J.K. "The 1948 Referendums." Heritage Newfoundland & Labrador, 1997. https://www.heritage.nf.ca/articles/politics/referendums-1948.php.

Hiller, J.K. "The Confederation Election of 1869." Heritage Newfoundland & Labrador, 1997. https://www.heritage.nf.ca/articles/politics/election-confederation-1869.php.

Hiller, J.K. "Newfoundland and Canada: 1864–1949." Heritage Newfoundland & Labrador, 1997. https://www.heritage.nf.ca/articles/politics/confederation-1864-1949.php.

Hiller, J.K. "Whiteway, Sir William Vallance." *Dictionary of Canadian Biography*. 2003. http://www.biographi.ca/en/bio/whiteway_william_vallance_13E.html.

Hiller, J.K. "The Newfoundland National Convention, 1946–1948." Heritage Newfoundland & Labrador, 1997. https://www.heritage.nf.ca/articles/politics/newfoundland-national-convention.php.

Hiller, James and Melanie Martin. "Develop or Perish." Heritage Newfoundland & Labrador, 2006. www.heritage.nf.ca/articles/politics/develop-or-perish.php.

Hiscock, Philip D. "*The Barrelman* Radio Program, 1937–1943: The Mediation and Use of Folklore in Newfoundland." PhD diss., Memorial University, 1994.

"History." St. John's International Airport Authority. https://stjohnsairport.com/about/corporate-information/history/.

Hoffmann, K.W. *History of Telecommunications in Newfoundland*. St. John's: Newfoundland Historical Society, 1978.

Hong, Kim. "My Life in Newfoundland." In Chinese Association of Newfoundland and Labrador, *Reflections of the Chinese Community*, 32–33.

Hong, Robert. "'To take action without delay': Newfoundland's Chinese Immigration Act of 1906." Honours essay, Memorial University, 1987.

H.N. "Review of *Tuberculosis in Newfoundland (1945)* by T.O. Garland and P. D'Arcy Hart." *The British Journal of Tuberculosis* 41, no. 1 (1947): 30.

Hui, Ann. *Chop Suey Nation: The Legion Cafe and Other Stories from Canada's Chinese Restaurants.* Madeira Park, BC: Douglas and McIntyre Ltd., 2019.

Jackson, Doug. *On the Country: The Micmac of Newfoundland.* Edited by Gerald Penney. St. John's: Harry Cuff Publications Limited, 1993.

Jenish, D'Arcy. "Raising Steel." *Legion Magazine,* November 28, 2009. https://legionmagazine.com/en/raising-steel/.

Jolly, Margaretta and Liz Stanley. "Letters as / not a Genre." *Life Writing* 2, no. 2 (2005): 91–118. https://doi.org/10.1080/10408340308518291.

Jones, Iris. "He Was a Student Minister and I Was a Jubilee Guilds Fieldworker." *Decks Awash* 7, no. 2 (1978): 26–27.

Kealey, Linda. "Historical Perspectives on Nutrition and Food Security in Newfoundland and Labrador." In *Resetting the Kitchen Table: Food Security, Culture, Health and Resilience in Coastal Communities,* edited by Christopher C. Parrish, Nancy J. Turner, and Shirley M. Solberg, 177–90. New York: Nova Science Publishers, 2007.

Kelly, Ursula A. and Meghan C. Forsyth. *The Music of Our Burnished Axes: Songs and Stories of the Woods Workers of Newfoundland and Labrador.* St. John's: ISER Books, 2018.

Kennedy, John C. "The Impact of the Grenfell Mission on Southeastern Labrador Communities." *Polar Record* 24, no. 150 (1988): 199–206.

Kidney, J.G. and E. MacLaughin. "Streptomycin in the Treatment of Pulmonary Tuberculosis: A Presentation of 11 Cases Treated with Streptomycin at the Newfoundland Government Sanatorium." *Journal of the Medical Association of Eire* 22, no. 127 (1948): 3–8.

Korneski, Kurt. "Planters, Eskimos, and Indians: Race and the Organization of Trade under the Hudson's Bay Company in Labrador, 1830–50." *Journal of Social History* 50, no. 2 (2016): 307–35. https://doi.org/10.1093/jsh/shw057.

Lake, Edward F.J. *Capturing an Era: History of the Newfoundland Cottage Hospital System.* St. John's: Argentia Pilgrim, 2010.

Lawson, Gordon S. and Andrew F. Noseworthy. "Newfoundland's Cottage Hospital System: 1920–1970." *Canadian Bulletin of Medical History* 26, no. 2 (2009): 477–98.

Leddy, Lianne C. *Serpent River Resurgence: Confronting Uranium Mining at Elliot*

Lake. Toronto: University of Toronto Press, 2022.

Leddy, Lianne C. "Intersections of Indigenous and Environmental History in Canada." *Canadian Historical Review* 98, no. 1 (2017): 83–95.

Letto, Douglas Mervyn. *In Cain's Footsteps: [People of the Labrador Straits]*. Paradise, NL: Blue Hill, 2000.

Luby, Brittany. *Dammed: The Politics of Loss and Survival in Anishinaabe Territory*. Winnipeg: University of Manitoba Press, 2020.

Lukins, Sheilah Roberts. *Bottoms Up: A History of Alcohol in Newfoundland and Labrador*. St. John's: Breakwater Books, 2020.

Lush, Gail Ruby Shirlene. "Nutrition, Health Education, and Dietary Reform: Gendering the 'New Science' in Northern Newfoundland and Labrador, 1893–1928." Master's thesis, Memorial University, 2008.

MacDonald, Joe, dir. *"I Just Didn't Want to Die": The 1914 Newfoundland Sealing Disaster*. Montreal: National Film Board of Canada. 2018.

MacKenzie, David. "The Indian Act and the Aboriginal Peoples of Newfoundland at the Time of Confederation." *Newfoundland and Labrador Studies* 25, no. 2 (2010): 161–86.

MacKenzie, David. *Inside the Atlantic Triangle: Canada and the Entrance of Newfoundland into Confederation 1939–1949*. Books Collection. Toronto: University of Toronto Press, 1986. https://doi.org/10.3138/9781487576493.

MacLeod, Malcolm. *A Bridge Built Halfway: A History of Memorial University College, 1925–1950*. Montreal: McGill-Queen's University Press, 1990.

Malone, Greg. *Don't Tell the Newfoundlanders: The True Story of Newfoundland's Confederation with Canada*. Toronto: Alfred A. Knopf Canada, 2012.

Manning, Susan M. "Contrasting Colonisations: (Re)Storying Newfoundland/Ktaqmkuk as Place." *Settler Colonial Studies* 8, no. 3 (2018): 314–31.

Mar, Lisa Rose. *Brokering Belonging Chinese in Canada's Exclusion Era, 1885–1945*. New York: Oxford University Press, 2010.

Markham, Nigel. "'Murmuring Against God': Inuit-Moravian Confrontations in Late Nineteenth-Century Labrador." *Newfoundland and Labrador Studies* 36, no. 1 (2021): 87–115.

Martijn, Charles. "Early Mi'kmaq Presence in Southern Newfoundland: An Ethnohistorical Perspective, c. 1500–1763." *Newfoundland Studies* 19, no. 1 (2003): 44–102.

Matthews, Michelle and Angela Robinson. "Newfoundland Mi'kmaq Place Names; Ktaqmkuk: Across the Waters." Qalipu First Nation. https://qalipu.ca/qalipu/wp-content/uploads/2018/11/Ktaqmkuk%20Handbook.pdf.

McAllister, R.I., ed. *Newfoundland and Labrador: The First Fifteen Years of Confederation.* St. John's: Dicks, 1966.

McBride, Michelle. "Electrifying the Island." Heritage Newfoundland & Labrador, 2001. https://www.heritage.nf.ca/articles/economy/electrifying-island.php.

McManus, Katherine. "Before the 'Fogo Project' There Was Florence O'Neill: A Glimpse of Early Adult Education and a Dedicated Advocate." In Cullum, McGrath, and Porter, *Weather's Edge*, 36–47.

McNeish, Sam. "Celebrating Otto Kelland's Legacy." *SaltWire*, February 12, 2018. https://www.saltwire.com/newfoundland-labrador/news/celebrating-otto-kellands-legacy-185788/.

Mercer, Keith. *Rough Justice: Policing, Crime, and the Origins of the Newfoundland Constabulary, 1729–1871.* St. John's: Flanker Press, 2021.

Miller, Leonard A. "The Newfoundland Department of Health." *Canadian Journal of Public Health* 50 (June 1959): 228–39.

Million, Dian. "Felt Theory." *American Quarterly* 60, no. 2 (2008): 267–72.

Moffatt, Ian. "Confederate Hauntings: The Spectral Legacy of Nationhood in Contemporary Newfoundland Fiction." Master's thesis, Memorial University, 2015.

Mondou, Mathieu. "Social Assistance in Newfoundland and Labrador." In *Welfare Reform in Canada: Provincial Social Assistance in Comparative Perspective*, edited by Daniel Béland and Pierre-Marc Daigneault, 239–54. Toronto: University of Toronto Press, 2015.

Morgan, Jennifer. *Almost Home: The Sinking of the S.S. Caribou.* St. John's: Breakwater, 2012.

Murray, Hilda Chaulk. *More than Fifty Percent: Woman's Life in a Newfoundland Outport, 1900–1950.* St. John's: Flanker Press, 2010.

Natcher, David C., Lawrence Felt, and Andrea Procter, eds. *Settlement, Subsistence, and Change among the Labrador Inuit.* Winnipeg: University of Manitoba Press, 2012.

Neary, Peter, ed. *White Tie and Decorations: Sir John and Lady Hope Simpson in Newfoundland, 1934–1936.* Toronto: University of Toronto Press, 1996.

Neary, Peter. "'A Mortgaged Property': The Impact of the United States on Newfoundland, 1940–49." In *Twentieth-Century Newfoundland: Explorations*, edited by James Hiller and Peter Neary, 179–94. St. John's: Breakwater Books, 1994.

Neary, Peter. *Newfoundland in the North Atlantic World, 1929–1949.* Books Collection. Montreal: McGill-Queen's University Press, 1988.

Newfoundland and Labrador Women's Institute. Accessed January 27, 2022. https://www.nlwi.ca/about.html/.

Newfoundland Historical Society. *A Short History of Newfoundland and Labrador*. Portugal Cove-St. Philip's, NL: Boulder Publications, 2008.

"Newfoundland National Convention, 23 January 1948, Debates on Confederation with Canada." 1865–1949 Confederation Debates. https://hcmc.uvic.ca/confederation/en/lgNFNC_1948-01-23.html.

Newfoundland Telephone Company Ltd. *Along These Lines: A History of Newfoundland Telephone*. St. John's: Newfoundland Telephone Co., 1979.

Noel, S.J.R. *Politics in Newfoundland*. Toronto: University of Toronto Press, 2020. https://doi.org/10.3138/9781487577964.

NONIA. Accessed February 20, 2022. https://nonia.com/about-us-2/.

Overton, James. "Brown Flour and Beriberi: The Politics of Dietary and Health Reform in Newfoundland in the First Half of the Twentieth Century." *Newfoundland Studies* 14, no. 1 (1998): 1–27.

Overton, James. "Moral Education of the Poor: Adult Education and Land Settlement Schemes in Newfoundland in the 1930s." *Newfoundland Studies* 11, no. 2 (1995): 250–82.

Overton, James. "Self-Help, Charity, and Individual Responsibility: The Political Economy of Social Policy in Newfoundland in the 1920s." In *Twentieth-Century Newfoundland: Explorations*, edited by James K. Hiller, 79–122. St. John's: Breakwater Books, 1994.

Overton, James. "Public Relief and Social Unrest in Newfoundland in the 1930s: An Evaluation of the Ideas of Piven and Cloward." *Canadian Journal of Sociology* 13, no. 1/2 (1988): 143–69.

Paddeck, Mark. "The Guy Philosophy." *The Express* (St. John's), February 3, 1993.

Paine, Robert. "Smallwood: Political Strategy, and a 'Career' of Rhetoric." *Newfoundland Studies* 3 (1987): 217–26.

Paine, Robert. "The Persuasiveness of Smallwood: Rhetoric of *Cuffer* and *Scoff*, of Metonym and Metaphor." *Newfoundland Studies* 1 (1985): 57–75.

Pallister, Hugh. "Order for Establishing Communication and Trade with the Esquimaux Savages on the Coast of Labrador, 1765." In *Labrador Boundary Dispute Extracts from Charters, Acts Etc.*, 1915. https://collections.mun.ca/digital/collection/moravian/id/17308.

Pamack-Jeddore, Rosina. "What Confederation Has Meant for the Labrador Eskimo." *Decks Awash* 3, no. 5 (October 1974): 6–7.

Parks Canada. "Joe, Sylvester: National Historic Person." Parks Canada Directory of Federal Heritage Designations, https://www.pc.gc.ca/apps/dfhd/page_nhs_eng.aspx?id=1971.

Paul, Jasmine. "I'll never forget my experience reading them and I will be going back again to do it again sometime for my own pleasure." Twitter, 5:13 p.m., January 13, 2023. https://twitter.com/jnp709/status/1614012753684975627.

Penashue, Tshaukuesh Elizabeth. *Nitinikiau Innusi: I Keep the Land Alive.* Edited by Elizabeth Yeoman. Winnipeg: University of Manitoba Press, 2019.

Perlin, A.B. "History and Health in Newfoundland." *Canadian Journal of Public Health* 61 (1970): 313–16.

Perry, Adele. *Aqueduct: Colonialism, Resources, and the Histories We Remember.* Winnipeg: ARP Books, 2016.

Perry, Jill Samfya. "Nursing for the Grenfell Mission: Maternalism and Moral Reform in Northern Newfoundland and Labrador, 1894–1938." Master's thesis, Memorial University, 1997.

Ping, Bill. "William Ping, 1909–1939." In Chinese Association of Newfoundland and Labrador, *Reflections of the Chinese Community*, 49.

Ping, William. "Chicken Balls and Baymen." *CBC Atlantic Voice.* St. John's: CBC Radio, 2020. Chicken Balls and Baymen: A documentary about Chinese immigration | CBC News.

Porter, Marilyn. "'She Knows Who She Is': Educating Girls to Their Place in Society." In Cullum and Porter, *Creating This Place*, 146–78.

Porter, Marilyn. "'She was skipper of the shore-crew': Notes on the History of the Sexual Division of Labour in Newfoundland." *Labour/Le Travail* 15 (1985): 105–23.

Power, Iris. "Joey's 'Girl Friday.'" *Atlantic Guardian*, June 1954, 23–24.

Procter, Andrea. *A Long Journey: Residential Schools in Labrador and Newfoundland.* St. John's: ISER Books, 2020.

Qwul'sih'yah'maht (Robina Anne Thomas). "Honouring the Oral Traditions of the Ta't Mustimuxw (Ancestors) through Storytelling." In Strega and Brown, *Research as Resistance*, 177–98.

Rennie, Rick. "Buchans: The Making of a Company Town." Heritage Newfoundland & Labrador, 1999. https://www.heritage.nf.ca/articles/economy/buchans-town.php.

Rennie, Rick. "Industrial Disease and the St. Lawrence Mines." Heritage Newfoundland & Labrador, 1998/2019. https://www.heritage.nf.ca/articles/economy/industrial-disease.php.

Rennie, Rick. "Iron Ore Mines of Bell Island." Heritage Newfoundland & Labrador, 1998/2016. https://www.heritage.nf.ca/articles/economy/bell-island-mines.php.

Rennie, Rick. "Mining." Heritage Newfoundland & Labrador, 1998. https://www.heritage.nf.ca/articles/economy/mining.php.

Rennie, Rick. "Work and Life in the Bell Island Mines." Heritage Newfoundland & Labrador, 1998/2019. https://www.heritage.nf.ca/articles/economy/bell-island-work.php.

Richard, Agnes M. *Threads of Gold: Newfoundland and Labrador Jubilee Guilds Women's Institutes.* St. John's: Creative Publishers, 1989.

Riggs, Bert. "Jack Higgins: Newfoundlander Through and Through." Heritage Newfoundland & Labrador, 2000. https://www.heritage.nf.ca/articles/politics/jack-higgins.php.

Roberts, Edward. "How the Baby Bonus Came to Newfoundland." *SaltWire,* September 29, 2017. https://www.saltwire.com/atlantic-canada/federal-election/how-the-baby-bonus-came-to-newfoundland-28364/.

Rollmann, Hans. "Edward Patrick Roche." Heritage Newfoundland & Labrador, 1999. https://www.heritage.nf.ca/articles/politics/biography-edward-roche.php.

Rompkey, Ronald. *Grenfell of Labrador: A Biography.* Toronto: University of Toronto Press, 2019. https://doi.org/10.3138/9781487580506.

Rowe, Frederick William. *The History of Education in Newfoundland.* Toronto: Ryerson Press, 1952.

Royal Commission on Labrador. "Report of the Royal Commission on Labrador." St. John's: The Commission, 1974.

Royal Commission on Renewing and Strengthening Our Place in Canada. *Royal Commission on Renewing and Strengthening Our Place in Canada.* St. John's: The Royal Commission, 2002.

Ruiz, Rafico. "Sites of Communication: The Grenfell Mission of Newfoundland and Labrador." PhD diss., McGill University, 2014.

Ryan, Shannon, Martha Drake, and Cater Andrews. *Seals and Sealers: A Pictorial History of the Newfoundland Seal Fishery Based on the Cater Andrews Collection.* St. John's: Breakwater, 1987.

Sanger, C.W. "Seal Fishery in the 20th Century." Heritage Newfoundland & Labrador, 1998. https://www.heritage.nf.ca/articles/environment/sealing-fishery-in-the-20th-century.php.

Sanger, C.W., A.B. Dickinson, and W.G. Handcock. "Commercial Whaling in

Newfoundland and Labrador in the 20th Century." Heritage Newfoundland & Labrador, 1998. https://www.heritage.nf.ca/articles/environment/whaling-in-the-20th-century.php.

Sears, Fred C. "The 1933 Labrador Garden Campaign." *Among the Deep Sea Fishers* 32, no. 1 (April 1934): 8–12.

Sharpe, Kenny. "In/Between the Walls: A Rare Look inside the Waterford Hospital." CBC Newfoundland and Labrador. https://www.cbc.ca/news/canada/newfoundland-labrador/rare-look-inside-waterford-hospital-photos-1.3457722.

Smallwood, Joseph. Foreword to McAllister, *Newfoundland and Labrador*, n.p.

Smallwood, Joseph R. "Memorial University of Newfoundland—'a live dynamic centre of learning [and] culture.'" Edited by Melvin Baker. n.d. http://www.ucs.mun.ca/~melbaker/jrs1949.htm#N_2.

Smallwood, Reg. *My Brother, Joe: Growing up with the Honourable Joseph R. ("Joey") Smallwood.* St. John's: R. Smallwood, 1995.

Smith, Jean. "Flowers Cove." *Among the Deep Sea Fishers* 45, no. 2 (July 1947): 36.

Smith, Sidonie and Julia Watson. *Reading Autobiography: A Guide for Interpreting Life Narratives.* Minneapolis: University of Minnesota Press, 2010.

Smith, Sidonie and Julia Watson, eds. *Getting a Life: Everyday Uses of Autobiography.* Minneapolis: University of Minnesota Press, 1996.

Snell, James G. "The Newfoundland Old Age Pension Programme, 1911–1949." *Acadiensis* 23, no. 1 (1993): 86–109.

Soo, May. "The Four Generations of the Tom Family." In Chinese Association of Newfoundland and Labrador, *Reflections of the Chinese Community*, 54–55.

St. John's Daily News. "Chinese Become Citizens of Canada." June 13, 1951.

St. John's Daily News. "Chinese Residents Become Citizens." February 14, 1941.

Stanbridge, Karen. "Framing Children in the Newfoundland Confederation Debate, 1948." *Canadian Journal of Sociology* 32, no. 2 (2007): 177–201. https://doi.org/10.2307/20460631.

Statistics Canada. "Hourly Wage Rates in Select Building Trades by City, 1901 to 1974." July 17, 2014. https://www150.statcan.gc.ca/n1/pub/11-516-x/sectione/E248_267a-eng.csv.

Statistics Canada. "Long Run Provincial and Territorial Data." November 2, 2018. https://www150.statcan.gc.ca/t1/tbl1/en/tv.action?pid=3610022901&pickMembers%5B0%5D=2.1&pickMembers%5B1%5D=3.1&cubeTimeFrame.startYear=1949&cubeTimeFrame.endYear=1949&referencePeriods=19490101%2C19490101.

Stoler, Ann Laura. *Along the Archival Grain: Epistemic Anxieties and Colonial Common Sense.* Princeton: Princeton University Press, 2009.

Story, George M. "Guides to Newfoundland." *Aspects: A Publication of the Newfoundland Historical Society* 2, no. 2 (1980): 18.

Strega, Susan and Leslie Brown, eds. *Research as Resistance: Revisiting Critical, Indigenous, and Anti-Oppressive Approaches.* 2nd ed. Toronto: Canadian Scholars' Press, 2015.

Strikwerda, Eric. "Newfoundland and Labrador Maligned: Taking Stock of Nutritional Health in Rural Newfoundland and Labrador, 1912–1949." *Acadiensis* 47, no. 1 (2018): 118–39.

Sutherland, Dufferin. "'We are only Loggers': Loggers and the Struggle for Development in Newfoundland, 1929–59." PhD diss., Simon Fraser University, 1995. Proquest NN17130.

Tanner, Adrian. "The Aboriginal Peoples of Newfoundland and Labrador and Confederation." *Newfoundland Studies* 14, no. 2 (1998): 238–52.

Tchen, John Kuo Wei. *New York before Chinatown: Orientalism and the Shaping of American Culture 1776–1882.* Baltimore: Johns Hopkins University Press, 1999.

Tenth Census of Newfoundland and Labrador, 1935. Vol. 1. St. John's: Department of Health and Welfare, 1937.

The Telegram. "Bell Island Icon Dies at 100." July 14, 2012.

The Wayfarer. "In the News." *The Daily News.* March 8, 1945.

The Western Star. "Sanatorium Officially Opened." June 6, 1952.

The Western Star. "Tests of New Anti-T.B. Drug Lead to Optimism." April 8, 1952.

Thomas, David, Simon Fowler, and Valerie Johnson. *The Silence of the Archive.* London: Facet, 2017.

Thomas, Gordon W. "Winter Plane Trips." *Among the Deep Sea Fishers* 47, no. 2 (July 1949): 35–36.

Thoms, James R. *Just Call Me Joey.* St. John's: Creative Printers and Publishers, 1969.

Thorpe, Jocelyn. "It Matters Where You Begin: A (Continuing) Journey Toward Decolonizing Research." In *Methodological Challenges in Nature-Culture and Environmental History Research,* edited by Jocelyn Thorpe, Stephanie Rutherford, and L. Anders Sandberg, 131–44. London and New York: Routledge, 2017.

Trouillot, Michel-Rolph. *Silencing the Past: Power and the Production of History.* Boston: Beacon Press, 1995.

Truth and Reconciliation Commission of Canada. *Honouring the Truth,*

Reconciling for the Future: Summary of the Final Report of the Truth and Reconciliation Commission of Canada. Truth and Reconciliation Commission of Canada, 2015. https://ehprnh2mwo3.exactdn.com/wp-content/uploads/2021/01/Executive_Summary_English_Web.pdf.

"The United Nations Declaration on the Rights of Indigenous Peoples." Government of Canada, 2007, last updated June 21, 2023. https://www.justice.gc.ca/eng/declaration/decl_doc.html.

Valverde, Mariana. *The Age of Light, Soap, and Water: Moral Reform in English Canada, 1885–1925*. Toronto: McClelland & Stewart, 1991.

Vernon, Karina. *The Black Prairie Archives: An Anthology*. Waterloo: Wilfrid Laurier University Press, 2020.

Vollprecht, Inge and G.J. Vollprecht. "Makkovik." *Periodical Accounts of the Work of the Moravian Missions*, no. 164 (1956): 48–52. https://collections.mun.ca/digital/collection/cns_permorv/id/16696/rec/1.

Walsh, Bren. *More than a Poor Majority: The Story of Newfoundland's Confederation with Canada*. St. John's: Breakwater Books, 1985.

Warren, Gail Denise. "Voluntarism and Patriotism: Newfoundland Women's War Work during the First World War." Master of Arts research report, Memorial University, 2005.

Webb, Jeff A. *The Voice of Newfoundland: A Social History of the Broadcasting Corporation of Newfoundland, 1939–1949*. Toronto: University of Toronto Press, 2008.

Webb, Jeff A. "The Responsible Government League and the Confederation Campaigns of 1948." *Newfoundland Studies* 5, no. 2 (1989): 203–20.

Weld, Kristen. *Paper Cadavers: The Archives of Dictatorship in Guatemala*. Durham: Duke University Press, 2014.

Wetzel, Jerry, Pat Anderson, and Douglas Sanders. *Freedom to Live Our Own Way in Our Own Land*. Edited by Peter J. Usher. Conne River, NL: Ktaqamkuk Ilnui Saqimawoutie and the Conne River Indian Band Council, 1980.

Whalen, David J. *Just One Interloper after Another: An Unabridged, Unofficial, Unauthorized History of the Labrador Straits*. Forteau, NL: Labrador Straits Historical Development Corporation, 1990.

Whitcomb, Ed. *A Short History of Newfoundland and Labrador*. Ottawa: From Sea to Sea Enterprises, 2010.

Whithead, Joshua. *Jonny Appleseed*. Arsenal Pulp, 2018.

Wright, Miriam. "'The most modern dining hall in the city': Chinese Immigrants, Restaurants, and Social Spaces in St. John's, Newfoundland, 1918–1945." *Acadiensis* 50, no. 1 (2021): 5–33.

CONTRIBUTOR BIOGRAPHIES

Sonja Boon is an award-winning researcher, writer, teacher, and flutist. Author or co-author of five books, including the memoir *What the Oceans Remember: Searching for Belonging and Home* (WLU Press, 2019), she is passionate about life stories, archives, and feminist theory.

Vicki S. Hallett, an associate professor in the Department of Gender Studies at Memorial University, is the author of *Mistress of the Blue Castle: The Writing Life of Phebe Florence Miller* (ISER Books, 2018).

Angela Antle is a writer, artist, MUN interdisciplinary PhD candidate, and documentary producer descended from tough Trinity South stock.

Terry Bishop Stirling, a native of St. John's, taught Newfoundland and Labrador history at Memorial for over thirty-five years. A long-time executive member of the Newfoundland and Labrador Historical Society, she is also an active public historian.

Jessica Bound, a settler writer and artist who lives in Treaty One territory, holds a BA (Hons.) and MA from the University of Manitoba.

Andreae Callanan, the author of *The Debt* (Biblioasis 2021), lives in St. John's, Newfoundland and Labrador.

J.T.H. Connor, John Clinch Professor of Medical Humanities and History of Medicine, Faculty of Medicine, Memorial University, is also cross-appointed as a professor of history, Faculty of Humanities and Social Sciences.

An independent historian, **Heidi Coombs** has a PhD in history specializing in twentieth-century outport nursing and rural medicine in northern Newfoundland and Labrador. She is past president of the Newfoundland and Labrador Historical Society.

Linda Cullum loves historical sociology, gender studies, and the smell of archives.

Elizabeth (Libby) Dane hails from the mainland but has lived in Town since 2014. She is an arts worker and academic but is first and foremost a community member.

Lesley Derraugh (she/her) is a feminist and hospital administrator, living in her hometown of St. John's with her partner and their dogs. She wishes more people wrote letters.

Violet Drake (she/her) is a white settler, disabled, queer and trans artist, writer, and cultural worker born and raised in Lawn on the Burin Peninsula. Her work has been exhibited and performed at artist-run centres, festivals, and classrooms throughout Ktaqmkuk (Newfoundland).

Sheila Hallett is negotiating the rapidly changing world of Newfoundland and Labrador. She earned a Master's degree from Memorial University and most importantly raised a wonderful family and is blessed with a remarkably talented grandson.

Joanne Harris is a first-generation townie with Ktaqmkuk Mi'kmaq, French, English, and Scottish roots from the bay and the bush an island apart. They are a proud Rabbittownie with a penchant for doggos, axe throwing, veg growing, improvising, and procrastinating.

Gemma Hickey is a renowned human rights activist, global speaker whose efforts have changed the legal landscape in Canada, and author of the highly acclaimed memoir *Almost Feral* (Breakwater 2019).

Robert Hong, whose father came to Newfoundland from China in the 1930s, earned his BA (Hons.) and MA in history from Memorial University. He spearheaded the Chinese Head Tax redress movement in Newfoundland and Labrador in the mid-2000s.

Daze Jefferies (she/her), an artist, writer, and educator born and raised in the Bay of Exploits on the northeast coast of rural Ktaqmkuk (Newfoundland), holds a Master of Gender Studies from Memorial University.

Mi'sel Joe, LLD, CM, is District Traditional Chief of the Miawpukek First Nation, appointed as such by the late Grand Chief Donald Marshall in 1983. He is the author of *Muinji'j Becomes a Man* (Breakwater Books, 2003) and co-author of *My Indian* (Breakwater Books, 2021).

Sharon King-Campbell, a poet, theatre artist, and scholar based in Ktaqmkuk/Newfoundland, is the author of *This Is How It Is* (Breakwater Books, 2021) and is currently pursuing a PhD at Memorial University. More information is available at sharonkingcampbell.com.

Kate Lahey, a writer, musician, and educator who holds a PhD from the Women and Gender Studies Institute, University of Toronto, is also a postdoctoral fellow and course instructor at Memorial University.

Julia Laite is a professor of history at Birkbeck, University of London, where she works on the history of women, crime, sexuality, and migration in the nineteenth- and twentieth-century British world. Her latest project addresses the troubled history of settler colonialism in Newfoundland.

Dr. Shannon Lewis-Simpson, an educator and researcher originally from Holyrood, now lives in Harbour Main. She tries not to get into too many political arguments with her family.

Dave Lough has lived and worked in Labrador and has studied and practised community economic development in Canada's north. He edited *Voices of Inuit Leadership and Self-Determination in Canada* (ISER Books, 2020).

In 1917, teenager Mac Morgan started a printing business in his parents' basement, where his friend Joey Smallwood was a frequent guest. Today Mac's granddaughter, **Jennifer Morgan**, has revived Morgan's Printing Office as a letterpress fine art practice, still based in St. John's.

Emily Murphy is a Master of Gender Studies student at Memorial University. When she's not studying, she enjoys fiction of all sorts and smashing the patriarchy.

Sheila O'Neill, a member of Qalipu Mi'kmaq First Nation and a founding member and past president of the Newfoundland Aboriginal Women's Network, holds a BA and BEd from Memorial University and is co-author of *My Indian* (Breakwater Books, 2021).

A little fishy, **Jasmine Paul** is an artist, writer, academic, and fifth-generation Placentia Bay fish harvester who is passionate about folklore and traditional inshore fisheries. When she is not fishing, writing, or studying, she can be found in the woods.

Andrea Procter, the author of *A Long Journey: Residential Schools in Labrador and Newfoundland* (ISER Books, 2020), has a PhD in anthropology and has been learning through collaborative projects with Indigenous communities in Labrador for twenty years.

Colleen Quigley is a Performing Arts Archivist and Head of Memorial Libraries' Archives and Special Collections (ASC), the archival home of the Smallwood fonds.

Shruti Raheja (she/her) is a recent graduate of the Master of Arts in English program at Memorial University, situated on unceded Beothuk and Mi'kmaq territory. She is passionate about justice, education, and storytelling as a means to imagine and create more equitable societies.

Amy Sheppard has been a practicing social worker for nineteen years and has lived in Newfoundland and Labrador most of her life. A recent PhD graduate, she is now enjoying teaching and spending a little more time on hobbies, such as backyard farming and Strong Woman Competitions.

Sarah Simpson, currently a student living in Harbour Main, enjoys chemistry, fine arts, and exploring libraries and archives.

Originally from the island of Newfoundland, **Gina Snooks**, PhD, is a gender studies and feminist scholar who explores women's life stories. Gina's reflection honours the women who have come before her, particularly her Nan Whalen and the woman whose telegraph inspired her writing.

Jocelyn Thorpe is a settler scholar and associate professor of Women's and Gender Studies and History at the University of Manitoba in Treaty One territory, where she directs the Centre for Creative Writing and Oral Culture.

Patricia Way is a Labradorian, retired teacher, and genealogist who is focused on Labrador's people. She received an honorary doctorate from Memorial University for her work in these areas.

Miriam Wright earned her PhD in history at Memorial University and is an associate professor of history at University of Windsor. Her research includes work on the Newfoundland fisheries, Chinese immigration to Newfoundland, and sports and race in southwestern Ontario.

INDEX